THE SKULL

BENEATH

THE SKIN

THE SKULL

BENEATH

THE SKIN

Africa After the Cold War

MARK HUBAND

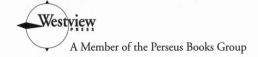

A Member of the Perseus Books Group

For Marceline

Published in 2001 in the United States of America by Westview Press, 5500 Central Avenue, Boulder, Colorado 80301-2877, and in the United Kingdom by Westview Press, 12 Hid's Copse Road, Cumnor Hill, Oxford OX2 9JJ

Westview Press books are available at special discounts for bulk purchases in the United States by corporations, institutions, and other organizations. For more information, please contact the Special Markets Department at The Perseus Books Group, 11 Cambridge Center, Cambridge MA 02142, or call (617) 252-5298.

Find us on the World Wide Web at www.westviewpress.com

Library of Congress Cataloging-in-Publication Data
Huband, Mark.
  The skull beneath the skin : Africa after the Cold War / Mark Huband.
    p. cm.
  Includes bibliographical references and index.
  ISBN 0-8133-3598-1 (alk. paper)
    1. Africa—Politics and government—1960– 2. Africa—Colonial influence. 3. Africa—Relations—Foreign countries. I. Title.

DT30.5 .H83 2001
960.3'2—dc21

2001045498

Designed by Heather Hutchison
Set in 10 point Janson by the Perseus Books Group

The paper used in this publication meets the requirements of the American National Standard for Permanence of Paper for Printed Library Materials Z39.48-1984.

10   9   8   7   6   5   4   3   2   1

Contents

ACKNOWLEDGMENTS

THE TEN YEARS OF EXPERIENCE that have provided the material for this book have been enriched and guided by many friends, colleagues, and acquaintances. Their advice, encouragement, and readiness to nurture me in the craft of journalism and to provide hints as to its limitless value opened my eyes to places and events in which I could have become lost but from which it became possible to emerge with a tale to tell. I will always be indebted to Michael Holman, Africa editor of the *Financial Times*, for first sending me to Abidjan and for encouraging me through example and advice for more than a decade. Stephen Smith, formerly of *Libération* and now of *Le Monde*, inspired me always to step a little closer to the story I sought to tell and to work a little harder than I might otherwise have done. Ann Treneman, formerly foreign editor of the *Observer*, fought hard to ensure that while the world, the British media in general, and her own colleagues in particular, sought to ignore the 1994 genocide in Rwanda, her pages told the story starkly. Elizabeth Blunt, formerly West Africa correspondent of the BBC, kept me fed and focused during some of the darkest days in the history of West Africa, as did Edith Odemo, whose help in Nairobi is an enduring memory of Kenya. I would also like to thank Martin Woollacott of the *Guardian* for having helped me lay a few ghosts to rest. At Westview Press I would like to thank Karl Yambert, Jennifer Chen, and Meegan Finnegan for their great help, encouragement, and commitment to the reporting of Africa, as well as Silvine Farnell for her sensitive and encouraging editing, which enhanced the quality of the manuscript. I am extremely grateful to Chris Walker, head of the graphics department at the *Financial Times*, for taking on the task of providing the maps for this book and to Jim Stephens for having contributed photographs of Somalia, Sudan, and Kenya and to my parents, Ann and David Huband for reading and commenting on the proofs of this book. But my greatest debt is owed to Marceline, my wife, for sharing her wisdom and fortitude when both often seemed in short supply.

Mark Huband
London, UK

PROLOGUE

THE ROAD SOUTH FROM THE BORDER wound through the dense forest of northern Burundi like a thread tracing its course through a medieval maze. The tranquility of that October morning in 1993—the calm, and the routine stamping of official papers and passports at the border post at the end of the bridge that marked the end of Rwanda to the north—conspired with the pleasant weather to suggest the atmosphere of another normal day.

As became clear after I crossed the border and traveled south, the biggest challenge was how to answer the question of what was normal and what was not. It had been six days since Burundi's president, Melchior Ndadaye, and seven of his ministers, had been bayoneted to death by middle-ranking officers from the army paratroop regiment. The hundred or so officers seized the national television station in the capital, Bujumbura, and proclaimed the creation of the Comité nationale du salut publique (CNSP: National Committee of Public Salvation). The coup brought an end to Burundi's already tense transition from military dictatorship to democracy. That transition had led to Ndadaye's election four months earlier on June 1[1] and the election of a parliament dominated by his Frodebu party.[2] The CNSP survived for only four days. The officers behind it were isolated by others within the armed forces who were reluctant to take the risk of being associated with a coup that opposed the path upon which other army officers had set Burundi two years beforehand.[3] But the collapse of the CNSP and the eventual arrest of its leaders did not mark and since has not marked the major turning-point sought by the architects of African democracy—neither in Burundi nor elsewhere. It did not mark a confirmation that the major shift—away from dictatorship, military rule, bad government, and clan-based elitism—had been achieved. Instead, it allowed the more cautious members of the armed forces to regroup and resume their key role within the political life of the country.

At heart, the history of Africa since the end of the Cold War has been dominated by such clashes between entrenched, illegitimate, and generally highly destructive regimes dependent upon brute force, and populations from within which have emerged voices intent upon exposing not just the brutality of those regimes, but also their serious political, economic, bureaucratic, and developmental shortcomings. Dictatorship has failed to meet the needs of the people. Absolute power and relative weakness are the twin causes of the fragility that has faced most of Africa's governments in the four decades since the European powers began the process of decolonization and the newly independent continent found itself lured, forced, or tempted into the global superpower conflict. For although they may have wielded power through the institutions of fear necessary to suppress their populations, the elements of which these regimes were comprised remained individually weak. The ill-disciplined individual soldiers, the corrupt command structures, the rivalry within the upper ranks, and the very illegitimacy of the regimes themselves, all were the elements determining their effectiveness. Faced with a serious threat, they were generally unable to show that behind the facade of power they had substantial force at hand.

With such failures having dominated the history of the forty years since the end of colonialism, the questions of "Who are we?" and thus "What kind of countries should we be creating?" are what now boil explosively at the heart of the continent's political debates, as the possibility of a new, post–Cold War, true independence emerges across the continent. Vital to finding any answer is the need to conclude how best the past should be understood, and what guidance it may offer for the present and future.

The Nigerian academic A. O. Ikelegbe describes colonialism as having been the axe that tore African tradition away from its roots, setting populations adrift, with little opportunity to draw upon the experience of the past.[4]

By contrast, the Kenyan writer Ali Mazrui asserts that autocratic, nondemocratic systems are not the result of the continent having suffered the violent rupture with the past; rather, "[In] some ways they follow the patterns established by Africa's great leaders of the past,"[5] following what he calls the "Elder Tradition," the "Sage Tradition," or the "Warrior Tradition."

The first is "heavily paternalistic . . . [and] has a heavy preference for reverence and reaffirmations of loyalty towards political leaders,"[6] while the second is a system essentially intended to ensure that the sagelike qualities and prestige of the leader are of sufficient weight to protect him or her from political opposition. The third manifests itself in a "reliance on intimidatory leadership, primarily on fear and on instruments of coercion to assert authority,"[7] Mazrui writes.

The search for credibility among the many incredible leaders of postcolonial Africa brought with it the assertion that the creation of single-party rule in much of the continent lay closer to African tradition than did parliamentary democracy.[8] Today, the bankruptcy of this view has become widely ac-

cepted. Mazrui's view that African tradition has in a serious way been continued in modern systems appears unconvincing, given the nature of the leaders—most of them irresponsible dictators—who have attempted to claim the
authority of tradition. What has yet to take root is a broadly acceptable
process of transition from one form of rule to another.

The crisis of leadership and the weakness of traditional structures stem in
large part from rule having been personalized in a way that tradition discouraged. Moreover, the creation of personality cults around modern leaders actually drove an immovable wedge between past and present; their only qualification was to have seized power in an often bloody fashion, and in doing so
they had more often than not sown the seeds of disharmony that traditional
rulers were supposed to overcome. Their behavior has ultimately served
only to confuse the debate over whether there is any value in looking to the
past for inspiration.

Taking the latter months of the year 1989 as a cut-off point, the countries
of Africa that had been politically frozen in time, largely due to the role they
had voluntarily or involuntarily played in the Cold War, have been starkly
exposed to the reality of the imbalance between leaders and led. But the
value of the past as an inspiration for a new political dynamism has long been
doubted, as Olufemi Akinola baldly asserts:

> By the 1950s, Africa had become a "mental no-man's land," for indige-
> nous institutions, and moral codes had become subordinated to, but
> not eliminated by colonial socio-political structures. The result was a
> split personality that issued from the simultaneous existence in the
> same society of at least two mutually conflictual but interacting value
> systems.[9]

The vast majority of people faced detachment from the source of power
and the denial of any chance to use political means to find solutions to the
crises they faced. "The state is out of touch with the realities of the people,"
Akinola wrote in 1989, when pressure for change was building up.

The nature of resistance to democracy in the 1990s tells more about the
basis on which African political systems will develop in the twenty-first century than does the character of the democratic movements themselves.

The resistance to change has clearly been asserted most wholeheartedly
by the incumbent regimes, whose character evolved during the Cold War to
serve both domestic self-interest, as well as whichever outside power—the
United States, France, Belgium, the former Soviet Union, Portugal, Britain,
Libya, South Africa, or a juggled combination of these states—made them
the most attractive offer. Whatever the traditional elements of African rule
evoked by dictators such as Mobutu Sese Seko, the late president of Zaire, a

large part of the blame for the intransigence of Africa's despots can be laid at the door of the foreign powers, which leant vital credibility to some of the worst leaders the world has ever known.

Dominating U.S. foreign policy in Africa when the foundations were being laid in the early 1960s was a combination of ignorance about the needs and realities of newly independent states and a recurrent failure to understand the real meaning of the policies of Nikita Khrushchev's Soviet Union as it sought to involve itself in the affairs of the postcolonial world. A U.S. government policy assessment of the potential Africa offered the U.S. in 1963 stated, "We see Africa as probably the greatest open field of maneuver in the worldwide competition between the [Communist] Bloc and the non-Communist world. . . . The critical factor in African nation-building is leadership. In choosing countries for special emphasis, we propose to make a major effort to help dynamic and progressive leaders who are reasonably friendly."[10]

The end of the Cold War has left Africa orphaned by the superpowers, but aware that its destiny as a continent of nations is now in its hands for the first time in its history. It has been a birth wracked by disappointment, dashed hopes, and bloodshed.

The significance of the process of finding a sustainable, vibrant, and pacific alternative to the malaise that faces Africa today cannot be overestimated. The chapters that follow are intended to illustrate how sub-Saharan Africa has emerged from the decades of the Cold War. The abuse of power, the tool of violence, the failure to build functioning states, the readiness of Western democracies to connive in the destruction and squandering of Africa's material and cultural riches, all these were the hallmarks of the Cold War.

Stability on the continent will only be achieved if African countries are left to find their own solutions to the problems they face. The end of the Cold War may now offer the opportunity for Africa to achieve the independence it never really achieved when the European powers departed from their former colonies.

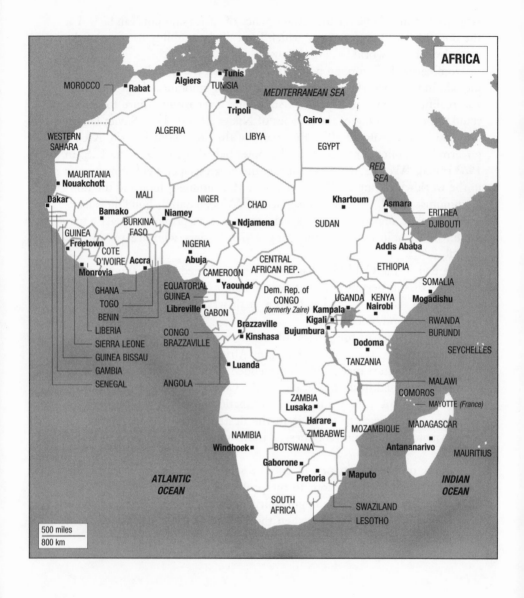

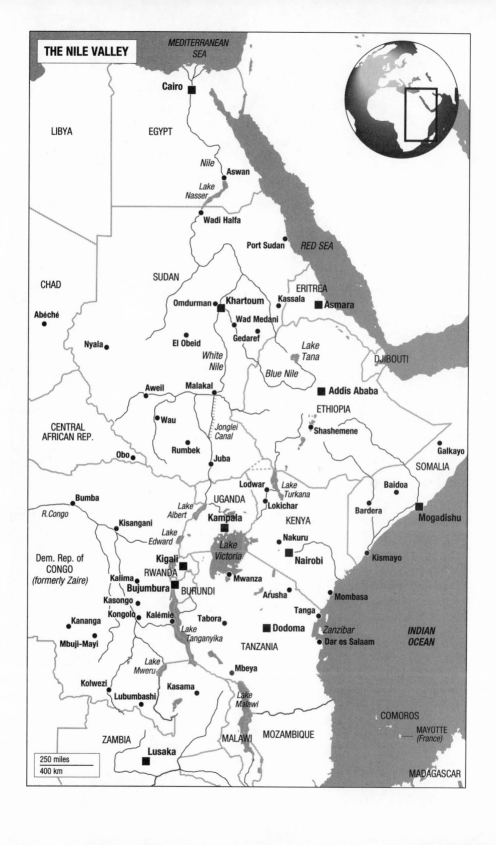

THE NILE VALLEY

MEDITERRANEAN
SEA

LIBYA

EGYPT

Cairo

Nile

Aswan

*Lake
Nasser*

Wadi Halfa

Port Sudan   *RED SEA*

CHAD

SUDAN

ERITREA

Abéché

Omdurman   Khartoum   Kassala

Asmara

Wad Medani

Nyala   El Obeid   Gedaref

DJIBOUTI

*White
Nile*

*Lake
Tana*

Blue Nile

Aweil   Malakal

Addis Ababa

CENTRAL
AFRICAN REP.

Wau

*Jonglei
Canal*

ETHIOPIA

Obo   Rumbek

Shashemene

Juba

Galkayo

Lodwar   *Lake
Turkana*

SOMALIA

Bumba   UGANDA

Lokichar

Baidoa

R.Congo

*Lake
Albert*   Kampala

KENYA

Bardera

Kisangani

Mogadishu

*Lake
Edward*

Nakuru

Dem. Rep. of
CONGO
(formerly Zaire)

Kigali   *Lake
Victoria*

Nairobi

Kismayo

Kalima

RWANDA

Kasongo   Bujumbura   BURUNDI

Mwanza

Kananga   Kongolo   Kalémie

Arusha

Mombasa

Tabora

Tanga

Mbuji-Mayi

*Lake
Tanganyika*

Dodoma   *Zanzibar*

*INDIAN
OCEAN*

Dar es Salaam

Kolwezi   *Lake
Mweru*

TANZANIA

Kasama

Lubumbashi

Mbeya

*Lake
Malawi*

COMOROS

MAYOTTE
(France)

ZAMBIA

MALAWI   MOZAMBIQUE

250 miles
400 km

Lusaka

MADAGASCAR

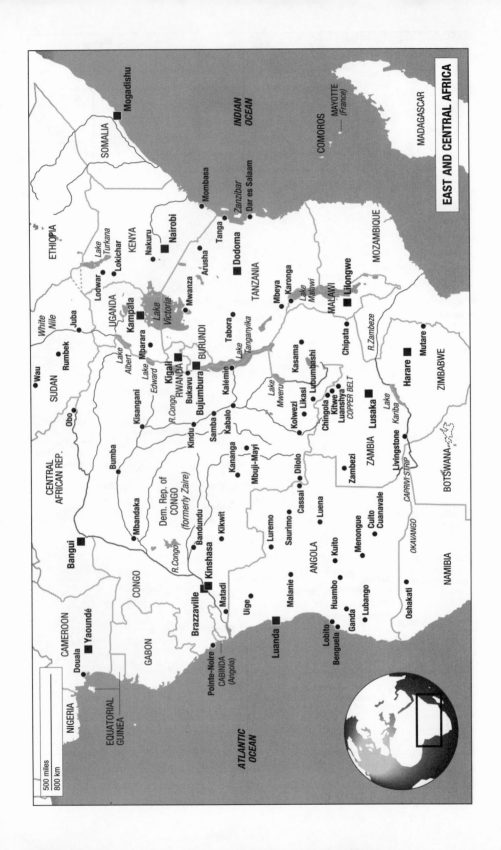

EAST AND CENTRAL AFRICA

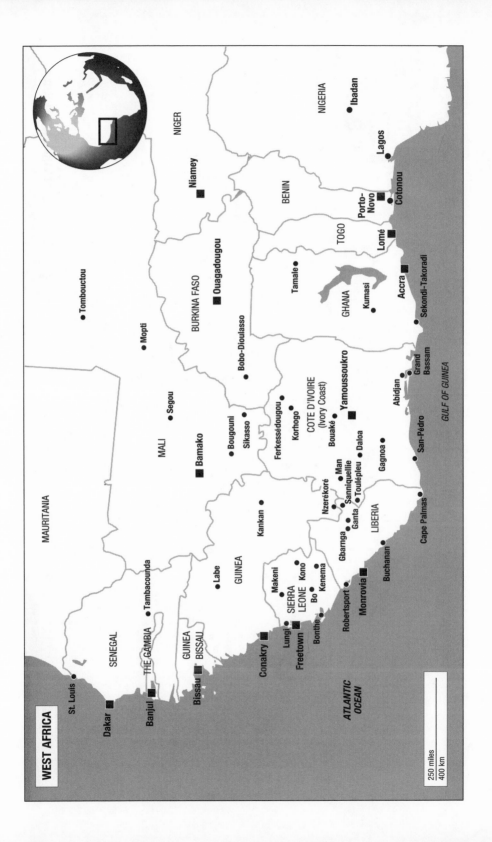

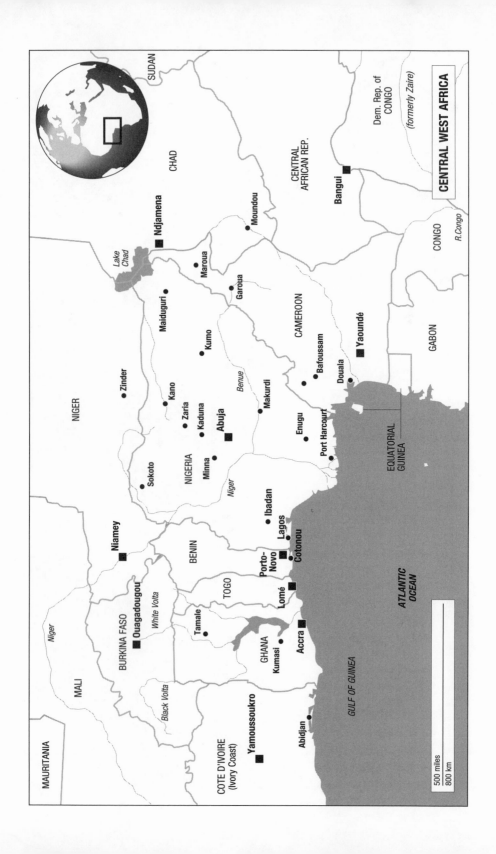

CENTRAL WEST AFRICA

PART ONE

Empty Promises

O N 29 JULY 1975, a U.S. C-141 military transport aircraft left Charleston, South Carolina, en route to Kinshasa, the Zairian capital, and onward to southern Zaire, which served as the rear base for the supply line to the U.S.-backed Angolan rebel movement, Uniaõ Naçiõnal para la Indepencia total de Angola (Unita; the National Union for the Total Independence of Angola), led by Jonas Savimbi. It was carrying a cargo infinitely more deadly than the combined firepower of the 25-ton loads of weapons stored in its hold. It was carrying the first dose of a poison that was to be fed into the veins of Africa, to support a war that was unwinnable and was the least promising means of resolving a political conflict that had riven Angola by the time independence was hurriedly foisted on the country on 11 November 1975. The plane took off after depositing its lethal cargo, and the first piece of a regional network was thus put in place by the United States. The network, created to feed U.S. allies in Angola and beyond, was dependent upon the enthusiastic complicity of African states, states whose despotic strengths and institutional weaknesses laid the groundwork for the collapse in the post–Cold War era of entire regions.

By 1975, the CIA already had a firm ally in Mobutu Sese Seko, the president of Zaire, whom the agency had bankrolled since 1960 and helped bring to power in 1965. A mere six-hour meeting with Jonas Savimbi and other Unita officials by a CIA official convinced the agency that the organization deserved military support in the fight over the future of Angola. The supply chain depended upon the support of neighboring Zaire, and Mobutu became a vital player on the U.S. team, to which, after the 1980 coup in Liberia, was added Samuel Doe. Doe was bought off with bribes, official aid, and military assistance to keep him sweet and so secure Liberia as a base of operations involving other U.S. interests in Africa, most importantly Angola. All three states, Angola, Zaire, and Liberia have now, the Cold War being over, been abandoned by those who once used them, left in ruins by wars fought over the empty promise that by taking the right side in the superpower conflict they could somehow expect a golden future. They have been left to pick up the pieces, alone in a vast wilderness into which they were encouraged to wander by the countries of the developed world to whose mix of flattery and deceit they succumbed.

I

SELL THE SILVER, STEAL THE GOLD

Mobutu and Zaire

A STONE PEDESTAL AT THE JUNCTION of a private driveway leading to the Villa del Mar commemorates Sir Winston Churchill as a *citoyen d'honneur* (honorary citizen) of Cap Martin. Off Avenue Churchill a shaded cul-de-sac leads to what was still on the day I visited, in May 1997, the French Riviera residence of Mobutu Sese Seko, which to my eyes seemed a monument of a different sort.[1] Iron gates, and a sign warning unwanted visitors that guard dogs might be snarling on the other side of the wall, hid the villa, estimated to be worth $4.3 million. The Villa del Mar is the largest of a cluster of luxury homes dominating a small hill leading down to the Mediterranean at Roque-brune-Cap Martin. A nearby real estate agent ran through the prices of mansions and villas in the surrounding streets, while in a shop opposite the couple that ran a newspaper shop and grocery store talked of how Mobutu's children used to come buy sweets and toys with large-denomination notes. A copy of the *International Herald Tribune* lay on the counter, with an account of the advance by rebel forces across the savannah and forest of the collapsing Zairian state dominating the front page. A world lying thousands of miles away, the inhabitants of which, every summer until only a few years beforehand, had arrived in a convoy of sleek cars in these streets, was reduced from being the geopolitical drama of the dynamic days of the 1960s, to a black-and-white

3

souvenir photograph of a time that was rapidly passing into history. The closed shutters of the magnificent villa overlooking the sea would soon have a new owner, perhaps proud of, though possibly disturbed by, the cachet that for some the previous ownership by an eccentric African leader might add.

Villa del Mar was one of twenty villas, mansions, and ranches amassed by Mobutu in Belgium, Côte d'Ivoire, Switzerland, Morocco, and elsewhere, whose combined value by the time of his downfall amounted to around $37 million. In addition to the numerous homes, Mobutu owned a hotel and a coffee plantation in Brazil. The largest concentration of properties was in the wealthy suburbs of Brussels, the Belgian capital, where he owned a total of nine buildings ranging from office blocks to châteaux, mansions, and parklands in the residential districts of Uccle and Rhode St. Genèse. In Paris, a few meters from the Arc de Triomphe, was a vast first-floor apartment at 20 Avenue Foch, while an alternative holiday home to the Villa del Mar was the $2.3 million, 12-bedroom Casa Agricola Solear estate at Areias de Porches, in the Portuguese Algarve, where Mobutu stored his 14,000-bottle wine cellar. Across the border in Spain were hotels in Marbella and a luxury home in the Madrid suburb of Las Lomas at Boadilla del Monte, valued at $1.38 million when it was bought in 1983 in the name of his sister-in-law.

I watched from Europe as a country whose length and breadth I had traveled, collapsed. As it fell apart, and the name Zaire came to be expunged from the map of the world, the resurgence of interest in Mobutu's fortune, the tales of vulgar excess and tasteless grandeur, which emerged as his demise approached, reduced the truly horrifying impact of his three decades in power to a level of banality with which his former allies among the democracies of the West could feel comfortable. Few fingers have been pointed meaningfully and seriously at Mobutu's allies, even at the grotesque waste of foreign financial assistance or at the scale of theft, which would have been impossible without the complicity of Western bankers, business people, politicians, and security services.

I was able to complete the search for much of his visible fortune in three days as the clouds were gathering over his rule. From the suburbs of Brussels, I wandered the boulevards of Paris, then took a quick flight down to Nice and a drive along the coast road to the mansion at Roquebrune. A further swing through Madrid and a few hours on to the Algarve would have encompassed much of the real estate empire. Further afield, Morocco, Côte d'Ivoire, Senegal, and Brazil would have taken a little longer. But most of it was there for the viewing, with nothing hidden. The entire world knew something of what Mobutu had, and long after questions started to be asked as to how he obtained it, the allies of the Zairian leader were still being fêted at his country homes.

His bank accounts, meanwhile, have remained largely hidden from view. Prior to his fall, the only attempt by Western governments to identify these accounts was made in 1992, when the United States, France, and Belgium examined holdings in their own countries. France and the United States abandoned plans to freeze his assets, on the grounds that they amounted to very little, while Belgium claimed it would have lacked sufficient legal instruments if it had pursued the seizure of his personal liquid financial assets, which were reckoned by U.S. officials to have peaked at around $4 billion. In a 1982 International Monetary Fund report,[2] the banks identified as having dealt with Mobutu and his financial front men included Banque Bruxelles Lambert, Paribas, Crédit Commerciale, Midland Bank, and Union Bank of Switzerland. In April 1997, Switzerland's Federal Banking Commission asked twelve leading Swiss banks whether they held accounts in Mobutu's name, to which they all replied that they did not.

The refusal of the Swiss banking system to accept that its share of the responsibility for the predicament of many African economies is as shameful as its role in the laundering of funds stolen by Nazi Germany from the Jews of Europe. It is a chapter in Africa's history that has yet to be opened, despite some efforts made as a result of enormous pressure in recent years. With the Cold War over, Switzerland is one of the isolated pieces in Africa's jigsaw of tyranny remaining to be turned fully face up. But its role was only a part of that jigsaw, as years of active support for Mobutu led Western governments and business people on an endless dance, which for twenty of his thirty years in power was marked by the silencing of critics, the sidelining of doubters, and the ridiculing of dissenting voices—often as much in the West as in Zaire itself, as Western governments sought to flatter the man who exercised power in Central Africa.

PICKING THE PLUMS

For much of its history, Zaire was as much symbol as reality. Even before the invention of Zaire, during the short life of the independent Congo, and even prior to the rushed Belgian departure, the country typified, symbolized, and conjured up images of Africa to the outside world, in a manner which has done much to form the continent's reputation beyond its shores. Central to the image in the formative years of the 1960s and 1970s was Mobutu, army chief of staff of the Congo at independence in 1960. Mobutu's emergence as a key political figure in the newly independent Congo in 1960, as well as the role he played during the turbulence of the 1960–1965 period, was the result of a plethora of factors at whose heart lay a combination of diplomatic failures, political blunders, greed, egomania, and ignorance, from which all of Central Africa has suffered ever since. Although there is little point in debating what might have happened had Mobutu never existed, the fact of the external support that assured his survival, rise, and domination necessarily raises the question of whether the experience gleaned from supporting such a character has been adequately understood.

"The U.S. stepped in at independence because the place was a plum financially,"[3] said John Stockwell, former CIA chief of base in Lubumbashi in 1967, and later chief of the CIA Angola task force, which equipped, advised, and paid Jonas Savimbi's forces in Angola. Stockwell's claim tells only half the story, however. Within a week of Congolese independence, on 30 June 1960, the army had mutinied, and the new government of President Joseph Kasavubu and Prime Minister Patrice Lumumba was completely unable to restore calm. Madeleine Kalb gives a clear picture of the way the situation looked in her remarkable study of U.S. policy during the period, *The Congo Cables*:[4]

> [U.S. ambassador Clare] Timberlake believed that anarchy in the Congo would have repercussions far beyond the immediate crisis: it would play directly into the hands of the Soviets by providing an opportunity for radical forces to take over and undermine Western interests in this rich and strategic part of Africa. At the same time he realized that the only action capable of preventing anarchy—intervention by Belgian troops—would also play into Soviet hands: it would antagonize the new Congolese government and give the Soviets an excellent opportunity to stress their anti-imperialist solidarity with the new African states.[5]

The United States sought to engineer an intervention by Belgian troops under the banner of the United Nations, as a means of deflecting the accusation that Belgian action was reminiscent of the colonial practices that had come to an end a week earlier, after seventy-five years of Belgian rule. The chaos that reigned in the immediate aftermath of Congolese independence can barely be said to have had a political direction. All sides were caught in a maze of emotion, anger, resentment, and suspicion. The variety of political programs that existed within the fragile Kasavubu government made it largely powerless. It represented a variety of aspirations, rather than a defined program with the political and administrative tools to implement it. The response of the European states was influenced by a mixture of fear for the security of their own nationals and concern for the protection of their vested interests. It was small wonder that this self-interest further enflamed the already intense suspicion of the Europeans among many—though certainly not all—of those around Kasavubu and Lumumba.

The role of foreigners in the immediate post-independence history of Congo was pivotal, and it was as significant in determining the direction the country took in the 1960–1965 period as the actions of Congolese politicians themselves. The continued Belgian military presence in Congo after independence, with attendant demands by Kasavubu and Lumumba that they leave, was a vital factor. The government not only appeared to have little control over its own army, but also could not even force the departure of the foot soldiers of the former colonial power. Its credibility in tatters, the Lumumba government severed diplomatic ties with Belgium, and appealed to the Soviet Union to consider intervening. Such an appeal inevitably played into Belgian hands, lightening the task of the Congolese government's critics in Belgium, who were attempting to portray it as pro-Soviet. Both the USSR and the United States, meanwhile, were keen to play the Congo crisis out on the floor of the United Nations and then among the ranks of the UN force, which began arriving in Congo on 15 July 1960.

With the arrival of the UN force, the complexity of the crisis worsened. Lumumba, the outspoken prime minister, was deemed procommunist at every turn. For Lumumba, the major impediment to the assertion of political independence was the continued presence of representatives of Belgian authority, namely Belgian troops. On 17 July, the UN received an ultimatum from Kasavubu and Lumumba, stating that unless Belgian troops left the country, the government would formally ask the Soviet Union to intervene. The move alienated Lumumba—who was being seen as the power behind Kasavubu's throne—from those within the UN who sought to play a middle role between the superpowers and the former colonizers. As Kalb puts it, it also "increased the pressure on Premier Khrushchev and probably forced him to become more deeply involved in defending Lumumba's interests than he had originally intended."[6] Kalb also asserts that the ultimatum drove a wedge between the United States and Lumumba. Within two days the United States was considering ways of overthrowing Lumumba:

> Only prudent, therefore, we plan on basis that Lumumba government threatens our vital interests in Congo and Africa generally. A principal objective of our political and diplomatic action must therefore be to destroy Lumumba government as now constituted, but at the same time we must find or develop another horse to back which would be acceptable in rest of Africa and defensible against Soviet political attack.[7]

Essential to any understanding of what kind of a threat Lumumba really represented is an understanding of the real intentions of the Soviet Union, which were far less threatening than the CIA in particular was determined to portray them as being. Kalb's account of the variety of reactions by U.S. policymakers reveals the extent to which reactions to Lumumba and the reality of Congo on its own terms was seen entirely through the prism of superpower rivalry. Lumumba's emergence on the political scene was increasingly viewed as the result of deliberate manipulation by the Soviet Union of the chaos in the Congo. To attribute such success to Moscow's strategists in itself betrayed the extent to which the United States had failed correctly to read the influence and capacity of its superpower enemy.

Crawford Young and Thomas Turner, in their authoritative history of Mobutu's first three decades in power, have also spoken of "the limited understanding on the part of both Soviets and Americans of the determinants of [Congolese] internal politics."[8] Defenders of U.S. support for Mobutu in the 1980s, when the Reagan administration sought to reignite the Cold War and called in the credit it felt was its due from allies like Mobutu, drew upon some of the most spurious and groundless arguments to justify this renewed involvement. In a 1984 verbal exchange between William Colby, CIA director in the mid-1970s, and John Stockwell, Colby asserted:

> The question we faced in the Congo was whether that country, which had just gained independence from Belgium, would be run by some toadies of the old Belgian mining companies or by men aided by Che Guevara and supported by the Soviet Union. The CIA found a midpoint between those extremes—it helped Joseph Mobutu, then a nationalist member of the Congolese forces, become the third alternative.[9]

Colby's argument is neat but disingenuous. Rarely if ever during the 1960–1965 period did the United States equate the threat of the continued domination of the Congo by Belgian business interests (which had led to Belgium supporting the secession of Katanga in 1960) with the threat to U.S. global influence posed by the Soviet Union. His analysis also presupposes that the United States had good reason to take a principled stand against these two alternatives, and then sought the third way by supporting Mobutu. Again, this is disingenuous. True, it is still debated whether the CIA actually offered assistance to the Belgian-backed secessionists in Katanga in 1960, even though no one disputes that Ambassador Timberlake paid an official visit to the breakaway province on at least one occasion. Whatever the true U.S. position regarding Katanga and the Belgians, however, what remained of much greater importance was the gulf between the reality of Lumumba and the impression he gave. As the American academic and expert on the former Zaire Michael Schatzberg makes clear, Lumumba did not in reality represent the threat the United States portrayed him as being:

> With the clarity of hindsight . . . , Lumumba was probably no more than a populist and nationalist politician, albeit with increasingly radical tendencies. It is doubtful that Soviet ideology or academic Marxism influenced him. . . . We should also remember that Lumumba appealed to the West for assistance in terminating the Katanga secession and in removing Belgian troops from his country before requesting Soviet aid. Indeed, Lumumba's travels in search of assistance took him to the United States, but never to the Soviet Union. . . . But these initiatives did not, and perhaps could not, alter official Washington's strong prevailing perception of Lumumba as a tool of Soviet interests. If Lu-

mumba was, in fact, sending signals to Washington, they were drowned out by international static.[10]

For Lumumba, the pressing need was to assert independence and turn a real corner away from colonial rule, in the face of apparently insurmountable domestic political problems that were not of his making but the result of the mixture of internal aspirations and external pressures imposing themselves on the "plum" of his vast country. Kalb, in her account of how U.S. policy-makers were reading the crisis, is largely blind to Mobutu's personal ambitions, and treats him as Colby depicts him. The CIA's backing of the Katanga secession and the ambiguity of the U.S. position when responding to Lumumba's calls for the West to help his fragile government reassert control over the country were key elements in forcing him to turn to Moscow. But Moscow did not step in, except by initially backing the UN and ultimately finding itself isolated from most African states at the UN Security Council.[11] The presence of Soviet advisers in Kinshasa, providing their advice to Lumumba as the United States and other Western powers dithered over how to react to the crisis in 1960, is simply insufficient evidence of a Soviet intention to launch a military operation to reclaim Katanga, bolster Lumumba, and create another Fidel Castro in the heart of Africa.

Although it took fifteen years, as well as the revelations of John Stockwell and others, to be exposed, the real force behind U.S. policy was not the balancing of political options claimed by former CIA director William Colby. Instead, it was the covert activities of the CIA itself, which followed its own agenda, dominated by the intrigues, naïveté, and conspiratorial mentality of the shadowy world of spies and agents. At the moment of independence for a country like Congo, the potential for U.S. policymakers in the Republican administration of President Eisenhower to possess a genuine understanding of what the country was going through was admittedly slim. Hardly surprising then that U.S. policy reflected instead the simple perspective of the CIA. Simplification appeared a particular skill of the CIA, as revealed when Lawrence Devlin, the CIA station chief in the Congolese capital Leopoldville (later renamed Kinshasa) cabled headquarters on 18 August 1960: "Embassy and station believe Congo experiencing classic Communist takeover Government. . . . Whether or not Lumumba actually Commie or just playing Commie game to assist his solidifying power, anti-West forces rapidly increasing power Congo and there may be little time left in which take action to avoid another Cuba."[12]

Scaremongers such as Devlin, who later profited from his relations with Mobutu by becoming a businessman through his connections to the future Zaire's diamond industry, did not appear to feel it was necessary to ascertain unequivocally whether Lumumba was a "Commie" or not, and it was in this atmosphere of ignorance and prejudice that U.S. policy took shape.

By addressing what it regarded as the need for a solution to the Congo's domestic crisis with a strategy—the Eisenhower-approved assassination of Lumumba—in fact intended purely to confront alleged Soviet expansionism, the United States assisted in creating the conditions which were to prevail in the country for the next thirty years. In 1960, however, it was not the case that instability in the Congo provided an atmosphere necessarily conducive to Soviet expansionism, even if the USSR had intended it. Lumumba sought assistance from all sides, and received little, as Stephen Weissman says:

> Lumumba's appeal for Soviet military aid to counter a much larger Western intervention in Katanga may have been unrealistic given the U.S.'s violent reaction; but it was not the result of Soviet-exploited "personal instability" since it arose from his group's basic political formula of militant nationalism. Nor were his actions guided by "pro-Soviet" advisers as the Americans charged. For example, two of his most trusted counselors, Press Secretary Michel and Ghanaian ambassador Din, opposed Lumumba's decision to accept Soviet aid. The Prime Minister's most influential colleagues were other [Congolese] nationalists. Even after the arrival of Soviet military equipment and technicians Lumumba manifested his independence by inviting Western technical assistance, recalling Belgian judges and teachers, and meeting with African diplomats who hoped to achieve a compromise between the impatient Prime Minister and the cautious UN Secretariat.[13]

Nevertheless, Devlin "reported to headquarters that he was serving as an adviser to a Congolese effort to eliminate Lumumba."[14]

The momentum for U.S. action accelerated, as if Mobutu's CIA-backed coup, which overthrew Lumumba on 15 September 1960, was the key to a political solution to the country's domestic crisis. Lumumba was taken into the protective custody of the UN. As Madeline Kalb wrote:

> Up to this point the U.S. Embassy and the CIA had taken a similar approach to the problem of Lumumba: They were both trying to force him out of office and to destroy him politically. Now that he was out, their priorities were somewhat different: while [U.S. ambassador Clare] Timberlake saw his dismissal as a victory for the forces of moderation and was ready to move to the next phase, the CIA continued to view Lumumba as a major threat to the U.S. position in Africa and stepped up its efforts to destroy him in a literal, physical sense.[15]

Mobutu's overthrow of Lumumba placed the apparently moderate Kasavubu in a more secure position as head of state, gave Mobutu the power the CIA had regarded as necessary to assure them that their influence was secure, and led to the closure of the Soviet embassy and the expulsion of Soviet diplomats and advisers. In Washington, however, these events were not seen as enough. On 26 September 1960, "Joe from Paris," the CIA's chief of technical services, whose real name was Sidney Gottlieb, arrived in Leopoldville with a vial of poison and Eisenhower's approval for the assassination of Lumumba.

By his critics, Lumumba was portrayed as a radical, unpredictable, and highly unstable political firebrand. His were the politics of a passionate, rather than a deep-seated ideology. But just as academic politics did not necessarily play a vital role in the direction taken by Lumumba, the same can be said of Mobutu. The chaos that pervaded political life in the newly independent Congo created conditions in which Mobutu's close ties with the West could be cemented by financial inducements that the Soviet Union barely seems to have matched, although funds were channeled through Ghana and Egypt to the Lumumbist political camp. The strength of the U.S. strategy in 1960 lay both in pursuing the diplomatic track via the embassy, and the covert track via Devlin's contacts with Mobutu. What the embassy could not win in terms of arguments, particularly at moments when Mobutu appeared to waver in his view of Lumumba in the days following his coup, the CIA could buy with mountains of cash with which to keep the chief of army staff sweet. Through Mobutu, the CIA was able to infiltrate the Binza Group, pliable and opportunistic civilian politicians surrounding Mobutu, which included the foreign minister, the finance minister, and two senior security ministers, all of whom were recipients of CIA funds and advice.[16]

The CIA's direct influence over Mobutu's military command—however unruly that command may have been—coupled with its influence over an influential section of the political class, allowed substantial CIA infiltration of the political field. This level of infiltration, René Lemarchand, Belgium's leading scholar on Africa and the continent's former Belgian colonies, asserts, amounted to "nothing less than an attempt to hamper the growth of individual loyalties to the newly emergent state. . . . One is impelled to wonder whether such practices do not constitute one of the most serious disabilities faced by Third World governments in their attempt to achieve a minimum level of national integration."[17]

From the earliest days of Mobutu's rise to influence under Lumumba, money played a key role in determining the direction of the "indecisive colonel,"[18] first with $1 million in UN funds approved by Lumumba, which were used on 1 September 1960 to pay the Congolese army led by Mobutu, in an effort to discourage them from roaming the streets of Leopoldville and stealing. As Kalb puts it,

> If UN money, however inadvertently supplied, gave Mobutu his first big boost, it was the additional money supplied by the CIA and by the Western embassies in Leopoldville that kept him in business from then on. . . . [The] indecisive colonel would never have taken the plunge if he had not been assured of major

outside assistance. From that time on . . . Mobutu always had plenty of cash to
pay his soldiers, even when the Congo's treasury was empty.[19]

Payments were also made to Kasavubu before Mobutu's coup ousted Lumumba.[20] Much of the financing for the anti-Lumumba camp was channeled
through the regime of Fulbert Youlou, president of Congo-Brazzaville, on
the other side of the Congo River. According to John Stockwell, the United
States was spending $1 million per day on its operations in the Congo by
1961.[21] Stockwell, a close associate of Lawrence Devlin, relates how Devlin
would always take large sums of money when he visited Mobutu, usually in
the region of $25,000. By the mid-1960s, Mobutu was refusing these sums as
too paltry, suggesting how quickly he had grown to assess his own value,
more in terms of millions than thousands. His self-evaluation was based on
what Stockwell estimates could have been as much as $25 million in CIA and
other U.S. funds, which passed through Mobutu's hands in the early and
middle 1960s.

Joe from Paris was overtaken by events, despite the best efforts of Devlin,
and the CIA's death squad become responsible for Lumumba's death. On 17
September 1960, the events that would place Congo in the U.S. camp for
the following three decades were falling into place. The scene was the UN in
New York, where African states keen to prevent the Cold War finding a
foothold on the newly independent soil of Africa voted in favor of a UN ban
on individual countries sending troops to Congo. The move was clearly
aimed at preventing the Soviet Union from honoring the commitment it had
tacitly made to Lumumba. The resolution thus spelled the end of Lumumba's hope that troops would be sent to allow him to retake Katanga,
which would have been his last hope of strengthening his own position. By
then, Mobutu had already ousted Lumumba. But the issue facing the superpowers was what to do with the former prime minister.

Nikita Khrushchev himself arrived in New York on 19 September, but he
was treated disdainfully by the United States and found the African members
of the UN largely opposed to his self-chosen role as a defender of African
nationalism. The Soviet leader had lost. The United States had successfully
used the cover of the UN to isolate Lumumba and thereby his allies in the
outside world, which had led to his downfall at the hands of Mobutu. At the
UN, there was little for Khrushchev to defend or gain, with regard to the
Congo. He could not expect Lumumba to be returned to power, as the UN
secretary general, Dag Hammarskjöld, had found that the UN strategy for
the Congo was untenable and inoperable if Lumumba remained prime minister, owing to UN reliance upon U.S. logistical and financial support. The
expulsion of the Soviet diplomats, the closure of the Soviet embassy, the isolation of the Soviet Union at the UN by African states, and the failure of
Khrushchev successfully to seize the mantle of a defender of Africa, sug-

gested that much was going the American's way. Simultaneously, however, Lumumba himself and certainly his supporters in Leopoldville remained a political force with which the "moderate" Kasavubu and other strands of political opinion had either to contend or confer. And so Lawrence Devlin still wanted Lumumba dead, and U.S. diplomats insisted on reminding the UN that "the Russians had 'not given up hope of returning' to the Congo,"[22] though quite how they intended to do so was never made clear.

As the UN sought a strategy that would advance the cause of finding political stability in the Congo itself—apart from the Cold War engagement of Moscow and Washington—it found the military junta created by Mobutu incapable of working with the UN, which had hitherto been the vital cover for advancing the U.S. campaign against Soviet influence. Mobutu needed a civilian aspect to his military government, which required the convening of parliament and thus meant that Lumumba might be rehabilitated politically as a parliamentary deputy. This possibility further intensified U.S. determination to murder Lumumba.

On 27 November 1960, a few days after Lumumba's last hopes of gaining credibility at the UN faded with the rejection by the assembly of the right of his representatives to occupy the seats of the Congolese delegation, he escaped from the guarded UN residence in which he had been held since Mobutu had ousted him. Immediately, Devlin, the CIA, Lumumba's political opponents, and Mobutu's Armée Nationale Congolaise (ANC: National Congolese Army) began scouring the country and throwing up roadblocks along the route from Leopoldville to Lumumba's home town of Stanleyville (later renamed Kisangani), to ensnare the deposed prime minister. U.S. ambassador Timberlake even went to the lengths of borrowing a helicopter from President Youlou of Congo-Brazzaville to aid in the search of Congo's democratically elected premier. When eventually he was captured, on 2 December, he was brought back to Leopoldville covered in bruises and blood, his spectacles broken, and immediately presented to Mobutu, whose troops beat him savagely in front of foreign television cameras. Ambassador Timberlake worried about the "movie recordings . . . [being] a gift of atomic bomb to Soviet bloc and friends."[23]

Stanleyville, where Lumumba had been heading when he was apprehended, had by then become the major source of political resistance to Mobutu and the junta in Leopoldville. The United States said Soviet aircraft were flying supplies to the self-proclaimed legitimate government of Lumumba's close ally Antoine Gizenga, which had established itself in the town. But the U.S. accusation was untrue, and Khrushchev, although sympathetic to Gizenga, was no more forthcoming with aid to Gizenga than he had been to Lumumba. Gizenga's supporters nevertheless mounted a military campaign, seizing territory in the west and center of the country. On 13 January 1961, Lumumba was freed by mutinous troops in the camp where he was being held, at Thysville. For a few hours he was again free, before the mutiny was quashed. Even before the Thysville mutiny, Mobutu and Kasavubu had asked Moïse Tshombe, the leader of the secessionist Katangese, if he would take custody of Lumumba, thereby putting him at the mercy of his most virulent political enemy. On 17 January, Lumumba was flown to Elizabethville (later renamed Lubumbashi). The aircraft landed, and Lumumba and two other prisoners, watched by UN soldiers and the Belgian mercenaries who led Tshombe's army, were beaten on the runway, thrown into a truck, and taken away. They were never seen again. Three days later, John Kennedy became president of the United States.

"CONGO NEEDS MARTYRS"[24]

By the beginning of January [1961], it was generally accepted by officials and diplomats in the Congo, even in far-off Stanleyville, that a change could be expected from the new [Kennedy] Administration—and if it was a change that would be welcomed by Gizenga and [UN representative Rajeshwar] Dayal, it was ipso facto a change that would not be welcomed by Timberlake, Devlin, Kasavubu, Mobutu, Tshombe, or the Belgians. . . . It does not seem far-fetched to suggest that much of the sense of urgency in the first few weeks of January which led to the death of Lumumba came not from the internal situation in the Congo, troubling though that may have been, but from fear of the impending change in Washington.[25]

U.S. policy toward the Congo in the months after independence assumed that convinced Marxists had infiltrated the ranks of both Congo's and Africa's nationalist movements. It also assumed, conspiratorially, that Moscow's influence within these movements was extensive and unquestioned by the movements, as well as the governments that emerged from them. Finally, it assumed that the "loss" of newly independent states to the "Soviet side" spelled the death-knell of U.S. influence. The rigid character of U.S. interference in the Congo, its use and abuse of the United Nations as a tool of its policy, and the U.S. reliance on such dubious figures as Mobutu to forge a "third way" were what characterized the U.S. involvement. Even though the actual political situation was far from being the pure East-West conflict the CIA's myopic operatives on the ground sought to portray it as being, the Congo seemed to the United States a theatre in which, "[in] the zero-sum terminology of the Cold War, U.S. success was a Soviet failure. Mobutu closed the Soviet embassy after his coup and Lumumba's demise ended whatever meager opportunities the Soviets might have had to increase their influence at the expense of the West."[26]

The death of Lumumba created a new rationale for U.S. involvement in Congo's affairs. The Soviet threat might have been neutralized, but the

United States was now faced with the prospect of having to help steer Mobutu, President Kasavubu, and other players on the political scene in a manner which would prove the value of having done so much to oust the elected prime minister. The U.S. had, after all, encouraged and supported a coup d'etat, planned an assassination, played with the fire of the Cold War on Congolese soil, and finally seen that all its efforts were just the beginning of three years of even greater instability than that which had prevailed in 1960. Three years of civil war followed Lumumba's death. The Soviet Union might have been sent packing from Congo, but the real conflict had yet to be fought.

The question remains as to whether U.S. support for Lumumba and the courting of the Lumumbists by the West, rather than their subjection to a Cold War rhetoric that never emerged from the heart of the Congo conflict but was imposed upon it from the outside, would have helped avert the bloodshed that followed. With a few exceptions, the Cold War in Africa was never as clear-cut as the Cold War superpowers necessarily felt obliged to portray it. Even the CIA admitted to doubts about whether Lumumba was actually a "Commie." He died as a result of a rivalry between enemies whose war was not even being fought in his country, but in the corridors of the UN, along the Iron Curtain, above the skies of the Soviet Union by U2 spy planes, and between the strategists of Washington, Langley, and the Kremlin. Lumumba's interest was ultimately in achieving personal power in his own country, as his appeals to the United States, the USSR, and the UN for assistance in putting down the Katanga secession showed. East-West ideology was way down his agenda. He was prepared to take from all sides.

By asserting the mixture of arrogance, pride, and dignity which radical, populist politicians are bound to do at such momentous points in the history of their countries, Lumumba frightened people off. Force of personality—the fiery Lumumba, the sinister and charming Tshombe, and the stolid Kasavubu—was a key aspect of the conflict. Lumumba was probably the wrong man for the job at that time. A firm, steady hand would have been more appropriate in the post-independence chaos of Congo. But by demonizing him ideologically, the United States assisted in slamming the door on Congo's aspirations and altered the expectations of independence. Instead of encouraging a flowering of nationhood drawing upon the variety of perspectives that a vast, new country like Congo clearly contained, the United States distorted the troubles naturally associated with the new life of independence into a sinister and bloody battle between extremes, from which Congo is still suffering in the twenty-first century.

Long before his second coup d'etat, on 24 November 1965, Mobutu had come to be regarded by the United States as an ineffective military leader.[27] His political indecision was already well known in 1960, and he had slowly withdrawn from direct political involvement in 1961, to concentrate on his

military duties. But he then proved himself wholly inadequate at leading the
national army against the Stanleyville rebels of Antoine Gizenga, which enjoyed the backing of Egypt. The political situation in Congo demanded political compromises, which would reintegrate Katanga and dissolve Gizenga's
Stanleyville rebellion. It took the Congolese army until 19 January 1962 to
end the Stanleyville uprising and arrest Gizenga. The issue that then faced
the pro-Western Congolese government of Prime Minister Cyrille Adoula
was the ongoing secession of Katanga, which only ended after the UN had
launched a military offensive against the separatist "Katanga Gendarmes"
and finally forced the Katangese leader Moïse Tshombe to leave the territory
on 21 January 1963.

Five months later, Mobutu arrived in Washington for a two-week visit. On
the lawn of the White House, Kennedy told him: "General, if it hadn't been
for you, the whole thing would have collapsed and the Communists would
have taken over."[28] U.S. goals had certainly been achieved, and Kennedy's at-
tribution of this success to Mobutu is a mark of how simple were the objectives
of U.S. policy. Congo was by then a country in ruins, without credible leadership, a country that had faced the whirlwind of the Cold War due more to the
paranoia of the outside world than the convictions of its indigenous political
players. Lumumba had never been a new Fidel Castro. Nor was Congo another Cuba. But in 1960 it had been the possibilities rather than the realities
that mattered.

Mobutu's second coup was a mark of the political failure that had characterized the entire period of superpower manipulation in Congo since independence. The "victory" over communism had never really happened, as
such a conflict had never really taken place. The victory that had been
achieved had in fact marked the end of the period of post-independence eu-
phoria, without laying the foundations for a durable political dispensation.
The United States saw Mobutu as a figurehead they could sell—when necessary—to *American* public opinion. Support for Mobutu could not be directly
linked to a firm knowledge of what was best for Congo, as the chaos out of
which Mobutu had emerged was of a kind that could never provide any best-
case scenarios. Accordingly, the United States had to promote Mobutu as the
man who had ended the Soviet threat, and thus as being a part of the policy
that had saved Congo from a worse fate. By 1965, there was no proof that
Mobutu was capable of doing any more than giving successive U.S. administrations the opportunity to show their own electorate that the United States
had a presence across the globe, and that that presence was bearing fruit as
far away as Central Africa. Mobutu's failure to engender any real discipline
in the soldiers he led, who were and remained, for his entire rule, a major
cause of Congo's and Zaire's insecurity, was largely ignored.

What was also largely ignored until the mid-1970s was the scale of
Mobutu's graft, which by 1962 was reckoned to have brought him so much

financial assistance from foreign powers that he was already thought to be a millionaire.[29] The consequences for the development of Congo and the surrounding countries of Central Africa were disastrous. To be effective, the CIA had to identify individuals or small groups of individuals with which it could do business. Lemarchand's judgment on the effects of this policy fit Congo perfectly: "The net result of CIA involvement in the internal politics of African states has been to greatly accentuate the dependence of their institutions on ethnic and regional particularisms, and sometimes on a very special category of occupational groups—i.e. mercenaries. . . . [That] it has had a profoundly detrimental influence on the stability of their political and military institutions is . . . undeniable."[30]

Officially, Mobutu sought to follow a path of nonalignment. He traveled widely, in Africa and beyond, and sought to play the role of mediator in the continent's quarrels, a role in which he rarely achieved success. Throughout, he remained a pragmatist, who had learned during the crisis of 1960–1965 that the best way to survive was, as Mobutu himself said on more than one occasion, to "fly high above the toads" and then step in as a safe pair of hands.

The Angolan conflict, which is examined in Chapter Two, tested the principles of Zaire's foreign policy. That policy moved to counter and exclude the leftist Movimento Popular de Libertacaõ de Angola (Popular Liberation Movement of Angola), the MPLA, from government, despite the view of the Organization of African Unity (OAU) that a solution to the conflict (which had erupted in 1974) had to be sought in the form of a coalition of the MPLA, the Frente Naçiõnal de Libertacaõ de Angola (FNLA: National Liberation Front of Angola), and the Uniaõ Naçiõnal para la Indepencia Total de Angola (National Union for the Total Independence of Angola), or Unita. Mobutu sought to use to his advantage not only CIA interest in the conflict, but also the animosity of his newfound Chinese allies toward the MPLA and its Soviet backers.

For Zaire and Mobutu, Angola was a chance to leap onto the world stage as a major Cold War player, in a game offering the potential of establishing a regional political dispensation that would hold the key to southern and central African development. However, the same weakness that had plagued Mobutu during the crises of the early 1960s returned. His own army, which he sent to fight alongside the FNLA, was ineffective. A clandestine CIA operation was exposed and halted, and the Chinese, ill-prepared to take on their Soviet adversaries, got cold feet and backed off from offering support to the FNLA on a scale that could match Cuban and Soviet support to the MPLA. Young and Turner state the case baldly:

> Diplomatically as well as militarily, the defeat could hardly have been more complete for Zaire. The MPLA was installed in Angola . . . ; the South African

and CIA intervention had swung African opinion solidly behind the
MPLA. . . . The vision of an Angolan triumph that would confirm Zaire as a
hegemonic regional power had thus become the nightmare of an embattled
Zaire, again cast into diplomatic isolation, anew the pariah state of tropical
Africa. This disaster, great as it was, was soon eclipsed by the relentless on-
slaught of the economic crisis.[31]

MONEY MAKES THE WORLD STAND STILL

In June 1967, the International Monetary Fund granted Zaire a one-year
standby credit of $27 million. Such was the health of the world copper mar-
ket, the country did not use the money. Mobutu did not like the IMF,[32] and
in 1975 he did everything he could to avoid IMF involvement in discussions
intended to secure funds to repay $887 million in Zairian debt owed to
ninety-eight banks around the world. But by the end of the year, Mobutu
had no choice but to turn to the IMF, having failed to see an upturn in copper prices, whose fall that year marked the end of his dream of Zaire as a
great power and himself as a great statesman. By 1982, Zaire was on the
verge of default. Within two years, the impact of a stringent package of IMF
economic austerity measures agreed on in 1983 began to take hold. More
IMF funds were released, but a full recovery was dependent upon a revival in
copper prices, coupled with increased foreign aid. Again, the price recovery
did not happen, and the foreign aid did not come. In 1986, Mobutu responded to the lack of foreign aid by limiting repayments on foreign debt to
20 percent of the national budget.

There is no doubt that the nature of the political regime—rather than the
vast extent of Zaire's social problems—was essentially to blame for the exac-
erbation of the economic crisis, which began seriously to bite after 1975 and
from which the country was never to recover. Mobutu's source of power was
essentially his control over economic resources, which he could use to retain
influence and buy domestic political support. In 1977, when the country began to reel from the economic collapse, the Mobutu family appropriated $71
million from the Central Bank of Zaire.[33] A trail of such theft has been left
across three decades of Mobutu's rule. Between 1970 and 1994, Zaire received $8.5 billion in grants and loans from Western donors, an assessment
based on IMF and World Bank documents.[34] Export earnings for the same
period, less a five-year gap for which figures are not available, were $10.7 bil-
lion, according to the IMF—a small sum for a country with such abundant
mineral resources. The patronage network that sustained Mobutu in power,
which included his ravenous family as well as the 10,000-strong Presidential
Guard, cost him millions of dollars that were handed out in cash. Stockwell
estimates that as much as $20–$25 million from the CIA could meanwhile
have passed through Mobutu's hands,[35] though a former U.S. National Se-

curity Council official, Roger Morris, estimated that much of what he said amounted to $150 million of U.S. funds was unaccountable funding from the CIA.[36]

Following the outbreak of the Angolan civil war, CIA funds destined for the Unita forces were delivered to Mobutu, but Mobutu did not routinely pass them on to Jonas Savimbi, the Unita leader. Mobutu quickly began to exploit his strategic importance, to serve the system of embezzlement he was creating. "Early on we channeled $1.4 million via Mobutu intended for the Angolans. But Unita came to us soon after to tell us, 'We're hungry. We can't do anything.' None of the money had gone to the Angolans, and our efforts to get Mobutu to pass the money on were futile," said Stockwell, recalling that the incident took place during the CIA directorship of George Bush, who would cement a close relationship with Mobutu that lasted well into the Bush presidency. "The CIA knew all along he was pocketing huge amounts of money," Stockwell said.[37]

By the late 1970s, according to an IMF report that was never published but widely leaked, Mobutu used his stolen funds to buy the allegiance of Western politicians, including a former Belgian prime minister. The report, completed in 1982 and written by a team of IMF officials installed in the Central Bank of Zaire (CBZ) under the leadership of Erwin Blumenthal, was an indictment of the entire system of government in Zaire.[38] Blumenthal had in 1964 been an adviser to the Katangese secessionist leader Moïse Tshombe, a fact Mobutu used against him when he later condemned the IMF.[39] He was then appointed to the West German Central Bank, before being appointed director general of the CBZ in 1978–1979. His secret 1982 report concluded that "there is no, I repeat no, chance on the horizon for Zaire's numerous creditors to get their money back. . . . Mobutu and his government show no concern about the question of paying off loans and the public debt. . . . [There] was, and there still is, one sole obstacle that negates all prospect: the corruption of the team in power."[40]

The "team in power" had as its main aim the use of state funds to retain that power. Blumenthal details the cavalier attitude toward the state finances that characterized the behavior of Zaire's military and political elite. The nature of the regime was well known by the early 1980s. What the CIA had known for two decades had been exposed publicly by Nguza Karl-i-Bond, the former foreign minister, in his book *Mobutu, ou l'Incarnation du Mal Zairois* (Mobutu, or the Incarnation of Zairian Evil), published in 1982. Karl-i-Bond listed the amounts the Mobutu family had stolen, and he was quite clear that it was not merely endemic corruption that had plunged Zaire into crisis. He made it clear that the raison d'être of the system, its very purpose, was corruption. "[Meanwhile] the West knows well enough what is happening in Zaire and what takes place every day under Mobutu's dictatorial and corrupt regime," Karl-I-Bond wrote.[41] He continued:

We are told that without Mobutu there would be chaos. Frankly, what is it that is taking place on the economic and social areas, if not chaos? The country has been through two wars in Shaba, and cannot be sure that there will not be other troubles. . . . The West's argument, according to which without Mobutu there would be chaos and the *balkanization* of the country, does not stand scrutiny. On the contrary, Mobutu has created all the conditions for the destruction of the country. The entire country, every day, is a powder keg. Everybody knows it. There's only one explanation: The West is defending its economic and strategic interests in Zaire.[42]

Both Karl-i-Bond's and Erwin Blumenthal's portrayals of the routine plunder of state finances was ignored by both foreign donors and governments, who thereby became complicit in the creation of the conditions which inevitably led to Zaire's collapse. Regional geopolitics determined that this collapse would happen. Blumenthal's report coincided with the buildup of Cuban troops in Angola, whose presence cemented U.S. support for Mobutu. By 1988 there were 50,000 Cuban troops on Angolan soil. IMF figures meanwhile show that the fund offered nine loans worth SDR 231 million[43] to Zaire between 1967 and 1982, when the Blumenthal report was completed. But three times this amount was offered by the fund between the year the report was written and 1989, in the full knowledge of the corruption Blumenthal had exposed. Blumenthal identified special bank accounts held in the name of the Central Bank of Zaire at seven foreign banks in Brussels, Paris, Geneva, London, and New York, holding millions in export earnings that had not been remitted. A key example of payments made to the special accounts reveals the amounts involved. In 1978 Zaire's state-owned copper and cobalt giant Gecamines was instructed to deposit its entire export earnings—which by 1989 had reached $1.2 billion—into an extrabudgetary presidential account. Despite this material and documentary evidence, which included account numbers and the amounts deposited, the IMF continued to sign standby agreements with Zaire.

Meanwhile, official presidential appropriations granted by Zaire's parliament accounted for 30–50 percent of the budget for capital investment from the late 1960s, reaching $65 million a year in 1988. Mobutu received funds for "political institutions," including the Mama Mobutu Foundation and the ruling Mouvement Populaire de la Révolution (MPR; Popular Movement of the Revolution). Blumenthal was unequivocal: "Every negative act has as its instigator Mobutu himself, even if there is never any proof, though nobody at the Central Bank nor in the government is able to take a personal initiative, even if the President wanted it."[44] A World Bank report containing data for the period 1980–1987 revealed that in 1986 the presidency officially received $15 million, though the World Bank document shows that Mobutu spent $94 million and the political institutions $172 million that year, revealing the extent of other sources of funding.[45] A further World Bank study, published in 1989, showed $209 million of the year's state expenditure was appropriated for what the Central Bank of Zaire itemized as "other goods and services."[46]

Intense debate within the United States regarding the advisability of U.S. support for Mobutu centered, unsurprisingly, on the strictest definitions of immediate U.S. interests rather than the harm that the process of protecting those interests might do within Zaire itself. On 31 March 1977, John Stockwell threw the entire debate over U.S. Cold War aims in Africa wide open when his letter of resignation to Admiral Stansfield Turner, the director of the CIA, was published in the *Washington Post*. Stockwell's letter demolished the entire U.S. rationale behind its policy in southern Africa, asserting for example that the MPLA was "the best qualified to run Angola; nor was it hostile to the United States."[47] Writing in the wake of the invasion of Shaba province by the Angola-based Katanga Gendarmes, on 8 March 1977, Stockwell asked: "[Having] encouraged Mobutu to tease the Angolan lion, will [the United States] help him repel its retaliatory charge? Can one not argue that our Angolan program provoked the present invasion of Zaire which may well lead to its loss of Shaba's rich copper mines?"[48] By 1977, Young and Turner concluded in their study of Mobutu's Zaire, "the old illusion in Zaire and the West that the economic crisis was a passing epiphenomenon had been thoroughly dispelled."[49]

Driving to the heart of U.S. policy, Stockwell's further devastating condemnation of U.S. action added fuel to the fires of doubt about U.S. engagement with Mobutu, when he referred to the death of Lumumba: "In death he became an eternal martyr and by installing Mobutu in the Zairian presidency we committed ourselves to the 'other side,' the losing side in central and southern Africa. We cast ourselves as the dull-witted Goliath, in a world of eager young Davids."[50]

Even so, a year later, on 18 May 1978, the *Washington Post* presented the second invasion of Shaba as coming at a time "of intense Western, and particularly American, concern about expanding Soviet-Cuban activities throughout Africa. In this context the possible fall of Mobutu and his replacement by a pro-Soviet leader must take on special meaning for both Washington and Moscow." Such inept reporting, raising the prospect of a neat transfer of power from one superpower camp to another on the basis of an incursion that was taking place hundreds of miles from Kinshasa and that never had the intention of overthrowing Mobutu, reflected the myopia that dominated U.S. analysis. Again I quote the *Post:* "The issue at stake is at once simple and complex: can the Carter administration sit by and risk the overthrow of Mobutu when the prospect, although still very far from clear, is a likely new leadership in Zaire supported by Angola, Cuba and the Soviet

Union." Such ridiculous conclusions clearly expose how little was known in the United States of the reality of Zaire, the intentions of its neighbors, and above all the viability of such claims.

The absence of an organized opposition to Mobutu throughout the high Cold War was a vital reason why there was no real danger of such a takeover. "[It] can be stated that the tremendous capacity of the Zairian state to resist the noxious effects of the ... crisis, despite many predictions about its imminent downfall, results from its clientelist character. Indeed, given the exclusion of such classes as peasants, workers, and the unemployed from clientelist relations, the chances of a viable political alliance between these classes and the client fraction of the national bourgeoisie are minimal," one writer asserted after the Shaba incursions, concluding that internal opposition could barely be amassed to oppose Mobutu.[51] By implication, the possibility that the incursions from Angola could have created the broader political conditions for Mobutu's overthrow simply did not enter into the thinking of those who knew Zaire well.

The polarization along superpower lines of the issues facing Zaire in 1977 and 1978 was a simple way of avoiding substantive analysis of the situation facing Mobutu, which involved not a political threat but an economic one, owing to the potential loss of the Gecamines copper and cobalt mines. In 1981, Lemarchand argued, "the threat of a Communist takeover in Zaire can no longer be used as a plausible scapegoat for throwing our weight unconditionally behind Mobutu."[52] The Communist threat to the Western economic interest in copper and cobalt mines supposedly presented by the Angolan-backed Katanga Gendarmes was a convenient pretext by which Mobutu and his allies in the West could galvanize support for his regime. "The scale of the Soviet-Cuban intervention in Ethiopia just before Shaba II supplied new arguments for globalists in the U.S. policy community, who argued that Shaba II bore the hallmark of Soviet machinations and required direct confrontation,"[53] Young and Turner asserted.

The more rational view appeared to prevail shortly after the 1978 Shaba rebellion, when the United States announced itself ready to establish contacts with the MPLA government in Angola.[54] Even so, President Jimmy Carter was obliged to blame Cuba and Angola for Zaire's troubles,[55] as they were accused of training the Katanga Gendarmes, and by implication undermining the U.S.-Soviet spirit of detente then prevailing. Western countries—notably France and the United States—knew, however, that the problems Zaire faced were domestic. The IMF had been allowed sufficient access to Zaire's accounts so that at the end of 1977 "it rescinded Zaire's eligibility for higher tranche credit, noting that the country was not meeting arrears, and that indeed it had no notion of what Zaire was doing."[56] The economic crisis eventually led to the conclusion that Zaire should allow receivers into its financial institutions. It was then that the Blumenthal team was appointed, whose report, as I have indicated, made such damning reading—yet was never published or acted upon.

With the end of the Carter administration, and the revival of the Cold War in Africa by the Reagan team after 1981, whatever pressures there had been on Mobutu were eased. George Bush, the new vice president and former CIA director, who was described by Mobutu himself as a man who "knew Zaire's problems backwards . . . [and] is [an] intelligent, open and sensitive man, with strong convictions,"[57] had met Mobutu thirteen times by 1989 and had invited the Zairian leader to his family home. Central to Mobutu's usefulness to the U.S. government was his role as a conduit for arms to Jonas Savimbi's Unita movement in Angola, following the repeal in February 1985 of the Clark Amendment, which had banned such aid. Aside from this logistical role, Zaire was by the early 1980s of no real economic use to anybody, except the diamond dealers prepared to take the risk of remaining there. It was a country which would go nowhere except downhill, in which "the politico-commercial class in intense pursuit of its short-term advantages, wound up destroying the means of their livelihood."[58]

RAGS AND RICHES

"Vous êtes les bienvenus (you are welcome)," pouted a woman with a deep voice, luscious lipstick, tight white jeans, and a chic handbag. We were a thousand miles from the coast, but the fish had been excellent. Stars shimmered over the darkness of central Zaire, as the wives of the company executives of the Minière de Bakwanga (MIBA: Bakwanga Mining) diamond mine at Mbuji-Mayi glittered, sparkled, and sipped the last of the chilled red wine. Leaving the restaurant, we walked to the Cosmos nightclub, where we ran the gauntlet of the welcoming women. Fluttering their eyelashes, they told us that, as guests of honor, we could avoid the long queue by entering through the kitchen. The Cosmos club throbs from 10 P.M. till morning. The woman who had bidden us welcome sashayed into a corner seat. She was joined by another, then another, until finally there were five. The mirrored globe suspended from the ceiling began to turn, lights flashed, and the ladies took to the floor, their handbags piled in a heap between them.

"They're all employed as chauffeurs by me at the diamond company," said Mabele Musamba, the deputy managing director.[59] Then his smiling wife leaned over and whispered in my ear. "You know they're all men," she said, pointing at the group. "They dress up like that every Saturday night, just to entertain everybody here in the Cosmos. It's fun, don't you think? They're just part of the scene here now." I looked at the group. The music changed to a slow dance number, and each one of them turned to a man, embraced him, and waltzed slowly across the dance floor. Nobody raised an eyebrow. It was the only club in town, where business executives, diamond diggers, dealers, company apparatchiks, and transvestite chauffeurs all socialized.

"Comment t'appelles-tu? (What is your name?)" The youngest of the transvestites introduced himself as Sylvestre, took my hand and led me to the dance floor. "Tu es de quelle nationalité? (You are of what nationality?)" His words oozed with hilarious affectation as we talked. He said he was married with three children, and that his wife was quite happy, that he came out on Saturday nights dressed as a woman, and no, whatever outsiders said about African conservatism about gender role models, he and his friends were never harassed.

Mbuji-Mayi, capital of the province of East Kasai, is close to the heart of Zaire, a town where, when I visited in October of 1994, the joie de vivre seemed to have intensified at a pace matched only by the degree of national decline. Saturday night at the Cosmos was the weekly highlight, in a life that no amount of hard work could improve. Every month, diamonds were being dug up from the pits surrounding the town. Most were smuggled out of Zaire. As the roads did not extend far from what had become a city-state in the heart of Zaire, people who wanted to leave took the plane. The airport had the trappings of an international terminal. There were direct flights to Tanzania, Zambia, and South Africa, and anywhere else the smugglers and dealers wished to go.

Since control of the diamond industry had been "liberalized" in the early 1990s, hordes of prospectors and dealers had descended on Mbuji-Mayi. Where once the market stalls had groaned under the weight of aubergines and tomatoes, they now carried diamonds, piles of them, lying on worn wooden counters beneath torn canopies that protected dealers and customers from the hot sun. "I tell you, we have some rules here," said a skinny dealer in a bright, silken shirt. He held up a tiny set of scales, and placed a few obsolete Zairian coins into the dish on one side. Then, from a small paper bag, he poured brown, rough diamonds into the other dish, until the scales were balanced. Diamonds sparkled on his wooden table. It was the same on the next stall, and on all the others. Diamonds everywhere, being sifted and sorted and examined by keen eyes set in serious faces. Deals were done, and bundles of Old Zaire notes changed hands. The dealers handed over the gems, throwing the money in cardboard boxes they kept beneath the tables. Then, on Saturday nights, the diamonds all come out to play; diamonds worn by women who had bought them, or had them bought for them, or dug them up illegally and then had them polished and set in gold. And there it all was, in the Cosmos nightclub, where Sylvestre and his friends danced among the diamond-clad women, taking their husbands away from them for a few dances, then returning them, before rushing to the bathroom to check on their makeup.

By August 1993, Mbuji-Mayi was exporting $25 million worth of diamonds[60] every month. By September 1994, the value had fallen to $13 million, as smuggling through Brazzaville and Bujumbura rose to account for 80 percent of the output. A 1.5 percent tax levied on diamonds was supposed to come to the state, and by 1994 was the only source of income to which the government could turn. But uncontrollable frontiers and the venality of the regime meant that money never arrived. By 1991, the products of other major sections of the economy were meanwhile being smuggled out of the country, including up to 60 percent of the coffee crop.[61] "It's an exaggeration to say that everybody is relying on diamonds. But all the politicians are relying on diamonds for their cash," said Mr. Amuri, the official at the Central Bank of Zaire in Kinshasa who was responsible for valuing the diamonds that were not spirited directly out of the MIBA in Mbuji-Mayi and sold in South Africa. Zaire was committing suicide, drawing the lifeblood from its own veins, while the people watched from the shacks, the roadsides, the slums, the closed factories, from beside the broken railroads and the banks of the churning, aimless river. The suicide was full of pain and fear, as people who thought they could escape the rising flood started to find that the collapsing edifice that had nurtured them had a tight hold despite its weakness.

"You know that Mobutu provides me with my security," said Jonas Kadiata Mukamba, quietly closing the door of his office. "Mobutu is the one who can guarantee whether or not I get home safely at night. He is the one who I am relying upon for my safety in Kinshasa. After Ceaucescou he is the last of the dictators. I'm frightened of him. So frightened. With one million Rwandans in the country, I am frightened."[62] Mukamba was a pillar of the establishment with which Mobutu had surrounded himself. On 17 January 1960, he had been sent to Thysville on a mission. Patrice Lumumba had trusted him. That day he visited Lumumba where he was being held, having been instructed to tell the deposed prime minister that there had been a coup d'etat in Leopoldville and that he was to return to the capital to form a new government.[63] Lumumba's trust was Mukamba's ticket to fame and fortune. Lumumba agreed to leave with him and was taken to the airport from where he was flown into the hands of Moïse Tshombe at Elizabethville and beaten to death, or perhaps shot. It thus became as much in Mukamba's interest to later resurrect Lumumba as a national hero as it was in Mobutu's, in the hope that they could hide their real role. For more than thirty years they pretended, Mukamba dependent upon Mobutu and vice versa. Now the system was unraveling, and nobody needed to believe anybody anymore. Time was running out, Mobutu was losing his grip, and that was why Mukamba was frightened of him.

"Mobutu Sese Seko: our salvation" said a rusting sign at an overgrown roundabout on the edge of Mbuji-Mayi, on the road from the airport. It was a cruel joke. At the airport, jets left directly for South Africa, Tanzania, and

Zambia, importing everything from bars of soap to matches and ignoring Kinshasa altogether, as Mbuji-Mayi sought to function outside the collapsed system Mobutu and his cronies were milking for all that it had. A policeman halted the traffic to allow some school children to cross a road that passed between modest but once elegant villas set amid trees and lawns.

"Mbuji-Mayi isn't just the main source of income for Kasai, but is the main support for the entire economy of Zaire. When the politics isn't going well nothing else goes well. Everything stops," said Kassembe Etete, vice-governor of East Kasai, the province at whose heart the diamond town lay.[64] "The misery of the people is the opponent of Mobutu," he said frankly of his political master, as he sat fidgeting nervously in his dark office behind a large desk, beneath a youthful photograph of the president. "There's a state, with a majestic river, and institutions of law and administration. But we have been subject to the crisis that never seems to end. We are the sacrificed generation. Why should you worry about not being promoted, when the salaries are not being paid? The president has accepted that he should implicate himself. Now there's a government that has found there is no money in the central bank. But that government wants to inspire people. In that sense there's a state," he said, riven with anxiety, incapable of hiding the fear that made him sweat and fidget endlessly.

Diamonds clattered onto the weighing machines behind the security glass and art deco front of the headquarters of the *Minière de Bakwanga*. Fifty thousand people were relying on the mine for their livelihood, while beyond the panners, diggers, scrapers, and *clandestins*, who crawled over the pits like ants, were one million residents of Mbuji-Mayi who lived off what the prospectors earned. The potential was vast, with up to fifteen years of the kimberlite reserves in which diamonds are found remaining to be tapped. Of the ten rock formations housing the kimberlite, six had been exploited since an English prospector had found the first diamond in Mbuji-Mayi in 1918. Now, 800 guards patrolled the mine to chase out the *clandestins*, whose work had doubled the output of the MIBA site since 1982, but who were largely responsible for the fact that up to 10 percent of the diamonds from the area were being stolen. Their theft, however, kept the local economy rumbling on, isolated from the rest of the country by distance, an island sitting on the great empty plains of central Zaire. Politics, distance, fear, and disillusionment tarnished the glitter, the wealth, and the fun of a Saturday night at the Cosmos. When officials from Kinshasa arrived in Mbuji-Mayi to enforce acceptance of the New Zaire (NZ)—the currency Mobutu forced upon the country in October 1993 as a means of reasserting the sovereignty of the discredited regime—the population refused. The Kasaians supported Etienne Tshisekedi. Troops beat people in the streets, to force them to use the new currency. They still refused. Only MIBA accepted the New Zaires in its shops.

"There are enough Old Zaires here, though the military tried to seize them," said Tchbobo Mfuamba, MIBA's technical director.[65] "Here we have the Old Zaire, the New Zaire, and the U.S. dollar. If I want to go to other parts of the country outside East Kasai, I use the New Zaire and the dollar." Within a year of the New Zaire being introduced, its value had tumbled, to a rate of NZ1.7 million to the dollar. Meanwhile, the Old Zaire had retained its value in Mbuji-Mayi, a symbol of how the town existed as a separate enclave in the dying country. "You know the truth," said an accountant at the mine, who had been hovering in the doorway waiting for the chance to speak to a foreigner. "There are some dictators who are good and others who are bad. And the one we have is bad. But you know that people don't want to talk. They are too frightened really to talk. They won't be frightened of you. But you know I feel I may as well talk, because when I'm dead I won't be able to say anything. But the people are on their knees."

Others tried to remain hopeful, forcing themselves to remain optimistic in a horrifying way that instead exposed their anxiety, as they tried too hard to deny that the catastrophe was already upon them and that a few more weeks, months, or even years would just be a period spent awaiting the inevitable. "Having all the currencies: it's democracy," said Kalonji Mbwebwe, general administrator of Mbuji-Mayi's Coca Cola bottling plant.[66] "We're not in a federal state. But what does a businessman do? If people accept Old Zaires or Swiss francs, then I will use them. There's no monetary pluralism, even if different money is circulating. We are in a period where people are trying to eat." He was proud of the factory, and the fact that it kept functioning, bottles clattering on conveyor belts through machinery squirting Coca Cola or Fanta. MIBA gave the factory the water and the sugar, and the concentrate was imported from Atlanta, Georgia, via South Africa. The market limit of the 1,944 liters sold per year was imposed by the fact that the roads had collapsed 130 kilometers beyond the town.

Along the road to the east, where the town gave way to the prairies (which need to be seen to be believed), Charles Tshinguvu, the *chef de la cité* (chief of the city) of Mbuji-Mayi, had his land. He grew maize, which MIBA bought from him and distributed to its workers in lieu of salary. The town had become self-sufficient in food, he said, the subsistence level this feat had created for the diggers of the diamonds seeming symbolic of the collapse. While the leaders profited from the diamonds, the workers were paid in food. Mr. Tshinguvu drove further on, across the prairies, to where the gush of a fast-flowing river broke the silence. The Tshala dam stood out against the clouds and the lush grasslands. Careful maintenance kept the turbines working, powering every house in Mbuji-Mayi, as well as the mine, and the computers of Mbuji-Mayi University. "Students come from Zaire, Rwanda, Burundi, Angola. It's the most serious university in central Zaire. We don't take just anybody," said François Kabilenge Mukendi, the university accountant.[67] His desk was piled high with one-million-denomination Old Zaire notes. The university had opened in 1990, with courses in science, economics, law, medicine, and applied science, and by 1994 had attracted 759 students, 15 visiting professors, 2 permanent professors, and 14 assistants, all set on preparing students for a future their country's leaders had ensured they would not have.

The isolation of Mbuji-Mayi and much of the province of East Kasai in which it stood, as I saw it during that visit in 1994, was more a reflection of the weakness of the Mobutu regime than a mark of any regional assertiveness or a shift toward a spirit of federalism. Mbuji-Mayi did not know where it was going then, and it is now plunged deep into the destruction wrought by the civil war that overthrew Mobutu in 1997 and that has been raging ever since. Further south, the illusory fires of rekindled federalism, which glowed temporarily in Shaba—the renamed Katanga—in the early 1990s, evoking the secessionist spirit of Moïse Tshombe, were a world away from the sentiments of the diamond town. "In Shaba there are two tendencies: pro-Mobutists, and those against Tshisekedi. Some people in Shaba aren't Mobutists, but they have been stirred up by Nguza and Kyungu," said Louis Kabungo Mukendi, a leading local member of Tshisekedi's Union démocratique pour le progrès sociale (UDPS: Democratic Union for Social Progress), referring to the Shaba governor, Gabriel Kyungu wa Kumwanza, and his discredited political mentor, Nguza Karl-i-Bond.[68] "We don't want Tshisekedi to come. If he comes here there will be deaths. There's not enough security. The mass of the population would chase after him. There would be deaths. We don't need him to come to galvanize the supporters," he said of his own party chief, a further sign of how hope of political advances in the country had disintegrated owing to the bitter nature of the battles the political heavyweights in faraway Kinshasa had fought with each other. "The risk of civil war is real and the temptation is big. [But] we are for a democratic battle, not a civil war. But among the masses there's an impatience to take up arms."

By the mid-1990s, the desperation of all sides in Mbuji-Mayi, from Mukamba the diamond king to the provincial officials of the beleaguered opposition, had been intensified over tortuous months and years, during which the sinister political atmosphere and the ruthless determination to continue their graft by those with access to Zaire's riches had denied the country a way out of its catastrophe. Mbuji-Mayi could not be allowed to find a political path of its own, because its diamonds were sustaining the theft of the crooks in Kinshasa. Meanwhile, its natural support for its native son—Etienne Tshisekedi—could not be strengthened and therefore be allowed to become formidable and meaningful, as the regime was not serious about letting the opposition take real power. By 1994, the Central Bank of Zaire (CBZ) was itself buying substantial quantities of diamonds, using local currency, though without repatriating the foreign currency it earned when it sold the diamonds abroad. To buy the diamonds, the regime used a group of Lebanese businessmen to organize the printing of local currency, first in Brazil, then in Argentina, sending inflation soaring to 24,000 percent. The sale of diamonds through unofficial channels, which denied the state any income through taxes, allowed the elite around Mobutu to amass funds abroad, over which Kengo wa Dondo, the prime minister, had no control.

A stuffed leopard grimaced in the hallway of Kengo's white villa on the river's edge in Kinshasa, the animal a symbolic reminder of the omnipresence of the leader who had long ago adopted the animal as his mascot. "The problem with our country is that when people gain certain privileges they don't want to lose them. The situation now facing us is such that those with privileges risk losing both those privileges and losing their lives,"[69] Kengo told me when I saw him in the autumn of 1994, ponderous understatement being a mark of his political style. He told me he was about to recommend the dismissal of the governor of the CBZ and his replacement with another, perhaps less venal candidate. It was a battle he would lose the following week. While Mobutu would not overtly prevent the means whereby he and his cronies could, in Blumenthal's words, "make no distinction between the expenditure of the state and their personal needs,"[70] Kengo was listing the items on the mounting roll call of catastrophes that was to be the undoing of Zaire: "Since I came in I have had nothing but misfortunes: the forged money, the Rwandans, the CBZ governorship battle. If I find it impossible to do my job, I will leave. I don't know if I will leave the country for my own personal security. Why can't this country realize its dream?"

He, who had twice been prime minister and long built his fortune on the corrupt foundation that Zaire's regime provided, knew the answer. "People know that what Kengo does isn't going to lead to concerted changes for most of them. And they are preparing for the consequences. Even Mobutu isn't secure in Kinshasa. The population threatens him, which is why he stays in Gbadolite," General Singa, the former head of the intelligence service, had told me a few days before I had seen Kengo.[71] "So, Mobutu doesn't control the country. Kengo is not accepted by the people. The reality is that only Etienne Tshisekedi is accepted by them." Tshisekedi was at that time banished to his house in Limete, where his predictions were becoming as dire as those of Kengo. "Zaire is a country that has become unsavable and has isolated itself. Zaire has no real friends in the outside world," he said.[72]

The storm was gathering. The night was hot and there was no moon to light the way along the endless, unlit road to N'djili, Kinshasa's grim airport, as I made my way out of Zaire at the end of what had been a particularly unnerving visit. On a previous visit, a senior official of the Service Nationale de l'Information et de Protection (SNIP: National Information and Protection Service) at the airport had grabbed me by the arm and hauled me into an office in the broad light of day, locked the door, and held out his hand as he demanded $300 "pour le service" (for the service). Silence had ensued as we sat, staring at each other, until a loud banging on the door had forced him to open it. Outside was Vincent, the head of the airport immigration service. "I am so so sorry for what they have done to you. It creates such a bad impression of our country. I hope they did not ask you for money," he had said, as he freed me from the clutches of the SNIP, his face blushing with embarrassment and anger.

After this incident we got to know each other. He was perhaps living proof that hope should not be abandoned, even as the country reborn as Congo disintegrates now at the hands of rival armies from across the region. He was not only an honest man in dreadful circumstances, but was able to condemn the system in which he lived, despite the power it had to either sustain him or leave him to die. He refused my offers of help for his family. Vincent's dignity was not a ploy, and he guided me through the airport on innumerable subsequent visits, while neither asking nor expecting anything in return. "We are all responsible for this terrible crisis," he said when we met again that evening in October 1994, his own dignity apparently meaning little to him. "All of us have contributed. And now we have nobody to lead us out of it. But I promise, we are not all like that."

2

THE SKULL BENEATH THE SKIN

Angola and the Cold War

SOMETIME EARLY IN THE MORNING, before dawn, when the military checkpoints were gunmen's shadows and the blackened buildings rose, their expressions as blank as the devastated faces of the people, out of the darkness against the starlit sky, a brazier glowed beside the road to the airport. It was August and the southern summer, but the shivering cool of autumn filled the night. Perhaps it was the breeze from the ocean that cooled the city and cradled the trees lining the streets, whose architecture had barely changed (except for the bullet holes) since the beginning of the conflict in 1975; they seemed to emerge straight out of the country's history. The city of Luanda bore the marks of its pain, its destruction exposing the depths of its calamity. However, it had been months since there had been any fighting there.

In a dingy apartment block Vladimir the TASS correspondent, one of the 400 Russians remaining from a previous Soviet presence of 5,000 personnel, sat half-naked and hunched over his desk, bemoaning the fact that his wife and child were forbidden by Soviet-era rules to accompany him to such a place; he tapped out his reports and sent his telexes to Moscow, a chronicler of the last days of the defeated Cold War power's African "empire." False hopes lay ruined in the doorways, where families huddled for shelter, and everywhere at night shadows lingered in the shadows—gunmen, thieves, police, trapped in the hopeless spiral of twenty years of war, then twenty-five years, war forever threatening to crash into streets which for now were deserted but for the shadows.

"Do you know the joke about Angola?" asked Joao Neto, as he sank his third South African beer in one of Luanda's numerous bars called simply Americano. "It was the time of the Creation and people were complaining that God had given Angola an unfair quantity of valuable resources—diamonds, oil—that sort of thing. And so God replied: 'Ah, but you haven't yet seen the people I'm going to put there.'" The bar, which was around the corner from the apartment where I was staying, disappeared into lugubrious shadows at its far end. The apartment belonged to Katia Airola, a tough, kindly Finnish woman who ran the government press center and took young reporters like me into her care, with a view to helping them along in a difficult country, while trying to compensate for their ignorance of a horrifying war with careful explanation of what had happened, was happening, and would happen.

There was rain in Luanda, and clouds, and in the summer of 1993 I had the overwhelming sense that the city and the country were little different from the days and weeks in 1975 when the war, whose third or fourth chapter I was witnessing, had begun. Thirteen years of war against the Portuguese colonizers of Angola had failed to oust the Europeans, until 25 April 1974, when the dictatorship of Antonio de Oliveira Salazar was ousted by a military coup in Lisbon, and Portugal rapidly quit its African colonies of Guinea-Bissau, Mozambique, and Angola. "I remember the wooden crates the Portuguese made to take their possessions back to Europe,"[1] Katia reminisced of that other time of false hopes: "The line stretched from the port all the way up the hill. There were so many crates, because the Portuguese knew they couldn't spend their Angolan currency in Portugal, so they bought anything they could here, in order to sell it when they got home. They emptied the shops. There was nothing left. The shelves only filled up in 1991, during the peace. But now they're empty again."

"We see a good possibility that war will continue here over the next six to eight months," said Joe Schriver, the U.S. embassy spokesman in Luanda.[2] "It appears that Unita isn't going to return to the negotiating table until there's more pressure on them. That's why it's important for the government to establish its control over the country." More war was the answer, apparently. Then the two sides would be forced to talk. But the talking had already happened. And his analysis echoed as far back as 1975, and forward to the early twenty-first century, throughout which time war has been proved merely a sign of failure, and certainly not "politics by other means." Nothing had come out of war, and the superpower logic that war could somehow create the conditions for peace exposed the same shameful ignorance that had transformed Angola into a theatre of the Cold War in 1975. Nothing had been learned. U.S. policy in

Angola, as in much of sub-Saharan Africa, was so deeply flawed that it would have been preferable that there had been no policy at all. The results could not have been worse. In 1991, Unita and the MPLA government had talked, and they had signed the Bicesse accord to end the war, which it was agreed would lead to an election in 1992. The election was held, Unita lost, and Jonas Savimbi's troops transformed Luanda into a bloodbath, before being driven out of the city and back into the hills, where the full-scale war erupted again, and is still raging, more than a quarter century after independence, forty years after the first shots were fired. But by then, one superpower had collapsed, and the other was interested only in easing its way out of the catastrophes its policies had done so much to create.

My Enemy's Enemy Is My Friend

I had been waiting for more than two hours, in a luxurious, sprawling villa almost hidden by the thick trees covering a slope on the edge of Cocody, rich suburb of Abidjan, the capital of the Côte d'Ivoire. A telephone call and a summons had interrupted the calm prevailing throughout the daylight hours of Sunday in the Ivorian capital. The villa had been the gift to Savimbi of Felix Houphouët-Boigny, the Ivorian president, one of Unita's stalwart supporters. The surrounding streets were quiet and empty, as a large gate swung open onto a drive cluttered with gleaming Mercedes'. Ivorian paratroopers lounged on chairs near the back door. John Marques Kakumba, Savimbi's resident representative in Abidjan and a relative by marriage of Felix Houphouët-Boigny, approached in impeccable dress and welcomed me and two colleagues with equally impeccable grace. We waited inside, until suddenly a door opened, and in the forthright style of his wife's brother-in-law—Mobutu Sese Seko—Savimbi strode into the large reception room swinging a carved cane, an enormous diamond glittering in a gold ring on his finger. The smiles were as for old friends, or at least acquaintances, though neither I nor my colleagues from the small group of journalists living in Abidjan had met him before. The charm was overwhelming, the theatrics beginning with the offer to conduct our discussions in whichever language we cared to name.

Jonas Savimbi's actions were, are, and will continue to be much more significant than the ideological content and substance of his pronouncements. The contradictions in his statements, the opportunism that led the CIA to open its lines of communication and supply with the Unita leader, and the brutality with which he has disposed of his critics during his lifelong effort to take power in Angola have, more than with any other of the U.S. Cold War adventures in Africa, been vital in pursuing a policy that has, at its heart, shameful disregard for the ordinary people trapped in a conflict from which they have nothing to gain.

The pressures on the United States, and in particular those "foot soldiers of foreign policy,"[3] the CIA, to respond to the emerging rivalries and political factions in Angola in the era of post-Vietnam U.S. humiliation, were admittedly substantial. The FNLA, led by Holden Roberto, which had been formed in 1962 to fight the Portuguese, had been intended as a united front of all Angolans against the colonizers. Then in 1973, prior to independence, it had received arms and 112 military advisers from China at its base in Zaire. Having realized—very late in the day—that the Portuguese colonialists were about to lose their power, the United States began a rapid search for somebody to back. In July 1974, the CIA stepped up its funding of the FNLA,[4] which had first received U.S. support from the Kennedy administration.[5] Prior to Angolan independence,

> Nixon and Kissinger bet on the tenacity and staying power of the white regimes to protect American interests, but it was a losing bet from the start. . . . [Furthermore it] appears that Kissinger was initially unaware of the complexity of the external support for the Angolan parties at the time he entered the imbroglio. . . . For example, he never took into account the fact that the Soviet Union had dropped all support for the MPLA only one month before the Portuguese coup or that the Soviets continued to withhold support for a period of approximately seven months. Nor did it apparently bother him that the "anticommunist" party he chose to back was receiving most of its support from the People's Republic of China, Romania, and North Korea. Kissinger called this the "pro-Western faction," an appellation which few Americans questioned.[6]

By 1974, the CIA's mistaken view was that the FNLA was the most formidable military force in opposition to the MPLA, the leftist movement that held sway in Luanda at independence. The sequence of events that led to the entire Angolan political-military scene being co-opted by the Cold War superpowers then began to take shape. The United States led the way, with its support for the FNLA. John Stockwell, the chief of the CIA Angola task force at the time, subsequently wrote:

> In February 1975, encouraged by Mobutu and the United States, Roberto moved his well-armed forces into Angola and began attacking the MPLA in Luanda and northern Angola. In one instance in early March they gunned down fifty unarmed MPLA activists. The fate of Angola was then sealed in blood. The issue could only be decided through violence. . . . Although allied with the MPLA through the early seventies, the Soviets had shut off their support in 1973. Only in March 1975 did the Soviet Union begin significant arms shipments to the MPLA. Then, in response to the Chinese and American programs, and the FNLA's successes, it launched a massive airlift.[7]

The instrumental role the United States played in escalating the military nature of the conflict is clear, its activities acting as a catalyst for the acceleration of Soviet military support for the MPLA. Prior to Angolan independence, attempts had been made by the FNLA and MPLA to overcome their differences. But a key element in their rivalry was the nature of the support they sought outside Angola during long periods in exile during the 1960s. The FNLA succeeded in gaining substantial political support from the United States during the late 1950s. Roberto began receiving the rather miserly sum of $6,000 as an annual retainer from the CIA in 1961, and it was increased to $10,000 in 1962.[8] Successive U.S. administrations in the 1960s nevertheless generally regarded the support of fascist Portugal, a Cold War and NATO ally against the Soviet Union, as too important to be compromised by whatever support they might wish to lend to the movements fighting for Angola's independence from Portugal.[9] Meanwhile the MPLA leader Agostinho Neto sought and received support in Western Europe and various African countries, though only limited material support from the Soviet Union until 1975.

The character of Cold War support for the rival movements during the 1970s, together with the civil war which that support played a key role in escalating, drove an immovable wedge between the rival movements, exacerbating the political differences between them and dragging the causes of the war far from their actual roots and onto the world stage. Among the real local issues was the one of race: "Many of the unfriendly exchanges between the MPLA and the FNLA dwelt on the question of race. Pointing to the FNLA's characterization of it as a movement dominated by *mesticos* [Angolans of mixed African and European descent], the MPLA in turn accused Roberto's front of being racist."[10] Throughout 1974, following the coup in Portugal which created the conditions for Angola's independence, Savimbi, according to Fred Bridgeland, a close observer of Angola, sought to reconcile the three rival political movements in Angola.[11] Bridgeland cites Savimbi as saying of a planned Unita-MPLA meeting, "As we are bound to work together to form a new government in Angola, we must cease attacking each other and mobilize the people for freedom. We want to prepare the ground for talks with the Portuguese so that we go to meet them not as rivals but as equals."[12]

On 5 January 1975, Savimbi, Neto, and Roberto signed a trilateral agreement in Kenya, under the guidance of Jomo Kenyatta, the Kenyan president, which recognized the right of each other's parties to exist and the need for a political transition following independence. Although it is perhaps a distraction to attempt to ascertain which of the warring factions first placed the trilateral agreement under strain by resorting to arms in the days immediately after independence, the contradictory claims are stark. Stockwell, the CIA operative charged with launching the United States fully into the Angolan war, asserts that Soviet arms did not arrive in the hands of the MPLA until 1975—after the

United States had sent supplies to the FNLA.[13] Bridgeland, whose account of
the rise of Savimbi is prone to paint a flattering portrait of the Unita leader,
contends that the MPLA was being supplied by Moscow during the last four
months of 1974.[14] Stockwell's account of the CIA operation in 1975–1976,
however, suggests that the actual sequence in which arms arrived is relatively
unimportant. The United States had decided to back the FNLA first and then
Unita, in both cases apparently on the *assumption* that the MPLA would take
Angola into the Soviet bloc, because of its declared Marxist leanings and the
political support it had received from Moscow during the 1960s.

William Minter, a leading U.S. authority on southern Africa, bluntly
characterizes the context in which this support was forthcoming:

> The primary motives for active U.S. intervention against the MPLA in 1974–75
> were not based on Angola or African realities at all. The Angolan crisis came
> when U.S. Cold Warriors were feeling particularly vulnerable. The U.S. client
> state in South Vietnam faced its final collapse. The Watergate scandal in Wash-
> ington was unseating a president and reinforcing doubts about the reliability of
> U.S. power. Popular revolution and a Communist Party strongly linked to
> Moscow posed a threat in Portugal itself, a NATO country. For Henry
> Kissinger, global considerations were paramount. Washington might have to re-
> treat from Indochina, but closer to home, it had to show the Soviet Union it
> could still defend its turf. Hard-line tactics had succeeded in overthrowing Pres-
> ident Salvador Allende in Chile in 1973, and might work in Angola as well.[15]

Broadly speaking, however, Soviet policy in Angola, as elsewhere in
Moscow's low priority regions of the Third World, was in general responsive
to events on the ground, rather than proactive. When a vacuum appeared,
the Soviets would offer assistance.[16] "In the face of its diminishing influence,
Moscow [after Khrushchev] began to streamline its policy towards the
[African] continent. From that time, it was to consist of concrete relations
with African regimes, relations not solely based on ideological affinities."[17]
Soviet diplomatic activity, dominated globally by its search for parity in nu-
clear weapons with the United States, was much of the time as strongly influenced by the desire to assert its socialist credentials, as part of its rivalry
with China, as by the ideological schism with the United States. Even so, the
MPLA under Neto established its key alliances abroad with the Communist
parties of Europe and elsewhere, and managed to retain Soviet support, despite lengthy periods during which Moscow cooled to the MPLA as it became wracked by internal disputes and factionalism.

Having chosen who to support, on the basis of what they were *not*, the
CIA then found that "Roberto and Savimbi never cooperated to the point of
telling us about their other allies: the Chinese, the Portuguese, and South
Africans."[18] Such discretion may have lain behind the view, expressed to me

during an interview in 1993 by Chester Crocker, U.S. assistant secretary of state for African affairs in the 1980s, when he said bluntly: "I never trusted Savimbi."[19] As the political reality was essentially derived from an under-standing—or lack of it—of the *military* reality, the CIA strategy and the intelligence gathering that filtered through to Washington's *political* decision-makers in 1975–1976, developed in response to perceptions of the real or imagined military threat posed by the Soviet assistance being provided to the MPLA.[20] Clearly it spiraled on both sides. On 14 October 1975, South Africa invaded Angola from Namibia. Within a few days of independence on 11 November, Cuba sent the MPLA 4,000 troops to supplement its 1,500 advisers already in the country, while the Soviet Union sent tanks, and Cuba subsequently sent a further 4,500 troops. China, the Soviet Union's other rival, continued to support the FNLA.

GUNS AND IDEAS

Did the rivalry between the MPLA and first the FNLA and later Unita warrant the incorporation of Angola into the theatre of the Cold War, and was the global character of the conflict consistent in nature with the pattern in which the local conflict had escalated? In 1964, the MPLA founder, Mario Pinto de Andrade, had announced: "During this phase of the national liberation struggle, there is no question of pledging our policy to either of the two blocs dividing the world. The only promise we make to the two blocs is that we will honestly seek to exclude attempts at establishing a cold war climate among the Angolan nationalists and to prevent the implications of international intrigues in the Angola of tomorrow."[21]

Agostinho Neto's later admission, in a 1969 radio broadcast, "That people fighting for independence will take aid from wherever they find it, is clear. To win our independence we should even take aid, as they say, from the Devil himself,"[22] was theoretically no less true for the MPLA than its rivals. Five years earlier, Holden Roberto had used practically the same phrase, though ostensibly as a challenge to the United States to support the FNLA or see him seek assistance from the Soviet Union. What prevented Neto's threat from being realized was the stipulation by the United States that it would only back the side that was fighting against the apparent interests of the Soviet Union. Guimaraes considers the MPLA as having been "intent on bringing the Cold War into its power struggle with the FNLA and Unita."[23] In 1964, the Soviet Union had declared open support for the MPLA in its opposition to the Portuguese colonial government,[24] though refraining from committing significant material support in order to avoid damaging its own relations with Lisbon.[25]

The role of ideology in the Angolan conflict must be seen against the background of the increasing radicalization of independence movements around the world in the late 1960s, and in particular the example set to independence movements by Vietnam following the U.S. defeat. Even so, the polarization of the Angolan conflict was accelerated post-independence by the conditions set by the United States in return for providing aid to the FNLA and Unita. The rivalry was cemented, whereas, at least in the first stage of the post-independence war, it had been a much more flexible rivalry from the protagonists' point of view than the global superpowers wished it to be. "There was . . . a definite ideological basis for the relationship that the MPLA came to develop with the Soviet Union. But both the Angolan movement and Moscow demonstrated the capacity to be pragmatic and transcend the ideological character of their relationship, especially if there were political gains to be had."[26] Such pragmatism did not exist on the U.S. side, which appeared to have no substantial ideological affinity with the armies it supported, the aims of the FNLA and Unita at that time having no more proven credibility as promising a brighter future for Angola and its people than that espoused by the MPLA. Faulty judgment was a constant feature, with the United States first opting to increase support for the FNLA in the belief that Roberto's force "would provide the most stable and reliable government."[27] The haphazard nature of CIA decisionmaking, as elucidated by Stockwell and revealed by his own readiness to opt to support Unita after a visit to Savimbi which lasted only a few hours on 20 August 1975,[28] reveals the extraordinarily cavalier attitudes that contributed so much to the transformation of Angola into a blood-soaked wasteland riddled with bullet holes and strewn with land mines.

In 1965, following a four-month period in China, Savimbi had written that the struggle to achieve Angolan independence was not an "ideological struggle":

> It has to unite all. . . . It is a democratic national struggle of a popular nature. This struggle has to incorporate everyone from the sincere chief who dislikes the odious Portuguese colonial system up to the most enlightened revolutionary, . . . from the isolated peasant in the valley and the mountains who only gets from his work his poverty to the contract laborer who does not even know the warmth of home.[29]

The unity he publicly espoused during the war for independence was nevertheless unlikely to endure into the post-independence era, when the nature of the rivalry inevitably changed, as it had done throughout Africa after independence movements became independent governments in the early 1960s. Moreover, in 1964 Savimbi had strongly criticized Holden Roberto for pandering to "American imperialism" and given that pandering as a reason for his resignation from the FNLA.[30] But did the struggle after independence then automatically become an ideological one, in a form in which the United States could responsibly become involved? Such was the shameful abuse of global military power, that the era of U.S.-Soviet detente that benefited Europe was irrelevant in the battlefields of the Third World, where instead there was total war. No meaningful effort was made by the United States to discuss Angola directly with the Soviet Union, in an attempt to avoid an escalation.[31] That escalation served the superpowers too conveniently, as a stick to beat each other, while the theatre of Angola was sufficiently distant from the United States to prevent it ever becoming the televised, photographed disaster of Vietnam. Without U.S. troops on the ground, the potential for arousing American public opinion was in any case nonexistent. For Angola, meanwhile, the damage has been devastating, has benefited nobody, has brought no victory, has condemned the country to a dark age, as the victim of that commonly used post–Cold War designation, "the forgotten war."

The Angolan war escalated, despite assertions by the protagonists that the country should not become the stage for a Cold War clash. In the same statement in 1965 cited above, written in a letter to former American missionaries who had worked in Angola, Savimbi had warned against an "ideological struggle . . . which might lead to a direct or indirect confrontation of the great powers."[32] What appears in part to have shifted his perception was the rivalry emerging between the opposing factions with regard to how to harness African political tradition to the modern era of independence, as elucidated in his assertion that "political and economic theories which are supported in atheistic attitudes do not fall in line with the feelings of Africa. The African believes in a higher Being, whatever his name may be or whatever the place he is worshipped. There is an ancestral force which transcends man."[33] Debate over such issues of identity and consequently of political organization and governance, which war cannot resolve, are closer to the heart of the Angolan conflict than disputes emerging from the now dead ideologies of East and West. The continuation of the conflict for more than a decade since the end of the Cold War suggests this to be so.

Even as the Cold War raged, all sides nevertheless generally stressed centralizing, national, and—to vastly varying degrees—nontribal political agendas,[34] despite the fact that until the launch in 1990 of the peace process, there was only a minimal cross-tribal presence in the rival movements. Of the MPLA, Minter writes:

> [Individuals] of any ethnic origin could advance within party and state structures. The centralization of authority, however, combined with taboos on the use of ethnic divisions as the basis for patronage or affirmative action, meant that under-represented groups could not openly mobilize patronage networks to advance their ethnic cohorts. . . . Of the contending parties, Unita probably came closest to representing an "ethnic" party. By their numerical weight and educational advantages, Umbundu speakers overwhelmingly dominated the Unita officer corps. . . . Still, its sub national appeals were more often couched

in regional rather than ethnic terms. . . . Despite its strong ethnic base, Unita
aspired to national leadership rather than to ethnic separatism.[35]

On 15 January 1975, Angola's three rival movements signed the Alvor
Agreement, under Portugal's guidance, which was to have been the basis for
a peaceful transition to independence. But according to George Wright,
"even while the three nationalist movements were being brought together by
Portugal, the means to undermine the political solution was occurring. This
was directly related to decisions by external patrons to continue providing
military assistance to the FNLA."[36] He continues:

> In October [1975], the Soviet Union resumed military assistance to the
> MPLA, heightening United States and South African concerns. The Soviet
> Union's renewal of military assistance was primarily a response to China's
> move to aid the FNLA. The Soviet Union preferred a political solution in An-
> gola, but it did not want the MPLA marginalized in any settlement. The Soviet
> leadership also recognized that the Ford presidency was weakened because of
> Vietnam, the Watergate affair and Nixon's resignation, allowing the Soviet
> Union an unprecedented opening to assist a Third World ally. Previously the
> Soviet Union had been cautious in Angola because it did not want to under-
> mine detente, but once Kissinger excluded the Soviet Union from the Middle
> East negotiations [after the 1973 Arab-Israeli war], the Soviet leadership de-
> cided it had no reason not to protect a Third World ally.[37]

Guimaraes claims that the ideological content of the MPLA political program "remained an important factor in keeping the two movements (the
MPLA and Unita) apart,"[38] but still he writes that it "is difficult to find only
one reason for the failure of Angolan nationalist movements to form a common front. Perhaps, it was due to personalities: both Neto and Roberto were
strong leaders and may not have wished to share power."[39] He hardly gives
the impression that rigid adherence to ideology was clearly the divisive element that led to a political conflict with some ethnic and personal overtones
becoming a horrifying total war lasting more than a quarter of a century. In
July 1974, prior to Angola's independence and the escalation of superpower
backing for the Angolan political factions, Savimbi had convened the annual
conference of Unita and called for the FNLA and MPLA to create a National Democratic Liberation Front with Unita, which would negotiate for
independence. The conference also made it clear that Unita had no intention of serving in a transition government without the participation of the
FNLA and MPLA.[40] As William Minter writes: "[MPLA] unity with the
FNLA would have been difficult in any case, but was definitively ruled out
by Cold War imperatives of CIA patronage. The [Unita conference] guidelines mandated excluding any possible leftist influences, such as the MPLA,

rather than building national unity. With the Congo crisis, actively combating any possible Soviet influence became the top U.S. priority in Africa. Angola, so close to the epicenter of that conflict, could not possibly be insulated."[41] Minter continues:

> Roberto's non-cooperative leadership style was notorious, raising questions whether other FNLA leaders might have been more receptive to reconciliation with the MPLA. Savimbi's monomaniacal quest for the top position and undying resentment of Luanda society, as well as his skill at ingratiating himself with different constituencies and sponsors, arguably played decisive roles in leading Unita into alliances with the Portuguese military, South Africa and other external sponsors. Neto's poetic sensibility and personal dedication, which even won recognition from most opponents, were coupled with an introverted leadership style which hampered communication with internal and external opponents.[42]

U.S. policy never sought to reconcile the warring sides. Instead, it created the conditions in which a local war became a global conflict, in which it hoped simply that it would back the winner. It embarked on this policy with the only gradual realization that, as Stockwell makes clear, "The glaring weakness of the program was a lack of information about our allies and about the interior of Angola. We were mounting a major covert action to support two Angolan liberation movements about which we had little reliable intelligence. Most of what we knew about the FNLA came from Roberto, the chief recipient of our largesse, and it was obvious that he was exaggerating and distorting facts in order to keep our support. We knew even less of Savimbi and UNITA."[43] The CIA appeared only to have a sense of what Roberto and Savimbi were *not*: They were *not* supported by the Soviet Union, and despite the lingering presence of China and Savimbi's occasional praise for Maoist guerrilla techniques, they did not appear to be of the political left. But even attributing ideological motives to U.S. support for the FNLA and Unita is at times difficult. Both Guimaraes and Wright assess Henry Kissinger's view of the situation in Angola as simply a clash between American power and Soviet power.[44]

War Without Winners

U.S. policy in the mid-1970s was led by the CIA and Kissinger, acting with barely any reference to other policymakers until after the U.S. commitment to the anti-MPLA forces had become entrenched. Kissinger was also concerned to retain the support of Mobutu Sese Seko, who hoped to see his relative, the FNLA leader Holden Roberto, installed in Luanda under his guidance and influence. Kissinger's efforts were thwarted, not by Soviet and Cuban power, but by Congressional resistance to his warmongering, which led to assistance to the FNLA being terminated in 1976 following the passage of two Congressional amendments. The Tunney Amendment to the 1975 Defense Appropriations Bill in the Senate terminated financial assistance to U.S. operations in Angola. The Clark Amendment to the 1975 Security Assistance Bill specifically called for a complete termination of funds to Angola. Despite these amendments, the polarization the U.S. role in the conflict had created during the bitter war of 1975–1976 was just the beginning.

A vengeful Kissinger sought to undermine the MPLA, which nevertheless achieved widespread diplomatic recognition in 1976. Meanwhile, the consolidation of the MPLA in Luanda was followed by a turning of the tide against Mobutu, who faced two insurgencies from Angola, in 1977 and 1978, by former supporters of Katangese separatists exiled in Angola since the demise of the Katanga secession in 1965. Following the fall of Richard Nixon, the unremarkable term in office of Gerald Ford and the Democratic victory in 1976, President Jimmy Carter admitted what most already knew: "We should realize that the Russian and Cuban presence in Angola, while regrettable and counterproductive of peace, need not constitute a threat to United States interests, nor does that presence mean the existence of a [Soviet] satellite on the continent."[45] Even so, the Carter administration refused to recognize the MPLA–led People's Republic of Angola, largely due to its concern not be seen within the United States as "soft on Communism."[46]

By 1981, when President Ronald Reagan strode onto the world stage with a desire to stoke the fires of the Cold War in Africa and elsewhere, Angola was ripe for a return as the target of the same willful and shameless destructiveness the CIA had helped facilitate six years beforehand. This time, however, U.S. support for Unita was more complex. The Clark Amendment, which prohibited direct U.S. assistance to Unita, was the hurdle Reagan sought throughout his first term to have removed. It was not until 11 June 1985, however, that the administration achieved this goal, advocates of repeal asserting that Angola "was a place where we can achieve victory, a psychological victory, which will give strength to free men across the world."[47] The amendment was repealed by 63 votes to 34.

Although diplomatic ties between the United States and the MPLA government were at that time years away, Luanda terminated such diplomatic contacts as had existed with the United States in response to the American move. This put on hold the strategy of "constructive engagement" that Chester Crocker, U.S. assistant secretary of state for African affairs, 1981–1988, had attempted to put in place, which it was intended would lead both to Cuban and South African forces withdrawing from Angola and to Namibia, the territory occupied by South Africa, gaining independence. With the repeal of the Clark Amendment, pressure mounted for military assistance to be sent to Unita. Reagan signed an order permitting $13 million of assistance, despite some in the administration arguing that doing so would limit the chances of successfully pursuing Crocker's multilateral strategy for Angola and Namibia. The U.S. media, critical of a resumption of military aid, also argued strongly that such assistance would ally the United States too closely to the apartheid regime in South Africa, with whom the CIA had anyway long worked intimately, and whose interests Crocker's constructive engagement policy was intended to protect in pursuit of regional peace. The passage of the Comprehensive Anti-Apartheid Act by the U.S. Congress in late 1986 also brought a chill in the U.S.–South African relationship and appeared to threaten Crocker's policy.

At odds with Congress, the Reagan administration ignored the critics. In 1986, the CIA provided Unita with TOW and Stinger antiaircraft missiles, antitank weapons, 106mm recoilless rifles, ammunition, and fuel. In 1987, the value of this assistance increased to $30 million, and to $50 million by 1989. Destabilization of the MPLA was the intention of the Unita-South Africa-U.S. strategy, and that strategy claimed a sickeningly high level of success, with the deaths of 435,000 people—among them 331,000 children—between 1981 and 1988. By the end of this period, antipersonnel mines had killed 40,000 Angolans. Meanwhile, lost revenues to the Angolan economy during this period amounted to $40 billion, and the total value of physical infrastructure destroyed in 1975–1988 has been put at $22 billion.[48]

More even than in 1975, the Angola of the late 1980s was a theatre of the Cold War totally removed from the roots of the indigenous conflict. As George Schultz, U.S. secretary of state under Reagan, made clear in his preface to Crocker's account of his peace policy in southern Africa, the "global" approach to diplomacy in the region succeeded in bringing about a South African withdrawal from Namibia and the departure of Cuban troops from Angola. "Confronting us at every turn was the Soviet Union, with the ideological contest of the Cold War at a stage of growing tension," wrote Schultz.[49] But ultimately it did not end the war in Angola, because it did not address the issues behind the war. The 1988 accord is discussed later in this chapter, but here it is worth mentioning that its implementation, which saw Cuba and South Africa withdraw their forces from Angola, and Namibia granted independence from South Africa, is widely regarded as not having been the result of the pressure on the MPLA created by the escalation of U.S. military assistance to Unita after 1985. Nor was it the case that Crocker's policy created the atmosphere of change that ultimately led to the end of apartheid in South Africa; rather, the peace agreement undermined the African National Congress (ANC)—the only meaningful opponent of apartheid—by denying it bases in Angola. In fact, the peace accord "greatly minimized the threat to white South Africa of the ANC," writes David Kyvig in his assessment of Reagan's foreign policy. "[The] main original thrust of constructive engagement—support for the reform efforts of white South Africa—had produced no meaningful progress at all."[50] In short, more death and destruction care of the CIA was not what ultimately brought the sides to the negotiating table to hammer out a settlement. The shifting positions of sanctions-hit South Africa, together with the momentous political shifts in the Soviet Union under Mikhail Gorbachev, had a much greater impact, against the background of war-weariness among Cuban troops on the ground in Angola. As William Minter writes, "If the U.S. had been willing more quickly to distance itself from Pretoria, Moscow was eager for compromises in a region that most Soviet policy-makers saw as marginal."[51]

The U.S. diplomatic absence from Luanda, together with the failure fully to understand why the MPLA remained suspicious of Savimbi, was a key cause of U.S. inflexibility and served Washington's negotiators poorly. Add to Crocker's distrust of his ally, Savimbi, which he made clear to me in an interview,[52] the lack of real knowledge necessary to work with all sides toward peace, and the nature of the U.S. role is made clear. If the United States had been a broker rather than a player, it might never have gotten itself into the position of supporting so determinedly a guerrilla leader who ultimately proved himself to be completely at odds with the ideals which had, at least for the consumption of U.S. policymakers and their constituencies, been the justification for lending him U.S. support in the first place. U.S. and South African support for Holden Roberto and subsequently Savimbi was the catalyst which led to an escalation of Soviet and Cuban support for the MPLA. Throughout the 1975–1976 war, and during the revival of proxy wars around the world throughout the Reagan years in the 1980s, the Angolans—the living, breathing, dying, and suffering victims of the war—were of no consequence. Their suffering simply did not matter. In fact, in the minds of U.S. strategists as far back as Kissinger, that suffering barely appeared to exist.

Queues formed outside Luanda's graveyards when the battle for the city erupted on 31 October 1992, after President Jose Eduardo dos Santos won 49.75 percent of the presidential vote to Jonas Savimbi's 40.07, and the MPLA 53.74 percent to Unita's 34.1 percent in the legislative elections.[53] "The MPLA has not undergone the minimal internal transformation. Their frame of mind is still that of the one-party state,"[54] Savimbi had confidently asserted to me, nodding his head vigorously, standing erect with his hands clasped behind him in the house in Abidjan that Sunday afternoon in December 1990, before the electoral contest had been held. "Free and fair elections are the way you can effectively end the conflict in Angola. But when they have an army, they can still impose themselves by force." A key element of the peace accord signed in 1991 had been the prior demobilization of troops, the dilution of the military rivalry, and a diminution of the potential sources of the violence that had plagued the country. Theories as to whether war or elections are the solution to Angola's crisis have tripped easily off the tongues of the players for as long as conflict has raged. "We have agreed that the ceasefire will only take place when the political parties are able to operate freely. The ceasefire will only be signed when the MPLA gives a date for elections," Savimbi went on, stressing the role of force, the pressure of arms, and the ever present potential for a resort to violence if the discussions, agreements, treaties, and commitments came to nothing. Above all, a lack of trust prevailed between the launch of the negotiations that ended a year later in the signing of the 1991 peace accord and the elections of 1992, which were quickly followed by a catastrophic collapse when Unita failed to accept its defeat.

Ill will against Savimbi as a creature of the Cold War and a protégé of the United States, bolstered by a "Devil's pact" with the apartheid regime in South Africa, reached the point at which he had no alternative but to negotiate directly with his enemies in the MPLA. The waltz he had danced with successive U.S. governments was over. Was it clear who had led and who had followed? "The civil war was the result of our own problems" he told me. "But once the Soviet Union said they would stop supplying the MPLA once there is a ceasefire, the MPLA realized it could not afford not to listen."[55] Who was listening and who was not was perhaps not the issue. The 1991 Bicesse Accord brokered by Portugal effectively marked the end of U.S. political support for Unita. Both Unita and the MPLA were left to face the question of whether for sixteen years they had been fighting a war on behalf of the superpowers or a war whose causes were closer to home. Neither the United States nor the Soviet Union were sensitive to the indigenous characteristics of the war. For them, the conflict was entirely proxy. But by the early 1990s, the real Angolan war, a war between Angolans, was about to start:

> The fact is that the underlying struggle for power had yet to be resolved. Granted, the international intervention complicated the course of the civil war in Angola and brought external considerations to bear on it. But the domestic political conflict at the heart of the civil war had developed before international actors had become involved and continued after they had left. Of course it was not a linear process by which an internal conflict developed and was subsequently externalized. It was a dynamic relationship in which the parties to the domestic struggle for power looked outward to foreign backers, whose intervention, in turn, served to feed the internal conflict, and so on. . . . In sum, the Angolan civil war was a domestic conflict for power which was internationalized with consciousness and purposefulness by the rival movements. Defining it as an East-West proxy war does not explain the Angolan civil war.[56]

Foreign involvement in the conflict appears all the more shameful when analyses, such as that of Guimaraes, reach such devastating conclusions. All that the foreign involvement in Angola did was to make an already bloody conflict an even bloodier one. Nobody in Africa won the Cold War, because all the theatres—Somalia, Zaire, Angola, Liberia, and elsewhere—lie in ruins, while the rotten skull beneath the skin of the West's favored "friends" has been exposed. The readiness of the local actors to internationalize their struggle for power, under the mantle of political principles to which their respective backers could relate, was a mark of the crisis of leadership that has prevailed across Africa for much of the four decades since independence was first achieved on the continent. Acceptance of the military solution, which has dominated the seriously flawed though more often deliberately short-sighted U.S. thinking from the time of John Stockwell's first foray into Angola in 1975, only ceased when the United States no longer saw the benefit to itself of war. The realities of the indigenous political struggle were inadequately recognized in the 1991 accord, where the international factors were most at play, and after which U.S. military assistance to Unita dried up. Already by November 1993, as Karl Maier, an American journalist, wrote in his account of the Angola of the 1980s and early 1990s, "In the New Angola ideology is being replaced by the bottom line, as security and selling expertise in weaponry have become a very profitable business. With its wealth in oil and diamonds, Angola is like a big swollen carcass and the vultures are circling overhead. Savimbi's former allies are switching sides, lured by the aroma of hard currency."[57]

EMPTY RAIL TRACK, EMPTY ROAD

Dawn broke over Luanda. A mockery of day. What was there to wake for? The city had doubled in size to three million in less than one year. Seven million more had fled to the coastal areas as the Forcças Armadas Angolanas, the Angolan Armed Forces (FAA), the new national army created as part of the peace pact, steadily pushed Unita back onto the plateau of central Angola. A Hercules lumbered along the runway of Luanda's *4 Fevereiro* airport. I left behind the shadows, the sinister devastation, the darkness, and the rain. South, along the coast, the Atlantic Ocean broke white and foaming onto the lush grassland that reached down to the water. By then, August 1993, Unita had control of 70 percent of the territory, while the MPLA areas were overflowing with 70 percent of the 12 million population. At Melange, Saurimo, and Luena, the FAA was fighting to protect enclaves of displaced people being fed by the UN World Food Program (WFP). The towns were surrounded by Unita and defended by the FAA, while Cuito and Menongue were out of reach of the aid flights, as Unita closed in on the FAA garrisons and the hungry, lonely people who scraped by for another day of life as best they could. In the southern provinces, drought was forcing the herders of Namib province to find buyers for their cattle, so depriving themselves of their long-term livelihood in pursuit of immediate survival.

The fragile economy that had emerged during the 1991–1992 period of peace had rapidly collapsed. The routes that had opened to bring food from the highlands to the towns and cities had closed again. Angola, which in 1993 was earning $4 billion a year from its oil exports and spending 50 percent of the national budget on arms, was being kept alive by food aid. The WFP had been asked by the United States to slow down the delivery of its food aid for the last three months of the year, as the scale of the crisis was exhausting the supply, 80 percent of it from the United States, amounting to 8,000 tons per month to meet the needs of two million people.

The WFP Hercules lumbered over Lobito and dropped down to Benguela. The hub of the rail track that had once linked the heartland with the coast was silent. The FAA had taken Benguela earlier in the year and had pushed east toward Ganda. Benguela, to which the riches of the African earth, the cobalt and the copper of southern Zaire, and the harvests of the Angolan highlands, were once transported by rail, was a dead town. Pleasant villas, arranged along neat streets, lay empty. A town that should have been bustling was home only to ghosts, or children with no games left to play. There was no center to it, nowhere obvious to go to establish an idea of what it was that was taking place there. The WFP drove us out of town and along the coast toward Lobito, the major port for southern Angola. The road passed between empty fields, past lush trees, and then veered across a river by way of a metal bridge. The bridge was guarded at either end by FAA troops, dubbed the Ninjas, owing to the futuristic bright blue riot gear they wore. The high-collared flak jackets and Star Wars–style helmets had been donated by the then West German government as a gesture of goodwill, one that left the troops stifling in the heat and oddly out of place in a country where riots were unlikely to be mounted by people so weakened by hunger.

Lobito had once been a center for processing crops grown in the surrounding area, in particular sugar. The town's state-owned sugar factory had been a major employer, until the MPLA government had decided to end state sugar production. The fields of sugarcane were sold to private owners, who rapidly stopped producing sugar and began growing more lucrative crops. As a result, Angola stopped producing sugar altogether, and then began importing it, while the former employees of the factory, on whom 2,000 families of Lobito relied, were forced out of work, in the name perhaps of the country's post–Cold War shift away from a command economy to a more liberal economic regime. The harvests of Lobito's fields went straight to Luanda, while 123,000 people in and around Benguela faced starvation, and those at work in agriculture earned 50,000 kwanza, equivalent to $1 per month. To earn a little more, they had dismantled the tin roofs of their former homes in the compound of the sugar factory and sold them in Lobito.

Beyond Lobito were the salt flats and the destroyed village of Beiro des Salinas, where it was not even the problem of displaced people that was most stark, but the hunger and anxiety of the people who had watched the war come and go, and had remained in their homes and then found their liveli-

hoods disappear before their eyes. "The FAA had destroyed the village because it wanted to use the site where the village was," said Xavier Da Sirva,
who had watched the pillage.[58] "They expelled everybody, and took away the
windows and doors, so all the houses fell down. The people have been dis-
persed around the region, and the soldiers have never said anything to us
about it. They just came and stole everything." The FAA—planned as the
glue of national reconciliation—had quit Beiro des Salinas, without apparently using the site for any identifiable purpose. We left the ruins behind and
drove back to Benguela, to the emptiness of the streets, the chilling back-
room of a war alternately raging and pausing to the east along the rail track.

Jaime Azulay, the correspondent for the *Journal d'Angola* and a contributor
to the Portuguese service of the BBC as well as the Portuguese news agency,
drove us around in his white Land Rover, from which he had removed the roof
and windows, leaving the vehicle like a box on wheels. He had the run of the
streets. He took me to his office in a large, empty square in the center of the
town. It was evening when he opened the door of what had once been a shop,
with a large display window and a glass door on one side. It was tempting to
imagine that perhaps in the past it might have been a shop selling provisions,
perhaps a hardware store, tempting to imagine that at some point there had
been a period prior to war, when the only vehicle in a town was not owned by
a reporter dispatching his stories down the telex wire, to a world that might or
might not have been listening to what he had to say.

Jaime's office, its papers and files piled high, the telex machine willing to
spread the news from where it stood in the corner, created an overpowering
sense of isolation. The war, Angola, the devastation of the civilian population, the years and years of outrageous and indefensible superpower dab-
bling in the country, all were made more horrifying by the existence of a
small, warm office, whose function was to ensure that the history did not go
unrecorded. The outside world's knowledge of some of the big events of the
century had been formulated on this quaint desk, while packs of mangy dogs
trotted across the dimly lit square outside. Trapped between the dramatic
pronouncements of the previous decades, and the ghastly reality of death,
hunger, and loss, which the superpowers' lofty words in their own lands were
never intended to admit, the small office in Benguela was perhaps where a
true understanding of the situation may once have lain, before the reports
emanating from the office found their way into the hands of those in the outside world who eagerly leapt upon them, with the aim of transforming them
into propaganda with which to fight their cause. Somewhere between the reporter's notebook, the telex tape, the radio airwaves, and the newspaper
stands, the progagandists intervened with the "promises and lies"[59] that have
ravaged Angola as much as the weapons and hunger.

The Cold War was over, the streets were empty, and "Savimbi is making
war because he has arms and guns. He has plenty of both. He can pay a little

more. He has a lot of money."[60] So Honorio van Dunem, one of fifteen Unita parliamentarians who had deserted Savimbi when he reverted to war after losing the 1992 election, told me over tea at Luanda's Hotel Tivoli. He had represented Unita in Dakar, Senegal, before becoming the organization's representative in the Zambian capital, Lusaka. "Savimbi is everything but a democrat. It's a shame he has destroyed the opposition. He is a cynic. He always told us that politics and power are the same, and that they can't be divided. Even so, he would not win an election as leader of Unita," van Dunem had said.

Having gone on for so long, and passing through so many different historical phases, the crisis seemed as much about the capacity to adapt to a changing world—or the lack of that capacity—as it was about the original issues over which the protagonists had gone to war. What Savimbi had been to the United States of Kissinger and Reagan was simply not adaptable to the needs of Angola in the 1990s. He could not accept that a new set of rules, requiring a review of strategy and ambitions, had been forced upon the country. True, neither side had shown democratic credentials in the past, but the collapse of the Soviet Union gave its allies no choice but to adapt if they were to survive. Denied his role as champion of a global cause, what had Savimbi become? "The rebellion has no legitimacy," a U.S. diplomat had told me in Luanda. To Savimbi and the Unita force that had stayed with him, the rebellion was no less legitimate than it had always been. Nor was it more so. When the United States decided it no longer had an interest in championing Savimbi, he lost all legitimacy, even that of a local warlord intent on power—which is in fact what he had always been. The silence of Jaime's office made it seem *the still point of the turning world*, a place where the true purpose of the conflict, the horror of its longevity and the greed and arrogance that had fed it and savaged its victims beneath the guise of ideology, all could be clearly seen. It was just another war, brought on by the hunger for power, whose history was neatly piled up on Jaime's desk, in manila files, which may fade, rot, or go up in flames before the fighting is over.

Before leaving Luanda, Katya Airola had raised the possibility of the air force providing transport to the FAA-held territory in the east, away from the coast, along the rail track. Early one morning we drove to Benguela airport from the empty center of the town. The terminal was empty. For hours we waited, until almost noon, when the sky came alive with the clatter of a helicopter's whirring blades. An ancient Russian helicopter bearing Aeroflot insignia swayed and swung like a huge drunken bird onto the runway, barely touching the tarmac, hovering on soft tires as though always about to take off. We ran to a partially opened door on its side, blasted by the downdraft, pulled open the door and scrambled inside, without even asking whether this was the transport Katya had been thinking of. Inside, some other journalists sat bemused by our sudden arrival, with Jaime, who had left for Luanda the previous day, sitting among them. In the darkness at the rear were the anxious young faces of new FAA recruits, sitting awkwardly in their uniforms as they handled their unfamiliar guns and wondered if this journey would be their last. With the door barely closed, the hulk took off and left Benguela behind, flying low, dodging from side to side as it barely missed the trees. We flew for less than one hour, sliding through the barrage of an imagined battle, the pilot clearly exhilarated, the passengers suffering in the hold. We touched down at Ganda and jumped out, and the helicopter immediately took off, leaving us stranded, on the deserted edge of a town that had been captured by the FAA a month beforehand.

We walked along a hot road into the town. There was nobody to see, no sounds of war, no sign of life along the neat streets, lined with curbstones and other details of urban life, making the emptiness all the more eerie. It was as if a wind had swept all the people away, while leaving the town apparently unscathed. As we reached a crossroads, a military vehicle approached us from the direction we had walked. An officer was driven past without acknowledging us. He stopped a little further ahead to speak with some soldiers we had not noticed and then drove on. We turned up a hill, and ahead of us some children were standing on the street. A boy sped past, pushing himself on a wooden scooter. As he passed, the front wheel fell off, and he lay on the road in the wreckage of his broken toy. Further on, at the market, the space between the near empty stalls had become a somber meeting place for war victims, limbless men dragging themselves around on rickety wooden crutches and subdued children begging for money and cigarettes. A shoeshine boy dressed in clothes blackened from top to bottom plied his trade hopelessly, while women offered unripe tomatoes, peanuts, and small heaps of salt for sale, and men sold twists of tobacco and marijuana, explaining that there were so few people with cash or goods to barter that there was barely any business.

Colonel Jose Manuel de Souza, the young officer who had passed us on the street earlier, reappeared. We were driven to the military headquarters, and then drove with him to the edge of town. The men of the FAA would take us on patrol, out into the rural area they had captured east of Ganda. The journey was taking us deeper into the country, first to the desertion of Benguela, then on a ride in a helicopter full of young soldiers, then onward in a military truck, then on foot through a forested land of rolling hills and fields littered with land mines, fields the farmers had no choice but to cultivate even though that meant gambling with death. We walked for an hour or more, in a ribbon across the rich earth.

We stopped at Vindongo, a hamlet of neat huts, where the people were slowly starving. "Unita has complicated our lives," said Maria N'guare.[61] Malnourished children stared at us as we passed in a line, women offering to sell withered and blackened bananas as we walked on. The villagers were eating manioc leaves, too frightened here to work the fields. "If we bought maize in the market, Unita would come and take it from us when they were still here. They would take our clothes. A lot of people are going to die of hunger. Around 150 have already died. The children and the old people are the ones who are dying," Maria N'guare said, as the troops walked on, oblivious perhaps, helpless certainly. We walked on to Atuke, a village surrounded by minefields where it was thus impossible to grow any crops. The mud-brick huts had no roofs. People lay on the ground barely moving. A woman suckled a crying baby. The people had left a nearby village because Unita had stolen their remaining food. "We have nothing," said Domingues Kalende. "No money. No food. Nothing."[62]

TRAIN TO NOWHERE

General Marquez Correia smiled broadly, donned his aviator sunglasses, and commanded us to follow him. Walkie-talkie in hand, he strode out of his military headquarters hurling orders at his men, who scurried off in all directions. Troops gathered in the cool shade of the purple-blossomed jacaranda tree that dominated the parade ground of the headquarters of the Angolan armed forces in the rebel-surrounded eastern town of Luena, one of five towns under siege by Unita. Luena and two other towns were accessible by air. The pilot of a small executive jet, which had taken us there from Luanda two days after leaving Benguela, had flown high to avoid Unita's antiaircraft fire, and then corkscrewed down to Luena, spiraling downwards over the town at a startling speed, before landing. Marquez, a short, bearded man with gold thread sewn onto his epaulettes, was in charge of the town. "We will take you to the front," he said. There was no turning back. This was the FAA—publicity-aware, modern, and apparently confident.

From the terrace of his headquarters, Marquez ordered us into the back of a new Brazilian jeep. Within five minutes he had assembled a unit of fifty men, one truck to carry them, and a convoy of jeeps. Then there was a rumbling in the distance. It grew louder, and around the corner roared two grimy Russian T-54 tanks. We left town, led by one of the tanks, and headed for the bush, then transferred to the leading tank, which crashed through the scrub blasting out black soot as it roared toward the front line. After about an hour we reached the front. Although the army had established a security zone around Luena, it remained cut off by land. Government troops emerged from trenches a hundred yards off the road. They showed us old AK-47 machine guns, bullets, and Chinese-made mortars captured from Unita. Then they showed us the bodies of two dead rebels. One had his left hand tied to a shovel, though nobody explained why. The other had shoes held together with plastic tape. By contrast, the FAA troops with us all had new boots and smart uniforms. A gunshot rang out as the tank began to re-

trace its tracks. When Marquez reached inside the vehicle and pulled out an
ancient rifle, the gloss of the new model army slightly dimmed. Nobody had
pulled the trigger. But it had fired all the same.

The gloss of the FAA had lost its sheen long before, in fact. In Luena, the illegitimacy of armies as essential to the solution of the problem seemed starker
than anywhere else. Two armies had entrapped each other. Unita surrounded
the town, but was unable to seize it. The FAA could defend the town but was
unable to break out of it. Trapped by both were the people. They were gathered at the railway station. They had been there for months. Thousands were
packed on the tracks, living on a train that had halted in a siding and would go
nowhere. The track was overgrown. The station still held the symbols of its
purpose. But now the people came there to stop, the country having stopped,
with nobody going anywhere. The tracks disappeared into the distance, seeming to beckon those at the station on a journey, when in fact no journey could
take them into a future any different from the horrors of the present. The FAA
fought in its trenches, and Unita pounded them with heavy weapons, while the
people cowered, waiting to move on and for the country to emerge onto the
horizon they could see at the end of the overgrown tracks.

Picking up the pieces in the early 1990s would have required recognition
that Chester Crocker's diplomacy, which had led to South Africa and Cuba
withdrawing their military presence in Angola and to Namibia's gaining its
independence, had not addressed the fundamental issues behind Angola's
war. Crocker had only extricated the United States from a situation into
which it should never have plunged in the first place. Angola had gained
nothing from the U.S. military support to Unita, following the repeal of the
Clarke Amendment in 1985. Ultimately, the United States could only seek
to install a legitimized Unita by way of elections. Post-Cold War it would
have been unacceptable for Unita to seize power in the manner the United
States had envisaged as acceptable in 1975–1976 and later, during the 1980s.
The 1992 election result said it all. America's man lost, and the failure to install Savimbi democratically marked the end of the strategic relationship that
had been built up with the Unita leader.

Dominating U.S. policy after 1988, when agreement for the withdrawal
of Cuban and South African troops was reached, was the demand for "national reconciliation." When the United States committed itself to maintaining its support for Unita in the interim, the implication was that moves toward creating such reconciliation lay with the MPLA. As the U.S. acting
assistant secretary for African affairs put it, "The [Bush] administration believes that lasting peace and national reconciliation can take place only in a
scenario in which there are no losers, only winners."[63]

U.S. policy straddling the end of the Cold War and beyond the Bush presidency into the Clinton years was dominated by the gradual realization that the
principles that had determined the actions promoted by conservatives

throughout the 1980s no longer had currency in the 1990s. The Cold War's victors were not about to enjoy the spoils, at least in Africa, largely because the principles they had held were so out of step with the reality. The view that Savimbi would be the proxy winner of a proxy war, because he had apparently committed himself to a certain stance during that war, became more and more obviously untenable. The United States came to see negotiations as the key to a solution and at the same time adopted a new strategy of beating the MPLA when it could be blamed for apparently appearing recalcitrant or obstructive. With such a move toward a negotiated end, the end of the Cold War came to be marked as much by the unraveling of much of U.S. policy in Africa, as by the undoing of the Soviet Union. The conservative principles that had underpinned U.S. policy with such an impact over so many years simply could not address the underlying issues that were the reason for the Angolan conflict having erupted. Conservatives in the U.S. Congress insisted that the Bush administration maintain military assistance to Unita, largely to punish the MPLA for its refusal to disintegrate and surrender to Unita.

The MPLA, with its oil revenues, was less dependent upon foreign assistance than Unita, despite a variety of arms embargoes imposed upon it. It was widely recognized as the legitimate government of Angola, despite attempts by Herman Cohen, assistant secretary for Africa under Bush, to characterize Unita as one of two governments operating in Angola. To save face, U.S. policy in the early 1990s attempted to address the issue of Angola's "national reconciliation" as if the end of the Cold War had created the conditions for such reconciliation. The end of the superpower rivalry did not create the conditions for national reconciliation. It simply created the pressure for such moves, as it was by then in the interests of the outside world that these moves take place, in order to replace Cold War rivalry with the New World Order and Western dominance, following the collapse of the Soviet Union.

More than in most regions of the world, the conflicts in southern Africa enveloping Angola, South Africa, and Namibia, as well as in Mozambique, revealed the enormous influence of Washington lobbyists. The $600,000 retainer paid by Unita in September 1985 to the public relations firm Black, Manafort, Stone & Kelly was a first step in ratcheting up the pressure on Congress to reemphasize the Angolan conflict as a Cold War showcase, whose outcome was vital to U.S. interests. The anti-MPLA publicity generated by the lobbyists suited the political bias of the U.S. administration. Meanwhile, Crocker's decision to engage in diplomacy, derived from his conviction that the Namibian and Angolan conflicts were interlinked and should be addressed in tandem, necessitated that U.S. policy in 1981, after the election of Ronald Reagan, should "recognize publicly the legitimacy of Unita's struggle and maintain pressure for Cuban withdrawal, while also pursuing an internationally acceptable settlement in Namibia. . . . [The] shift to tacit linkage was the correct move. It strengthened my right flank in Washington. It would avoid rubbing everyone's nose publicly in a new Angolan condition," Crocker wrote in his southern African memoir, *High Noon in Southern Africa: Making Peace in a Rough Neighborhood*.[64] Linkage for Crocker clearly involved not only Namibia, Angola, Cuba, and the Soviet Union, but also policies that would allow him to deflect the accusation among Washington's hawks that a deal with the MPLA— the Marxists, who made a barely noticed conversion from Marxism-Leninism to democratic socialism in 1991 only *after* a peace accord had been struck—was tantamount to yielding to Communist influence. Crocker himself explains the attraction of the linkage thus:

> The Cuban withdrawal link would bring pressure on Luanda to reconcile with UNITA. It would prevent a Namibia settlement from occurring at Unita's ex-pense. Cuban withdrawal from Southern Africa was inherently attractive in its own right, and in terms of U.S.-Soviet relations. Finally, it would give us the leverage we would need to obtain South African cooperation on Namibian in-dependence.[65]

Against this background of multiple linkages, the motives behind U.S. policy during the peace process should be regarded less as an attempt to bring an end to the appalling suffering the superpower war and South Africa's exploits in Namibia and Angola had created, than as a second-tier strategy to install Unita as the government of Angola by way of a strategy that "would challenge the legitimacy of the Cuban presence *and* the MPLA regime that depended upon it."[66] Crocker's diplomacy was thus a one-sided effort, intended to undermine the MPLA and to put Savimbi in power. This was the purpose at the heart of the "reconciliation" that had polarized An-gola's political currents since the mid-1970s, in a manner that the Cold War involvement was primarily responsible for making irreconcilable.

With the end of the Cold War, attempts to portray U.S. diplomatic ef-forts in southern Africa as having brought the end of the conflict in the re-gion were being cast into serious doubt. U.S. policy, particularly by way of the long established intelligence sharing between the CIA and the Bureau of State Security (BOSS), South Africa's security service, as well as the CIA-Unita-South Africa linkage, had essentially served to prolong the conflict, as William Minter states:

> It is a logical fallacy to conclude simply from the historical sequence that U.S. aid to Unita facilitated either the 1988 or the 1991 settlement. . . . [In fact the] Soviet Union in the 1980s, far from pursuing an aggressive expansion of influ-ence in southern Africa, aimed to limit its involvement—without, however, be-ing forced to withdraw or seeing its allies collapse under joint South African and U.S. pressure. If the U.S. had been willing more quickly to distance itself from Pretoria, Moscow was eager for compromises in a region that most So-

viet policy-makers saw as marginal. Despite the appearance of close Soviet-Angolan alignment, the mutual commitment was far from unconditional even in the Brezhnev years.[67]

The Angolan war suited the U.S. need to assert itself in a variety of theatres. Across the world, the scenarios took little account of genuine national needs and local realities, which were ignored in the platitudes and ambitions of Cold War friends and foes. In Afghanistan, as in Angola, past U.S. support for one side has made subsequent reconciliation on a national level a pipe dream, owing to the militarization in the 1980s. Ultimately the Cold War was all about the assertion of power, rather than a political and diplomatic search for solutions to national conflicts. The United States abused its power grossly. The end of the Cold War exposed the paucity of its real commitment to Savimbi, as it leapt aboard the process preceding the 1992 elections. This shift necessitated tacit recognition of the Angolan government, despite only formally recognizing the MPLA in 1993, after the election of President Clinton and the MPLA's election victory an entire year beforehand.

Shifts by the United States were accompanied, though not necessarily inspired, by worsening human rights abuses committed by Unita and the collapse of efforts to rekindle the peace process that had been agreed on in 1991. They were also accompanied by a rejuvenated United Nations under Secretary General Boutros Boutros-Ghali, which oversaw the Angolan election in 1992 and was then formulating its bold strategy for rebuilding Somalia on the other side of the continent. The UN, as will be examined in Part 4, sought to insert itself as the post–Cold War arbiter, ready and able to pick up the pieces left by the old conflict and redraw the map of the world. The post-election debacle in Angola and the catastrophe faced by the UN in Somalia in 1992–1993 left this hope in tatters. Even so, the pressure on Unita to abide by the election result and comply with the peace agreements it had signed was brought to bear by the UN. On 26 September 1993, the UN Security Council imposed stringent sanctions upon Unita, including an arms embargo and a variety of other measures, which forced the organization into a fresh round of peace talks in Lusaka in November 1993; the talks resumed after a break in March 1994.

The Lusaka Protocol signed on 20 November 1994 allowed for power sharing, Unita's disarmament, and its incorporation into the FAA along the lines envisaged in the 1991 Bicesse Accord. But throughout, serious doubts remained as to whether Savimbi was seriously engaged, in part due to his absence even at the signing ceremony in Lusaka. Subsequent events have shown that he was using negotiations as a stalling tactic, allowing him time to consolidate territory from which to pursue a war of attrition against the government, financed by the one commodity left to him after the loss of his political currency—diamonds. In 1998, Unita-controlled areas of Angola produced $225 million's worth of diamonds,[68] more than one-third of Angola's total $685 million that year. This however marked a slump on previous years, notably 1996–1997, when miners in Unita-controlled areas produced $750 million's worth of diamonds. Between 1992 and 1998, Angola's official diamond sales to the outside world were controlled by a Unita official, until the UN imposed a ban on diamond sales by Unita in an effort to thwart the Unita war machine. Subsequently, diamonds worth $150 million were produced in Unita-held areas in 1999.[69] However, the UN ban led Unita to sell diamonds through corrupt officials within the Angolan government, resulting in De Beers, the South African company which controls 60 percent of the world's uncut diamond supply, suspending all purchases of Angolan diamonds.

The unraveling of the Lusaka peace process resulted less from the shortcomings of the text signed by Unita and the MPLA than from the fundamental clash of characters that lies at the heart of the Angolan conflict. Savimbi, as he subsequently made clear on numerous occasions,[70] simply could not accept playing a secondary role within a power-sharing government. His objections appeared to have no ideological root, nor did he have any principled objection to the MPLA government that had defeated him at the ballot box. The establishment of a government of national unity and reconciliation (GURN) on 9 April 1997, which saw sixty-three Unita deputies sworn into the Angolan National Assembly inaugurated two days later, was not followed by Unita meeting its commitment to disarm and hand over territory to the GURN. By the same process, the central government was to assert administrative control over the entire territory of the country by 28 February 1998. The UN responded to Unita's refusal to disarm and surrender its territory by imposing increasingly tough sanctions on it, culminating in Unita's suspension from the National Assembly and the subsequent defection of fifteen Unita deputies from the organization and their creation of a rival "New" Unita, which was legitimized by the MPLA as quickly as the Savimbi faction was declared politically criminal.

Unsurprisingly, the rise in tension and the fracturing of Unita became a precursor to further war. This erupted in December 1998 and has continued into the twenty-first century. Even though he has been able to continue the war, Savimbi has become increasingly isolated. This isolation became clear in October 1999, after the fall of the town of Bailundo to the FAA. The fall of the town had a symbolic importance, which resonated through Unita's political hierarchy, leading some to conclude that "Savimbi's grip on Unita cadres, many of them from Bailundo, is weakening. The town's aristocrats regard him as a commoner from the minor kingdom of Andulo, dismissing the idea that he is their people's natural leader. . . . Others from the Bailundo elite say it's time for Ovimbundu from the royal line . . . to assert their traditional rights."[71]

3

GREAT GAME, DIRTY GAME

The United States and Liberia

> Had we been candid about the standards of government in
> Liberia it would have been very damaging to U.S.
> interests. . . . Great powers don't reject their partners just
> because they smell.[1]
>
> Chester Crocker, former U.S. Assistant Secretary
> of State for African Affairs

IT WAS AN EARLY EVENING IN FEBRUARY 1993.[2] A Cadillac taxi had
swept me into the quaint streets of Georgetown from the bland order of
Washington. I was dazed by the normality. Students wandered through the
neatly kept grounds of Georgetown University. One had directed me to the
university's tall, new, red-brick, multistory block, where classes for high-
fliers, future diplomats, and potential leaders and policymakers were held in
bright rooms with newly varnished desks facing blackboards where the intri-
cacies of American foreign policy were outlined and discussed.

"I don't believe in trust in diplomacy. I look at performance. I never
trusted Savimbi," said Chester Crocker, the architect of U.S. Cold War
strategy in the sub-Saharan Africa of the 1980s.[3] He had retired from diplomacy when Ronald Reagan left office, his experiments with Africa reduced to
diagrams on a faculty blackboard. "But with Liberians one had a quality of
dialogue because they really thought of themselves as honorary Americans.
This meant that it was very candid—on both sides. During the Cold War,
diplomacy with Third World states was something like running a singles bar:
They come to New York and go shopping."[4] He never once paused, except

to say how busy he was and that I couldn't keep him long, and to ask if I had read his new book.

The post of U.S. assistant secretary of state for African affairs is reputed to be more like the post of president than any other within the U.S. executive. Because nobody else really cared about Africa, the assistant secretary could formulate and implement policy with an incomparable degree of independence. Gunrunning to right-wing rebels, propping up criminal dictators, or strengthening juntas with mercenary firepower, all have been, at some point, part of the assistant secretary's armory.

On 12 April 1980, when Samuel Doe emerged from behind a bush in the grounds of Monrovia's presidential executive mansion, America was about to find some new friends in Africa. They might, in Crocker's words, smell, but it was a smell that could be contained. Crocker had to wait another year before being given the fiefdom of the State Department's Africa office. Meanwhile, the Carter administration kept the channels of communication open with Doe, so that the Cold War warriors of the Reagan years could inherit a continuity of policy, with which they could work or not as they pleased. "Liberia was not the object of coveting by anybody. It wasn't as if the Soviets were waiting to come in," Crocker said. "And we had the executive mansion pretty well wired. So we knew what was going on. Womanizing until 3 A.M."[5]

At its height, in the mid-1980s, the U.S. embassy in Monrovia had the largest staff of any U.S. embassy in sub-Saharan Africa. The combination of the apparent absence of an outside threat, as asserted by Crocker, and the simultaneous importance, reflected in these staffing levels, that Liberia held for America—whether or not it was vulnerable to being *lost* to the Communist bloc—hint at the nature of the American relationship with Liberia. "Liberia was our own colony," a senior State Department official, with long experience of the country, told me. "We wanted this place to work. Part of it was military assistance. We wanted to professionalize the military. It was a failure. It was an unmitigated failure."[6]

America's Liberian colony was really born on that April day in 1980 when Doe seized power. Even though previous Liberian presidents had enjoyed a special relationship with America, some had also established themselves, though to markedly varying degrees, as African leaders of note. By the time most African countries were fighting for independence during the 1950s, the independent Republic of Liberia was already over 120 years old, run by a tiny elite of Americo-Liberians, the descendants of freed slaves who had been dispatched to the West African coast in the 1840s after the American Colonization Society secured their freedom and then obtained a home for them from the indigenous African tribes on a stretch of swamp along the coast of present-day Liberia. William Tolbert, the president overthrown by Doe and his fellow coup makers, as well as his predecessor, William Tubman, presided over an aristocratic system of government for a combined total of thirty-six years. They had preserved the privileges of the Americo-Liberians by owning the country, running it through Masonic lodges from which the indigenous tribes were excluded and suppressing dissent with ease.

The U.S.-Liberian relationship was rooted in the historical role the United States had played as the country that had passed legislation in 1807 outlawing the importation of slaves. It had followed this by facilitating the efforts of the American Colonization Society to free slaves in the United States and transport them to West Africa.[7] By the time Doe seized power, this relationship had reached the point of rupture, inevitable in relations between two such vastly different states whose differences had remained unspoken for so long. "With Liberians one had a quality of dialogue because they really thought of themselves as honorary Americans,"[8] said Crocker. "During the Cold War period, when diplomacy with Third World states was something like running a singles bar, they came to New York and went shopping. Had we been candid about the standards of government in Liberia it would have been very damaging to U.S. interests. Not just us. The British and French also played the game," he said.[9]

Crocker's cynicism, which reached its peak when the United States recognized Doe's election as civilian president in 1985, after a poll which even Liberia's vice president admits was riddled with fraud, is made all the more horrifying in light of his recognition that "Liberia's not an object of coveting by anybody. It wasn't as if the Soviets were waiting to come in."[10] His outspokenness was replaced by a more resigned sense of despair when Herman Cohen became assistant secretary of state for African affairs on the election of George Bush in 1989. Still, the Cold War permeated every aspect of U.S. policy, while the Doe regime's human rights abuses were undoubtedly creating the conditions for serious popular unrest. Its instability and excesses had already led to numerous attempted coups d'etat from within its own hierarchy, but, as Cohen said,

> Doe was somebody we had to live with. We didn't feel that he was such a monster that we couldn't deal with him. [U.S. recognition of] the 1985 election must be seen in the context of the times. At that time every West African election was rigged. But then the Cold War was raging. And here was a guy who believed the U.S. was right and the USSR was wrong. The U.S. started out by supporting a democratic solution. That was why we never took sides [in the war]. This was to make up for [recognition of] the 1985 election. By the time [Doe] was overthrown, he didn't have a single friend in Washington.[11]

On the outbreak of civil war on 24 December 1989, the United States took on the role of an observer, while exerting occasional pressure in the form of calls for greater discipline within the Armed Forces of Liberia (AFL) or letters encouraging Doe to step down and go into exile.[12] Later, it generally supported and helped finance the regional Economic Community Monitoring Group (Ecomog) military intervention, though criticizing the force for becoming engaged as a fighting faction. Herman Cohen never once spoke to President Bush about Liberia throughout 1990,[13] despite the obvious seriousness of what was taking place in a country whose political path had been so heavily influenced by U.S. interests, and which, in the opinion of one senior U.S. official, "was our own colony."[14] Very quickly, the United States deserted its colony, however, as its strategic Cold War importance disappeared.

RONALD REAGAN AND CHAIRMAN MOE

Although many of those who became Doe's enemies throughout the 1980s continue to feel that Tolbert's overthrow was the necessary prerequisite for the realization of their political aspirations, the brutality that followed that overthrow pushed even some of the most ardent opponents of the old Americo-Liberian regime to feel within days of the 1980 coup that everything was going very wrong. In fact it appears to have been relatively easy to slaughter Tolbert and his ministers. But what then? In fact, due to the absence of any kind of plan on the part of the coup makers, Doe was really owed very little by the Liberian population for his part in the overthrow, and the failure to govern well quickly isolated Doe from the more educated people who had supported him—people with ideas about how to give the country a fresh start.

Unfortunately for Liberia, Ronald Reagan's America did not see things this way. America did not care who was in power in Liberia, as long as they served the U.S. interest. American policymakers like Chester Crocker are keen to portray this as reflecting a charitable attitude on their part. But if, as Crocker appears to believe, there was no East-West battle for Liberian hearts and minds during the Cold War, then why was there really a need for America to accept Doe and his atrocious regime, if the risk of *losing* Liberia to the Soviet Union did not exist as a reason for keeping hold of it? "I consider the revolution of 1980 to have been a revolution, and the previous regime to have been an aristocracy. It was the first experience of democracy for Liberians," Crocker told me.[15] The bloody and, many would say, undemocratic slaughter of April 1980 had entailed tying several overthrown ministers to telegraph poles on the beach and shooting them with machine guns, while subsequent years were characterized by the murder of opposition figures and students. Thus it would appear that American policymakers on Liberia had decided to attempt the justification of state criminality on the basis that because it was being carried out by "people" as opposed to "aristocrats" it must therefore be democratic. Until well into 1990, after Doe's soldiers had committed some of the most atrocious human rights abuses ever seen in West Africa, the United States kept talking to him.

What is clear from Crocker's statements is that his judgment of performance did not extend to the performance of the United States itself. At every step American policy failed. It did not create a democracy in Liberia—ostensibly the condition for American aid—but instead propped up the Doe regime. Worse, it continued to give Doe money, pay the civil service, repay the International Monetary Fund, and finance the military. "We were basically subsidizing the government. Every month we would be running around trying to pay for Liberia's fuel imports and arranging bridging loans,"[16] said James Bishop, a former U.S. ambassador to Monrovia. Meanwhile, the appalling abuse of human rights was commonplace, and it prepared the ground for the war that was to destroy Liberia. "We sublimated [sic; subordinated?] our view of human rights in the interests of our strategic concerns," a senior U.S. State Department official who had served at the U.S. embassy in Liberia told me.[17]

The Cold War was the single biggest factor in our policy towards Liberia. The U.S. facilities in Liberia were the second factor. The U.S. desire to promote human rights was the third factor. The U.S. military mission [in Liberia] was reluctant to adopt a negative attitude towards the AFL. The mission had very good insights into what was going on. But overall their influence was limited, and if you look back over our ten-year experience in Liberia, we have to say it was a failure. We didn't depoliticize the army. Doe didn't want institutions to develop. We trod assiduously. But we were undercut by Doe. Doe manipulated us right from the beginning. His entire policy towards Libya was manipulation.

Our problem was that there were no good guys [after the war started]. The [U.S.] National Security Council was asking, Who do we support, a Libyan-backed insurgent or a semi-literate leader? The Libya angle bugged us. We would have liked to have targeted Libya and gone for Taylor. But supporting Doe was impossible. If Taylor had been committing atrocities it would have been easier. But there was nobody in the DoS [Department of State] saying that there was somebody they could support in Liberia.

For the United States during the 1980s, Liberia's importance lay in part in the form of strategic installations. Diplomatic communications from throughout much of Africa were relayed to Washington via a communications station outside Monrovia. The regional transmission station for the Voice of America, the U.S. government radio station, was sited in Liberia. It has now been moved to Sao Tome. The Omega transmission station, which allowed ships in the Atlantic and aircraft to navigate using triangulation, is still in Liberia, though it is now obsolete due to the development of satellites. From the military point of view, Liberia was perfect. American aircraft flying arms supplies to Savimbi's Unita movement in Angola stopped for re-fueling at Liberia's national airport at Robertsfield, en route to the bases in southern Zaire from which Unita was rearmed. Twenty-four hours' notice was supposed to be given for such arrivals, though the arrivals became so routine that the Liberians would simply be informed that an aircraft had landed, refueled, and departed. To facilitate this operation, Robertsfield was modernized and the runway improved. Financing for these improvements did not come in the form of foreign aid but from the U.S. Department of Defense. Militarily, the United States could call on Liberia in other ways. By agreement, the entire Liberian-registered merchant fleet—the biggest in the world, owing to its "flag of convenience" system, which allowed ships from any country to register in Liberia—could be called upon to assist American forces in time of war or U.S. national emergency.

In return America had no concrete obligations to Liberia. A military assis-tance agreement between the two countries did not actually oblige the United States to do anything. However, following the 1980 coup the desire to prop up its new partner in West Africa led the United States to grant $60 million in military aid. Although $42 million was to pay for improvements in the living conditions of the AFL, the rest went on military supplies. Accord-ing to James Bishop, these included 4,000 M-16 assault rifles, light weapons, mortars, and light artillery, as well as communications, trucks, and the refur-bishment of navy patrol boats. Bishop's confirmation undermines claims made during the height of Doe's terror, when U.S. officials would only iden-tify military assistance as having been spent on the improvements in living conditions at the barracks. Possession of 4,000 M-16s, in addition to weapons stocks acquired from elsewhere, essentially meant that most combat troops within the 6,300-strong AFL had access to a gun, should they be distributed. However, the bulk of the military assistance, particularly the lethal aid, went to Doe's Executive Mansion Guard—his private militia and personal body-guard—and the First Infantry Battalion. Both were dominated by his Krahn tribe, and both used their superior equipment, numerical strength, and the fear they instilled among the population to protect the evolution of Doe's regime on the path to criminality.

Meanwhile, popular redemption, of the kind Doe's Popular Redemption Council (PRC) government professed to intend when it seized power in 1980, had also to go beyond favors to the military. For this he needed more money.

It poured in.

Soon after the Reagan administration took over, Secretary of State George Schultz met Doe in Monrovia. "Schultz said after the meeting: 'Perhaps I made a wrong career choice, if it was people like that I was going to meet. Doe was unintelligible'," was the way James Bishop related Schultz's account of the meeting.[18] Nevertheless, that year the United States granted Liberia

$52.4 million in economic support, development assistance, and subsidies on rice imports. In 1982 it was $62.3 million, making Liberia sub-Saharan Africa's biggest per capita recipient of U.S. aid. Doe kept thousand of dollars in cash in a six-foot high safe in a corner of his office in the executive mansion. After his death he was also found to have held $5.6 million in an account at a branch of the now collapsed Bank of Credit and Commerce International in London. Philip Banks, a lawyer who held the position of justice minister in Liberia's 1990–1994 interim government, estimates that Doe and his cronies stole $300 million during their ten years in power.

OUR MAN IN MONROVIA

On 21 November 1983, a group of armed men attacked the Yekepa iron ore mine on Liberia's northern border with Guinea, in the hope that they could attract support from the local population and inspire a broader uprising against the regime. What became known as the Nimba Raid was organized by Samuel Dokie, a former minister for rural development, who had fled the country after falling out with Doe in 1983, when he refused to transfer $3 million from his ministry to Doe's personal bank account. Dokie was sacked over state radio and fled to Guinea, from which the raid was launched. Those allegedly involved in the raid, twenty-two of whom were charged with treason, mutiny, murder, and conspiracy, were all found guilty, but all except those found guilty of killing were pardoned. They duly left the country, to become the nucleus of the next coup attempt.

By 1990 Doe was boasting to senior American officials in Monrovia that he had survived thirty-eight coup attempts, and that his superiority as a military tactician was what would see him through the war that was by then raging. It is unclear how many serious coups were mounted against him during the 1980s. Following the Nimba raid, which Dokie had been warned by sympathetic friends was bound to fail, the next serious attempt was launched by Elmer Johnson, the Americo-Liberian nephew of Clarence Simpson, Jr., until 1980 the treasurer of President Tolbert's ousted True Whig Party. Johnson, an American resident, who had fought with the U.S. Marines in the 1982 invasion of Grenada, arrived at Robertsfield airport with a gun hidden inside a videotape recorder. He and an American, William Woodhouse, successfully entered the country, but were betrayed. The AFL surrounded the house they were staying in, and there was a shoot-out, during which Johnson lost an eye. He was arrested but relatively soon pardoned by Doe, just as most of those involved in the Nimba raid had been pardoned. Johnson gratefully accepted the pardon and then left the country to plan his next coup attempt.

Doe's custom of pardoning his enemies was part of an attempt to create a statesmanlike impression, in which it was believed mercy was an important element. According to his former vice president, Harry Moniba, Doe failed to learn anything from the coups mounted against him. "Doe was always finding himself in conflict because of the way he had come to power. The executions of April 22, 1980, turned public pressure against Doe," one former senior minister who was with him until almost the end, told me.[19]

In 1985, a third attempt was launched, this time by the then deputy commander of the Executive Mansion Guard, Colonel Moses Flanzamaton. Flanzamaton opened fire on a car Doe was driving through Monrovia but failed to hit his target. He escaped but was captured on 4 April, and in televised interrogations he said three opposition leaders had hired him to carry out the assassination and implicated an American working as an adviser to the security forces as being part of the operation. Flanzamaton also said he had been promised $1 million to kill Doe, half to be paid now, half later. Lack of evidence led to the hasty release of the opposition leaders, and the government said Flanzamaton was tried before the Supreme Military Tribunal. In fact no trial was held. He was executed by firing squad on 8 April 1985. The event was a blow for the Americans, because, as State Department officials have now admitted, Flanzamaton was spying for the CIA. Asked about Flanzamaton's role, Crocker said: "Any great power has both technical and human sources of intelligence. And probably has more than one. That's the way the world is organized. By regional standards in West Africa, Monrovia was a serious mission for the CIA."[20]

At points, secret intelligence resulted in disclosures necessitating action to steer their friend and ally away from paths that could undermine American interests. And of course money was the only way to do so. Doe regularly slammed the Libyans, because he knew it pleased America. But in 1984 the United States learned through intelligence channels that he had decided to pay Colonel Gadaffi a visit, with the possibility of renewing diplomatic relations. A senior Liberian government official, in office at that time, described the situation to me in an interview:

> The U.S. was very sensitive to the Libyan presence. In 1984 Doe was invited by Libya to make a state visit. Doe accepted the Libyan invitation. The U.S. didn't like the idea, and Reagan sent Vernon Walters to discourage the visit. Walters promised $5 million to Doe immediately without conditions. Doe knew that he could get more from Libya. His officials were already waiting for him in Tripoli. The trip may have led to the re-establishment of diplomatic relations. But after Walters' visit Doe canceled the Libyan visit.[21]

According to Crocker, he and his colleagues portrayed Libya to Doe as being unreliable. "We made it pretty clear to him that Libya just wasn't on," he said.[22] The American tactic to prevent this link being established was unashamedly admitted by a senior state department official: "Libya was important. We told Doe: This is the wrong thing to do. It might give these guys a foothold in the region. With regard to Libya we bought Doe off. There was a direct link [between aid and foreign relations]."[23]

The essence of Doe and his cohorts' strategy with regard to the United States are well reflected in an advisory memorandum sent on 22 March 1983 to Doe by his then minister of state and close adviser, Major John G. Rancey. The memorandum was intended to advise Doe on measures he should take if he wanted to keep power after the promised return to civilian rule in 1985:

> As you requested, per our discussion regarding possible strategies for remaining in office beyond 1985, it is my opinion that several essential steps will have to be taken if we are to minimize the effect such a decision will have upon your credibility as Head of State. Since it is obvious the greatest opposition will come from the Americans I think we should do everything humanly possible to placate them into supporting you, economically and politically. For this to happen however, the following moves must be considered:
>
> 1. Remove all known MOJA [Movement for Justice in Africa] and PPP [Popular People's Party] sympathizers from the public eye through reassignment or dismissal from the Government and private positions.
> 2. Re-establish diplomatic ties with the state of Israel.
> 3. Adopt a sharp stance in both domestic and international arenas against Soviet policy.
> 4. Dissipate all domestic opposition through strategy if possible; crush with force if necessary.
>
> It would be expedient to denounce Socialist philosophy and those individuals and governments associated with it including the Ethiopian and Libyan friendship with the Soviets. Condemn all Soviet expansion in Africa, especially Chad, and you will convince the U.S. that ideologies other than Western-based capitalism have no place in Liberia. It may be helpful to label any internal activists as Socialists.
>
> To be totally convincing in the "pro-American" attitude, it may be necessary to acquire a Foreign Minister with whom the U.S. will be comfortable, a distinction that Mr. Fahnbulleh does not enjoy.
>
> Once Liberia receives her blank check of support form [sic] America it is possible to begin the last, but the most formidable task, the total elimination of potential opposition. As we agreed in our discussion, it may be anticipated that the most vigorous opposition to your staying on will come from Nimba County. You may be assured that the leading voice will be that of your "friend" Thomas Quiwonkpa. . . . I am convinced that they are troublemakers who do not hesitate to organize themselves. You may recall that Nimba was the strongest base of the PPP. Nimbaians seem to love politics, thus, the removal of Thomas and supporters from the Army and positions of Government must

be gradual and most carefully planned. . . . Regardless of the risk, I believe you
will agree that Thomas and the other "Nimba heroes" must be totally discredited, if not totally eliminated. . . . I have no doubt that once these critical steps
are taken it is certain that the people of Liberia will overwhelmingly support a
continuation of your leadership in 1985.[24]

The letter reflects the complete absence of any kind of political philosophy in the regime, other than that of clinging to power. The readiness of the
regime to do absolutely anything to please the United States, knowing that
Reagan's America would only see what it wanted to see, meant Doe could
portray his domestic enemies as the "socialist" enemies of America, and
thereby "eliminate" them, almost in the name of the United States. Such
measures allowed both the Reagan administration and the Doe regime to parade each other as allies, though in a manner which usefully provided pre-
texts for policies that were ultimately to lead to the destruction of Liberia.

By 1985, Liberians opposed to Doe reacted with increasing disbelief at
the continued American support for the monster they had watched take
power. Rumors abounded that secretly America would like to see Doe overthrown, but that it was not acceptable for the United States to be seen to be
involved. This was not the case. It was the wishful thinking of a population
that was losing hope. The hope of many Liberians, that secretly America was
really on their side against their oppressor, appeared increasingly unrealistic.
America wanted Doe to remain. They liked him being there, as a senior U.S.
policymaker made clear in 1993: "We were getting fabulous support from
him on international issues. He never wavered his support for us against
Libya and Iran. He was somebody we had to live with. We didn't feel that he
was such a monster that we couldn't deal with him. All our interests were being impeccably protected by Doe. We weren't paying a penny for the U.S.
installations."[25]

The Reagan administration's contentment with Doe had its most memo-
rable moment when Doe honored his promise to hold civilian elections.
This he did on 15 October 1985.

"I have photographs of the cheating. The ballot boxes were filled before
the voting," Doe's former vice president, Harry Moniba, who retained his
post as a result of the malpractice, told me.[26] "The Liberian Action Party,
which declared itself the winner, was also cheating. [Doe's] National Democratic Party of Liberia cheated more carefully," he said. But the cheating did
not matter to America. Crocker, testifying to the U.S. Senate Foreign Relations Committee's Africa subcommittee on 10 December 1985, said: "There
is now the beginning, however imperfect, of a democratic experience that
Liberia and its friends can use as a benchmark for future elections—one on
which they want to build."[27] His comments came after two political parties
had been banned and prevented from running in the election, after a year

preceding the poll when opposition leaders had been imprisoned, and after a massacre of students on Doe's orders at Monrovia University on 22 August 1984, following agitation against Doe by students and academics.

American acceptance of the election result contributed to the view among many Liberians that the country it looked to for guidance must have a hidden agenda which would save them from Doe eventually, but which in the meantime it was necessary to believe was being concealed until the time was right to rid them of this monster.

STEERING THE SHIP OF STATE

After the election Chester Crocker, in a 23 January 1986 statement to a joint session of the American Congressional Subcommittees on Africa and Human Rights and International Organizations, said, "We learned that Doe was considering appointing to important positions in his new civilian government Liberians of proven talent who were not members of his party."

Thomas Quiwonkpa, Doe's fellow coup maker and later AFL chief of staff, who had fallen out with Doe and fled Liberia in 1983, did not understand that fundamentally the United States was happy with its ally in Monrovia, as long as Crocker could continue to find a balance between what he called in his 1986 testimony the "plusses and minuses" of Doe's conduct. Crocker told the joint session that "no outside observer could be certain who won those elections," though the United States accepted the result. A month later, on 12 November 1985, the very people Rancey had identified in his 1983 letter to Doe as "troublemakers" arrived in Monrovia, and for six hours Doe was overthrown.

According to the former U.S. ambassador James Bishop, American officials heard in the spring of 1985 that a coup against Doe was possible and that Quiwonkpa was involved. "We understood that it was going to be much earlier than when it happened. The report was that it would be staged in the summer. We gave the report credibility," said Bishop.[28] Another senior State Department policymaker has since confirmed that American embassy officials in Monrovia then went to Doe and informed him of the coup plot, "because we had reason to believe that he knew we knew, and would therefore think that if it took place that we were a part of it. We also tried to get word to Quiwonkpa to knock it off," the official said.[29]

Within six hours of arriving in Monrovia, where it was intended that Quiwonkpa would seek to attract the support of the men he used to lead as army chief, the plotters had been rounded up. Quiwonkpa was captured, tortured, castrated, dismembered, and parts of his body publicly eaten by Doe's victorious troops in different areas of the city. America's ally was safe. Mass slaughter then broke loose. The U.S. embassy, in a bid to downplay the slaughter (in a way that was repeated in later massacres during the war that erupted in 1989), said 400 people were killed by Doe's troops as they rounded up supposed plotters. The figure is reckoned by numerous Liberian eyewitnesses to have been as high as 3,000. Civilians who had celebrated in the streets of Monrovia when they thought the coup had been successful were driven to the beaches outside the city where they were massacred. Truckloads of bodies sped through the city from the grounds of the presidential mansion to mass graves outside Monrovia on the road to Robertsfield airport.

"In the short run, President Doe's government seems to have the power to govern," Chester Crocker said two months later, in his January 1986 statement to the joint congressional committees. "A key lesson of the November coup attempt is that the military units that counted—the first battalion and the Executive Mansion Guard—were loyal and effective." He went on to say,

> There is in Liberia today a civilian government based on elections, a multiparty legislature, a journalist community of government and non-government newspapers and radio stations. An ongoing tradition among the citizenry of speaking out. A new constitution that protects those freedoms, and a judicial system that can help enforce those provisions. The [Liberian] government is committed publicly to that system.

It was corruption rather than brutality that eventually began to irk the United States. Liberia's corruption was an issue for the American taxpayer, while human rights apparently were not. By the time of the 1985 election, the United States had given Doe $400 million. By the outbreak of war in December 1989, this had risen to $500 million. This was still less than the cost of relocating all the American installations sited in Liberia, and the refueling of arms flights to Unita would have been complicated to relocate. But it came nevertheless to be seen as an increasingly expensive price tag. Even though human rights abuses in Liberia were not playing a significant role in the cat-and-mouse game of the Cold War, pressure within the American opposition-led Congress eventually resulted in an attempt to stem the corruption, which was proving such a waste of American resources.

U.S. State Department statistics show that in the financial year after the rigged election and the post-coup massacres, Doe's government was accorded $55.9 million in U.S. aid. Doe had reneged on his promise of free elections, but he had held a charade that let both him and his financiers—the Reagan government—off the hook. On paper, an election had been held, and the Reagan administration could delude itself into believing that democracy really had blossomed, despite the election being condemned even in the U.S. Congress, and later by victors in the contest such as Vice President Harry Moniba, as one of the most rigged elections in history. For both Reagan—who once became famously confused as to the identity of his Liberian counterpart during a visit by Doe to Washington, referring to him as "President Moe"—and Doe, avoidance of the truth was in their mutual interest:

"I don't think we made any special effort to point out what our relationship [with Liberia] was. But here was a guy, Doe, who believed the U.S. was right and the USSR was wrong,"[30] said a key American policymaker. America's problem was, of course, that having nurtured its monster, there was the problem of keeping him under control. "Doe used to complain to me sometimes that he was just not getting as rich as some of the other African heads of state. He used to say: 'look at Houphouët-Boigny [of Côte d'Ivoire]. He has all that money. Why am I not getting that rich?'" one of his former confidantes told me.[31] His annual presidential salary of $35,000[32] was minuscule beside those of the habitual diverters of foreign aid he took to comparing himself with. He wanted more, for himself and his cronies; otherwise they would stop supporting him.

U.S. concern over the waste of U.S. aid money led, on 26 August 1987, to Doe, the U.S. Department of State, and the United States Agency for International Development (USAID) signing an agreement that allowed seventeen U.S.-appointed Operational Experts (Opex) to take over financial control of government accounts in the Liberian Ministry of Finance and at the National Bank of Liberia.[33] Opex officials were also to be present in the revenue, customs, and data processing offices of the Ministry of Finance, the Bureau of the Budget, and other key government offices. The Opex team, which produced its final, never published report in May 1989, worked on the basis, expressed in the report, of being "a last ditch effort on the part of the U.S. to assist Liberia out of its financial crisis."[34] It also said that Doe had "requested outside assistance to help control fiscal disarray in Liberia, and gave the team operational authority to implement management and policy reforms."[35] Doe was also to act as arbiter in any disputes that might arise during the operation of the Opex team.

The Opex report, which looked at the process of decisionmaking within the government rather than tracing where foreign aid money had gone, identified the close relationship between members of Liberia's largely expatriate business community and the Doe government. This relationship meant that businessmen, mostly Lebanese, Indian, and Israeli, were able to use personal contacts with Doe's kitchen cabinet to strike business deals that circumvented any budgetary controls the Opex team may have been trying to instigate, as the report makes clear:

Lebanese businessmen were among the most influential at the Mansion. A Lebanese-owned construction company obtained the first loan guarantees that specifically by-passed the Ministry of Finance and Opex. This deal established a precedent for other construction companies. . . . An Israeli firm obtained

payments for the construction of a new Defense Ministry directly from the
Mansion, financed by diverted forestry revenues collected by the Forestry Development Authority. . . . The vendor community in Monrovia, dominated by
the Lebanese and Indian businessmen, also contributed to the budgetary problem. The vendors who provide goods to the Government often overcharge by
two to three times the normal price. The Government was in arrears to most
of them, dating as far back as 1984, and the vendors rationalized the over-
billing as compensation for lost interest and for the risk of not being paid at all.
In this environment, vendors have a strong incentive to offer bribes to get early
payment.[36]

The report identifies eight different ways in which the economic reform
team was bypassed and decisionmaking and finances retained in the hands of
the executive mansion staff. This situation led the team to conclude that its
eventual failure was due to the fact that Doe's Liberia

was managed with far greater priority given to short-term political survival and
deal-making than to any long-term recovery or nation-building efforts. . . .
The President's primary concern is for political and physical survival. His pri-
orities are very different from and inconsistent with economic recovery. . . .
President Doe has great allegiance to his tribes people and his inner circle. His
support of local groups on ill-designed projects undercut larger social objectives.[37]

Although the evidence of Doe's determination not to allow economic reform
was made obvious by the Opex report, the issue itself was only a contributing
factor in his long-term decline. Nevertheless, this decline became impossible
to hide after the Opex team departed in November 1988, though the absence
of a published report deprived Doe's opponents of a weapon to further discredit him. It is unclear why the report was not published, though evidence
from the leaked copies suggest that to have done so would not have served to
improve Liberian government finances, nor would it have helped America
help its ally. As Crocker said: "Had we been candid about the standards of government in Liberia, it would have been very damaging to U.S. interests."[38]

WHO DARES WINS

On 19 December 1983, Doe had approved an arrest warrant for his former
deputy commerce minister and head of the General Services Agency (GSA),
Charles Taylor. The warrant was followed by an extradition request to the
U.S. government. Taylor had fled Liberia the previous year, accused of em-
bezzling $900,000 from the GSA. Even though the Liberian government

never sought the return of the money, it wanted to prevent Taylor from joining the ranks of exiled dissidents. Taylor, living in New Jersey, responded to the extradition order and the cancellation of his diplomatic passports by writing Doe a four-page letter, on 10 January 1984, that revealed his determination to take power for himself, while effectively blackmailing Doe and his government on the issue of the corruption allegations. Although Taylor had not been part of the 1980 coup, he was in Liberia when it took place. As a student in the United States he had been involved with the Union of Liberian Associations in the Americas (ULAA), and he had been invited to the country by President Tolbert.

He quickly secured a job with the new PRC government, but was later advised to leave, having fallen out with several influential members of the government. He went to the United States, as he wrote to Doe, "on a health mission abroad in an attempt to prevent my health from further deteriorating as the gravity of the situation was approaching crisis level." He did not specify the disease, and the letter continued:

> As I recovered from my hospital bed I had the privilege, thanks to the love of friends in and out of certain areas of Government, of receiving newspaper and other intelligence briefings [sic] from Liberia, that revealed information that was a direct threat to my life and existence. . . . The evidence was clear that my life was in immediate danger.
>
> . . . [On] many occasions we discussed the revolution in detail and disagreed on several issues, especially the mechanism for return to civilian rule. I still remember when you took a decision that persons having political ambitions for [the planned civilian elections of] 1985 should resign their positions with the government. I met with you on three different occasions during the period involved (and you can't deny this), and made it clear to you I had political ambitions of my own but didn't think I should resign and insisted that you withdraw the statement, but you refused to do so. I knew then that the vast differences in our political view could cause immense problems between us and I would have to prepare for the worst.
>
> There is no question in my mind about my services to the Government of the of the PRC. . . . You know very well that I did nothing without specific verbal or written instructions from you or a member of the PRC and now everyone is trying to play "MR. CLEAN," which you and I know very well is a lie. . . . Up to this point I have behaved responsibly as I think an ex-official serving in such sensitive position should. I have kept my mouth shut while newspapers have hypothesized and made guesses as to what happened at the agency over the three years under my leadership. You and I know what happened and why. I am not prepared to become the whipping boy, just because I fled to save my life.[39]

Taylor's letter admits not only that he was himself involved in official corruption, but also that the practice of corruption was sanctioned from the top level of government. Small wonder that, when the U.S. installed the Opex team three years later, it was a failure. The letter goes on to say that Doe should end the extradition proceedings against him and end allegations of his corruption, or risk consequences:

> I will have no alternative but to fight back by making public to the world everything I know about the PRC, about your own activities, financial transactions, and that of every council member all the many corrupt actions that you know I know of. I would not want this any more than you would. You know that I never embezzled any money and also you know that I served well. This is not a threat of blackmail as some may suggest. It is what I will do if you don't put a stop to these lies, just to protect myself and my image.[40]

Taylor's apparent readiness to connive at the concealment of corruption is revealing, as is the readiness to blackmail. Doe was apparently not convinced, however, and pursued the extradition. Taylor was arrested by the authorities in May 1984 and imprisoned in the Plymouth County House of Correction at Plymouth, Massachusetts, while awaiting the extradition hearings. He remained there until 15 September 1985, when he escaped in as yet unexplained circumstances. Taylor's versions of events, as reported to the people he subsequently spent most of his time with, are as varied as the relationships he shared with those people. Taylor told one of his confidantes that he and his two accomplices sawed through the bars of their prison cell for several days, lowered themselves to the ground on a rope made of bedsheets, and escaped into the night.[41] Taylor then drove to Mexico, before traveling to Ghana via France.

A VISIT TO THE COLONEL

Taylor arrived in the Ghanaian capital Accra to find the majority of Liberia's exiles involved in various plots against Doe. From Ghana Taylor went to Abidjan, Côte d'Ivoire. Before leaving Ghana, Taylor had made his first contact with Libya through the Burkina Faso ambassador in Accra. He began visiting Libya in 1987 and, using financial backing from the Libyan government, began assembling the nucleus of an army with which to invade Liberia and overthrow Doe.

The first Liberians to be enlisted by Taylor were a forty-strong group assembled by Cooper Miller, a former AFL soldier, who had stealthily brought his followers into Côte d'Ivoire from northern Liberia by telling the border guards on both sides that they were taking part in a football competition. They were taken to the Ivorian border town of Danane and then transported by bus to the central town of Bouake. From there they took the train to Ouagadougou and were installed at a military base outside the city. A second group of thirty Liberians, led by former Liberian soldiers Prince Johnson and John Duoe, was moved from Danane to Abidjan, then on to Ouagadougou and Tripoli. A third group was assembled in Danane in November 1988, following the same route, led by another former soldier, Paul B. Harris, who had been a member of the deposed Liberian president William Tolbert's personal body-guard before Samuel Doe's 1980 coup. The Libyans opened up their military facilities to the Liberians, many of whom had already trained in the Armed Forces of Liberia along American lines, and who found themselves increasingly disappointed with what they saw as the shortcomings of the Libyan war machine. One of the trainees provided a comprehensive account of the training they received:

While in Libya we did military training at Tarjura base. That included Libyan drill, which most found inadequate, then American infantry drill, supervised by Prince Johnson and Paul B. Harris, done on Fridays when the Libyans were at mosque and the Liberians could do their own thing. Then we did commando training, jumping from multistory buildings, and barbed wire training at the sea-side base, which was a former U.S. base before Gaddafi took over. Also we did guerrilla warfare training in Hodrabya, close to the desert. It was where the U.S. had trained soldiers to go to the Vietnam War. U.S. trucks, uniforms, and huts had been left behind there when the U.S. left the base, which was commonly called First September. At this base the Chadian war prisoners were kept. We gave them some of our green jackets to allow them to escape, though this only became known later on. Taylor wanted to recruit Chadians to fight with them against Doe and some of them did go with Taylor back to Liberia. When we weren't training some of us spent time in the base library reading books by Che Guevara, Karl Marx, Mahatma Gandhi and Fidel Castro.

There were twenty-nine nationalities training there, among them Mada-gascans, Haitians, Brazilians, black South Africans, Central Africans, Zairians, Sudanese, Ugandans doing aviation studies, Gambians, Martiniquans, Con-golese, Sumatrans, Colombians from the M-19 organization, Sri Lankans led by a colonel who was planning to overthrow Rajiv Gandhi, and Tamil Tigers based at Mataba, which was the revolutionary office and was called Alba by the Libyans. Also at that time Idriss Deby's Chadians were there, some of whom said they were from Centrafrique but were in fact Chadians. Even anti-Compaore Burkinabe were there training after infiltrating the camp. But Tay-lor helped expose them, which strengthened his friendship with Compaore [Blaise Compaore, president of Burkina Faso].[42]

Head of the Mataba training base was Moussa Kusa, to this day the head of state security in Libya, though most contact between the Libyan hierar-chy and their apprentices was made through his deputy, Dr. Moktar. The chief training officer was another Libyan, Mohammed Hassem, a weapons specialist also responsible for training Gaddafi's personal bodyguards and nicknamed "Wicked" by the Liberians. Lieutenant Joseph Magabe, a Zairian, was the second planning and training officer, who gave the Liberians lessons in map reading and reconnaissance. The teaching of military tactics and maneuvers was run by Abudadi, another Libyan, nicknamed "Desert Lion," who had fought with the Ugandan president Yoweri Museveni during the overthrow of Tito Okello's regime in January 1986, or so he claimed. As youthful as some of the Liberians was a seventeen-year-old Libyan antiaircraft weapons specialist named Glada, who had fought the Chadians in the disputed Aouzou strip and wore a black star tattoo on his shoulder that designated him as a warrior, the Liberians were told. Among the non-Libyan instructors were a Maltese named Amore, who taught sabotage and countersabotage techniques, and a Ghanaian known simply as Mohamed, who acted as an Arabic-English interpreter.

For battlefield training, according to the former trainee, the Liberians spent their days at the Halaka:

> The Halaka was a circle inside the desert camp and was basically used for exercises and learning hand-to-hand combat and barbed wire training with live ammunition. No Liberians were injured or killed during this, but Sumatrans were killed. Holmes navy base bordering Egypt and near to Saibar military base was where we did naval training. There we lost a man called Ernest Wemer, who drowned when he was dumped from a ship and told to swim back to shore. He was almost on the shore when the instructor deliberately disabled him. He was alive when his body was retrieved but he bled from his nose when brought on the shore. He died in hospital, where his body has been preserved.[43]

Despite securing the backing he needed for his group to prepare, as well as an apartment for himself in the Mataba base, a room at Tarjura, and the pseudonym Charlie Liberia, Taylor was still fighting rival Liberian dissidents for unchallenged leadership of the eventual move against Doe. Another Libyan, Mohammed Tallibe, was in charge of 200 Sierra Leoneans who had drifted to Libya, as well as having overall charge of the Liberians. Taylor preferred to deal with Dr. Moktar, whom he had convinced that he was the rightful leader of the planned insurrection against Doe. For Taylor the main irritation was the arrival of 100 supporters of Boima Fahnbulleh, a left-wing former foreign minister in the first Doe government, who were eager for the same type of training Taylor's 168-member group had already embarked upon. Tallibe fell out with Taylor because the Libyans accepted the Fahnbulleh group, which annoyed Taylor enormously. He knew that Fahnbulleh had substantial political credentials as well as credibility in the eyes of other regional regimes, to which Taylor himself was a relative unknown.

Playing with Fire

The Liberians remained in Libya until July 1989. Taylor had problems finding a friendly country bordering Liberia from which to launch the invasion,
and an attempt to overthrow him from within the rebel group shook his grip
and led eventually to his force splitting altogether after the invasion. Despite
the absence of a final destination, the recruits in Libya eventually began leaving. Some flew from Tripoli via Paris and then landed in Burkina Faso in
July 1989, while others flew direct to Ouagadougou. All the National Patriotic Front of Liberia (NPFL) had left Burkina Faso by the first week of November 1989, though more recruits were still being brought from Côte
d'Ivoire. The police in the central Ivorian town of Bouake at one point
stopped and arrested twenty-five of the new recruits, because some of them
did not have identity cards. They were forced to sweep the floor of the police
station, before eventually being released. They stayed in Bouake for another
day "to enjoy themselves before going to die," one of the recruits said. They
were then taken immediately to Danane in northwest Côte d'Ivoire, where
they were given the funds that would allow them to disperse among the border villages.

Meanwhile Taylor had gathered his commanders in Abidjan. In all, forty
had arrived by plane at Abidjan's Port-Bouet airport from Ouagadougou on
22 November 1989. At Port-Bouet they successfully bribed the custom officials and police to let all of them through the airport without being asked
any questions. From Abidjan they left for the Liberian border, arriving at the
village of Bin Houye in early December.

The idea was to push on three different fronts from Bin Houye, Danane,
and Guinea. In Bin Houye on 21 December, as they prepared for the push,
Taylor ordered all his troops to take a stone and swear over a pan of water,
"If anybody goes against me or plan [sic] to kill me, they will die." That day,
fourteen of the rebels crossed unarmed into Guinea from Côte d'Ivoire.
They were to receive weapons when they arrived at the Liberia-Guinea border, where the Guinean district commissioner had promised Taylor arms and
was expecting a large pay-off in return. By nightfall on 21 December the
fourteen had reached the Guinean provincial capital of N'Zerekore. They
waited for Taylor, but he had been stopped at the Côte d'Ivoire border and
did not turn up with the money for the district commissioner. Instead he
sent orders via a go-between that they should continue to move toward
Liberia even though they had no weapons. Suspicion of the group was
aroused among local villagers, and they were arrested by the Guinean police,
who escorted them back to Côte d'Ivoire.

While the fourteen were attempting to pierce through Liberia's border
with Guinea, a small group led by Prince Johnson crossed the border from
Côte d'Ivoire, straight into Liberia. They crossed from Bin Houye with two

single-barrel shotguns, and made their way toward the town of Butuo, where the AFL had a barracks and a plentiful supply of weapons. The plan had been to reinforce Johnson's group, but within days of crossing the border Johnson split with Taylor and embarked on his own campaign to seize power. Simultaneously, the third prong of the offensive, upon which Taylor had finally decided, collapsed as disastrously as the push from Guinea. As well as the invasion from outside, Taylor had decided to infiltrate people into Monrovia. They were all discovered and arrested after giving themselves away, and were made to confess who they were on Liberian state television. They also denounced Taylor and his Libyan connections, to the delight of the Doe regime, which at that time had had little idea of what was really happening along its northern and eastern borders.

The fourteen fighters deported from Guinea returned to Danane, where they tried to contact Taylor. There, they heard that the Ivorian authorities had arrested Taylor and others after cross-border shooting had erupted near Zouan Hounien, when AFL soldiers fired at rebels retreating across the border. Somehow Taylor had managed to escape and flee to Abidjan. From there he went to Burkina Faso. The shortage of weapons then became his major problem. The Libyans had waited for him to prove that he could launch an invasion. Now they had some degree of proof, though the arrests by the Ivorians and the failure of the Guinea and Monrovia attacks threw the entire invasion into doubt. It was not until early March that he was able to pick up the first batch of arms from Burkina Faso. The arms were hidden inside a lorry filled with yams, and included 57 AK-47 assault rifles, 157 Berretta machine guns, 150 hand grenades, 42 general machine guns (GMGs), and 27 rocket-propelled grenade launchers (RPGs). These weapons were taken to Zouen Hounien and hidden behind the village Catholic mission, before being taken into Liberia by NPFL troops, who had secured areas just across the border around Gborplay, a small village that became Taylor's base when he himself entered Liberia.

CLOSE YOUR EYES

"I believe that Liberians had a perfectly legitimate reason to believe that we had a responsibility to take a role in the war,"[44] Herman Cohen, Crocker's successor, told me, long after Liberia had become one of several of the largely hidden graveyards of U.S. Cold War policy in Africa. Cohen never once spoke directly to U.S. president George Bush about Liberia during the early years of the civil war, he told me.[45] Unlike Angola, Liberia had no cards to play in the post–Cold War era. Its strategic importance to the U.S. was derived from the weakness of its institutions, the retarded character of its system of government, and the absence of principle in decisionmaking. John

Rancey's 1983 memorandum to Doe shows clearly that the regime was unscrupulous and ultimately little more than a private gang holding an entire country to ransom. The United States successfully exploited this weakness by feeding the system of government created by Doe and his henchmen, receiving "fabulous support on international" issues in return, and giving what was ultimately the small amount of $500 million in return. Doe was cheap, Liberia was cheap.

Despite detailed exposés of the regime's abuse of human rights, in particular Bill Berkeley's *Liberia: A Promise Betrayed*, published in 1986 by the U.S. Lawyers Committee for Human Rights, the U.S. government showed no awareness of the severe impact of its policy, even though it had produced effects that threatened the very existence of Liberia. It would be wrong, however, to assert that Liberia fell apart simply because Doe was a bad leader and the United States a truly irresponsible godfather. Liberia itself, with its identity crisis, its uncertainty, its poverty, corruption, isolation, brutality, and tension, was easy to exploit. The United States fed money into the bloodstream of a country that, as anybody could see during the 1980s, was bound on a path toward self-destruction. U.S. policy derived from the need to lie about what Doe really represented. How is it possible to suggest, as Chester Crocker did, that the Doe regime was moving toward democracy in 1985?[46] It was not naïveté that led to this conclusion. Liberia was a necessary part of U.S. Cold War strategy in Africa, a country that could be bribed to oppose Gadaffi and to support other aspects of U.S. foreign policy, for example, to accept that recognizing Israel was in its national interest. The leaderships on both sides of the Atlantic Ocean could see the advantages to themselves. Maintaining Liberia's rottenness was essential if U.S. interests were to be served.

It is obviously a matter of conjecture as to whether Doe would have survived a decade in power if he had not had U.S. financial and military support. My assessment is that he would probably not have lasted that long but would have been overthrown from within the ruling elite and perhaps replaced by somebody even worse. Whatever might have happened, however, the "unmitigated failure" of U.S. policy in Liberia in the 1980s undoubtedly contributed to the ferocity of the bloodbath of the 1990s. Although ultimately it was Liberians who tore their country and each other apart, the potential for an explosion was undoubtedly greatly increased by the "character of government in Liberia," which the United States used as its Cold War tool and then dropped. Just as Crocker told me with regard to Savimbi, there was no trust in U.S. Cold War policy in Liberia. The difference between Angola and Liberia, however, was that, as Herman Cohen made clear, the historical relationship between the United States and Liberia was not negligible. Whereas the United States merely used Angola as a stage upon which it believed it was confronting the military power and expansionism of the USSR and Cuba, Liberia was an established if minor chapter of U.S. history. When it suited the United States to invoke these historical ties, it did so. As became horrifyingly clear after the first shots of the civil war were fired, Liberia was alone in paying the price (as I describe in Chapter 7), while the United States closed its eyes.

The civil war in Liberia embroiled much of West Africa in a diplomatic and military confrontation which has since brought instability and conflict to neighboring Guinea and Sierra Leone, Monrovia, Liberia, 1991 (photo: Mark Huband)

Prince Johnson, leader of the breakaway Independent National Patriotic Front of Liberia (INPFL), Monrovia, Liberia, 1991 (photo: Mark Huband)

Charles Taylor, president of Liberia, who launched a civil war against Samuel Doe's U.S.-backed government and has since used his position to back rebel movements in west Africa (photo: AP Photo)

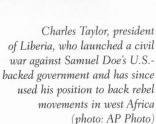

Liberian president Samuel Doe's forces rapidly became known for the atrocities committed during the civil war, Monrovia, Liberia, 1992 (photo: Mark Huband)

As the United States' sought a new role for itself in the post-Cold War 'New World Order', supporters of Somalia's warring factions voiced their suspicions of foreign intervention, and prepared to resist the foreign forces sent to Somalia in December 1992, Baidoa, Somalia, 1992 (photo: Mark Huband)

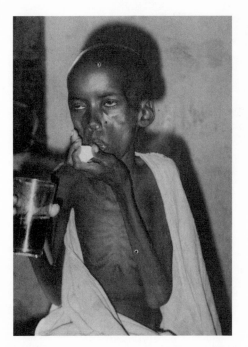

Famine created by the war which wracked Somalia had left as many as 350,000 people dead by the time foreign forces arrived in the country. Bardera, Somalia, 1993. (photo: Mark Huband)

International relief organizations played a vital role in feeding the survivors of Somalia's hunger and violence, but were themselves forced to hire gunmen to protect their efforts. Jaanaale, Somalia, 1993 (photo: Mark Huband)

Ali Mahdi Mohamed,
the Mogadishu-based
faction leader whose
conflict with Gen.
Mohamed Farah Aideed
contributed to Somalia's
descent into war and
famine, Mogadishu,
Somalia, 1993
(photo: Jim Stephens)

More than 20,000 foreign troops poured into Somalia in December 1992-January 1993,
in the hope that by protecting food deliveries they would be able to bring an end to the
worst of the suffering, Baidoa, Somalia, 1993 (photo: Jim Stephens)

Mohamed Sahnoun, the former Algerian diplomat appointed in 1992 as United Nations Special Representative to Somalia, sought to use painstaking diplomacy to bring Somalia's factions together, Mogadishu, Somalia, 1992 (photo: Jim Stephens)

Heavily-armed militia ruled the streets of Mogadishu and other towns and villages, controlling food supplies and holding much of the international relief effort to ransom by creating insecurity and demanding a high price for the provision of body guards, Mogadishu, Somalia, 1992 (photo: Jim Stephens)

Felix Houphouöt-Boigny, president of Côte d'Ivoire (center, with sunglasses), used a mixture of skillful manipulation and statesmanship to turn the country he led for thirty-three years into one of the most stable on the African continent, Abidjan, Côte d'Ivoire, 1991 (photo: Mark Huband)

Pro-Democracy movements burst out across the continent with the end of the Cold War. Thousands took the streets demanding an end to single-party rule, Abidjan, Côte d'Ivoire, 1990 (photo: Mark Huband)

Paul Kagame, President of Rwanda, has emerged as the key player in the politics of Central Africa. When extremists launched the genocide which led to the deaths of up to one million Rwandans in April-June 1994, Kagame led the Rwandan Patriotic Front (RPF) to occupy the entire country and force more than one million Rwandans to flee as refugees, Mulindi, Rwanda, January 1994 (photo: Mark Huband)

General Romeo Dallaire, the Canadian head of the UN military force sent to oversee Rwanda's transition to democracy, whose warning of the imminent genocide and calls for the UN to step in once the killing had started in April 1994 were ignored. (Photo: Mark Huband)

Victims of genocide, Nyarubuye, Rwanda, May 1994
(photo: Mark Huband)

PART TWO

The Time of the Soldier

But how do we avoid war? It's necessary for all groups to have
confidence in the state. For that, they need to be led by
democrats. For that there's a need for clarity and discussion.
But it's always the warlords who are in power. A warlord can't
become a democrat next day. It's the military that always runs
the country. The military can't create a democratic system,
because they know that if there's democracy they lose power,
because the people want peace. The army are frightened of the
people and the intellectuals. There's always a militarization of
the democratic process. In thirty-two years of independence
we have had twenty years of war. That marks the political
mentality. To democratize it's necessary to find a solution to
the military conflict. It's necessary to have a genuinely national
army, because now everybody wants their own army.

Gali Gata N'gothe

GALI GATA N'GOTHE, political opponent of Chad's military ruler,
Hissène Habré, whose assessment is cited above,[1] gets at the heart
of what typified the political struggles throughout much of the
continent—in particular West Africa—during the early and mid-1990s. The
call for democracy exposed military rulers and militarism itself as having
firmly divided the interests of the leaders from those of the led. Before the

arrival of colonial powers, rigid monarchical or chiefly rule in Africa did not generally wield power with the intention of creating discord between entire sections of the population. Republican militarism in the late twentieth century has subsequently made this happen. Why, and to what purpose? The structure of armies, the absence of law, and the weakness of democracy have fostered a climate in many African countries in which civilian political life cowers before the threat of military takeover. Where this is not the case, those holding military power have spent much of the past decade conducting a variety of transitions to political pluralism purely on their own terms, at their own pace. In so doing, they have attempted to ensure that the privileges they secured for themselves will not be denied them if one day they hand over power.[2] Ten years of agitation for democracy have now created the multiple-polarization of many African countries, though one out of which an interest-based rather than a community-based multiparty system may one day emerge.

With the advent of multiparty politics in 1989, what became clear was that a new relationship between the leaders and the led had indeed become established. Years of military rule, or civilian dictatorship with a strong military element, had created the need for change within the military itself. But even though agitation for multiparty democracy brought thousands of people out onto the streets of African towns and cities throughout the 1990s, it has yet to bring the fundamental change that is necessary. Populations were and are hungry for change. But the old elites were and are not. Key among these elites are the military officers, who have had most to lose if democracy takes root. On the popular level, democracy is understood and valued across the continent. Its enemies—and those of the people—are the armies that have resisted change. The major question now facing all African countries is how best to change the old, military structures, and replace them with a form of democracy appropriate to the continent's historical reality and therefore sustainable within the cultural life of its varied states and societies.

4

WHISPERS AND SCREAMS

Tribes and Armies in Burundi

AS THE ROAD WENT DEEPER into the forest, trees had been hacked down and dragged across it. Strands of lush grass grew beneath the trees, where the sunlight failed to reach. The trees across the road were barricades. The peasants of Burundi had done the same in 1972, when 150,000[3] people had been slaughtered, and in 1988, when a further 13,000[4] had died. They had machetes, knives, and spears, to confront troops armed with machine guns, and their only real protection lay in preventing the troops reaching them at all by blocking the roads. In a small valley, where the road turned sharply at a row of wooden shops, a drunken man lay on the ground murmuring, his trousers down at his knees, an empty bottle in his hand. Two young men appeared from nowhere and said the other shopkeepers had been killed the previous day. They pushed open the door of a shop, which was empty inside, the floor stained with blood. They took us to a small field in a clearing in the woods and showed us the grave of a woman who had been killed as she worked. They talked in Kirundi, the language of Burundi. Their pace quickened, and they beckoned us to follow them further, but they seemed to be taking us too far. Who were they? Why had they survived?

We turned back—the two journalists and the photographer I was with—toward the road. The two men wanted us to follow. But we left them, wondering what they had in mind for us, in that silent place. We drove on, edging round the great trees that at points still partially blocked the road. We learned later that the army had been here and cleared many of the barriers, which is why the occasional villages we passed through were deserted. The people had fled the army, either by disappearing into the forest or crossing the border. The army's reassertion of control had intensified fear, not brought security, despite a call by the prime minister, Sylvie Kinigi,[5] that the troops be allowed access.

On the outskirts of Kayanza we were stopped at a military checkpoint and ordered to report to the police station in the town. It was on the other side of a steep valley. We drove, and waited for two hours for whatever permission was required. We were the first outsiders to pass through the town since the killing had started. There was no official guidance for the police. The border had been open throughout the slaughter, but the makeshift barricades along the road had cut the country off from the outside world. The police and army adopted an air of concern for us. They asked us where we would be going, and we said we would just drive, until we reached Bujumbura. We were told to wait some more, but we told them we had only a short time, made our way back to the car, returned across the valley, and took the road east toward Ngozi.

"There are criminals on that road over there. On that hill."[6] Martin Sindaru pointed across a wide valley. We had stopped to speak with a small crowd of people gathered beneath trees on the roadside ten miles along the road from Kayanza at a small hamlet called Ifo Butegane. "Everything on our hill was calm. Then people went to get their weapons. And the pygmies came and wanted to massacre us, so that we would leave. We lived there. Now we have fled. The military have paid the BaTwa[7] to kill us. Ntanyandi Adrien, he's a former soldier, who has used his gun to intimidate us. He and his people got inside the houses and killed everybody they could find. The army gave him the guns. They're ready to kill everybody. We can't say how many have been killed, because they're still killing. They're all Tutsi who are killing. And now everything we had is gone. All our possessions."

A boy strolled by, wearing a T-shirt commemorating a visit by Pope John Paul II, who had visited Burundi some years earlier. The crowd watched intently, an occasional murmur erupting as a figure was discerned among the houses of the village they had fled. After standing and watching for almost an hour, Martin Sindaru said he would walk with us back to the village, called Karengura. We descended the steep valley side, seven or eight of us, and walked slowly across the lush green fields of the valley, leaping the streams and irrigation channels that cut through the thick grass.

The grassland gave way to crops, and the fields were ripe with thick green beans. Hardi, a four-year-old boy, lay on a checkered cloth in the bean field. The back of his head had been sliced open. His nose had been cut off, leaving a gaping wound where his face had been slashed in half. There was another gash on the top of his head. "His father, Damien, is over there. He is dead too.

And his mother. It was just an hour ago they were killed. There are more. You must follow," said Martin Sindaru, pointing to the edge of the bean field where the grass grew thickly. Blood had dried running from the father's mouth. His bare legs were bruised. A small spider crawled over the blue cloth with which the villagers had covered his body before they fled. Further on, the valley started to rise, and we reached the ruins of a small brick factory, beside which ran a path to the village. There was a heavy silence. The sun had almost reached its zenith. Silence, warmth, and the feeling of being watched from a distance by hidden faces combined with the lush beauty of the place to accentuate the sense of savagery, of helplessness, of humanity out of control. The figures we had seen from the other side of the valley had gone. The only person remaining was an old man sitting beside the path. Martin Sindaru asked him if there was anybody else left. "Yes. There are some. But most of them fled. They left me behind," the old man replied.

But the mud huts, with their thatched roofs, were deserted. The yards between them were filled only with upturned pots. The late morning heat combined with the whiff of dust to create a feeling of tranquility. The village lay along a soft grassy path that disappeared into a wood at one end. Among the smashed clay pots and rags a baby lay dead, covered in flies and dust. Blood around its body had turned purple. Then the piercing scream of a man cracked the air ahead of us. One of those accompanying us had fallen on his knees, beside a pit filled with banana leaves and branches, in which lay the mangled corpse of a woman, soaked with blood, a baby at her feet. The woman was the man's aunt.

The men had gathered beside the pit in which the woman lay. And as they moaned, they watched as she raised one of her arms and moaned with pain. She was alive, hours after she had been buried. Nobody knew who had buried her.

The grieving, tormented men with us gently eased her out of the pit. The baby slipped further into its depths. They made a stretcher with looped stakes on each side. We moved away from the village and back across the field. Miburo, the woman, was heavy. All the while she murmured: "Baby, baby, baby, baby." The men grew tired and hot. "Why should I carry her? My wife is somewhere over there. I should be carrying her instead," one of the men kept saying for the hour or more it took us to carry her back across the bean fields, the ditches, and streams, to the road. "She is wanting her baby. But there's no point in carrying a dead baby," said Martin Sinduro.

We drove Miburo to the hospital at Ngozi, five miles away. On the way we passed two more women and a baby, promising that we would return to pick them up. One woman had been hacked across her face. Dr. Rinat, the Russian medic at Ngozi hospital, came with us in the car when we went back along the road to collect them. When we stopped to pick up the other women he complained that we didn't have enough space for them all, as if this was the time to worry about being uncomfortable in the overcrowded vehicle. When we reached the hospital he said that behind one of the wards were sacks containing the parts of forty dismembered bodies. The hospital officials wouldn't give casualty figures, but everybody said all the patients were Hutu.

"The army has evacuated people from the rural areas to the towns, and has transported people to the hospitals," said a priest at Ngozi's small Catholic cathedral and seminary.[8] "So now they know where the Hutus are. Yesterday they came into the hospital and killed two people there, but nobody at the hospital will tell you about it." His words stunned us. We had brought the injured women to the hospital, and now had no idea what would happen to them. The sense of entrapment grew, as if the entire country had become a vast concentration camp. "The soldiers are committing terrible repression," the priest continued, quietly, aware that other people were watching him from a distance as he spoke. "I have to be careful. The people feel that peace may come eventually, so the soldiers are killing as many people as they can now, or they are paying other people to do it. These massacres are immense. Much bigger than in 1988. Then it was 5,000 people dead, but much of the country was calm. The massacres are everywhere now. We are worried. We are terrified."

It was four o'clock in the afternoon. We approached the barracks in Ngozi to speak with the army, but were turned away. The priest had said it would be a mistake to stay too long in Ngozi. He didn't say why. The sun began to fall over the seemingly endless, tree-clad hills. We stopped at the house of a Belgian businessman, who told us to get out of his compound as soon as we arrived. Two of the journalists said they wanted to return to Rwanda. The tension of the nearly deserted town had infected us. I wanted to continue to Bujumbura, which was between two and three hours drive away. But eventually we took the road back to Kayanza and the north. We drove through that land of death in the pitch dark, the only car on the road, fearful of whoever might emerge from the dense blackness of the forest that engulfed us as we slowly wound our way higher into the tree-clad hillsides, all plunged into complete silence, with never a light to be seen, nor any sound of life. Eventually we reached the border, crossed back into Rwanda, and reached Butare after midnight.

Early the following morning I drove south again toward the border and reached Bujumbura in the early afternoon.

A procession was moving silently along the Boulevard l'Uprona, the main street commemorating what had been the single party in the country, until it had lost the election four months beforehand. The mood was mournful, everybody mourning somebody, expecting that violent death was just around the corner. In such circumstances, the signs of apparent normality make the horror of what is taking place seem so much more nightmarish. People sipping drinks on hotel terraces, the few remaining foreigners buying patisserie at the Novotel cake shop, which its owner had named Les péchés mignons, or The Darling Sins, as if buying a sugary chocolate cake were the worst sin in Burundi at that time. Taxis plied the streets for trade. Shops did a little business. All these things take on an awful symbolism in the face of attempts to stifle humanity.

The procession was the first to take to the streets since the bloody slaying of Melchior Ndadaye. His supporters, two or three thousand of them, walked in near silence along the street carrying photographs of their dead hero. Placards read: "Disband the ethnic army," "No to the extremist Rwandan refugees who are massacring us,"[9] "Without foreign forces we say goodbye to democracy in Burundi," "Burundian army or ethnic army?" "Our hero is dead but our party is still in power." They filed slowly along the Boulevard l'Uprona, turned right along the Boulevard de l'Indépendance and gathered in a large open area in the shadow of the Stade Rwagasore. There they chanted and listened to speeches, their stern, worried faces watching intently, all facing the terror of knowing that they had no protection from the extremists who had led the coup attempt.

"The *putschists* want us out of the embassy so they can kill all the heads of the regime. They have stopped the *putsch* so they can get us out and can continue what they started on October 20," said Jean-Marie Ngendahayo, information minister in the Ndadaye government.[10] On the night of the coup several ministers fled their homes and sought refuge in the French embassy in Bujumbura. (As well as President Melchior Ndadaye, who was killed on 21 October 1993, seven ministers were executed by the coup makers.) Ngendahayo was one of the leading Tutsi members of the largely Hutu Front des Démocrates du Burundi (Frodebu: Front of the Democrats of Burundi) party led by Ndadaye. "The *putschists* want to prove that Frodebu can't rule. There was a military truck at every minister's home on the night of the coup. But they were too late. There are administrators, deputies, and churchmen dead. The army has been truly savage. And there has been tribal vengeance," he said. The surviving members of the government initially called for foreign military intervention to confront what they regarded as proof that the entire army[11] could no longer be trusted. "If you [foreigners] don't intervene while the government is here it won't be possible to control anything. Then the army will take power and the people will regard the government as weak. Then there will be a terrible clash between the angry population and the small, unrepresentative army," he said.

BLOOD OF A NATION

Beneath Burundi's surface, beneath the surface of current events, deep in popular memory, there is a time and place that long precedes the rise of militarism, in which the social fabric is not thought to have been dominated by a system of exclusion and repression. "Status, not ethnic identity, was the principal determinant of rank and privilege," writes René Lemarchand of the monarchist period in Burundi's history, which began long before the colonial period and continued even after independence in 1960.[12] "Not only were there significant discrepancies between the ranking and ethnic identity, but many variations could also be determined within the broad range of dependency relations subsumed under the term *Hutu*," he says. Privilege and power were not the preserve of a wide array of ranks and officers within an unanswerable armed force.

In the case of Burundi, it is difficult to characterize this divide in tribal terms, because there are no cultural differences between the tribes. No ethnic, religious, or linguistic differences exist between Hutu and Tutsi—neither in Burundi nor in neighboring Rwanda. Thus, it is not possible to argue with any accuracy that ethnicity is the fundamental cause of friction between the two tribes. Some other explanation must be sought. History does not bear witness to any age-old Hutu-Tutsi ethnic conflict.[13] Meanwhile, there is undoubtedly a minority that is called Tutsi and a majority that is called Hutu. But in the absence of cultural differences between them, some other distinction must be sought to explain the tension that erupts into violence. That distinction is not to be found in the normal daily life of Burundians, whose tribes for years appeared to live alongside each other in precolonial times and even since independence, without slaughtering each other. Instead it is to be found in the relationship between Burundians and the state, the country, and the institutions of the nation. Only on recognition of this fact will it be possible to begin identifying the areas in which it is necessary to reform the state to avert the recurrent crises.

It is, of course, not possible to ignore the particular ferocity of the violence once it erupts, within both Burundi and Rwanda, if only due to the part it plays in the search for a nonviolent solution. The scale and viciousness of the violence itself is remarkable, even by the sorry standards of other African countries wherein similar eruptions of violence have taken place. But the root cause of the violence cannot be explained in ethnic terms. So why, on a cool October morning in 1993, was the silence of northern Burundi's tree-clad hills only explicable as being the result of 440,000 people having fled the country into Rwanda[14] and 380,000 others into Tanzania and Zaire. In essence, what were they running from—tribal violence or military rule? The division between people and army, as well as between extremist and moderate, was clear. Even though the response of Hutu to the army coup attempt had been to target Tutsi, the conduct of the army lay at the heart of the crisis. The rapid escalation of the violence had been caused by the army then acting, it claimed, in defense of Tutsi civilians, who became the target of Hutu revenge after the killing of Ndadaye. The issue of the "institutionalization of the tyranny of an ethnic majority" will be more closely examined in Part 3. In the case of Burundi, it was the Tutsi military elite, under intense pressure from human rights groups and public opinion to open up the political system, who had been forced to allow the first moves toward democracy. These moves were made despite the soldiers having been under no illusion that their grip on political power would diminish once the majority had had the chance to vote.

The anxiety expressed by politicians like Jean-Marie Ngendahayo in the wake of the October 1993 coup attempt reflected the extent to which fear played a pivotal role in the evolution of the political scene. Most people wanted democratization, but they believed that tough measures would be required to protect it; hence the call for foreign military intervention. But the likely impact of an intervention[15] would have been to distract the country from the path of indigenous reconciliation, owing to the overpowering temptation that would have arisen to try and use the presence of a third force—a foreign military force—as a weapon against political opponents. Its presence, particularly in the face of extremist violence, would also have made the decision by individuals to choose between moderation and extremism more difficult, as the sight of one's compatriots perhaps becoming the victims of UN or OAU military action would have enflamed feelings and worsened the polarization. At that time, as the UN force in Somalia was facing one of the worst chapters in the UN's history, an intervention was in any case impossible to contemplate. Consequently, the Burundian army itself was the only potential source of security, if its moderates could be brought to the fore and its strategy and methods used to promote security by handling an enflamed situation with care rather than brutality.

Warriors of the Southern Hills

Lake Tanganyika lay like a slab of gray slate, dimly reflecting the morning light creeping through the heavy clouds that seem always to hang over Bujumbura. Across the water, Zaire rose in the hazy distance to the west; south was southern Africa, another world altogether, where the humidity and rain of the Great Lakes gave way to the dry warmth and blaze of jacaranda upon the plains of Zambia and the grasslands beyond. But Bujumbura cowered among its mountains, beneath the unchanging austerity of its gray sky, beneath the dull weight of its people's misery and fear.

The road south clung to the lakeside. I wanted to reach Bururi. It was from this southern province that the majority of Burundi's political leaders as well as the senior ranks of the army had been drawn since independence. Bururi had become the heartland of Burundi's military rule over three decades. The hold its inhabitants had over the political life of the country had forged the prevailing relations between Hutu and Tutsi, between the Tutsi clans,

and between moderates and extremists. The road passed a memorial to
David Livingstone and Henry Morton Stanley, the two nineteenth-century
travelers whose adventures had exposed central Africa to European influence, exploitation, and imperialism.[16] Had the impact of such travelers on the
European mind not been so profound, the tales of their exploits would have
seemed irrelevant, as the country turned upon itself and the future looked so
bleak. Livingstone had called Africa the "open sore of the world,"[17] and he
"believed he could find the means to heal it by making an 'open path' to [Eu-
ropean] civilization. The Nile, bringing trade and Christianity 3,000 miles
from the Mediterranean to the heart of Africa, would be the path—if only he
could find it."[18]

Bururi was almost deserted, its largely Tutsi population barely in evidence, the bright lush grass of the hills and the bright orange earth of the
roads a stark patchwork devoid of life. There were no signs of victory, nor of
a community threatened, just the emptiness left behind by families who had
fled in fear. Further on, we stopped at a roadside kiosk. A man sold us dried
biscuits and said the small village we were in was called Bononi, though it
didn't appear on any map. A priest approached us and, without introducing
himself, began to explain what had happened. "In this region," he said, "the
Hutu didn't simply start killing the Tutsi. It always depends on the local
commanders and administrators, as to whether the killing takes place. But
here the army came and pacified everything yesterday, and so the two tribes
didn't start killing each other."[19] In a few words he had again driven to the
heart of the issue. Where the authorities promoted the violence, it took
place. But when the authorities stepped in to halt the slaughter it didn't take
place. Just as in 1972 and 1988, the spiral of the violence had its epicenter in
the army and the other institutions of government. The state, rather than
the tribes, was the heart of the problem.

As we were talking, a large car pulled up, and two missionaries, Swedish
Pentecostalists as it turned out, smiled awkwardly with red faces, while a Burundian man in the back of the car offered his explanation for the relative
calm of the valley.

"You see, in the north, in the hills, the people are more conservative.
They didn't intermarry, so the tribes are violent against each other. But here,
in Bututsi province[20] the people are much calmer. The tribes are intermar-
ried, so they were calm when the president was killed." His explanation ignored the fear the Hutu in this Tutsi-dominated province would undoubtedly have felt had they decided to react to the death of President Ndadaye in
the manner seen elsewhere. The Tutsi majority of Bururi, together with the
normally heavy military presence in the area, would have acted to discourage
them. The valley, a meandering, tree-clad gorge, was swept by smoke. As the
Swedish missionary at the wheel of the car began to pull away, the Burundian
with her explained the coils of smoke we could see up ahead: "They're just

burning the bush to clear it for when the rains come. Everything's calm here. There are no houses burning."

A few miles further on we emerged from the valley and reached a main road. Northwards it went to Bujumbura. A few miles south was the source of the River Nile, which David Livingstone had never found, on the edge of the swamps which become the Gasenyi River, trickling ice-cold through the lush valleys as it flowed. A small pyramid marks the place where the river emerges from the earth's core and meanders through the most troubled region of the world, carrying with it many victims of the wars it passes through. The road ahead was empty, and we traveled further east, crossing the Bujumbura road. Small mud houses were closed and deserted. Nobody was working the fields. Animals had been driven away. We passed the Mahwah zoological center. A man with a long cane sat motionless in the entrance archway. Opposite, a body twitched on the ground at the foot of the steps leading up to a single-story house. Another lay face down in the mud. A third was splayed close to the road. Shoes, bags of food, and a few clothes lay smoking in a pit beside the house. The man lying at the foot of the steps turned over, his gaping eye-balls rolling as he peered across the ash-strewn garden. Blood poured from his right foot, which had been all but torn from his leg. From his neck down-wards he was soaked in blood, which had left a trail smeared down the steps. Only the murmurs of the dying men, and their soft breathing, broke the silence. The early morning sun had gone, replaced by cool wet air and the threat of rain. From outside the house, down the steps, one could see in the distance where smoke was belching further up the valley.

The tale was told by a man who appeared from nowhere, carrying a spear. "The army came at ten o'clock today. These men were passing through the village. The army locked them in the house, and then killed them. They killed them with their bayonets, and they used their guns," he said. "They're killing all the way up the valley. The smoke is from houses burning. They're killing—it's the Tutsis. These men in the house, they're all Hutus."

I pushed open the door of the house. It was like walking into a gaping wound. The walls, the floor, the ceiling were dripping with blood, as if the killers had chased their victims from room to room to kill them. Bodies, all men, lay on the floor, awash with blood. At first there appeared to be no sound. Then, a sound that could have been the scratching of an animal be-came instead the rasping breaths of wounded bodies. The dead were not dead. One man in the first room had his knees raised. He suddenly stirred and opened his eyes. He was alive, in complete shock, but apparently not in pain. It was impossible to see where he was wounded. We helped him to stand, he murmured quietly as we led him away from the carnage where his friends lay dead or dying, and he sat in the back of our car.

Five miles away, at a church in Butwe, there was a small clinic where the Burundian curate, Father Balthazar Bacinoni, said we had done well to bring the wounded man in. We told Father Bacinoni that there were three others in the house with appalling injuries and we weren't sure if they were still alive. He said he would have liked to go with us to bring them to the clinic, but that he was frightened. "They're killing all the way along the valley, all the way along that area. They're killing us, the church people,"[21] he said. Who are? The army? I asked him. "Well, who do you think?" was all he would say. But then he added: "I will go and find some soldiers to protect us." He got in his car and drove to Matana army post, five miles away. We followed. At Matana he told the soldiers what had happened; in effect he told the soldiers that some of their victims were still alive.

"You should go, leave the area. We'll take care of this. It's a security issue," said the army commander, Paul Rukuki. We drove back to Bujumbura and reached the city at dusk. I went to the office of the International Committee of the Red Cross and told them about the young man we had taken to the clinic in Butwe, where I thought his life might be in danger, as the army who it appeared had attacked him now knew that he was with the priest.

The following day I drove back to Mahwa and took the track that passed the house. A large tree trunk had been dragged across the road to prevent anybody traveling along it, but it was possible to drive around it. The body that had been outside the house had gone. The three who had been inside were also gone. At the side of the house was the freshly turned soil of a new grave. Nearby, the bodies of four other men lay in a six-foot-deep pit, partially covered with leaves and branches.

Leaving Mahwa behind, the dirt road passed between grassy slopes and clumps of trees. On the right, on the summit of a slope, a man stood watching the road. We stopped near a stream and got out of the car. He began walking toward us and was joined by another man who had been lying hidden in the grass. Then another man appeared and some women, until twenty or thirty people appeared, some walking, some standing still. The one we had first seen was walking fast, sweating, his eyes showing his fear as he drew closer, his breath sharp, his words rapid. He said that his name was Frederick Nimbesha and that he was a student.

> Twenty soldiers came this morning, firing off their guns. Everybody fled. We fled. The people fled from Murama. We don't know why they attacked. But there were no deaths this morning. Here we are Hutus, but there are also Tutsi. They got the soldiers. The Tutsis lived on the hill. When this started a week ago the Tutsis massacred the Hutu. There hadn't been any Hutu attacks on Tutsis. The soldiers weren't even in a military car. It was a government car, from the public works ministry. A red pick-up. We have heard the sound of gunfire from the other hills. We are staying in our houses. We are scared. I am frightened to go back to Gishobi, to the school.[22]

All the time he was talking he cast anxious glances along the road. Then suddenly he and the few others who had walked with him turned and fled back up the slope. The others who had remained on the summit disappeared onto the other side. Within seconds the hillside was deserted.

A cold wind blew off the hill as we left. A scatter of rain fell. We passed the bodies of five dead men lying beside the road. We turned a corner and a red pick-up truck filled with soldiers appeared ahead of us. We slowed but didn't stop. A colleague, Patrick de St. Exupéry, a correspondent for *Le Figaro*, spoke with them through the open window of the car and asked casually if the road was clear. An officer in the front of the car eyed us suspiciously, but answered that the road was clear. They watched as we drove off, round a corner and down a slope at the bottom of which twenty-two more bodies lay lined up beside the road. The rain began to fall harder, turning up the dust on the road, until it was falling in sheets. We turned off the road into the market square of Gishobi to wait for the rain to stop. A burned car lay in a ditch. Every shop in the square had been looted. The ashes of burned shops still lay smoldering. The sound of a door creaked in the wind, which caught the tin roofs and lifted them with a clatter. The people in the square watched us silently, refusing to talk, and when the rain eased we drove on.

Less than a mile away a group of people standing in the road stopped us among some houses. They were all talking at once, arguing with each other. "The military burned the houses," said a young man, Sibomana.

> It was only the Hutu houses which were burned. There were people killed—by bayonets. The rest of us ran away. We were all terrified. Everybody here is Hutu. The military came yesterday and burned our houses. They were not soldiers from Gishobi. If they come back we will be scared. When they came, they had four armored cars and three lorries. It was 11 A.M. We don't know how many they killed yesterday. They killed women and children. We have buried the dead, away from here. If we see a military vehicle, we run. There are Tutsi villages near Gishobi, but Tutsis never live in Gishobi. We don't know what is happening in Bujumbura. But things aren't going well. The president was assassinated. We are angry. Very angry. We didn't have arms to kill the Tutsis.[23]

Just as with all the other eyewitness accounts of what had happened, it was the army that was seen to have created the fear among the population. Evidence of Hutu and Tutsi civilians turning on each other before the army had arrived was less easy to find. While there is no doubt that the army intended to protect Tutsi civilians it saw as under threat, it also appeared to have polarized relations between the tribes. Certainly, Hutu civilians killed Tutsi in the aftermath of the coup, though as a result of the anger the Hutu felt following the slaughter of the Hutu president by Tutsi soldiers. The Tutsi had comprised around 780,000 of Burundi's 5.6 million population before the coup, and most of the 150,000–200,000 people estimated to have been killed during the few weeks of violence after the coup were Tutsi. Most of the Tutsi were thought to have been killed by activists of Ndadaye's largely Hutu Frodebu party, in revenge for the death of the president. The pattern of the violence therefore severely undermined the prestige of Frodebu, despite the presence of Tutsi ministers in the government. "In the medium term the best strategy would be to restructure the military, perhaps under international supervision, as part of an extended political transition program incorporating representatives of a broad range of political groupings,"[24] it was suggested at the time. "Currently, political life is characterized by disillusion and despair. The army is irrevocably sullied in the eyes of the Hutu population. Frodebu activists are discredited in both Hutu and Tutsi eyes for their role in the massacre of Tutsi civilians. Individuals trying to bridge the ethnic chasm can be counted on one hand."[25]

But the complete breakdown of order came as a result of military officers either backing the coup and using it as an excuse to slaughter as many Hutu as they could find, or failing to calm the situation by using methods other than violence. Either way, the army emerged as a having completely failed in its role as, essentially, a force of domestic law and order.[26] Instead, it succeeded only in enflaming feelings, which had initially burst out due to the actions of the original coup makers, and which were further fanned by the combination of its own savage methods and the entrenched distrust of the army that had been felt among Hutu since the 1960s.

We stopped at a Catholic mission a few miles further along the road from Gishobi. The nuns, from a variety of countries, seemed pleased to have visitors, but smiled as they said they had seen nothing and heard nothing and really knew nothing about what had been going on, because they had locked the gate and none of their lay staff had come to work for the past few days. They wouldn't even guess what might have happened to them. We left them cocooned in their untouched world, as the rain poured outside, and found ourselves on the outskirts of Gitega, Burundi's second-largest town.

A large redbrick church towered over the town, whose streets were almost as empty as the road we had driven along. Across a stretch of waste ground there was a camp from which smoke spiraled into the wet, gray sky. There were three camps on the edge of the town, housing 4,500 people.[27] A priest at the church wouldn't give us his name, but he talked quickly and quietly, as we stood in the corner of a vast courtyard surrounded by the walls of the church.

"The military came to find people at Le Sibou camp, next to the coffee factory," he said, as we watched a long column of blind children being led across the courtyard, each with its hand on the shoulder of the one in front as they smiled and chatted loudly. "They killed three by shooting them. The

Tutsis are guiding the army. Here in town it's like that. When there are whites in the camps the military don't do anything. It's like that. The military are terrified. They have been ordered back to the barracks, but they don't want to. They are a terrified minority."[28] He said that in Gitega the conflict had taken on a more political character, of Frodebu versus Uprona, and that consequently "it's been slightly ameliorated, whereas in 1972 it was clearly tribal. The refugees in the church are mixed. The tribes wanted that, because then if the army comes they won't be able to distinguish them. Once, the army came into the church looking for a Frodebu activist, but they couldn't find him."

The conflict between the tribes appeared, to some extent, to have been subsumed by a conflict between the political parties, the army, and the civilian population, as well as a conflict within the army itself, which remained the vital issue. Melchior Ndadaye had relied heavily on the support of four relatively progressive senior officers.[29] "[But the] army is restless. [The] small [political] parties are appealing to junior officers to complete the putsch. Senior officers are more prepared to respect the constitution but lack the political will to defend it against military pressure from below."[30] On all levels there was conflict, except on that of the purely tribal.

"It was a small group within the army. I am against them. It was a small group. I'm a loyalist. I am in favor of moves towards democracy," said Captain Augustin Nkunda.[31] He presented himself as a third-ranking military officer, stationed in Gitega. Although it was impossible to put aside some suspicion of his views, he tried to sound convincing, as we talked in the pouring rain outside the church wherein the refugees scattered to hide as they saw his military vehicle draw up outside.

"They are frightened of the army, because of what has happened before," he said, casting a glance at the refugees inside. "But if the local [Hutu] administrators start to work, they will be able to understand. They will work with the army." Government assessments later estimated that half the country's Tutsi administrators either fled or were killed following the coup, while three governors were also killed—it is thought by soldiers. "The coup was political, not tribal. It was more political. We are in the barracks. But why stay in the barracks? None of the military here supported the coup," Nkunda said. He was asked if, as the priest inside the church had suggested, the army was frightened. "There are political problems. The tribes have lived together. But the tribal question is a political one. I can understand the reaction of the people, the reaction of the peasants, to the death of the president. It's normal. But I'm an optimist. The defense minister could come here.[32] He could telephone me. But he hasn't."

The captain's telephone remained silent. Meanwhile, the coup revealed splits within the army that have dominated the course of events in Burundi ever since. Lieutenant Colonel Jean Bikomagu, the army chief of staff, proclaimed his loyalty to Melchior Ndadaye's successor, Cyprien Ntaryamira, and then, when Ntaryamira died in April 1994,[33] to his successor, Sylvestre Ntibantunganya. Bikomagu subsequently became increasingly isolated from the Tutsi hardliners within the army. The fear among Tutsi moderates was not that their strategy would be thwarted by Hutu initiating an extremist campaign against all Tutsi, but that Tutsi hardliners would use their ongoing domination of the army to seize the initiative before the coming of the event the hardliners most feared—the redressing of the ethnic balance within the army, which would mean Hutu rising up the ranks.

FAITH, HOPE, AND ILLUSIONS

Expectations of a solution following the October 1993 coup attempt were illusory. The event was really only the beginning of a period of disintegration along a multiplicity of lines, which has continued into the early twenty-first century. A few days after the coup attempt, the United Nations sent a special representative to Burundi, in the hope that a neutral outsider could help guide the rival parties toward a new dispensation, while also attempting to maintain the country on its path to democracy. That representative, Ahmedou Ould Abdallah, saw at first hand the depth of the crisis, without ultimately arriving at a workable solution. On leaving Burundi six months later, he summed up his conclusions:

> [There] are Hutu and Tutsi as a matter of status, not ethnicity. In the event of a mixed marriage the child would adopt the ethnic origin of the father. *Hutu* means *peasant* in Kirundi: theoretically, a Hutu can rise socially and become Tutsi. There are also the *Ganwa*, the aristocracy. In the conflict they identified themselves with the Tutsi. But I continue to believe that it is the political leaders of the '50s and '60s who held the ethnic groups hostage, concealing themselves behind ethnicity because they lacked any better political program. In Malaysia, Singapore, the former Yugoslavia or in Moldova, the same thing has happened.
>
> It's normal that in any cycle of violence, ethnicity becomes a means to an end: a refuge for the weak and innocent, a resource for those with ambitions to dominate or rise to power.[34]

In October 1993, the extent to which ethnicity had been used as a "resource" by the ambitious in the four months since Burundi had embarked on its first experience of democracy became clear. The failed coup and its aftermath revealed the extent to which those members of the armed forces who represented the extremist elements—whose activities most Hutu regarded as representative of the army in general and the Tutsi establishment as a whole—were isolated. Despite the response to the coup—the Hutu revenge, the Tutsi military counterrevenge—having polarized the mass of the population along tribal lines, the impression is clear that this polarization ran counter to the path that that same mass had been moving along since the election. There is no evidence that a full-scale civil war was likely following the election. The violence that has dominated the country throughout the late 1990s and that brought Major Pierre Buyoya back to power through a further coup in 1996 has been a response to the halt in the process of political reform, a process whose successful conclusion had been the hope of the majority. In the climate of fear and anguish that is at the heart of Burundian daily life, extremist minorities were able to derail a process that most Burundians had decided to embark upon.

In many ways the post-election politics of ethnicity had yet to have an impact on the population by the time the coup took place. The Frodebu government had appointed its own provincial prefects on taking power, but it remained a government that sought its own variant of ethnic balance, having a prime minister and other ministers who were Tutsi. The soldiers who led the coup feared the curtailment of their own power and the incorporation of the Hutu within the armed forces. By the time of the coup, stark political polarization had taken root. The coup was a military response to a civilian experiment with democracy. Despite the fact that it was Buyoya's Tutsi-dominated military government that had launched the moves toward democracy, the Hutu population saw it as their route to the franchise that had long been denied them. Democracy would mark the beginning of the end of the Tutsi dominance of Burundian political life, a dominance that would never have been possible had it not been for military rule. Any change in the ethnic balance of power would either imply an end to military rule altogether, or at the very least lead to the creation of an ethnically balanced army. The 1990s saw military rule across Africa being exposed as the least appropriate system for development, with its impact exposed at its most negative in countries where such systems were intended to preserve minority power. The majority of Burundi's Hutu accepted democracy, despite their overwhelming numbers, which made them at least theoretically capable of overthrowing the minority through an uprising. The past explosions of violence, in 1972 and 1988, deterred them from such acts, due to the ferocity of the military response. Only after democracy had been tasted and subsequently denied in 1993 did the Hutu uprising begin. Then, the complexity of Burundi's crisis became obvious. It was then that what really lay beneath the surface of the rivalry became seen in all its regional, political, ideological, and historical aspects.

It is true that ridding the country of military rule would have ended Tutsi domination, but the essential aim was rather to end military rule, and therefore minority rule through brute force. But to establish whether a viable and harmonious system could then emerge, it is necessary to establish whether the historical parameters of the Hutu-Tutsi relationship would or will in the future allow the leap of faith that such a move requires.

5

A City on the Lake

The Creation of Hutu and Tutsi

The young man I had taken from the house in Mahwa had survived. The Red Cross drove to the mission in Butwe and picked him up the day after being told that he might be in danger from the troops at Matana. They took him to the Prince Louis Rwagasore hospital in Bujumbura. The hospital is a long, two- and three-story building along a tree-lined avenue on the eastern side of the capital. The wards were dim and silent. I began to ask a doctor where I might find him and explained unclearly how he had been brought by the Red Cross from south of the city. The doctor had no idea what I was talking about, so I wandered through the wards hoping I might recognize him. At the end of a long room filled with beds surrounded by net curtains, a young man sat on the edge of a bed with a woman sitting beside him. They were both silent. He looked at me without any expression. I asked another doctor whether he was the one who had been brought from Butwe, and the doctor replied that he was. I stood for a minute, wondering what to say. He breathed, almost sighing, saying nothing.

"He hasn't said anything since he came here. This is his sister, who came here when the priest in Butwe said he had been brought to Bujumbura. He hasn't said anything at all." The doctor explained this with his arms crossed over his chest, staring down at the young man, who shifted his weight without changing his expression. The doctor explained to him and his sister who I was. The sister told him in Kirundi she knew who I was, that her brother was fine, and that I could go now. "They won't give us their full names, neither of them. They're worried," said the doctor, as he walked me to the hospital entrance.

The young man's wordless fear was chilling. The violence of the attack that he had survived somehow seemed less nightmarish than the fact of his having to now live in a climate of terror: terror on all sides; terror that only immense courage could overcome. "The other thing which you also notice, beyond the apparent calm and the slightly forced courtesy among the people that you meet, for example, the waiters in the hotels, are the clammy hands which you are always shaking," Ahmedou Ould Abdallah, the UN special envoy sent to Burundi within days of the coup attempt, related.[1] "I am sure that it is not the climate, but the tension, the ever-present sense of fear, which lies behind this. . . . When you stop to think about this sweating, and see it's caused by a sort of morbid paranoia, it's rather disturbing."

THE TIME OF KINGS

The absence of security that lies behind the fear is rooted as much in abstraction as in real historical experience. The juggling of governmental ethnic complexions over the years since the end of Burundi's first attempt to create national unity, an end marked by the assassination in 1961 of Burundi's first post-independence prime minister, Prince Louis Rwagasore, failed to convince the majority that a Hutu presence in government was anything more than symbolic. As with the taste of power the majority was later to experience during Melchior Ndadaye's short tenure as president, so Rwagasore's tenure—as head of a tentatively national Uprona party drawing on all elements of Burundian society—was a short taste of the liberty won with independence and the end of colonial power. "[By] projecting the present into the past, Hutu politicians end up with a vision of history totally at odds with every shred of evidence available," Lemarchand writes.[2] "[And] by doing precisely the opposite and refusing to acknowledge a Hutu-Tutsi problem, Tutsi politicians have consistently turned a blind eye to the radical transformation that followed in the wake of their own discriminatory policies."

History is, in many ways, unhelpful as a guide to understanding the cause of the conflict, owing to the way in which it has been used and abused by the protagonists. Its selective and often dishonest use by politicians means that the fact of Hutu and Tutsi having so much in common is ignored. Consequently the real meaning of *Hutu* and *Tutsi* is lost, their past social functionality forgotten, their particular contributions to social cohesion obscured in the popular memory, and their relations subsumed by political opportunism, as Lemarchand writes:

> [Traditionally] status, not ethnic identity, was the principal determinant of rank and privilege. . . . Thus, the ruling princely oligarchy (*ganwa*), forming a separate

ethnic entity different from both Hutu and Tutsi, stood at the very top of the so-
ciopolitical hierarchy; they were the supreme holders of power and privilege. . . .
Among Hutu and Tutsi, the pecking order was immensely more complicated. . . .
To argue . . . that the patron-client relationship served the Tutsi as a social mechanism for placing the Hutu masses into bondage is arrant nonsense. . . . The stability of the relationship owed much to the maintenance of a fair pattern of exchange between patrons and clients. . . . [But] once recast in the social fields of
ethnically homogenous nets, as happened after independence, patron-client ties
served only to accelerate the process of ethnic polarization.[3]

Functional social ties, it can perhaps be argued, served to prevent what
was perhaps a brooding if unacknowledged tension between the tribes from
erupting. All that was required was for the network that bound the tribes together to unravel. On the other hand, as Lemarchand points out, "[If] Hutu
and Tutsi increasingly tend to define each other in terms of mutually antago-
nistic categories, this is not because of ancestral enmities but because ethnic
identities have acquired a moral dimension—whether as a martyred community or a threatened minority—they never had before."[4]

Burundi's central political institutions predated similar institutions in
many European countries. Their collapse within a few years of independence could be used to suggest that the experience of colonialism had so
shattered their credibility that they could never recover, despite their long
establishment. Moreover, the arrival of independence could perhaps have
been regarded as the point at which the brooding tribal antagonism was—
finally—allowed to reach the surface. Again, history does not really bear
these hypotheses out. The precolonial period was characterized by a struggle for power within the royal class, the *ganwa*, which was set apart from
the Hutu, Tutsi, and Twa. "[The] Burundi kingship was never identified
with Tutsi supremacy; indeed, the Burundi kingship derived much of its legitimacy from its symbolic identification with Hutu elements. . . . [As] a
symbol of power and institution, the *mwami* [king] served as a powerful
unifying bond and a prime focus of popular loyalties."[5] Many of the characteristics of kingship emerged during the reign of Mwezi Gisabo
(1850–1908). Meanwhile, in 1904, signs of an emergent anti-Tutsi sentiment centered on the emergence of a Hutu chieftain, Kilima, in the north-
west of the country. Kilima is recorded as having ordered the slaughter of
Tutsi in the area, but Lemarchand says his actions did not reflect an "organized Hutu movement against Tutsi hegemony."[6] The emergence of such
regional chieftains is regarded as having heightened loyalty to the *mwami*,
who was seen as above tribal politics. Moreover, although territorial conquest by the *ganwa* class heightened resentment of that class among the
lower classes, it did not do so on an ethnic basis. Colonial rule—German
(1889–1918) and Belgian (1918–1962)—further heightened the impor-

tance of the *ganwa*, leading both Hutu and Tutsi to seek protection under the umbrella of royal power.

The arrival of the German imperialists coincided with severe economic hardship in Burundi, which, together with the burden of the colonial yoke, led to a retrenchment by the beleaguered population. After 1918, the Belgians consolidated their power by reducing the number of administrative chiefdoms, so as to limit the complexity of their rule through local powers. By 1945 there were no Hutu chiefs, all having been dismissed by the Belgians, leaving ten Tutsi, eight Batare, and seventeen Bezi. Following periods of unrest, the eight Batare chiefs succeeded in controlling areas that had previously been under Hutu chiefs. Generally, outbreaks of unrest were caused by economic crises and natural disasters, exacerbated by the weight of dues paid to the colonial power. A rebellion in the northwestern region of Ndora—the Inamujandi rebellion of March 1934—was characterized by a general resentment of all the rulers under which the majority—the Hutu—were by then living. Europeans, *ganwa*, and Tutsi were all condemned by the rioters, who called for the return of the "just King" to replace the rulers, who were by then the effective agents of the Belgians.

The Inamujandi rebellion took place in the chiefdom of Pierre Baranyanka, a Batare prince who had established close ties with the Belgian authorities. These ties made Baranyanka a favored candidate to replace Mwami Mwambutsa IV, a Bezi, whose ties with the colonial authority were strained. Baranyanka's close ties with the Belgians laid the foundations of the political landscape that was to emerge in postcolonial Burundi. Rivalry between Baranyanka and Mwambutsa simmered throughout the 1950s until 1959, when the colonial authorities announced a series of political reforms in response to the emergence of political parties. On one side stood Baranyanka's sons, who led the Parti Démocrate Chrétien (PDC: Democratic Christian Party) and retained close ties with Belgium, and on the other Mwambutsa's son, Prince Louis Rwagasore, who emerged as the leader of the Parti de l'Union et du Progrès Nationale (Uprona).

Belgian support for the PDC led to Uprona being popularly characterized as the truly nationalist party. The Belgians portrayed Rwagasore—a royal prince whose wife was Hutu—as a Communist. In the charged climate of the approach toward independence, such sentiments further enhanced support for Uprona. In the legislative elections of September 1961, Uprona won fifty-eight of the sixty-four seats. Rwagasore's credentials as a unionist endowed with many of the traits regarded by Hutu as those of the "just" leader thus gave Burundians a taste of nationhood. Then, on 13 October 1961, Rwagasore was assassinated by a gunman dispatched by the PDC, which some suggest had been encouraged to get rid of him by the Belgian authorities. Pierre Baranyanka's eldest son, Prince Jean Ntitendereza, was hanged for his part in the murder.

"Rwagasore's death, and the fact that the legitimacy of his role as a nationalist leader owed very little to constitutional niceties and virtually all to personal qualities, including that of being the *mwami*'s son, were critical elements in the background of the Hutu-Tutsi problem,"[7] writes Lemarchand. Unfortunately, he does not offer a detailed explanation as to how ethnic feeling in Burundi had evolved up to the point at which the country achieved independence. He suggests that the tensions within society were essentially derived from issues of economic differentiation, but he does not explain whether the emergent Hutu-Tutsi ethnic conflict had indeed always lain beneath the surface. The transition from economic to ethnic conflict is not adequately explained, simply presented as the result of Rwagasore's death. For his life, and therefore death, to have been so significant, it is necessary to offer more detail of what underlying ethnic tension Rwagasore had been able to calm. Equally, the shock of assassination was in itself sufficient to create a climate of anxiety.

The *mwami* remained the source of stability until the abolition of the monarchy in 1966, following a military coup. By then Uprona had become riven with internal rivalries along Hutu-Tutsi lines. Political leaders within both tribes came to view the monarchy as an inadequate vehicle for the centralization of the national administration. Meanwhile, the 1959 Hutu revolution in Rwanda—which saw the Hutu majority usurp Tutsi primacy on the eve of independence—had inspired Burundian Hutu, both by its republicanism and its termination of Tutsi domination. The momentum for a Hutu attempt to seize power was thus set in train—despite a residual Burundian attachment to the monarchy in some quarters. Events in Rwanda, which have had a variety of both direct and indirect impacts on Burundi (and vice versa), contributed more to the growing trend of historical mythmaking than to a political atmosphere conducive to reestablishing national interest and common ground. Around 50,000 Tutsi refugees fled from Rwanda to Burundi in 1959 following the Hutu overthrow of Tutsi rule. They came replete with stories of Hutu savagery, which fueled the tension within Burundi itself. From the Belgian point of view, the response of local administrators was to view the Hutu revolution in Rwanda—which had received crucial backing from Belgian-based religious organizations through the Catholic church in Rwanda—as a positive development, which had brought the majority to power over the Tutsi minority. The effect in Burundi of the emergence of Hutu rule was the bolstering of Hutu politicians and political groups. Just as Belgium supported the PDC political party, so it supported the Christian trade unions, the Syndicats Chrétiens, which in the eyes of Tutsi became what Lemarchand describes as "the Trojan horse of Belgian interests."[8]

The Tutsi response to the emergence in Burundi of Hutu groupings was to form the Jeunesse Nationaliste Rwagasore (JNR: Rwagasore Nationalist Youth). The group evolved into the radically anticolonial, anti-Hutu Jeunesse Revolutionaire Rwagasore (JRR; Rwagasore Revolutionary Youth). The JNR led anti-Hutu riots in 1962 in Bujumbura's Kamenge district, which left the president of the Syndicats Chrétiens and three other leading Hutu dead. A key result of the violence was felt within the still interethnic leadership of Uprona, which had been divided following the death of Rwagasore between camps led by the *ganwa* André Muhirwa and the Hutu Paul Mirerekano. Attempts to avoid a split between them failed and resulted in increasing polarization and provocations along ethnic lines. This split was made even more evident when the reality of Tutsi predominance within the bureaucracy became an issue, the Tutsi minority by 1964 holding twice as many senior civil service posts as the Hutu majority.

The political tension was temporarily broken in 1963, when Muhirwa resigned, at which point Mwami Mwambutsa, the king, reasserted his role by bringing the army and the gendarmerie under his direct control. But his ability to control events was severely hindered by the outbreak of rebellion in eastern Congo. The leaders of the Congolese Armée de Libération Nationale (ALN: Army of National Liberation) rebellion forged links with Burundi's Tutsi elite, who allowed the Chinese embassy in Bujumbura to transship arms to the Congolese en route from Dar es Salaam. Rwandan Tutsi refugees joined the ALN with the aim of creating a base from which to launch their return to Hutu-led Rwanda. To cement their ties with the Burundian Tutsi, they came to play a key role in the latter's struggle for power. In 1965 a Rwandan Tutsi refugee assassinated Burundi's Hutu prime minister, Pierre Ngendandumwe. Mwambutsa then held legislative elections, which saw Hutu win twenty-three of the thirty-three seats. Hutu exasperation was exacerbated, however, when Mwambutsa appointed a *ganwa* prime minister, reduced the number of communes, and limited the power of the local administrators, the *burgomestre*, which severely limited Hutu power despite their numerical majority.

The Hutu response was a coup on 19 October 1965, which left the prime minister dead and Mwambutsa a refugee in Uvira in neighboring Congo. Tutsi troops then rounded on the Hutu coup makers. Within six days they had executed 47 Hutu soldiers. Meanwhile, Tutsi officers formed a *conseil de guerre* (council of war) and rounded up Hutu politicians in Bujumbura. On 28 October, 10 were executed. Within three weeks a further 86 death sentences were handed down on Hutu politicians, among them Paul Mirerekano. The Hutu political elite was thus destroyed. Outside the capital, Hutu groups responded with attacks on Tutsi homes, leading to a violent response from Tutsi soldiers and members of the JNR that left around 5,000 Hutu civilians dead in the home areas of the dead Hutu leaders. His power disintegrating, Mwami Mwambutsa ended up in Switzerland, and he passed on his royal powers to Mwame Ntare III. But by November 1966 he too had been overthrown by a military coup d'etat while on a visit to Kinshasa. Pressure had been building within the Tutsi political establishment for the creation of a republic, which the *mwame* had resisted. Both sides waited for their chance, Burundi's monarch was the loser, and a republic was declared in November 1966, at the head of which was Captain Michel Micombero. The military had taken over.

THE MANY FACES OF THE PAST

The rise of military power is not to be understood in terms of providing the only alternative to the failure of civilian politicians to organize the affairs of state. To varying degrees a military seizure of power marks the assumption of power by individuals whose tendencies are instinctively antidemocratic. Military coups are ultimately irresponsible, and it is, as Samuel Decalo writes, "simplistic, ethnocentric, and empirically erroneous to relegate coups in Africa to the status of . . . a function of the political weakness and structural fragility of African states and the failings of civilian elites, thus ignoring fundamental behavioural dynamics and motivations."[9] Burundi is significant, as it has experienced military dictatorship and a military-led transition to democracy. Both have been accompanied by strong divisions within the armed forces that have exposed the variety of views and ambitions, as well as the immense tensions that exist within groups that to the outside world appear as though they ought to be homogenous in the face of supposed common enemies. "What the term *tribe* fails to capture are the complex hierarchies of power, status, and privilege that cut across ethnic identities and that once formed the axis around which revolved much of the country's social and political life," Lemarchand writes,[10] a view shared by Decalo:

> Seething with corporate, ethnic, and personal grievances that divide their loyalties, hardly national armies but armed factions reflecting wider societal cleavages, these mutual-advancement loyalty pyramids are only nominally beholden to military discipline and hierarchical command. One direct corollary is that when the military assumes political power, its own internal cleavages and competitions constrain its efforts and achievements over and beyond the immensity of the task and other considerations.[11]

Scholarly and journalistic concentration on Hutu and Tutsi, at the expense of other elements of Burundi's societal makeup, has led to these other aspects of what had been an extremely complex and functional social pyramid being given scant attention in the face of an emergent ethnic identity, which has effectively been born since independence and nurtured entirely within the atmosphere of tension which now prevails.

The failure of military regimes in general to gain broad popular legitimacy can be said to have at least one of its roots in the traditional perception of power. "Power traditionally was not personalized; the ruler did not rule to enforce his personal will. He was the living embodiment of the community-state's members' aims and aspirations as well as the axis of their political relationships, the symbol of their unity and integrity. Consequently, power was conceived in sacred terms and could only be held in trust," writes the Nigerian academic Eghosa Osaghae, perhaps somewhat idealistically, but nevertheless reflecting accurately at least the ideal to which traditional rulers would have been expected to aspire.[12]

Much of the postcolonial political agenda has been geared toward the creation of personality cults around modern military leaders whose only qualification was to have seized power in an often bloody fashion. This very process has more often than not sown the seeds of the disharmony that rulers were supposed to overcome and thereby driven a wedge between the past and present practice of wielding power. In doing so, the act of wielding power drove a wedge between populations whose traditional role had not changed since the precolonial era, and whose expectations of rulers remained what they had always been, and the new military rulers who could use modern methods—weapons, security services, surveillance techniques, and recourse to defense pacts with foreign powers—to cement their power, while drawing simultaneously on a selective use of tradition by favoring their own ethnic group in the division of the spoils of that power. Perhaps with too great a view to diminishing the role of the army itself, Burundi's military ruler, Pierre Buyoya, identified this in the context of Burundi:

> For political parties to have different programs and beliefs is difficult after the end of the Cold War. So, what other differences exist to allow different parties to be created within the multiparty system? Ethnic differences. But these [other] differences will come slowly. Our politics is simply about getting into power. Among the peasants there are no differences, because for them the [economic] problems[13] are all the same.[14]

SOLDIERS AND REPUBLICANS

Following the assassination of Rwagasore in 1961, an event which ultimately led to the seizure of power by the military in 1966 and the declaration of a republic, the failure of subsequent governments to build upon indigenous institutions or garner some benefit from the organizational legacy of colonial administration was made clear in Burundi. Thirty-two years later the weakness of the national structure was as pronounced. "My government is requesting that the international community assure the security of the country and institutions, so that the institutions aren't threatened by the *putschists*," Sylvie Kinigi, Burundi's prime minister told me in October 1993.[15] "The response [to this request] is still being awaited by the government. . . . [But] if the military don't return to the barracks, we will find ourselves in an irrevocable situation. We demand that the military end very quickly the actions they are carrying out—that is the massacres in some areas—in Gitega and Rugigi—which are continuing at the moment against the population."

The crisis facing the government stemmed from the fact that the moderates within the military appeared at that time to have no power to force their extremist colleagues to end their slaughter of Hutu civilians. It was not really the case that military orders were not being obeyed, but that these orders were not being effectively given, due to the breakdown of the command structure within the army itself. What then was the cause of that weakness of command within the most organized and—tribally speaking—the most homogenous institution in the country? Although military coups and military rule are often portrayed as the strong-arm alternative to the apparently weak civilian institutions, military rule is in fact subject to the same weakness as the rest of society.

Seldom have periods of military rule provided a respite from the long-term weakening of the state, seldom have security superstructures dominated by the military allowed civilian institutions to be strengthened, so as to facilitate a smooth transition of power back to civilian rule. Invariably, military rule is inspired by the desire of military regimes to rule indefinitely in their own interests, without the irritation of dissent to divert those in power from the pursuit of power, privilege, and personal enrichment. Broadening his theme from discussion of Nigeria to trends elsewhere, Akinola writes:

> The exclusion of popular groups from the political process . . . still finds forceful expression in the welter of bureaucratic-authoritarian regimes that dot the African political landscape today. . . . Being heirs to the colonial order, the political elite most probably holds a contemptuous and unpromising view of the underprivileged as [they do] of popular forces. . . . [The] African political elite has internalised the ethnocentrism of colonial officers so much that the typical non-privileged citizen is perceived as lazy, unimaginative, and perhaps incapable of engaging in rational thought on social issues.[16]

The complex practicalities of a transition from entrenched military rule to democracy have occasionally been used as an argument against launching the transition in the first place. In Burundi there was no excuse for delaying a transition on the grounds that the Hutu majority was not ready for the power such a transition would ultimately hand to them. Hutu did have experience in government—in the lower echelons—and even within the army—in the lower ranks. The Tutsi minority that had excluded them from real power had had no choice but to co-opt members of the majority, if the bureaucracy were to be sufficiently broad so as to function during twenty-seven years of one-party rule. When the time came, in the early 1990s, for the transition to democracy to take place, the "heirs to the colonial order" in the military regime had shifted the source of their authority so far from the traditional precolonial structures that the source of their legitimacy was impossible to identify. They neither appeared to be the answer to immediate problems, nor capable of creating an environment in which long-term solutions could be formulated by civilians. Meanwhile, the vast majority of people faced detachment from the source of power and the denial of any chance to use political means to find solutions to the economic crises they faced. "The state is out of touch with the realities of the people," Akinola wrote in 1989. Although he was writing of Nigeria, the same conclusion was entirely appropriate to much of the continent at that point.

Major Pierre Buyoya's decision to hold an election in which he, the Tutsi minority, and Burundi's military elite would in theory lose the stranglehold on power they had enjoyed since 1966 was intended ultimately to engender political pluralism with a view to safeguarding Tutsi interests. This would be achieved by creating a meritocratic system in which the past privileges of the minority would better equip them with the credentials to run the newly *democratized* bureaucracy than the majority, which would take years if not generations to catch up and achieve the qualifications to rule. The first apparent weakness of the transition lay in the failure to contend with extremism within Tutsi ranks. Even after the coup, the limitations on Buyoya's own vision were revealed when he asserted: "The Burundian army isn't an obstacle to finding a solution. The problem in Burundi isn't within the army. It's among the politicians. It's different in Rwanda. In Rwanda the military was very much more involved in politics. In Burundi we have a classic army. In 1965 there was a Hutu majority in the [Burundian] army."[17]

Unsurprisingly, Hutu disillusionment with democracy after the horrific violence of October 1993, was also influenced by suspicion of Buyoya's own motives. Buyoya in fact shares the motivation of Rwanda's Tutsi-led Rwandan Patriotic Front, which rejects the pursuit of the protection of the rights of the majority on the grounds that such a system would thereby exclude the minority—that is, the Tutsi minority. After years of suppression of the Hutu, the argument promoted by the Tutsi, in very general terms, is that it would be wrong to regard a transition to pluralism as ultimately intended to allow a dictatorship by the majority. On one hand it would appear that the Tutsi of Burundi remain intent upon further denying Hutu their rights. It is the result of that history of that repression and denial of rights that is now creating conflict. On the other hand, the democratic argument promoted by the minority is based on the thesis that democracy cannot be allowed to amount to a Hutu payback for Tutsi repression in the past. To make such a demand of the majority is clearly expecting a great deal. But the rationale behind it has to be seen as part of the uneven evolution of the state: The relative sophistication of entrenched military rule established over many years contrasts sharply with the stagnation of civilian life during periods of subjugation to that rule. In such a climate of uncertainty, it is necessary to broaden understanding of the value of change within the civilian population, on the assumption that a majority of people on all sides are in favor of peaceful coexistence, if only a way could be found to allow all sides to profit from it.

Buyoya himself made the extent of this challenge clear:

> The people don't really understand democracy. People have to understand the advantages of democracy. We have no experience of it. We have no democratic tradition. When a party comes to power here, it puts all its people in power in all areas. But that's something that can be adapted. It's necessary that the democratic system adapts to the African reality. There's a tendency in Africa to try and copy models from the outside. Africa has undeveloped countries. That's the African reality. There's the Africa of ethnicities and regions: They are the differences Africa has with other countries. The Western democratic model is an exclusive system. In Africa there are ethnic, regional, and religious differences. It's necessary to adapt the system to the Burundian reality—a country where there are ethnic groups in which one is the biggest and the other is the most dominant. The system should adapt to take into account the different ethnic groups. Each party should be multi-ethnic.[18]

Buyoya's frank assessment is based on the assumption that ethnicity is the key relationship, to which political reform must be addressed. It is a revealing assessment. For four days during the coup attempt of October 1993, he took refuge inside the U.S. embassy in Bujumbura, aware that he was associated in the eyes of his fellow Tutsi—the coup makers—as having at least in part engineered Melchior Ndadaye's rise to power. By dismissing the idea that different perceptions of politics—perceptions that cut across tribal lines—could have played a major part in the coup attempt and the subsequent Hutu response, he appears to have diminished the relevance of his own experiment. Voting patterns in the 1993 elections revealed some voting that did not fit into the anticipated tribal pattern. Moreover, the presence of Hutu and Tutsi in both Frodebu and Uprona revealed the existence of the horizontal division of both parties into moderates and extremists, rather than the vertical division of society into tribes. Although Buyoya recognized the existence of extremists and moderates on both sides, he was uncertain as to how the ethnic reality should affect the structure of parties and government. Either "the system should take into account the different ethnic groups," or "each party should be multi-ethnic." By implication, the need he identifies for the system to take into account the different ethnic groups is to suggest that the ultimate purpose of democracy—to create a fairer and more just society—should essentially favor the Hutu majority in its search for equality. But by calling for the system to prevent exclusion, he is obviously seeking to prevent the exclusion of the Tutsi minority. How, then, can multiparty politics foster such an atmosphere of inclusion, while simultaneously addressing the historical reality of Hutu exclusion, which was the central motive behind Hutu support for democratic change? "For most Hutu, nothing short of majoritarian democracy will do; yet precisely because it conjures up threats of ethnic domination, made all the more ominous by the Hutu's shared sense of past injustices unavenged, such a democracy is what most Tutsi wish to avoid at all cost,"[19] Lemarchand writes. Trust is perhaps the key determinant of the outcome, since trust will be necessary for any real change. Buyoya continued:

> The conflict of October 1993 was created by ethnic extremists on both sides who want exclusive power. They are afraid of having the other in power. In each group, the extremists are a minority. But they are very active. They are now afraid of a Hutu president and Hutu-dominated parliament. The people who massacred others throughout the country were extremists. There were hundreds of Tutsi who were eliminated by Hutu too.
>
> But the big majority of both groups are for democracy. They accepted a Hutu president. The nonmastery of the democratic process gave the extremists their reason for launching the massacres. They had the impression that the new system was going to favor the Hutu. That it was going to become an ethnocracy, particularly with the distribution of land.
>
> There were errors made in the democratic process. From the start of the democratic process we were going to see problems, but felt that over time we would see the system improve. I don't think we will go back to a one-party state.[20]

GHOSTS OF FEAR AND MYTH

The absence of trust is the most powerful element in hindering the future evolution of democracy and the move away from military rule or civilian dictatorship backed up by the iron fist of the army. The brutality of Burundi's army has left a permanent impression in the Hutu civilian psyche. "We all want to live together, but it's impossible. Impossible. They just don't want it," said Therese Minani, a Burundian Hutu refugee living at the Kigani refugee camp in southern Rwanda, as she stretched out her muddy legs at the entrance to her twig and grass hillside hovel.[21] She had been there before, in 1972, when thousands of Hutu had fled an outbreak of slaughter, and she escaped with her family to this same smoke- and mist-draped valley. "When there are both Hutus and Tutsis in the army, then it will go better," said David Nkurikiye.[22] "There were Palipehutu here. But they left. They didn't say why they were leaving. This was a refugee camp in 1988. Everybody knew where to come, because they had all been here before."

A series of camps along Rwanda's southern border with Burundi presented the same picture: thousands of people, smoke lingering in the pine forests, the staring vacant eyes of malnourished children. At the Saga One camp, a small boy wielded an axe he could barely lift. A small, half-naked boy was learning to walk among the splinters and smoke as he cried out for his mother. At Burenge it was the same, 40,000 people living crammed onto a rain- and windswept hillside. Malaria, cholera, and dysentery were common. A group of disturbed children wandered around grinning wildly. A child in the clinic gripped its mother's nipple in its mouth, but had no energy to suck. Stick crosses stood in the brown mud of the graveyard, stark against the wet gray sky, at the foot of the rolling waves of the camp's white plastic dwellings. A dark gray sky, about to burst with rain, threw the ripped-up forest into relief, with the last remaining trees standing skeletal against the clouds. "I came here because the soldiers came to our village throwing grenades into our houses," said Manda Tukahataza.[23] "They threw grenades and killed people. The [Burundian] soldiers have come into the camps [in Rwanda] to get people and take them back. And they could throw grenades here too," she said, as a barefoot man dug at the soft ground nearby. People watched him in silence, arms crossed, as the hole grew deeper. Then they placed the body of a child inside—a six-year-old girl. Her father buried her. The hole was filled, and everybody went away.

Buyoya asserted that the key motivation behind the violence that forces refugees to flee is the strategy of civilian politicians:

There's never been any conflict between the groups on the level of the village. There was no ethnic war before independence. The politicians transfer their political conflicts to the hills in the countryside. Certainly, when there's tension you can die because you're Hutu, or because you're Tutsi. It's exactly the same in Rwanda and Burundi. But if the leaders say nothing then the killings don't happen. What's the difference between Hutu and Tutsi? None. Their interests are the same. When I was head of state I was pressured by both sides. The extremist Tutsis from my own group I had to put down three times. From my own group. They got very close, and the force of extremism was very strong. And the Palipehutu attacked many times as well.[24]

Equanimity is as abundant among both Burundi and Rwanda's moderates as vitriol is among the two countries' extremists. Lemarchand identifies the weaknesses of the arguments in favor of democracy as advanced by Burundi's Tutsi minority and thereby exposes the fragile rationale behind the transi-

tion to democracy. In doing so, he lays out clearly the role played by historical denial in determining the future path both Rwanda and Burundi are
likely to take:

> It is among Tutsi intellectuals that ethnicity performs a vanishing act in the name
> of instrumental rationality. Only by denying their collective identity as Tutsi can
> they legitimately claim (1) that there is no real discrimination between Hutu and
> Tutsi, (2) that the quest for a political majority, as distinct from an ethnic major-
> ity, is the key to a healthy democracy, (3) that the verdict of history is entirely
> consistent with their present-day contention of basic social harmony between
> Hutu and Tutsi, and (4) that Hutu claims to represent the majority of the popu-
> lation are simply a thinly veiled manifestation of "tribalism," the bane of the
> African continent.[25]

The only sure claim that can be made about the relations between Hutu
and Tutsi in Burundi is that before the arrival of European colonialists they
were not rivals for power in the way that they have become since the Hutu
uprising in Rwanda in 1959, which had a ripple effect on its southern neighbor. Finding a way out of the bloody mesh of history is as much complicated
by myths as it is by reality. In this process, the Europeans played a role that
served to exacerbate rivalries, to a point where, at the beginning of the
twenty-first century, myth and reality have been so confused that the countries to which they apply are in fact barely functioning. The inheritance of
myths is perhaps the main feature that links the precolonial, colonial, and
postcolonial periods, as Lemarchand notes when he talks of ethnic identities
having "acquired a moral dimension—whether as a martyred community or
a threatened minority—they never had before."[26] With myths playing such a
role in the lives of the populations today, it is hardly surprising that the
countries have found it so difficult to resolve their political crises.

So where did the myths start? In 1858, the British explorer John Hanning
Speke, searching for the source of the Nile, passed through Uganda and later
western Tanzania, where he encountered Central Africans—the *Wahuma*—
an encounter that led him to offer "my theory of the ethnology of that part
of Africa inhabited by the people collectively styled Wahuma, otherwise
Gallas or Abyssinians. My theory is founded on the traditions of the several
nations, as checked by my own observation of what I saw when passing
through them. It appears impossible to believe, judging from the physical
appearance of the Wahuma, that they can be of any other race than the semi-
Shem-Hamitic of Ethiopia."[27] Speke asserts, as one part of his theory, that
the pastoralism of the Gallas, as opposed to the arable farming that prevailed
among "aboriginal Abyssinians," was mirrored in the relationship between
the Wahuma and the aboriginals of Central Africa, in the kingdoms of Uz-
ina, Karague, Uganda, and Unyoro, through which he traveled.

In these countries [or kingdoms] the government is in the hands of foreigners who had invaded and taken possession of them, leaving the agricultural aborigines to till the ground, while the junior members of the usurping clans herded cattle—just as in Abyssinia, or wherever the Abyssinians or Gallas have shown themselves. There a pastoral clan from the Asiatic side took the government of Abyssinia from its people and have ruled over them ever since, changing, by intermarriage with the Africans, the texture of their hair and color to a certain extent, but still maintaining a high stamp of Asiatic feature, of which a marked characteristic is a bridged instead of a bridgeless nose.[28]

Speke offers no historical evidence of Abyssinian expansionism into East and Central Africa, and uses only guesswork to explain how and why the Abyssinians effected such a decisive change in the demography of the region. He says simply that it took place "for reasons that cannot be traced."[29] He does not specify the situation in the then kingdoms of Urundi and Ruanda—modern Burundi and Rwanda—as his journey did not take him to those areas. However, the same process of immigration by supposed Hamitic peoples is the most common explanation given for the supposed physical differences between Hutu and Tutsi in both countries:

[Other Abyssinians] were lost sight of in the interior of the continent, and, crossing the Nile close to its source, discovered the rich pasture-lands of Unyoro, and founded the great kingdom of Kittara, where they lost their religion, forgot their language, extracted their lower incisors like the natives, changed their national name to Wahuma, and no longer remembered the names of Hubshi or Galla.[30]

Speke says of the Wahuma princes of Unyoro that they identified their forefathers as having come from the north, in the direction from which he and other Europeans had come. A division of the kingdom, at an unspecified date, led to the creation of two other monarchical lines, established at Nkole and Karague. Speke says of the Karague line that it was created "twenty generations ago," meaning perhaps as long as a thousand years before he visited the region in 1858. The Karague line was the most southerly of the Wahuma kingdoms, with its furthest outpost being that of the Watusi, "who are emigrants from the Karague of the same stock, overlooking the Tanganyika Lake from the hills of Uhha, and tending their cattle all over Unyamuezi under the protection of the native negro chiefs; and we also hear that the Wapoka of Fipa, south of the Rukwa Lake (in central Tanzania), are the same. How or when their name became changed from Wahuma to Watusi no one is able to explain."[31]

The history of invasion by the *Watusi*, for which read *Batutsi* or *Tutsi*, is the most potent of the myths invoked today, in the already enflamed political climate of the Great Lakes, to perpetuate the sense of injustice felt by the Hutu majority. The myth—perhaps true, perhaps not—completely obscures the fact of generations of intermarriage, the reality of *Hutu* and *Tutsi* in fact having become a question of status rather than tribe long before the colonial conquests of the nineteenth century, and the cultural assimilation of the two tribes. In times of conflict—or at times when extremist politicians have sought to create conflict—the only point of reference is a moment in the past at which the injustice of the present is supposed to have had its genesis, an injustice all must now seek to rectify.

It is unclear whether the myth of the invasion is one that prevailed among Hutu before Speke introduced the idea into the European mind, and that was then transferred to the colonial subjects when the two kingdoms fell into German and later Belgian hands. The Belgian role in pitting the two sides against each other—largely through the churches—had at its root, first, in the idea that the Tutsi were the superior invaders, who (if Speke is to be believed) may originally have been born of Asian stock. Second, there was the eleventh-hour realization that these same Tutsi were the keenest to see the back of colonialism and would agitate vociferously until the Belgians departed. Playing the colonialists to the end of the game, the Belgians helped implant the *mythico-history*, as Lemarchand calls it, by insisting on distinguishing between the tribes, equipped with Speke's completely baseless claims, which even he admitted were essentially founded on the shape of peoples' noses.

Colonialism undoubtedly polarized the elements of Burundi's social makeup in a manner rarely seen before on the African continent. In an invaluable study of the perceptions of history voiced by Burundian refugees in Tanzania, the American academic Liisa Malkki states categorically that, based on the numerous interviews she conducted in 1985–1986, "[Postcolonial] competition for political power—and not 'the old African problem of tribalism'[32] served to bifurcate the populations in Rwanda and Burundi into two opposing categories, Hutu and Tutsi, and to render other social divisions less meaningful and less powerful. The exclusive predominance of the ethnic bifurcation was at this level a markedly recent political phenomenon."[33] Malkki continues:

> The issue of who were the original, primordial occupants of the land now known as Burundi was central to the Hutu claim to rightful moral and historical precedence over the Tutsi, and to the Hutu people's status as "the true members" of the primordial nation, the aboriginal homeland. . . . [It] was very much a contemporary question concerning the "true essence" of the Burundian "nation" as it *should* be, and as it was, according to the mythico-history, prior to the arrival of the Tutsi "impostors" or "race of foreigners." . . . The exalted position of the Tutsi in Burundi, suggests the mythico-history, was

founded, not on divine or natural premises, but on deception and ill-gotten power.[34]

Malkki relates that the Hutu believed they had arrived in the first century B.C. from modern Katanga, in what is now the southern province of the Democratic Republic of Congo, had mixed with the indigenous Twa to create Burundi in an area where no country had previously existed, and had created a nationality out of the mixing of the two tribes. She dismisses the "Hamitic hypothesis" as a failed theory of historical reconstruction, but describes it as "having taken on a life of its own."[35] However mythical it may be, then, it must be taken into account, as it provides a key to understanding how the two sides regard each other's rationale for political action, and raises the fundamental question of whether or not the crises in both Burundi and Rwanda amount to the playing out of historical rivalries or are a response to immediate conditions. To this point, Malkki responds by making an interesting suggestion:

> Instead of looking at historical consciousness as a *thing* already formed, it may be more profitable or true to life to focus on the *processes* of its formation and transformation. Indeed, the Hutu case underscores the fact that here, historicity does not culminate in any closure which might permit it to be examined as a finite, bounded entity or structure. Rather, it is an ongoing process.[36]

Perhaps only a change in views of history will allow the popular consciousness to be injected with new elements that could break the cycle of violence, as until the past is seen differently the sense of grievance is unlikely to dissipate.

However, a changing consciousness of the past is unlikely to happen unless the conduct of the modern actors changes so that they no longer resemble, at least in the eyes of the people, those figures from the past perceived as responsible for the historical inequality and injustice. In 1988, Buyoya moved decisively to terminate the system of tribal apartheid practiced by the man he had overthrown a year earlier, Colonel Jean-Baptiste Bagaza. Ultimately he did so because within a year of staging his 1987 palace coup, he faced the worst outbreak of violence the country had seen since the carnage of 1972. Was this motive for changing the political direction of the country a real break with the past, or a ploy to ensure that the majority would never have the power of a majority, and the minority never be forced to accept its numerical deficiency? With violence still ravaging Burundi in the early twenty-first century, whatever motive once existed now appears barely relevant , and the question scarcely worth answering. Although the psychology and ideology of genocide at play in Burundi may have its roots in *mythicohistory*, the daily practice of rule is brutally realistic. Death really does lurk around every corner. Buyoya had no illusions:

The ideology of extermination exists among the extremists of the Hutu and Tutsi. In 1959, in Rwanda, there was extermination. It was that event in Rwanda that created the fear among the Tutsi in Burundi. In 1972 there was a civil war here. It's necessary to eradicate the ideology of extermination. It's difficult for outsiders to understand. To eradicate that ideology is a question of political development. How can it develop in a balanced way? Secondly, how do you punish the people responsible for it?[37]

Eradication is an all too common theme among the peoples of the Great Lakes. Terminating long-held beliefs, entrenched over generations, is the greatest challenge facing the region. The ultimate intentions of government are viewed with such immense suspicion that any similarity in form or content with past practice will always lead to a rapid evaporation of expectations of change, enflaming an already deeply entrenched cynicism, and quickly breeding violence. To break with the past, the country must see that the most potent images from the past have been consigned to an unrepeatable history. The most potent image of all is that of the soldier slaughtering the civilian. Buyoya's claim that the army in Burundi was not the problem is either naive or deceitful. The army has clearly had a key role in perpetrating the violence in Burundi's previous explosions, and it failed in 1993 to exercise sufficient discipline within its own ranks to bring a rapid end to the violence. Even this did not prevent Buyoya from portraying the situation a year later to me as follows:

In some ways one could say that a majority of the government is using a Hutu militia against the national army. The fundamental difficulty is in the political arena. It's paralyzed. Why aren't the militias here adequately confronted? It's because there's no willingness on the part of the government. The government must confront the situation. It's necessary that, on a cross-party basis, all the politicians condemn the violence and overcome the political divisions. The danger is great. Everybody's frightened. There are problems, but we haven't seen the government take measures. There's no political willingness to face the situation.[38]

By then what had emerged was "a thinly disguised form of military rule held together by networks of Tutsi politicians, youth gangs, armed militias, and army men."[39] Buyoya himself was not in power when he gave that diagnosis; he had lost the 1993 election, and he only took power again in 1996, when everything was falling apart. He then came back to power through a military coup.

6

JUGGLING THE JUNTAS

Zaire, Nigeria, and Military Rule

A dictator doesn't give democracy. Everybody sees that the
people are behind the opposition. Each party has its own
identity. But for the exertion of pressure we are united.
Mobutu has no more drastic measures to take. He is weak
because he has survived through a system of state terrorism.
The people have lived in fear. We have demystified Mobutu.
And now the people are moving.

Etienne Tshisekedi

ETIENNE TSHISEKEDI, the stubbornly resilient leader of Zaire's[1] main
opposition party, Union démocratique pour le progrès sociale (UDPS: Democratic Union for Social Progress), reflected in every one of his statements
during our interview the core truth about politics in Zaire and the nature of
the relationship between ruler and ruled—at the heart of Zaire's political life
nobody had any illusions about anybody else.[2] He, like the other political
opponents of the Mobutu regime, had no illusions as to what Mobutu Sese
Seko would be prepared to do to stay in power. Equally, they had no doubts
as to what it would take for them to seize that power. Relentless pressure was
the only weapon they had at their disposal.

The demographics of Zaire, the vastness of the country, the fact that a major incident in one region could take place without having any real impact on

events elsewhere, all played a vitally important role in the practice of politics. Only Mobutu had a meaningful nationwide presence, having built up a party machinery over twenty-three years in the form of the Mouvement Populaire de la Révolution (MPR: Popular Movement of the Revolution), to which the entire population had been ordered to belong since its creation in 1967. Moreover, his control over a gubernatorial network, security police, gendarmerie, and national army—however disorganized, ill paid, and unruly they were— provided him with at least a basis for nationwide influence and control.

"DIGNITY FOR AFRICA?"[3]

The unknown into which Zaire stepped on 24 April 1990, when Mobutu declared the country a multiparty state, in which two parties would be permitted to operate alongside the MPR, was less of a leap into uncertainty than a recognition that the long-awaited trial of strength between all the forces Mobutu had corrupted and repressed for much of his twenty-three years in power was about to start. Power through intimidation and manipulation was the heart of *Mobutism*, the amorphous creed under which Zairians lived. Mobutu's power lay with the security forces, even though the regime was not officially a military regime. "Mobutu's regime originated in a military coup d'etat and, like other such regimes in Africa, was imperfectly civilianized,"[4] writes Thomas Turner. As coercion and corruption lay at the heart of his power, Mobutu created a system of government in which there was no identifiable ideology in practice.

The evolution of non-politics had its roots in more than mere ambition on his part. It stretched back to the years 1960–1965, which had seen the collapse of the country:

> The public was highly ambivalent regarding politicians and parties. The term "politician" had become virtually synonymous with "thief" or "traitor," as was attested by the violence directed against members of the 1960 political generation during the 1964–65 rebellions. . . . At the same time, particular parties and politicians retained substantial credit with their respective constituencies. . . . Mobutu's problems were, therefore, how to break the hold of these parties on their respective constituencies, and how to work with the politicians without granting them access to their clienteles.[5]

In 1967 Mobutu diminished the influence of these parties by incorporating many of their leaders into the executive committee of the MPR. Meanwhile, "[The] Mobutist state required a legitimating myth which was distinctive, demarcating Zaire from other African states as well as from its own past, and yet which drew upon certain common themes in African nationalist thought."[6] Thus, the myth of Congolese nationalism dominated from 1966

to 1971, when it was replaced by *authenticité*, which was subsequently replaced by Mobutism.[7] None of these theories lent themselves to political
evolution; they were dependent upon the military backbone of the regime to
prevent change, which could only come by way of their overthrow and replacement.

Mobutu initially nailed his political colors to the mast with the *N'Sele
Manifesto* of 19 May 1967, in which he espoused nationalism, essentially in
the form of independence from foreign business control of the country's resources. By 1971, however, the need for an ideology that addressed the indigenous needs of Congolese, rather than their position in the global context, led Mobutu to assert his own primary position within the body politic,
with the assertion of authenticité:

> In our African tradition, there are never two chiefs; there is sometimes a nat-
> ural heir of the chief, but can anyone tell me that he has ever known a village
> that has two chiefs? That is why we Congolese, in the desire to conform to the
> traditions of our continent, have resolved to group all the energies of the citi-
> zens of our country under the banner of a single national party.
>
> It is the same concern for authenticity that has always led us to avoid found-
> ing our policy upon external advice, from whichever quarter. Among us, in the
> Congo, a chief must seek . . . counsel among the elders. He must inform him-
> self; but having taken counsel and informed himself, he must decide and re-
> solve the issue alone, in full cognizance of the problem. For it belongs to the
> chief to live with his own decision, to evaluate it, and to accept its conse-
> quences. . . . It is on this sole condition—because he will have weighed in ad-
> vance the consequences and accepted alone all the risks of his option—that his
> decision will be honest, and therefore good for the People and, finally, authen-
> tically democratic.[8]

Mobutu was never able to elaborate the real substance of authenticité.
Consequently, only the basic elements of the ideological phases through
which Zaire passed between 1965 and 1975 were retained, as the flaws and
inconsistencies were exposed by the irrelevance of theory in the face of the
dire poverty and deprivation facing the vast majority of the people. The passage toward Mobutism was consistent with what had preceded it. "Mobutu,
the quintessential man of action, evidently had neither the time nor the
amanuensis to convert his political reflections into an integrated holy book.
Thus the doctrine was to be discovered cumulatively in the teachings, the
speeches, the thoughts, and the actions of the president."[9] The value of the
ideology never really had a chance to emerge,[10] as Zaire's economic crisis
deepened in the mid- to late 1970s.

In effect, more than twenty of Mobutu's thirty-two years in power were
spent managing crises. During the period 1965–1976, he experimented with

systems of rule and was generally given a degree of popular support. But from 1977 until his demise in 1997 he was increasingly at odds with the people. Consequently, his rule is much more closely associated with the last twenty years of repression and conflict than with the first decade, in which the political identity of the Congo and later Zaire was created. As a result, Mobutism is a creed remembered for the increasingly brutal methods it used to survive, rather than for Mobutu's original search for the authentic identity of the state. It was the tools of repression that marked Mobutu's years, rather than ideologies intended to bring a brighter future.

> The social contract between the people and the government has collapsed. Mobutu began with good intentions when he took power. But it went to his head.[11]

With this simple conclusion, Nguza Karl-i-Bond seemed to sum up thirty years of Zairian history. We were sitting in the large villa in central Kinshasa which served as the headquarters of the party he led, the Union des Fédéralistes et Républicains Indépendant (UFERI: Union of Federalists and Independent Republicans). Zaire, it seemed, was perhaps on the threshold of a new era, that summer in 1991. A week beforehand, Mobutu had sought to counter growing opposition to his rule by naming Etienne Tshisekedi prime minister.[12] He said he had chosen Tshisekedi after consultations with the UDPS leader. At the time there was no confirmation that any consultation had taken place, and for hours it seemed the nomination had been made without the consent of the man being appointed—Tshisekedi—as a ploy by Mobutu to split his opponents. Tshisekedi and the Sacred Union, as it was called, of opposition parties had pointedly refused to accept that Mobutu had any role to play in the nomination of the prime minister. They had claimed that this power lay in the hands of a national conference of political parties and other interest groups, which was then going through the painful early stages of being convened before its scheduled opening on 31 July as the first stage of an effort to draw up a program of political reform. On hearing of Tshisekedi's nomination, his supporters thronged outside his walled bungalow in Kinshasa's tree-lined Limete district, begging him not to take the job. Mobutu's ploy failed, and on 25 July he reappointed Mulumba Lukodji, the technocratic prime minister he had sacked three days beforehand.

Tshisekedi had indeed agreed to take the post of prime minister. His acceptance of the post at a secret dinner he was said to have attended with Mobutu the previous week exposed the opportunism that lay at the heart of the opposition movement. There was no *unity*, and certainly nothing *sacred*, about the Sacred Union. Tshisekedi told his fellow members of the Union, including Karl-i-Bond, that he had accepted the post as a means of doing something about the dire state of opposition party finances. Most recognized, however, that basically Tshisekedi wanted to take power for himself and was prepared to break ranks with the rest of the opposition to do so, even if the result—had he gone that far—would have been the creation of a government made unworkable by the very fact of his having broken ranks. Such scenarios were normal. Within a year, Karl-i-Bond had also broken ranks and accepted the premiership. Following his ultimate rejection of the premiership in July 1991, Tshisekedi explained why he had decided not to leave the opposition after all: "Mobutu wanted me to be prime minister because he knows that the people have no confidence in him. But I have to be a prime minister nominated by the national conference. And he knows that if I am nominated prime minister by the national conference, I will have authority over the army."[13]

There was no way of knowing whether Mobutu really cared what the people thought of him. Clearly he felt he could play games with his opponents. But a significant reason for this conviction on his part was that he knew his opponents were also ready to play games. Tshisekedi, like many other members of the political opposition, had served in several Mobutu governments, having been minister of the interior before quitting in 1980. Mobutu believed he could use the threat of the exposure of their generally corrupt activities while in government to control the opposition. Part of Mobutu's failure in his handling of his increasingly emboldened critics, however, was his failure to realize that the public had no more illusions about the opposition than it had about him. Thirty years of corruption had tainted most of those who had tasted political power, including those who had broken with Mobutu in the late 1980s and in particular after the declaration of a multiparty state in 1990. In the absence of any virtuous political leaders, public opinion held to the core belief that it barely mattered who should lead the opposition, as long as the opposition was capable of overthrowing the core of the corrupt system, which was Mobutu himself.

Tshisekedi's claim that his seizure of political power would lead to an opposition government gaining control of the army assumed a great deal about the structure of the army and where its loyalties lay. He held that the failure to pay the army and the fact that it therefore suffered the same (or at least similar) levels of discontent and poverty as the rest of Zairian society would draw it toward sympathizing with the political opposition. At this time, the Force Armée Zairoize (FAZ: Zairian Armed Forces), was 81,000-strong—on paper. According to a well-placed foreign military source, 19,000 of those listed were fictitious names, included to allow senior officers to claim the salaries of nonexistent troops.[14] Alongside the FAZ, the Garde Civile (Civil Guard) numbered 12,000, under the command of General Kpama Baramoto, Mobutu's brother-in-law. Charged specifically with ensuring presidential protection was the Division Spéciale Présidentielle, the DSP, numbering 6,500 soldiers, and the only section of the armed forces to be equipped with the means of carrying out their assigned function. Mobutu's Ngbandi tribe from Equateur province dominated the DSP, whereas the Marine was largely from Bas-Zaire and the small air force mostly from

Kasai. Training of the different sections of the armed forces reflected Zaire's place in the world of the Cold War, with Egypt having trained the Garde Civile, Israel the DSP, and France the parachutists.

Despite the training, or perhaps as a deliberate result of the way in which the armed forces were structured, "There are no generals who could lead military action," according to the foreign military source quoted earlier.[15] The point is a vital one. Why had Mobutu created such a military structure, if it was not capable of fulfilling the function of protecting national integrity? What was the purpose of the army if it could not fight? The answer, given by the same source, reveals as much about the conduct of power in Mobutu's Zaire as it does about the reason behind Mobutu's fall and the disappearance of Zaire within hours of that downfall. Michael Schatzberg wrote in 1991: "Mobutu and his cronies believe the population has to see the implements of rule and coercive authority. As one Zairian general . . . put it: 'By its essential character as the holder of force, protector of institutions, and guarantor of public order, the Army incarnates Power.'"[16] Schatzberg went further, quoting the views of dissident Zairian parliamentarians:

> Zaire has never had an ethnically balanced or representative army. . . . Competence is rarely, if ever, a factor [influencing promotion within the military] since one of the things [Mobutu] fears most is an effective military establishment. . . . The more Mobutu's political and psychological insecurity has grown, the more he has relied on ethnic quotas in the military, and the narrower and more restrictive these have become. . . . Citizens from most of Zaire's regions had simply been purged from the armed forces. . . . [Recruitment] focused increasingly on the northwest corner of Equateur, especially the subregions of northern and southern Ubangi.[17]

Schatzberg recounts instances of soldiers from Haute-Zaire threatening villagers in Bas-Zaire with genocide.[18]

> The problem, ultimately, is that both citizens and soldiers know the latter are not present in the countryside to protect lives, property, or the state's territorial integrity. . . . [They] are present to intimidate and control the population . . . [and] are responsible for violently repressing revolts, strikes, rebellions, and any other regime-threatening manifestations of unhappiness with the *Mobutiste* social, economic, and political order,[19]

he writes, concluding his searing criticism:

> The [Zairian] state, when viewed from abroad, may well be weak according to certain evaluative criteria. . . . But, from the vantage point of villages and

towns, even a ragtag, underpaid, poorly disciplined, and utterly corrupt pla-
toon of Zairian soldiers represents a truly awesome power. Their often-chaotic
presence and occasionally anarchistic behavior constitutes a latent threat to
Zaire's people—a threat, moreover, they understand only too well.[20]

While Mobutu played cat and mouse with his political opponents in mid-
and late 1991, he also initiated a restructuring of the army, in an attempt to
improve its quality.[21] The aim was to create a rapid intervention force, which
would lead to the dissolution of the DSP, whose parachutists would become
a reserve force. The Garde Civile wasn't mentioned in the restructuring ordinance, but it was assumed they would become the police, with responsibility for borders. The one issue, however, that Mobutu failed to address adequately, if at all, in his restructuring plans was the dire economic condition of
individual soldiers. Between February and October 1991, military pay had
fallen by around 300 per cent in most sections of the armed forces. By the
time rioting, led by soldiers of the 31st Battalion, erupted in several parts of
the country in September, soldiers were eating one meal a day and were
barely able to support their families.

The political crisis that existed between the regime and the opposition in
late 1991 was reflected in the relations within the regime itself, as Mobutu
juggled with the complexion of the government in his efforts to ensure that a
political opening would not undermine him personally. The fallout from the
riots, which erupted in Kinshasa and later in Shaba that September, left
Mobutu's strategy of manipulation in tatters. "Why hadn't the army been
paid properly? It's the result of many years of economic growth, during
which time the salary has remained the same. Changes in the army salary are
part of a two-year [reform] program. You can't accuse me of provoking the
army. I found this situation [when I became prime minister]," a defensive
Mulumba Lukodji, the prime minister, told me in Kinshasa within hours of
the riots subsiding.[22] He continued:

> The troubles have been a big disappointment [for Mobutu], because the army
> and the security forces are the domain of the president. That's how, on the ba-
> sis of the constitution, we are organized here. He is responsible for foreign af-
> fairs, defense and security, and I'm responsible for the other sectors. The fact
> that he has invested so much in the army in the last years . . . you can under-
> stand his disappointment. For many years he has built his national credibility
> on his role as a peacekeeping African leader, in his own country and neighbor-
> ing African countries. To see his best troops behaving like they did has been a
> very very big disappointment for him. I used my personal contacts with the
> army to try and regain a position, and I think I succeeded in not antagonizing
> the forces involved in the operation.[23]

The rioting led by the 31st Battalion had been a shock to the government. Lukodji had been involved in raising $15 million owed as salary arrears to the troops, who had begun to be paid prior to the destruction. However, the troops had refused their pay, on the grounds that they were owed more. Three days later the violence erupted, leaving around 130 people dead and damage worth around $1 billion. Within a week, Lukodji was sacked. The combination of events during that tense week in Kinshasa plunged Mobutu into the midst of a political crisis that only the division and weakness of the opposition allowed him to survive. Key to the crisis was the army, as one political observer (who later advised Mobutu) said:

> There's a political conscience within the army. For twenty years they haven't revolted. But now they have had enough. Lukodji was aware of the crisis in the army. He received an ultimatum on Friday saying they had refused their pay. But why did they loot certain ministries? Because there is a political conscience. Mobutu knows that the army wouldn't shoot on the public. In that way the government is weak. The soldiers see the cause of change as being as much theirs as that of the people.[24]

The FAZ was drawn from families who were facing the hardship of Zaire's economic decline as dramatically as everybody else. Mobutu continued to make the calculation that his direct control of the defense ministry, in defiance of demands by the political opposition that the National Conference decide all cabinet posts, was essential to the prestige of the regime, as well as its survival. The question continued to arise as to why the army had rioted. Was it a protest against the regime, had it been encouraged by the regime as a means of raising tension and allowing Mobutu to regain powers he was threatened with losing, or was it simply an expression of extreme frustration? Kabuya Lumuna's conclusion above, that the riots were the result of the politicization of the army, suggests that there were elements of all three explanations lying behind the army action. Frustration with Mobutu, with the opposition, and with the plummeting living standards faced by most of the population had infected all sections of Zairian society, outside the coterie of officials immediately around the presidency. Mobutu's strategy of keeping the army weak to ensure it did not overthrow him had started to backfire, and the president sought to reimpose his control by reorganizing its structure and resisting the forces of political reform.

In the wake of the riots, Mobutu declared on state radio that the rioting amounted to an "insurrection. I could have used the forces that remain loyal to the head of state to apply the full force of military rule. But I preferred to use my wisdom," he said.[25] In fact, it is doubtful that the section of the armed forces to which he was referring—the DSP—would have confronted other sections of the army. The DSP was also said to be divided along ethnic lines between Mobutu's Ngbandi—which dominated the force—and other

ethnic groups, which ultimately strengthened the majority of the DSP in
their loyalty to Mobutu. Singa Boyenge, a senior FAZ general, told me, long
after the riots had crystallized the role of the army in the transition period,

> The generals see their chief as being the head of state. [The prime minister]
> couldn't replace the army chiefs, because he would court a conflict with
> Mobutu. The reason for the army generals remaining faithful to Mobutu is be-
> cause they're all from his tribe, the Ngbandi. All the other tribes are sidelined.
> Among the lower ranks there are other tribes, but they are marginalized.
> Money is also the thing which keeps the generals faithful. He gives them
> money. But tribalism is more profound.[26]

General Boyenge had been the head of the domestic intelligence service,
the Service Nationale de l'Information et de Protection (SNIP), as well as
having been defense minister and head of the gendarmerie. He had also led
Zaire's troops against the Katangese uprising in the 1977 Shaba war. According to Singa, there were lower ranks within the military that hoped to take
over the army if Mobutu's closest collaborators were ousted in army reforms.
These Mobutu faithful within the military were in Kinshasa, while units of
the DSP were in the capital as well as in Goma, Lubumbashi, and Gbadolite,
Mobutu's rural retreat in the far north of Zaire. The concentration of elite
troops in these areas had isolated them from the rest of the military, who
"haven't benefited from the corruption," Singa said.[27] But even within the
supposedly favored elements of the armed forces, there was discontent:

> The lower ranks are incapable of reacting to the inequalities within the army.
> Mobutu has concentrated all the army resources in Kinshasa. For the riots of
> 1991, the military knew about it beforehand. It was a reaction to the situation
> within the army. The army sees Tshisekedi as acceptable. It doesn't matter to
> the FAZ whether it is one person or another who is leading, even though
> Mobutu has ousted most Kasaians from the army. After a coup attempt in
> 1978, Mobutu ousted Kasaians, Bandundans, and Shabaians from the army.[28]

The period following the September 1991 army riot saw Mobutu forced
to address not only the fracturing of the military machine that had sustained
him, but also the impact of political pressure for change, as expressed in the
outlook of rank-and-file troops. Mobutu had not been successful in preventing the polarization of political views in the wider society from infecting the
army. To spread the load of the crisis, Mobutu was in great need of incorporating his main political opponents into government.

On 30 September 1991, Etienne Tshisekedi accepted the post of prime
minister with the agreement of other members of the Sacred Union. Mobutu
arrived late for their first meeting, at the Palais de Marbre (Marble Palace), in

a smart Kinshasa suburb. Tshisekedi arrived even later. Mobutu arrived in a convoy of three limousines guarded by a small armored car. Each of the limousines had blackened windows. The game, the challenge to any would-be assassin, was to guess which one Mobutu was in. The answer was only provided when an electric window slid down and the familiar leopard-skin hat appeared. Mobutu, the "Big Man," stepped out of the car, strode purposefully across a lawn surrounded by severe-looking members of the DSP hidden behind wraparound dark glasses. They walked past a dramatic mosaic decorating the entrance, which depicted a torch-bearing classical figure rushing into a wild wind that blew his wavy locks as he surged forward to an ill-defined victory while stroking a leopard that galloped at his side. The figure evoked the classical fantasy of Mobutism, the creed of Mobutu Sese Seko Kuku Ngbendu Wa Za Banga, the full name of the Zairian leader, which may be translated as "the indomitable warrior who goes from victory to victory leaving fire in his wake."

The spectacle was nothing if not sinister. Mobutu did not speak. He was clearly awaiting Tshisekedi, and was reluctant to enter the building before the archrival who had famously described him as a "monstre humaine" (human monster). Eventually Tshisekedi arrived. Mobutu was awaiting him in an anteroom. They met in a gloomy hallway. Some photographers asked them to shake hands. But they would not. They stood side by side, refusing even to look at each other, before Mobutu entered an adjoining room, where he sat at the end of a large table, at which the main opposition party leaders were already seated. Flanked by Tshisekedi on one side and Nguza Karl-i-Bond on the other, he stared blankly at the gathered media, before booming unequivocally: "Les journalistes peuvent partir" (the journalists can leave). But nobody left. Then he repeated the order, and the room slowly emptied, as the media left for a bar to drink beer that, despite the building being an official residence of one of the world's richest leaders, was sold at a premium.

It was revealing that, within four days of taking up his post as prime minister, the real prizes for which Tshisekedi had hoped when he accepted his position continued to evade him. Control of the army remained the key issue, as Tshisekedi made clear in our interview:

> I am prime minister in name, but I haven't actually taken on the functions. Mobutu [insists he] will stay as minister of defense and security. The army and security services have played a role in the condition of this country and in matters of human rights. I must have total control of defense. Mobutu doesn't see this. He is insisting that defense is his prerogative that he is not predisposed to give to another person. But this government cannot be anything other than a government of change, and should have total mastery of defense and security.[29]

The same day Mobutu told the French daily newspaper *Libération* that: "The instrument of power is the army. One of the attributes of the sovereignty of the country is the army. . . . I have nothing except the right to nominate and also the right to revoke. All that is in the constitution."[30] The implication was that he had the power to sack Tshisekedi, just as, he asserted in the same interview, his opponent's appointment as prime minister had in fact been his initiative. Two days later, however, Mobutu's determination to placate the political opposition while retaining real power for himself through control of the military led to the collapse of the accommodation. Mobutu had prepared for the inclusion of opposition politicians in government by, first, sacking the army chief of staff, General Manzembe Mayibanga, and replacing him with General Mahele Liyeko, who had been credited with preventing troops from ransacking Kinshasa airport during the riots earlier in the month. Many of the powers of the defense minister were then transferred to General Liyeko, in anticipation of a change in the political colors of the defense minister. Second, he insisted at the meeting in the Palais de Marbre that ten ministerial posts be reserved for members of the ruling MPR. This would have given the MPR a majority in the cabinet.

By 10 October, the tension felt in the immediate aftermath of the rioting had returned. Armored cars appeared on the streets; troops leered at visitors to Tshisekedi's house in Limete. Nobody was in control of this vast country. Kinshasa's gloomy, crumbling streets turned to lakes when the ever present rain clouds burst. The lingering odor of burning wood and a film of smoke seemed always to rise in the evenings, when darkness suddenly fell and the rivals for power in Zaire gathered in their homes to plot the future, encumbered always by the aching fear that the very mention of Mobutu's name continued to inspire in the people. "Mobutu has created a fear among the people of Zaire like the fear one has of animals," Tshisekedi told me, as we sat beneath a large canopy assembled in his garden in which party meetings were often held.[31] As night fell, and the city hummed, the fear intensified, and it became ever clearer that the fight was a fight to the death and that Mobutu would use every weapon he had to ensure that whoever died on the way, he would never be a sacrifice. Whatever talk there may have been of democracy, both its proponents and opponents knew where the real power lay, in part due to the brutality of their battle with each other, and in part because the fear of national disintegration was very real and necessitated a strong army at the behest of the government to suppress any such tendencies.

For Mobutu, his entrenched position within the army was, he clearly believed, the guarantee of his continuing role:

They want my head. They all want my head—the Belgians, the French, the U.S. If my wife isn't smiling in the morning, the West asks: Why isn't she smiling? *I* am change. The policies of democratization are mine. It can't happen without financial and military assistance. The road is not calm. And I am the

creator of that army. There were forty-four mutinies during the colonial period. That has not happened since I took over.[32]

He was correct in his assessment that he alone could guarantee a peaceful
transition. In fact he alone could guarantee a transition. Unless he decided to
guarantee it, it would not work—for the simple reason that he could and
would destroy it, if he felt it was not working in his interest. It was never the
case that Mobutu had created an institutional reality in Zaire that could
withstand gradual change. What he had created was a system of rule based
on the theft and redistribution of the country's resources, at the center of
which he remained. Change meant getting rid of him. His departure was always going to bring the collapse of that system. What was less certain was
the extent to which the country at large, with its tenuous attachment to the
centralized ruler, would collapse along with the system. As the transition
program ground to a halt, what became clear was that Mobutu's system was
sucking in all the resources of the country, merely to sustain itself.

As the country stumbled through the 1990s, along with much of the rest
of the continent, in which a variety of forms of repression backed by the
military were confronted by new reformist movements, it was the extent of
the past failure to create effective and responsible armed forces, which almost alone could have symbolized and perhaps even created the reality of
nationhood, that was most catastrophic. By the time Zaire finally collapsed, following the invasion of 1997, it was clear that Mobutu's system
could never have changed. The knots that bound it could either tighten or
snap. So they snapped. The army, which had been created as a means of internal repression, collapsed, along with the mythical state of which it was
part, and Zaire was no more.

ARMY OF THE PEOPLE, ARMY AGAINST THE PEOPLE

Our army fights with the desperation of a people who are threatened with extermination. The secret success of the Biafra army is the soul of Biafra. When I
talk about the soul of the army and the spirit of the army, these can in no way
exist in a vacuum. The spirit of the Biafra army arises from the spirit of the Bi-
afran people. Our army has been popularized and has become a people's
army. . . . In Nigeria it is not quite the same.[33]

Ojukwu's ideal of a people's army "rising from the spirit of the people"
could not have been further from what Nigeria managed to produce in the
decades following Biafra's defeat.

Almost thirty years after Odumegwu Ojukwu, the leader of Biafra and the
military commander of the army that plunged Nigeria into a devastating civil
war between 1967 and 1970, spoke these words, Nigeria finally emerged from

the plague of military rule. Thirty years of brutality, corruption, and wasted opportunities have debilitated the national psyche and threatened the unity of the country. The motivation behind military rule, and the response to it from within the civilian population, has perhaps been more starkly illustrated in Nigeria than anywhere else in sub-Saharan Africa. The dynamics of change have been exposed, by way of the transition back to a short-lived civilian government in 1979, the resumption of military rule in 1984, a flawed attempt to manufacture a return to civilian rule in 1993, followed by the tyranny of Sani Abacha, and most recently the return to a democratic system that followed his demise. The way the dynamics of change have operated has revealed above all the disdain with which the country's elites view the masses.

Africa's most populous country has been routinely manipulated by a succession of largely corrupt and disingenuous civilian governments alternating with military leaders whose success in taking power was usually their sole success. The ability of the military leaders to create the conditions for good governance was less hampered by the enormity of the task than by their own lack of interest in meeting such a challenge if it impeded their goal of self-enrichment. But rather than revealing an innate commitment to democracy and civilian rule, Nigeria's military state governors and senior army officers tended during the run-up to the 1999 elections to wrap themselves in a cloak of false generosity when—with a feigned air of benevolence toward the civilian population that so loathed them—they portrayed themselves as charitable and receptive in agreeing to give up their power. In fact they had no choice; the population had been brought to the boiling point by the brutality and venality of the Abacha regime. Despite their continued disdain of the population, however, the message from the military was that, in deference to the popular will, it would return to barracks forthwith. Only months beforehand, during the worst days of Abacha's junta, the same officers seemed content to disregard the fact that popular opinion had turned against them many years beforehand.

Ojukwu's ideal of a people's army "rising from the spirit of the people" could not have been further from what Nigeria managed to produce in the decades following Biafra's defeat.

The historical conditions that have fostered the climate in which military rule replaces civilian government are only one source of explanation for the appearance of military governments. The fact that more than a handful of military regimes have dominated the lives of the people of many African countries since their independence should not be seen as somehow "natural" to the condition in which those countries have found themselves. Nevertheless, it remains true that, by 1990, more than three decades after the first African colony became independent, "no election [had] ever ousted a ruling party from office."[34] History, or perhaps simply the succession of events that has led to armies taking power, cannot be ignored. In the most detailed account of the military rule of General Ibrahim Babangida between 1986 and 1993, the advent of military rule at key points in Nigeria's history since independence in 1960 is cast in the light of civilian failure. "In each case, military intervention was preceded by a broad loss of political legitimacy due to widespread corruption, poor economic performance, electoral fraud, political violence, and rising ethnic and regional conflict deliberately mobilized for political ends."[35]

Whereas in mature democracies there is a role reserved for the other side in the form of an official opposition, the shift from military to civilian rule means that the soldiers who have controlled the autocracy become, not the opposition, but the supposed guarantors of the security of the people by whom they have been ousted. It is a wholly different scenario, one that has few parallels outside the developing world. Of major importance, also, is the post–Cold War absence of ideology. This absence meant that the new era would always be marked more by personalities than political creeds. Ideas about political economy did not mark one party out from another during the early 1990s, when new parties emerged and incumbent regimes devised their strategies for clinging on to power. Opposition parties and individual opposition leaders became the symbols, in themselves, of change.

Almost alone among African countries, Nigeria has experienced a variety of systems, all of which have ended in failure. Even so, far from dampening hopes of creating a functional system of constitutional rule, the failures intensified the determination to alternately forge or await a workable formula.

> What became obvious in the seventeen years between the first [Nigerian] coup in January 1966 and October 1979 when the Second Republic was born and December 1983 when it was overthrown, was that the politicians had forgotten the mistakes and excesses that led to the overthrow of the First Republic. The public, on the other hand, had greeted the return to civil rule with euphoria, and in spite of the previous experience with politicians in the First Republic, demonstrated active support for the democratic process. So, what went wrong?[36]

Jimi Peters's main conclusion is that democracy remained weakened by the political conflicts that are an essential part of democracy itself. This situation was made worse by the greed of the civilian politicians, who had behaved in a way that undermined public confidence even before the return to civilian rule in 1979. Under the government of Alhaji Shehu Shagari, they secured financial and other perks, which

> created the impression of a group out to enjoy itself at the expense of the public rather than serve it. . . . They not only voted outrageously high salaries for themselves, but also demanded a number of prerequisites that included, amongst other things, flats provided with color television sets, air conditioners, telephones, living quarters for servants and uninterrupted water and electricity supply. Beer and soft drinks were sold to them at greatly reduced prices, and

parties organized monthly. . . . [The] feeling was that only on the question of their welfare could the politicians agree on anything.[37]

Corruption alone assured the functioning of the political party machinery,[38] and democracy was so weakened by the civilian-led system that it "had been in jeopardy for the past four years [1979–1983]. It died with the elections. The army only buried it. They didn't kill it. The politicians killed democracy," Peters quotes General T. Y. Danjuma, the army chief of staff in 1979, as saying.[39]

The 1 January 1984 military coup in Nigeria was justified by the new military president, Major General Muhammadu Buhari, as a response to the "halfhearted" manner in which Shagari's civilian government had attempted to confront Nigeria's vulnerability to global oil prices.[40] Five days later he said:

> While corruption and indiscipline had been associated with our state of development, these twin evils in our politics have attained unprecedented height over the past four years. The corrupt, inept, and insensitive leadership in the last four years had been the source of immorality and impropriety in our society, since what happens in any society is largely a reflection of the leadership of that society.[41]

But the Buhari regime, which had at first been welcomed, quickly came to be associated with draconian economic austerity measures, and moreover it failed to prosecute and punish most of those accused of corruption during the Shagari years.[42] Meanwhile, Buhari failed to watch his own back, and was overthrown by Babangida, following a power struggle within the military, on 27 August 1985. The changeover heralded the longest political transition in Nigerian history, and set the military and the civilians along divergent paths that, even with the election of the soldier-turned-civilian Olusegun Obasanjo in 1999, have still to meet.

The Babangida years gradually confirmed the popular distrust of the military, as Peters writes: "Although many have argued that General Babangida had a hidden agenda to perpetuate himself in office long before he got to power, I think the idea only became real when he saw how easy it was to manipulate the public, including its leading figures, and get away with it. . . . By the time society realized what was going on, things were out of control."[43] What has been most clearly exposed by military rule is that the social and political structural defects of civilian rule often used as the justification for the military seizing power are themselves the very source of military power, as is reflected in the attitude of military officers toward transitions to civilian rule. "[The] transition program of the Babangida regime stands out in bold relief in a post-independent Africa whose ruling regimes—military *and* civilian—have primarily sought to demobilize the people by reducing their involvement in politics, eliminating or weakening participatory structures and institutions, canceling elections, and neutralizing political opposition."[44] In such a situation, there is no level playing field. Taken as a whole, populations are either in the military or the civilian camp, and this defines many of their political interests. Civilians have played major roles in the military governments that have been imposed upon Nigeria, and indeed in most African countries that have endured army power.

From the perspective of the military ruler, the key priority is not the deliverance to the population of the promises made in the heady days following the coup. Much more important is the retention of power in the face of threats from within the ranks of the military itself. "The military was President Babangida's major constituency that he dared not displease" writes J. Bayo Adekanye,[45] a fact that, aside from leading to a careful ethnic balance within the army, ultimately led to "increased differentiation of the military from the rest of society, as measured by the huge privileges that came to be accorded to military status. It was as if the whole machinery of the Nigerian state were being put at the service of the military, both serving and retired."[46] So important is the need to keep the military happy, that it is little wonder that, faced with their own illegitimacy, military rulers are as preoccupied with looking behind them as they are with looking forward. Consequently, the character of the army determines the style and structure of rule, the system of preferment, and the allotment of resources. The needs of the people the coup was supposed to serve become secondary to the retention of power. An economic Structural Adjustment Program (SAP), introduced by Babangida in June 1986 while military officers were being provided with millions of Naira for the purchase of staff cars, had "for the military rulers, [brought] such destabilizing political effects that their instinctive reaction was to seek to buy more security through recourse to greater coercion and authoritarianism."[47]

Babangida was a master manipulator, capable of using all the means at his disposal to ensure that he remained all-powerful within the military. Moreover, he used that power to ensure that the increasingly bitter distrust of the military prevailing within the civilian political environment did not infect the army ranks. "A major focus of Babangida's management strategy toward the military as institution was aimed at preventing the armed forces at all costs from entertaining common cause with disaffected groups in civil society, even if this meant inciting the armed forces' latent antipathy against civil society."[48] He used instability as a weapon within the armed forces to ensure that nobody rose to such prominence or confidence that his own position as the supreme power could be questioned, in particular by those members of the military who were not part of the military government.

Babangida's long-drawn-out transition to civilian rule finally reached a conclusion with civilian elections on 12 June 1993, fought between two parties (the National Republican Convention—NRC—and the Social Democratic Party—SDP) that had been created by the Armed Forces Ruling Council (AFRC). Observers generally concluded that the elections had been conducted correctly, leading to the victory of Chief Moshood Abiola, the SDP candidate. He received votes from across the country, which in itself marked a break with the past tradition of regionally and ethnically based support. On 2 January 1993 a National Defence and Security Council (NDSC) had been installed, chaired by Babangida. On 23 June the NDSC declared the 12 June election result invalid, suspended the National Electoral Commission, and repealed all laws pertaining to the transition to civilian rule. An interim national government was installed under Ernest Shonekan.

More importantly, the interim period experienced a power struggle within the military hierarchy, which saw Babangida forced to resign from the NDSC under pressure from General Sani Abacha, the secretary of defense. On 17 November 1993, Shonekan handed over power to Abacha, and all talk of a transition to civilian rule stopped. Only with Abacha's death in 1998 and his replacement by General Abdusalami Aboubacar did the military—which by then had become so loathed that its activities risked creating the conditions for a civil war in Nigeria—realize that it had gone too far in engineering Nigeria's degradation for it to consider remaining in power.

To return to Babangida's role, it has been well summarized: "In the end, General Babangida outsmarted himself, as his constant manipulations alienated public opinion and trust rather than uniting the citizenry behind the government, while providing the former political class the opportunity to sow the seeds of more discord and disaffection."[49]

In the meantime, Babangida continued to regard civilians with disdain, their relationship with the armed forces centering, as he put it, on "the intractable question of *who does the military perceive must control its organization*. . . . [It] is the military who can work out a relationship that can lead to some civilian-military equilibrium and not the civilian political authority. I believe that it is only the military that can successfully lead the armed forces back to the barracks."[50] Babangida secured a mandate from the army to rule the country, which he retained through manipulation of army appointments. He did not create the conditions in which democracy could follow smoothly from this period of military rule, despite his pretense that his rule was somehow transitional:

[The] whole thrust of Babangida's rule was to increase rather than diminish political authoritarianism, for three major reasons. The first is the basic antidemocratic nature of the military *qua* military. The second . . . [was the] imposition of the economic reform package called SAP,[51] which tended to induce increased reliance on coercion and authoritarianism. And the third was Babangida's own personal leadership style and strategies, which led to relentless enhancement and centralization of the security and intelligence apparatus under the presidency. These authoritarian practices of the regime, using structures of the state power not markedly changed from the colonial era, were incapable of nurturing the democratic orientations among the citizenry essential for running a constitutional government.[52]

If the armies of Africa are not able to use their power to oversee transitions deemed essential to creating the conditions in which good government can take root, then where else does the power lie which will allow the creation of institutions which will bring a new dispensation? As in Burundi, the military in Nigeria was the source of the problem of good governance, the problem that—so Babangida claimed—he had seized power to resolve. At the heart of the problem lies the composition of the armies, and the use of that composition to sustain the ruler in power. Babangida promoted, dismissed, and retired senior officers throughout his eight-year rule. He manipulated the military hierarchy by mixing religions, tribes, and generations, as a means of preventing a concentration of power outside the presidency. Coupled with the alienation of the army from the civilian population—an alienation created by the disparity in material wealth and exacerbated by the routine brutality of the regime, as well as its venality and corruption—the result was a transition that led to an election in 1993 whose result proved unacceptable to the military, and brought the reimposition of military rule. The army and the people were simply moving in opposing directions, with the former barely regarded as a guarantor of security for the latter, or even necessarily as a guarantor of security for the nation.

It was the growing realization of this fact, not only in Nigeria but also across the continent, that forged much of the political landscape in the 1990s. Institutional weakness, even collapse, is a thread running through African history, as political polarization has exposed national institutions as being little more than interest groups. The inherent weakness and isolation of these institutions—in particular the armies, which have defined the character of so many governments—have ultimately emerged to haunt the leaders who have used them to assert the myth of their own power yet deliberately kept them weak.

The 1990s exposed the rawness of the power of regimes whose internal structures simply lacked the capacity to act on behalf of the nations they claimed to serve, so isolated were they from the populations they dominated. In contrast to the Babangida juggling act, however, the many dangers facing Nigeria as a result of the practices of the 1993–1998 Abacha regime had at their core the failure to achieve a balance within the army itself:

After a stopgap period of about four months, the leadership of the country again went to the Hausa/Fulani of the north when General Sani Abacha, a Hausa, assumed power. That Abacha has held on to power against the will of many people in the south, especially among Abiola's[53] ethnic group, the Yoruba, has further aggravated the north-south ethnic tension. An indication of the indignation felt by many Yoruba people for the Abacha regime is their attempt to ostracize those Yoruba elements in the government. Although the government still clamps down on opposition, many individuals and the media especially in the [non-Hausa] south continue their opposition.[54]

The failure to maintain a regional balance within the military had ignited the brewing conflict that erupted into the 1967–1970 civil war.

An intense inter-ethnic hostility between the Igbo and the Hausa-Fulani was related to the pattern of killings which took place during the two *coups d'etat* of 1966. In fact they led to a complete breakdown of order and discipline within the military organization itself. Ethnicity battles had eroded the *esprit de corps* of the army and regionalist philosophy had gained popularity.[55]

The devastation caused by the war and the military defeat of the eastern Nigerian republic of Biafra by the Nigerian federal army "fully militarized the processes of government,"[56] a development facilitated by the sudden increase in Nigeria's income from petroleum in the mid-1970s, which allowed extensive restructuring, and a sudden escalation in wealth that appeared as some sort of compensation for the horrors visited on the population during the war. In the process, the states of the Nigerian federation became closely tied to the central, military government, in whose hands the oil wealth lay and from whose coffers grants to the states were disbursed.

As Babangida prepared for the handover of power, originally intended to be on 2 January 1993 but then delayed until 12 June 1993, a key concern was to create the conditions in which a future military coup would be unlikely, by professionalizing the army in a manner likely to terminate the political aspirations of its recruits. However, "the only sure way to reinstate a dominant professional ethic in the army would be a sweeping purge of senior ranks—a course of action which Babangida clearly could not contemplate."[57] Still, the process of transition through which Babangida took Nigeria, culminating in the 12 June election, was too tortuous, expensive, and complicated to be simply written off as a roundabout way of ensuring ongoing military power and continued military access to state funds. When the election result was annulled, was it because Babangida didn't like the result—the victory of Moshood Abiola—or was it because he had never intended to hand over power in the first place? The most likely scenario is that the election itself—intended to be a handover of power by the military—bore all the hallmarks of a *civilian seizure* of power. Babangida was not being fêted as the man who returned Nigeria to democracy; instead, he was merely regarded as the man who had led the country down a tortuous path, during which frustration grew, anger rose, poverty worsened, and the corruption of the military hierarchy abounded as never before:

> The political environment surrounding the 12 June presidential election is crucial to understanding the attitude of the government both in organizing and then in scuttling it. [It] is not likely that General Babangida truly intended to hand over power by organizing the election. It was the hostile political environment that compelled him at least to appear to be doing so by going forward with the election. This environmental factor can be explained at the national and international levels.[58]

Just as Babangida had had little real choice but to embark on some sort of transition program, so he had no choice but at some point to reach the conclusion of that program. His decision to annul the poll on 23 June and call a fresh presidential election isolated him,[59] confirmed popular suspicions—if they still needed confirming—of the military government, and set Nigeria adrift. Babangida's specific reasons for annulling the election, which was declared generally free and fair by independent election observers, were indeed barely credible. He said there had been a

> tremendous negative use of money during the party primaries and presidential election . . . [and] documented and confirmed conflict of interest between the government and both presidential aspirants, which would compromise their position and responsibilities were they to become president . . . [and that] to proclaim and swear in on the basis of the 12 June election, a president who encouraged a campaign of "divide and rule" among Nigerian ethnic groups would be detrimental to the survival of the Third Republic.[60]

Above all, Babangida's statement exposed his deep-seated disdain for Nigerian civil society. The political climate was so charged that the most inflammatory act the military regime could carry out would be to tantalize the public with promises of an end to military brutality, graft, and dictatorship, and then deny them the fruits. This was the ultimate form of divide and rule: creating a division between the army on one side and the population on the other. On all these counts, the Babangida years will forever be notorious. The catastrophic downward economic spiral was in large part the work of the corruption that became a way of life during the Babangida presidency; to make such an accusation against the civilians was a mark of such shameless and overweening arrogance, that it was bound to unleash popular condemnation. Equally, his alleged concern over the power play cited as reason to question the credibility of the civilian candidates is likely to have been inspired by his own concerns for his own position within the army, where political pressures had turned Babangida into a beleaguered figure with limited personal political support.[61]

To add a final insult to popular hopes, Babangida revealed his most telling reason for annulling the election. The election, he made clear, had not healed the problem of nationhood. Nor, despite all the time he had taken to create the conditions in which such issues could be addressed, had he perhaps ever intended it to do so. What Babangida in his arrogance failed to acknowledge was that there was indeed a lessening of these very ethnic divisions in the nationwide response to his decision to defy public opinion and annul the election. The military government had itself meanwhile exacerbated ethnic tensions in areas where such tensions had erupted during its term in office. Yoruba discontent, the closure or censoring of newspapers owned by southerners, and tribal and religious tensions, were all the result of a distinctly partisan strategy conducted by the military government.

However devastating the fallout from Babangida's annulment of the election was for the Nigerian population, the most immediate impact was felt within the army itself. The military was divided between those who had prepared for a handover of power as being the most propitious step, and those who remained content to see Abiola, a southern civilian, denied the presidency. Abiola had scored highly in the military vote, and had courted military officers prior to the election. The divisions within the army culminated in the 18 November 1993 coup led by General Sani Abacha. Abacha's seizure of power was in retrospect hardly surprising, though at the time certainly a shock. It seemed to confirm the flimsiness of all that had preceded it. Abacha made the usual promises of a return to civilian rule, at some date in the future. But within hours he had launched Nigeria's headlong plunge into its darkest years of violence, political turmoil, and instability since the civil war. The entire country was left reeling from the brutality of the regime. In the process, the isolation of the military from the people was cemented. Recognition of this isolation emerged from the military side only with the death of Abacha, the accession of General Aboubacar, and the rapid and real transition he initiated, which culminated in the inauguration as president on 29 May 1999 of Olusegun Obasanjo, a former military ruler who had swapped his uniform for civilian dress.

Thus, Nigeria's army left power, disgraced, undoubtedly enriched (Abacha alone was believed to have stolen up to $4 billion), and above all isolated from the people whose lives and livelihoods it was supposed to protect, but for which it in fact represented the greatest single threat. Even though it remains an open question whether Nigeria was any more ready for civilian rule in 1999 than it had been in 1993, the cruelty and decay of the Abacha years fully exposed the immense shortcomings of military rule. The execution in November 1995 of Ken Saro-Wiwa, the writer and leader of the Ogoni people in their conflict with the government, and eight other Ogoni activists, was a gesture of pure brutality.[62] It exposed not only the cruelty of the government, but also the weakness of civil institutions, in particular the justice system. As with Babangida, the execution also revealed the horrifying lengths to which the

Nigerian military was prepared to go to taunt the civilian population that it regarded with such disdain. But the brutality bore no fruit. Nigeria's suspension
from the British Commonwealth in the wake of the Ogoni executions isolated
it internationally. Abacha had become a remote figure, and his sudden and
timely death in 1998 was the surprise departure that Nigerians had theretofore
only been able to dream of. "Thank God that evil man has gone," said Wole
Soyinka, the Nigerian Nobel Prize–winning author.

Meanwhile, nothing had been gained by the excesses of military rule. Until
1999, Obasanjo's handover of power to Shagari in 1979 had stood alone as an
example of the Nigerian military handing power back to civilians. In their
study of democracy and security in post–Cold War Africa, Amadu Sesay and
Abiodun Alao assert that it was the pressure for democratic change in the
post–Cold War period that succeeded in breaking the cycle of coups and
counter-coups which had entrapped Nigeria, as well as other countries, despite
occasional intervals in which generally shaky civilian governments had taken
over.[63] The nature of military rule, concentrated as it is in the hands of a few
autocrats, who often find they are as much at odds with each other as they are
with the people over whom they rule, has been in itself the major cause of the
failure of that rule to bring solutions to the economic and social problems that
have traditionally undermined civilian governments and created the conditions in which soldiers have left the barracks and taken over. Failure, coupled
with brutality, as well as the venality of the successive military regimes in
Nigeria, has been the recurrent theme, whichever assortment of officers has
seized power. Babangida played a personal role in every coup staged in Nigeria
between 1966 and 1985. But while the senior military personalities may have
been different, their failures were generally what united them.

The failure of the state has been felt most dramatically when it has not
only used its military structure to rule, but has also sought to infect civil society with its own weaknesses. The extreme consequences of both the isolation
of the state from the interests and needs of the people and the determination
of the state to undermine popular attempts to compensate for these weaknesses were vividly displayed in the Zaire of Mobutu, where the military was
the most important element of an institutional structure designed to be weak
while it sucked the country dry. In isolating themselves from the people so
dramatically, Nigeria's successive military rulers had taken much the same
path. But was military rule by its very nature responsible for this decline?
There is no doubt that it was, and in the 1990s, it came to represent the opposite of nationhood, institution building, and national identity. This was especially true in states like Liberia, which, instead of using their limited resources to build democracy, collapsed into civil wars that revealed the true
character and intentions of armies.

7

THE DEADLY HARVEST

Liberia At War

THE RUSTING CARCASS of an abandoned Cadillac lay beneath a colonnade at the base of the national bank's multistory headquarters.[1] I heard music playing. I had heard the song many times without knowing who played it. It became the song of the war for me, but nobody could tell me who was singing with the pain of a man who had suffered, who was looking for hope when everything around him seemed hopeless and the rules he had been raised to abide by no longer seemed to apply in the difficult world into which he had been thrust. It was July 1990, and more than a year later I stopped beside the road for a rest in the heart of the Cameroonian rain forest. A truck drove by playing the song, and I chased after the driver and found him in a bar and asked him the name of the singer, and he slowly wrote it down on a piece of paper for me, so I could buy a copy of it and play it, to remind myself of the afternoons spent in Monrovia, the city of the dead.

Prince Johnson's troops sat on deck chairs in the shadow of the national bank. They all smiled and said hello as I walked up to them. Three men in civilian clothes, sitting on the ground nearby, smiled and said hello too, but were then told by the soldiers to be quiet.

"Terrible. Terrible," the militiamen said, shaking their heads, as we talked about the massacre of civilians by Samuel Doe's troops in Monrovia's St. Peter's Lutheran Church a few days beforehand. "That's Doe," they said. Their lack of emotion made it appear almost as if they were not involved in what was going on. They didn't appear to regret not having been able to save those people, nor did they seem to feel a sense of failure at having been unable to do so, despite being part of the faction led by Prince Johnson, a faction that drew its core support from the tribe that had sought refuge in the church.

Moses, the soldier in charge of the group, instead reflected the relief of somebody who *had* been saved by Prince Johnson. Moses was not a redeemer. He was one of the redeemed.

"I have been waiting for Prince to come," he cried out, tears welling up in his eyes, and then falling down his quivering cheeks. "Now I can rejoice. He is going to steer our ship. I would rather die than see him fail," he half yelled, half moaned. Then he turned on the three men in civilian clothes sitting on the ground nearby. "Meantime, all you can do is loot and steal from innocent people. And now we are going to kill you," he yelled at the three cowering men crouched on the pavement strewn with glass and bullet cases. As he spoke three other rebel soldiers began kicking the prisoners where they sat on the ground. They beat them with their rifle butts, and kicked and kicked, as the men writhed on the floor, thin, hungry, and terrified.

Moses opened the trunk of the wrecked black Cadillac. The sun was hot that afternoon.

"And this is what they stole," he said, pointing inside at bottles of pink champagne and tins of beans and luncheon meat. "Now we are going to kill them. Because we have suffered. My family has suffered so much because of Samuel Doe. They have suffered so much." He began to cry again, uncontrollably, big tears rolling down his face. "We have suffered so much," he said, as his fellow soldiers put their hands on his shoulders to comfort him, embarrassed and smiling.

One of the rebels led me a few yards away from the looters, who remained crouched on the ground. One of the looters scuttled past me on all fours. He ran out into the road. They chased him. They opened fire. The shooting went on and on. Then the man lay on the road without moving. They turned to the other man. His face was cracked with tears.

"Don't be afraid. There's nothing you can do," Moses told me, as if to reassure me. "Go on. Write it down. Prince's army kills looters."

The second man prayed to his executioners, begged them. Then he scurried under the Cadillac. They forced him out from underneath by opening fire at him where he hid. He crawled out from beneath the car and lay on the ground wounded. Five of the soldiers pointed the barrels of their guns at where he lay. Blood pumped out from inside his pink T-shirt as they shot and shot and shot. The man curled his left leg beneath him, slowly.

Then he was still.

They offered me rice.

We ate among the spent bullet cases. A man walked past on the road pushing another man in a wheelbarrow who had a bloody wound in his leg.

The man pushing said the injured man was his brother. The rebels rounded on him.

"We saw you in uniform firing on us this morning. We're going to kill you." They prepared their guns. I moved in between them and the injured man, saying his injury meant he couldn't do much harm. Why didn't he just disappear?

"The pressman thinks he should just disappear," Moses said to the others. "Where can he disappear to?"

I told his brother to push the wheelbarrow out of the city. But the injured man kept arguing, justifying, denying the rebels' accusations that he was part of President Samuel Doe's army. I told him to get out before he was killed, and looked over to the bodies of the looters. He kept arguing. The rebels aimed their guns. I told the brother to get out of sight, and he wheeled the injured man away, and the rebels ate more rice, and I said good-bye and walked farther up Broad Street toward the Ducor Hotel. The injured man was lying farther up the hill, bleeding heavily. The wheelbarrow had tipped over. The brother was asking some people peering out of a house if they would help him. Some children nearby were throwing sticks at a lime tree, trying to bring down the unripe fruit.

Writing of Liberia—a country never officially colonized, but one that experienced a form of radical change similar to that undergone in the former European colonies, when Samuel Doe overthrew 130 years of Americo-Liberian rule in 1980—Basil Davidson concludes:

> Men like Doe are the children of their own ancestral cultures. But they are also the product of an alienation which rejects those cultures, denies them moral force, and overrides their imperatives of custom and constraint. Such cultural hybrids . . . may be said to have become "lost between two worlds"—and this saying has at least the merit of suggesting the mental confusion in which their seizure of power forces them to live.
>
> They turn to the AK-47, and use it with the blindness of the damned, at which point their power rebounds upon itself and becomes a route to suicide. It has happened in every culture dispossessed by another, and thereby riven to its roots. . . . The pathology is explicable, but only in terms of alienation. The ancestral cultures of the peoples of Liberia, as with those of neighbors near and far, knew plenty of abusive violence. But they possessed rules and regulations for the containment and repression of abusive violence; and these were the rules and regulations, before the scourge of the slave trade and the colonialism that followed it, that enabled them to evolve their sense and value of community.[2]

The suggestion is that the militaristic leaders of Africa's modern nation states have been alienated from the indigenous traditions that, if preserved, could have nurtured these states in a manner allowing a sustainable and productive marriage of established tradition and modern needs. The variety of political traditions in precolonial Africa has been broadly categorized into either centralized or segmented structures.[3] The apparent incomparability of Africa's precolonial political structures with European structures prevalent during the early years of European contact with sub-Saharan Africa contributed to the view among European academics—as well as African academics influenced by European attitudes[4]—that the continent had few or no internal checks and balances intended to avert the abuse of power. This view has led to the conclusion that dictatorship was Africa's precolonial norm. Consequently, the tendency has been to explain postcolonial dictatorship as building on precolonial traditions. Clearly the complexity and variety of systems of rule that existed in the past, and continue to exist in the early twenty-first century, is sufficient proof that no single explanation is adequate.

The question remains, however, why dictatorship has been so common. Specifically, it is necessary to ask whether the environment into which the newly independent states were born, itself *produced* these dictators, or whether they were in fact attempting to recreate aspects of the traditional systems from which Davidson says they were alienated, only this time on a *national* scale, perhaps thereby creating the alienation in the process. It should be remembered that such alienation has not always led to atrocities on the scale seen in Liberia under Doe and during the civil war that eventually toppled him. In instances where a degree of political pluralism has been sought in the late 1990s—in Ghana and Uganda, for example—the intention of those in power has been to prevent the internal regional and ethnic pattern from being projected onto the national level by attempting to create various forms of non-party democracy. The result of these attempts has ultimately been to prevent any viable opposition from organizing at all, thereby allowing the incumbents to remain in power beneath a deceitful gloss of democracy. Meanwhile, the real political relations between opposing groups are denied an effective and functioning institutionalized framework.

Wars have formed a part of the African landscape as the tragic accompaniment to the birth of democracy on the continent. In doing so, they have exposed the reality that democratic institutions alone can bring an end to the deadly harvest, born of years of misrule, that is now being reaped. Wars have not only halted the progress of change, but have also nurtured the conditions in which regimented militarism has acted to weaken states, institutions, and pluralist attitudes. Wars have fostered extremism and fear, causing the process of alienation not only to create numerous local dictators who are "cultural hybrids . . . lost between two worlds,"[5] but to plunge entire populations into the same confusion. Child soldiers, criminal warlords, the unemployed youth, and the dispossessed are now practicing war on the basis of spurious ideologies, using tribal identity as a pretext for conflicts that have in fact lost any traditional cultural consensus or meaning.

The Keeper of the Key

"It's been a very dark period in this region. It was unfortunate that there was ever a war in Liberia. To a great extent, it was unfortunate that the region had to get involved in this war."[6] Charles Taylor, chairman of the National Patriotic Front of Liberia (NPFL), the former civil servant who launched the Liberian conflict on 24 December 1989, was sitting staring at a space on the carpet of the Hôtel L'Amitié, the sand-colored luxury hotel that rises up out of Bamako's sandy streets.

Eleven months after the war had erupted, Liberia lay in ruins, a byword for horror, a nation torn apart. In response, the leaders of West Africa had gathered in Bamako, Mali, for the third attempt at a peace accord between the warring sides. "Whatever one is fighting for, could be achieved through peaceful means," Yoweri Museveni, Uganda's president, there in his role as the chairman of the Organization of African Unity, told the Bamako conference.[7] He continued:

> It's not necessary to fight until the end. If you fight up to some stage, you can easily replace fighting with negotiation. This has been pertaining in Liberia for the past four to five months. We can easily change this armed conflict into a vibrant democracy.
>
> Africa in general must take a hard look at armed conflicts. Our continent is one of the most armed in the whole world.
>
> When the Europeans were taking slaves from here, it was not only the Europeans who were taking slaves. Africans were assisting them. One chief would be in conflict with another chief. So it's incorrect to say that the Europeans were the only ones taking slaves. Are we, the present generation of African leaders, going to be like our forefathers, who failed to see our genuine African interests, when each one was trying to preserve a micro interest? What is going to be our role?

I had last seen Charles Taylor a month beforehand, in Gbarnga, the town in central Liberia he had established as his capital and military headquarters in October 1990. That year and for years to come, I spent weeks and months in Liberia, initially advancing with the NPFL as it progressed through Liberia in the first months of 1990 and then reporting from Monrovia, the capital.[8] The trip to Gbarnga in October was a turning point. Taylor had decided to install himself as president. Samuel Doe was dead, killed on 9 September 1990 by the faction led by Prince Johnson, which had broken with Taylor within days of the civil war being launched.[9] Meanwhile, Monrovia, the prize Taylor had sought, had been tenuously occupied by peacekeeping troops led by Nigeria and Ghana. These Ecomog (Economic Community Monitoring Group)[10] troops arrived at the port of Monrovia in late August and remained there for several weeks before moving into the city center and the suburbs, with the aim of driving a wedge between the rival factions.

The sending of the peacekeeping force marked the high point of attempts by Nigeria's military rulers to assert their ambition of a regional role, and was in many ways the climax of Nigeria's experience of military rule. The army-led political solutions President Babangida professed to seek for Nigeria's domestic problems were exported to Liberia, with the same mixture of poor political-diplomatic strategic thinking, ill-resourced logistical back-up, and a lack of clear vision that dominated the military governance of Nigeria itself. The result on the ground in Liberia was that, on all fronts, Taylor was isolated. He had been prevented from capturing Doe, and he then found the seat of government occupied by foreign troops who had no intention of handing it over to him. Meanwhile, he had seized most of Liberia's territory, and was using this control to restart the logging, iron ore, diamond, and gold mining industries, which sustained his war effort for a further seven years.

Some writers have asserted that had Taylor accepted the Ecomog intervention immediately, he might have become president under whatever formula for peace the Ecowas (Economic Community of West African States) states had worked out with him and the Liberian opposition in exile. Stephen Ellis concludes:

> By accepting Ecomog in 1990, Taylor could have become president with Nigerian support since he controlled most of Liberia at that juncture and already had some international backing. His failure to do this meant that, once Ecomog had intervened to secure Monrovia and had installed a puppet government, the conflict became intractable. Taylor was obliged to rethink his assumption of imminent victory and to make other plans. . . . Charles Taylor's hope in 1990 was to displace Doe as soon as possible, and assume the presidency himself, at which point he might hope to end the war, receive international recognition and run the state patronage machine in his turn.[11]

Ellis's view fails to take into account the progression of events that had led to Taylor's rejection of the peacekeeping force. When the idea of Ecomog first arose in July 1990, Doe was still alive. Following Babangida's seizure of power in 1986, Doe had become a significant ally and business partner of the Nigerian president. Taylor could not assume that Nigeria and the other Ecowas states—the West African regional states that had sent the Ecomog force—would sideline Doe if the NPFL agreed to a ceasefire and peace talks. Equally, Taylor knew that his strength would continue to be drawn for a considerable time from the strategic alliances of which he was part. Coupled with the support he had received from Libya[12] through his connections in

Burkina Faso,[13] Taylor in the early months of 1990 came to be seen by the government of the Côte d'Ivoire as a credible alternative to Doe, whom the Ivorian president Felix Houphouët-Boigny had long despised. Côte d'Ivoire, a key state within French-speaking West Africa, also retained a strong economic rivalry with Nigeria and vigorously opposed the Ecomog intervention, owing in part to its domination by Nigerian and Ghanaian troops.

These factors influenced Taylor in his opposition to Doe from the regional perspective. Meanwhile, he could not assume, prior to Doe's death, that Doe would have withdrawn from the political scene if the NPFL had ceased fire. Doe himself said he was "not going to surrender the sovereignty of Liberia to any other country, big or small. Or indeed any regional organization. . . . It is absurd and illogical for anybody to ask a Liberian to leave Liberia and stay in another country."[14] It was not a condition of the Ecomog arrival that Doe leave the country, and Doe retained a rump support within the Armed Forces of Liberia (AFL) and those members of his ruling clique who had not fled Liberia. Doe's death in September 1990 would only really have changed Taylor's attitude toward Ecomog had it been his troops, rather than those of the rival Independent National Patriotic Front of Liberia (INPFL) of Prince Johnson, who had killed the president. Meanwhile, the same Ecowas talks in Gambia that had created Ecomog had also created the Interim Government of National Unity (IGNU). The IGNU was to be installed under Ecomog protection for an initial twelve months, during which time elections would be planned. In the circumstances, it was not surprising that Taylor rejected Ecomog, denouncing it as a Nigerian-led attempt to deny him the fruits of war and rejecting an offer of six seats in the IGNU. Ellis's theory is thus on uncertain ground.

The president of IGNU, Amos Sawyer, had become increasingly suspicious of Taylor long before the Banjul meeting, at which the creation of the IGNU had been agreed on. In fact the aim of Ecowas and its troops was ultimately to prevent Taylor becoming president at all, owing to the widespread expectation that were he to do so he would likely become as dictatorial as Doe. "To see Doe replaced by something like another Doe would be too much for the Liberian people to take. Charles Taylor is predisposed to arbitrary rule, and his use of coercion is similar [to Doe],"[15] according to Sawyer. Taylor's installation of himself as president in October 1990 was the result.

"Among the lessons learned in the past ten months, is the lesson of the absolute reliance on God," Enoch Dogolea, a lay priest and Taylor's vice president until 2000,[16] told the gathering of Taylor partisans during Taylor's installation as head of state in the sun-filled hall of a long-abandoned school surrounded by forest interspersed with patches of grassland south of Gbarnga.[17] "We must see our suffering not as a curse and a punishment, rather we must see our suffering as discipline. Discipline like a father's correction of his son. You will certainly be destroyed because of your disobedience to the Lord your God," Dogolea cried. He turned to Taylor as he was about to take his oath of office and told him: "Keep peace with the people. Hear their cries. The chief architect of national construction is the Lord." The horror of Liberia perhaps did bear a resemblance to an imagined purgatory. In the school hall, as Taylor received various oaths of allegiance from his ministers a few yards from where I was standing, a young boy, perhaps twelve years old, approached me with a Kalashnikov rifle slung around his neck and demanded I give him the camera that hung from my shoulder. It was a reminder of the true extent of Liberia's collapse that one of the armed child soldiers who had played an infamously bestial role in the ranks of both sides' armies during the previous ten months could so have lost all sense of where he was. The boy cocked his gun and sneered at me, before being calmly told by an adult that he should leave me in peace.

Dogolea's assertion that Liberia's war was somehow a process of readjustment of an unruly child, or taken a few stages further perhaps a kind of exorcism, heightened the sense of desperation, anxiety, and misery into which the war had plunged Liberians, by highlighting the psychological motivation of the war and diminishing the significance of any ideological content. The political momentum that had both created the conditions for war[18] and ultimately brought those isolated and dispossessed by Samuel Doe's years in power to the point where they could forge a military alliance able to confront Doe's forces[19] was not retained once the war erupted. The NPFL sought support from within the northern areas of the country traditionally inhabited by the tribes of some its senior figures.[20] Meanwhile, the Armed Forces of Liberia, the country's national army, rapidly fragmented.

"The atrocities by the AFL were caused by stupidity, ignorance, and a lack of discipline," General Hezekiah Bowen told me. We were sitting in the Barclay Training Centre (BTC), the Monrovia city center barracks that housed the AFL command.

I had first met Bowen in August 1990, during the afternoon of a day that had begun with my attempt to cross the front line dividing the city into rebel- and government-held areas. Within minutes of our crossing, AFL troops had surrounded me and two colleagues, shooting into the air, demanding that we follow them down a mud track between shacks toward a mangrove swamp, which we knew had become one of their numerous killing grounds because we had seen bodies floating from there. Terrifying minutes passed like hours, until we finally found ourselves talking with General Bowen, who was full of apologies for the way we had been treated.

By then I had lived in Monrovia for almost two months, watching with growing horror as the city was torn apart, as AFL troops executed suspected NPFL sympathizers on street corners, on the beach, or, as I later learned, at

an airstrip on the eastern edge of the city. The terror grew worse as Taylor's
NPFL drew closer from the east and north, and Prince Johnson approached
from the west. The city's people were trapped by the advancing rebels and
terrorized by the AFL forces, whose desperation and failure to confront the
rebel advance led to them turning on both the civilian population and AFL
soldiers from tribes which broadly supported the rebel forces.[21] "The army
discipline fell apart, and people just started accusing everybody of being a
rebel," Bowen told me during the April interview.

> The speed of the rebel advance frightened the soldiers in Monrovia. The Gio
> and the Mano[22] in the AFL were all arrested, even though I had used them to
> fight in Nimba early in the war. Dubar[23] had ordered their arrest. Two hun-
> dred Gio and Mano soldiers were confined to the post stockade. Doe visited
> them in July and said that they should be released. But these soldiers didn't feel
> safe. Most fled and joined the rebels. Others stayed and were killed.
>
> The army leadership at the time was very poor. The tribal links meant that
> there was no law and order within the AFL. The Krahn[24] would say, referring
> to all members of other tribes: "It's nothing but snake. If it's a small snake,
> chop it. If it's a big snake, chop it." People were doing things on their own.

Instead of the conduct of the war serving to create the conditions that
would allow those who launched it to build a new country, free from the
brutal autocracy of the kind that developed under Doe, the conflict reaffirmed the trends that Doe had allowed to become entrenched within the
practice of government. "I have risked my life. No matter who killed Doe,
I started the process. At least I was steadfast enough to start this process.
They expect me to curl up and hide under a rock. It's very unreasonable,"
Taylor told me, as darkness fell a few hours after he had inaugurated himself as president in Gbarnga.[25] He was bemoaning the fact of the Ecomog
force having acted to deny him the prizes he considered his due. "If they
want to end the conflict, they don't have to back me. You don't have to respect what I stand for," he said, in his ice-cold, air-conditioned bungalow,
which had been renamed the Executive Mansion, the name of the Monrovia presidential residence. Our discussion had followed a dinner in a hall
beside that in which he had been inaugurated, at which the hundred or so
people sitting in the dusk light had spoken not a word. It was supposed to
have been a celebration, but there was little sense of achievement, only a
hollow feeling of worry for the future. Least of all was there any certainty
as to what Taylor did stand for, the war having wrenched wide the wounds
which Doe was undoubtedly responsible for first opening, but which the
horrors of the war made it seem that Taylor was least likely to heal, if liberation was indeed his aim.

WARRIOR DREAMS

On Sundays after the lull in the fighting that had gone on during the summer of 1990, Monrovia's churches filled up with the survivors. When there had been war in the city there was just day and night, and people stayed inside their homes and died of hunger in their beds. But when the fighting seemed to stop, sometime in the autumn, and the city was quiet, people left their homes to pray in the churches and beg for food. On Mondays it was time for work, so normality must have been returning, or so people liked to say. But that was because nobody any longer knew what normality was. Nobody knew why the war happened as it did. Nobody really knew what could bring it to an end. There was no reason for it to end. The country had been carved up, and the only reason for the apparent return of normality was that nobody had decided to shatter the temporary peace.

Telephone cables drooped across Monrovia's streets. Sometimes the electricity supply was switched on, and piercing blue sparks leapt out of the houses as junction boxes exploded at the sudden surge of power after months of darkness. In the clinics and hospitals, the ghosts of the war could never be laid to rest. Every day, a child died at the city's Island Clinic. Amid the stench of the children's ward, a twelve-year-old boy lay in a cot, being fed intravenously by a drip, gasping for breath, his eyes half closed. He had been operated on for appendicitis, but it was the wrong diagnosis, and the doctors had no idea what was wrong with him. He would not last the night, a nurse said.

Many of the dead from this first of the three wars that together comprised Liberia's civil war had been buried by 1991. What remained were memories of the nightmare. In October 1992, the second phase of the war broke out, between the National Patriotic Front of Liberia (NPFL) and the regional Ecomog peacekeeping force, sent in late August 1990 to enforce a ceasefire and push the sides toward a solution. The renewed fighting in 1992,[26] then later in 1993 and 1996, proved that any expectations in 1991 of a permanent peace had been premature. By the end of the first year of the war, there were at least 30,000 people under arms in Liberia, most of them teenagers, though some as young as nine or ten years old.

An understanding of the background of the fighters who came to characterize the Liberian conflict, with their horrifying readiness to maximize the terror and pain that swept through Liberia with such ferocity, is vital to establishing the real nature of the conflict. Such an understanding is particularly important when one examines the question of how far tribal loyalties, culture, and practices determined the course of the war.

The purpose of the war was not clearly tribal, in that the motive behind Charles Taylor's invasion of northern Liberia in December 1989 was not specifically to overthrow one tribe and replace it with another. Even the avowed aim of some rebels to end the domination of the Krahn—the tribe to which President Samuel Doe belonged—was not necessarily due to cultural rivalry, but instead a result of the resentment that had built up toward all Krahn as a consequence of the favoritism shown them during Doe's decade-long presidency. Tribal loyalties did play an important role in determining which side individuals chose to fight for. However, even this issue was not clear-cut. The Armed Forces of Liberia (AFL), the government army, retained soldiers within its ranks who were members of the tribes regarded by the government as automatically sympathetic to the rebel side. Their presence within the ranks revealed that the tribal favoritism practiced by the Doe government prior to the conflict was not necessarily a deterrent to these tribes joining the army, and that any latent tension between them and Doe's tribe was not necessarily ongoing.

What changed this apparent ambiguity was the war itself, and the climate of suspicion that erupted when the fighting broke out: "Colonel Mania was left in charge of BTC in late June. Then massive killing started. The killing of AFL soldiers from the other tribes," Isaac Roberts, an AFL officer, told me.[27]

The Loma and the Gio[28] had a strong presence in the AFL. They became the main victims. From late June [1990]. These killings took place every day and every night. Michael Tilly ordered these killings. I worked with Tilly at the free port. Tilly was brave. Tilly always wanted to be the first in the battle. He was a captain. But he was more powerful than the generals. He was a warrior. He would drink blood from a skull. He would say, "*Mo Koo. Mo Koo.* I am a devil. I am a devil." This would happen at night. At the port. He would say, "The only way to be a strong warrior is to taste the blood of whom you kill." Other brave fighters could see fire in Tilly's eyes. At the port he would kill soldiers who wouldn't fight. The skull he drank from was a very old skull. I saw him drinking blood.

Michael Tilly,[29] whose atrocities played a key role in determining the image of the AFL, was instrumental once the war started in asserting the primacy of the Krahn within the AFL and creating the climate of suspicion that led to the isolation of the other tribes who served within the force. "The Krahn were dominating the AFL. They wanted all the weapons and supplies. The Krahn had all the machine guns, while all the other tribes were given shot guns," said J. Barcee Cooper, an AFL officer who deserted its ranks and joined the NPFL in 1990.[30]

At BTC there were people being held in the cells who were mostly Gio and Mano [AFL] soldiers who were kept there after being accused of being rebels. Then in the night, the Krahn soldiers would go into the cells and pick people out at random and then take them onto the beach to kill them. They never buried them very well. Then after a while they stopped burying them. When non-Krahn soldiers came to the Freeport, Tilly would ask: "*Ma Bleh You*, are you my countryman?" Then he would kill them. The soldiers would go there for rice, and he would ask them if they were Krahn. Tilly killed hundreds of non-Krahn soldiers.

Prior to the war, ethnic identity had been subject to economic and demographic pressures, as well as the whims and preferences of local politicians in pursuit of power, all of which had led to dilution. "By the 1980s . . . [the] most successful exponents of local politics were those who were appointed to a chieftaincy on the grounds that they represented a given tribe, and it was in their interest to maintain that each clan or tribe had a distinctive culture and ancestry which required autonomous administration,"[31] writes Stephen Ellis, in his study *The Mask of Anarchy*. "Chiefs became cultural brokers, translating the value of 'tribal' society to the Americo-Liberian elite, and *vice versa*."

The impact of the high culture of Liberian tribal lore and practice upon a war that seemed, at least to Western eyes, a tribal conflict has been vastly more complex. Prominent in the Liberian conflict were the shifting and even the collapse of authority. Ellis writes:

> Although almost all the fighters believed that it was possible to obtain spiritual medicine which would make them invulnerable to bullets and successful in battle, they were at the same time contemptuous of those individuals who, according to the traditional values of their home areas, should have been able to provide them with this. . . . Only the most exceptional *zoes*[32] were regarded by the irreverent NPFL fighters as having really impressive power."[33]

Ellis refers to the practice among fighters on all sides of eating human flesh as a means of both gleaning the strength to ensure success in battle, and being seen to be observant of practices emanating from the ritual of eating. But he also voices doubts as to whether the practice—which is integral to the initiation practices of the secret Poro society led by the zoes—was being practiced with conviction by the young fighters. He concludes: "[For] the fighters, the manipulation of spiritual power, including the eating of human flesh, was not only likely to give them a greater chance of success but was also one of the signs of adulthood. Since many of the fighters were young, often barely teenagers, it suggests that they regarded the battle as tantamount to an initiation into adult life."[34]

The transition from practitioner of tribal rites to warrior engaged in supposedly tribal war is not a convincing explanation of what took place in the lives of the fighters in Liberia, despite the repeated references to tribe and tribal conflict by all those involved. Instead, the war presaged the collapse of Liberia, not only physically but also—perhaps more importantly—culturally.

It was in fact the social glue provided by tradition that collapsed. "The leadership in the AFL at that time was very poor,"[35] said General Bowen, who was promoted to chief of staff of the AFL following the death of Doe in September 1990: "The Krahn would say, referring to all members of other tribes: 'If it's a snake it's a snake. If it's a small snake, chop it. If it's a big snake, chop it.' The atrocities were due to stupidity, ignorance and a lack of discipline. The tribal links meant that there was no law and order within the AFL," he told me. The AFL collapsed because tribal loyalties prevailed within it. But those tribal loyalties were an inadequate alternative to national concerns, because the tribal structure was irrelevant to the real conflict, which was essentially a fight for personal power.

It would seem logical that if the teenagers—many of them delinquents freed from jail to swell the numbers of Liberia's armies—who later committed many of the worst atrocities felt they had done such things on the basis of traditional tribal or religious conviction or practice, their later reflections upon what they had done would be colored by the sense of righteousness rather than regret or guilt. A war that lasts seven years, that engulfs the entire population of a small country, inevitably creates a generation of people who have known nothing but war. Those who knew early teenage life before the war are perhaps in a better position to reflect upon what has taken place, than those who witnessed the first violence at a very young age and subsequently became involved. A momentum builds up.

Among those who withdrew from the conflict, after first being immersed fully in its horrors, were teenagers from all sides who left the fighting altogether by taking advantage of the lull that prevailed in Monrovia following the arrival of the Ecomog peacekeeping force and the installation of an interim government in 1990–1994. It is among them that the dislocation and schizophrenia are most intense, and among them that the wide variety of interpretations of what it was they were doing is most starkly revealed. For some, far from being a war justified by the defense of traditional loyalties, the war seemed to be an aberration, in which they had engaged as "other" people, not as themselves, and in which they disguised themselves in order to hide from their true selves. For others it was a social duty, which also required the adoption of another personality, induced by protective medicines and charms.

One NPFL fighter, Elijah McCarthy, told me how it was for him:[36]

We captured ten AFL soldiers on Old Road. They put up their hands and we killed them. We cut their heads off. I don't feel good killing. I have knifeproof. But he is my enemy. I wear my charms—they are *Sonkaley Goa*. I have my medicine. It is *Seke*. I'm not sure what's in it. It was given to me by a medicine man in Saklepie. If you take the medicine then you can't have sex or eat raw cassava or palm oil. If you do, the medicine will spoil. I keep the medicine because everybody knows I'm a rebel. I wear a ring and two fetishes on rope round my neck. If you are my enemy, the ring will burn me. If somebody is my enemy at the checkpoint then I will know because my ring will tell me. If somebody is my enemy I will take him on one side. People beg. They say: "Please don't kill me." But I don't trust them. They are in my territory. I have killed fifty people. I cut their heads off or shot them. They begged for their lives, but I didn't trust them.

My people in my area like me. I did things for them. If I think about the war I feel bad, because here's my own country and we have damaged our country. Now everybody has an enemy. I don't kill innocents. I kill my enemy. I would do it to them before they did it to me. When you kill any AFL soldiers, you search their pockets. While they're bleeding you check the pockets. You see if they have any money.

McCarthy, like numerous fighters from the NPFL, the AFL, and the INPFL breakaway rebel faction, had been taken into the care of a rehabilitation program, the National Readjustment Commission, launched by the interim government in 1991. "Most of the rebel fighters were criminals before the war—petty thieves, pickpockets, troublemakers. At least 80 percent of them were like that. They have impressive criminal records," said John Nimley, who ran the center.[37] "During the war they knew that force could get anything. They thought that the same could be done here. But they are now being made to feel that they can't do that here. The fighters say that they felt good, and that now they don't. It shows that people can be two people at the same time."

After the war, the presence in the killers' dreams of the victims of their violence during the war shows that they were haunted by their own behavior, rather than gratified by or proud of what they had done. Boima Brown, an AFL fighter, told me:

I dream about the people I killed. Those who I saw face to face. I can see them. When I see them, I see them all sitting round a table. But we're not talking to each other. Nothing happens. They don't talk to me. The only thing is that they're wearing white gowns and white hats and white gloves. I don't see their bodies at all. I can't see their faces even. But I know it's them. There are forty-three of them. They don't even talk to each other. But I know it's them. Forty-three of them. All the people I killed.

We had our protection. If a bullet hits you, you just take it out. I never die. I think only that I did bad during the war. In my other dream, I came across one of my enemy. He said to me that I was going to be killed. He gave me his name and said I would be killed. He said I was the enemy. I killed his brother in real life, and his brother came in my dream. But his brother was the one I killed.[38]

The confusion of real life and the world of dreams seemed, with all those who had deserted the ranks of the armies, to have left the former combatants isolated rather than having brought them into closer proximity to the spirit world, from which dreams are regarded as a message.[39] "Most of the time I'm fighting in my dream, executing people," said Isaac Roberts, a former AFL fighter who had deserted the government and later joined one of the rebel factions.[40] "Other times I am being tied up and being taken to an execution ground, and I am going to be executed. The person who has tied me and is going to execute me is my commander. He is going to execute me at the same execution ground where I had killed people in reality." Above all, his dream suggests an enormous sense of betrayal and distrust, and the feeling that he was perhaps no better than the people he had killed and that the people on whose behalf he had killed could turn against him.

It would be a mistake to deduce too much from the experience of the dream world of Liberia's warriors. However, the spiritual aspect of the war, which only rarely involved evocation of spirits as a source of power but included the regular use of narcotic drugs to inspire courage or forgetfulness, suggests that the "tribal" or traditional aspects of culture were at most selectively applied to the reality of war. Granted, the examples cited above are from individuals who had deserted, and were perhaps less committed to the various causes they joined, despite the ferocity of violence that they admit to. But the lasting impression from these fighters is that, far from celebrating tribal identity, by way of the pursuit of ritual, they are haunted by what they have done. Their experience seems to have troubled them deeply. This tends to support the contention that rather than being a tribal war, beyond the obvious fact that it pitted identifiable tribes against each other, the Liberian war instead destroyed the tribal identity of the country, by undermining the authority of the guardians of that identity.[41] Thus Ellis speaks of the *unmasking* of the masked individuals invested with the power to evoke the power of ancestors:

> The act of exposing the masks of secret societies to public ridicule, as happened in the war, is thus tantamount to destroying the possibility of communication with the spirits since it is impossible for them to assume visible form. . . . Once the Bush Devil has been unmasked, he can no longer serve to keep people in their proper places in society, to prevent individuals from transforming in ways which are dangerous to others and to ensure orderly progress from one phase of life to another, such as from childhood to adulthood. This is a disturbing prospect when it is a mainstay of social order.[42]

The Liberian war above all exposed the impact of collapse on the level of the already shaky state, as well as on the level of local power and authority. But instead of this collapse leading to a genuine reversion to tribal loyalty or identity, disintegration left every individual isolated, alone in a sea of uncertainty, an uncertainty perhaps ultimately due more to the proven weakness of tradition than the failure of an already failed nation state.

Make War Not Peace

Rain swept across the lush meadow stretching from the verandah behind Prince Johnson's bungalow down to Stockton Creek. The soft notes of an electric organ oozed out from behind the net curtains hung across the French windows. A soldier sang as he splayed his hands across the keys of the organ.

"If you're a white man, you will be beaten. If you're a black man you will be beaten," he moaned, eyes closed, voice lilting.

Prince sat behind a desk at the end of the sitting room, which had become a cluttered operations center. A kitsch pastel portrait of Christ carrying a lamb on his shoulder had been nailed to the wall behind him, bearing the message: "Look at me and be saved." On another wall a small photograph of Yasser Arafat introduced an element of politics into the room. Prince's desk was a shrine to lofty aspiration, with a golden penholder, elaborate paper knife, small flags, a Model-T Ford in shiny metal. Prince had become an executive, and he now had the desk to prove it, while he mused over the issues of the day and yelled orders at a small secretariat at the other end of the room, whose members were furiously typing press releases and shuffling paperwork.

"Do you want to see my film?" Prince rasped. Refusing his offers was not easily done, and we were led out onto the verandah, expecting to see a visual account of Prince's adventures and exploits. A large color television was wheeled out, and Prince's wife said that she would fast-forward the video so we did not have to see ordinary shots of rebel troops. Behind the screen the rain fell across the meadow. The organist played on in the sitting room. We were given chairs in the front row. The rebels gathered in rows behind us. The singer became more passionate. The man in the next seat kept talking as the screen burst into life. A group of children played in the meadow beyond the verandah, yelling to those of their friends gathered behind us watching the film.

Samuel Doe looked out of the television screen. His face was bruised and bloody. Rolls of flab oozed out over bloodstained white underpants, which were all that he was wearing. His arms were tied tightly behind his back. The organist's plunging notes grew to a crescendo in the room beside where we were sitting, the room in fact where Doe had been sitting when the film was taken.

"I want to say something, if you will just listen to me," Doe, half-smiling, half-sneering, tells his captors. Samuel Varney and another of Prince's men, John Yormie, stroke Doe's head, which has been shaved, we are told, with a broken bottle.

"You untie my hands and I will talk. . . . I never ordered anybody's execution."

The camera moves to Prince, who is sitting behind the desk, with the same pink and blue portrait of Christ watching impassively from above him on the wall.

"I'm a humanitarian," Prince rasps. "Cut off one ear," he calmly tells his men.

The television audience sat gripped in total silence. Prince sat slightly slumped on a chair beside me, watching himself give the order to begin the torture, his hands clasped in semi-prayer. The camera swings to Doe, where he is sitting with his legs stretched out in front of him, his arms tightly tied behind him. A knife flashes in the bright light. The camera gets close. Doe is forced to lie down. The camera cannot catch the moment. An arm can be seen sawing, as a scream pierces the verandah, the meadow, the whole world. And the organist stopped, and there was silence.

Doe sits up, shaking his head violently, as his captors grapple with him. Then he is seen to blow down on his own chest, and the rebels sitting beside us say that Doe is trying to use magic to make himself disappear.

"I beg you," Doe says.

One grabs his head and forces him down onto the carpet, as the sheen of the knife catches the light, and a second scream sends the birds flying away from Prince's verandah, as the action shows Prince chewing the sawn flesh of his prey, holding an ear high above his mouth and then lowering it down.

For a few seconds the audience sat in silence, then they clapped, and a small fishing boat on Stockton Creek sent ripples across the brown water.

The action moves to the end of Prince's garden, where Doe sits bound and naked, barely recognizable, the stumps of his ears bleeding.

"Varney, I'm dying," Doe tells Prince's deputy.

"1985," says Varney, the year of the rigged elections, the failed coup, and the horror that followed it.

"We know you," another rebel soldiers tells Doe. Then Yormie says:

"We are asking you in a polite manner now: What did you do with the Liberian people's money?" But Doe refuses to say, and the knife comes out again.

"My penis. No, please, not my penis."

Tahseen, the Palestinian who had been in the city throughout and eventually thrown in his lot with Prince in August, appears on the screen. It then becomes clear that during the torture he has been holding the camera. Tahseen tells Doe to repeat after him:

"I, Samuel Kanyon Doe, declare that the government is overthrown. I'm therefore asking the armed forces to surrender to Field Marshall Prince Johnson." Doe repeats the words. His tyranny is over. Somebody says: "fuck" offscreen and is reprimanded.

"Don't abuse the man," the rebel is told.

"I want to talk. I need pee," says Doe. Then the screen went blank.

Prince Johnson and his men captured and tortured Samuel Doe on 9 September, three weeks after Prince had signed a ceasefire agreement with the AFL, in which they had agreed to fight together against Charles Taylor. Prince's film has been a best-selling video throughout West Africa ever since the event. Prince was incensed when he heard the day after the torture that Doe was dead. After that first day, he had ordered that Doe be locked in the bathroom of the bungalow and a guard be put on the door. Doe was still alive, but bleeding profusely. After being dumped in the bathtub at Caldwell, Doe spent several hours banging his head against the side of the tub and the walls of the room, eventually bringing on the hemorrhage that killed him. Prince, on hearing this, was disappointed because he said he wanted to put Doe on trial.

My two friends, Stephen Smith of *Liberation* and Patrick Robert of *Sygma*, and I walked silently to our car. The sound of the engine intruded on the vision of the world into which Prince's film had given us a glimpse. As we left, there were none of the fake pleasantries with which one usually engaged Prince, who had declared himself interim head of state following Doe's death. After that numbing film show, there was nothing to say. We all wanted to get out of his compound. It was sickening being there, being pressured by the presence of his protocol team, the sound of typewriters in the secretariat, the desk laden with his executive toys, all these things forcing us to behave in a way that confirmed the myth that he was a liberator. More than any other figure, Prince Johnson supported the view that in Liberia there was, and perhaps remains, an enormous gulf between the lofty ideal of liberation and the base reality of the country, in which savagery ruled and humanity was, like the Krahns' snakes, being "chopped."

Stephen drove the car out of Prince's gate, which squeaked shut behind us. We were not supposed to understand his film, or to sympathize with it. His film was for him and his people. I realized that it was an example, albeit extreme, of the gulf between myself and the people I had spent so much time with. Though my instinct was to try and understand, to empathize even, I knew nothing about them. They knew more about me and the world I came from. They knew how to use Western technology—to capture on video the scenes from the life they were leading, just as anybody with a video camera would have done.

Black rainclouds hung over the junction of the compound road and the muddy track that, to the left, went to White Plains and to the right back into the city. There, we had first seen the INPFL troops on parade when they had reached the city in July. Now, on the right, two men in bright white underpants were being led by Johnson's troops into a small hut at the side of the road. On the left a group of INPFL in uniform were standing on a patch of grass. A naked man was before them on his knees, holding up his hands as he begged the soldiers not to harm him. From inside the car we could hear nothing. We could only see, as one of the soldiers brought a machete hard down from above his head onto the palms of the man's pleading hands.

We had sailed from Freetown on a cargo ship with 1,200 Nigerian troops being sent to reinforce the 4,000-strong Ecomog force. Early on the morning of 1 October 1990, Ecomog troops pushed out of the Monrovia free port and began taking up positions within Prince Johnson's area of the divided city center. The frontline between the INPFL and the AFL troops still occupying the executive mansion lay where it always had, close to the defense ministry, along the road that ran through the city cemetery. Prince's troops fired barrages up the hill toward the AFL, just beyond the bright green defense ministry building. A blood trail off the street led to the back of a hut at a crossroads controlled by Prince's men, and the body of a man in civilian clothes lay in the mud with the back of his head shot away.

By next day the same crossroads was silent. It was 7 A.M. Ghanaian troops had gathered at the junction and convinced the INPFL to stop firing. Then, in the silence that followed, in the face of drizzling rain, the Ghanaians walked out of the protection of the buildings, pushed aside a metal fence that lay across the road, and began walking up the hill to where the AFL were positioned. Stephen, Patrick, and I walked with them, surrounded by white-helmeted troops. Nobody had any idea how the AFL troops would react. I had had no contact with them since crossing the line in August. Six weeks later—their president tortured to death, their politicians fled, their army run by the remaining sadists and murderers who knew that to leave would mean certain death—what had they become? As we walked up the hill I felt panicked and wanted to turn back, but the presence of the Ghanaian guard gave some reassurance, and we approached the top of the hill.

The AFL troops were all young, most out of uniform. There were some who looked more like college students than soldiers, with tortoise-shell spectacles and casual clothes. Nearly a thousand AFL troops had immediately turned themselves over to Ecomog when Doe was captured and had been herded into the free port and some evacuated to Freetown, Sierra Leone. The estimated thousand who remained in the Executive Mansion were the die-hards, who had been burning shops and looting the city after Doe's death, yelling: "No Doe, no Liberia," from the backs of the pick-ups in which they tore through the city, as Prince's men attempted once again to advance toward the mansion.

But that morning, the Ghanaians who confronted the AFL troops revealed the concern that, at that time, inspired the motives of the peacekeeping force among the soldiers who were sent to Liberia. They talked and pleaded and promised these traumatized, hungry, haunted killers that Ecomog was there to help them. It was an amazing sight, right from the time the brave Ghanaians had walked up the hill without knowing whether they would be shot at; the motive of the soldiers was to help end the suffering, because if Liberia was suffering then it meant that everybody in the region was suffering. Only other African soldiers could have appealed to the AFL in that way, without malice or condemnation of what the AFL had done in the previous months. The aim was to end the slaughter.

"Leave the job to me, and wait for me to establish peace. I will help to see to your needs, but I demand that the center of the city is ours," the Ghanaian colonel in charge told the gathered AFL, who had been lined up in a ramshackle and barely containable guard of honor for the Ecomog troops, the first outsiders they had seen for months. But after three or four minutes the atmosphere suddenly changed. The AFL became agitated, and they demanded to know who we reporters were. The Ghanaian colonel's eye caught mine, and he signaled for us to leave immediately; five of his men surrounded us and walked us back down the hill.

A week later, on 10 October, the Ecomog commander, Major General Joshua Dogonyaro, a close friend of Babangida and a member of the Nigerian junta's Armed Forces Ruling Council (AFRC), strode purposefully along the runway at Monrovia's Spriggs Payne airfield toward the sound of gunfire and the swamp at the end of the pockmarked tarmac.

White bones sprawled down the slope and across the mud into the mangrove swamp at the end of the runway. Fingers gripped the lush grass. Legs lay entwined beneath crumbling ribs, skeletal puppets performing a medieval *danse macabre*. Skulls lay in the cool shade of the undergrowth. Beyond the branches of the mangrove the swamp lay thick with bones, picked clean by insects.

Doe knew about this place, just as he knew about St. Peter's Lutheran church. Did he get what he deserved? Who was I to say? Rumors have it that the AFL held trials at Sprigg's Payne airfield during the summer, and when the accused were found guilty they were taken to the end of the runway and hacked to death or shot. I wondered, for only a few seconds, what it must have been like to be brought to this place, to see as we had just seen, the end of the runway, then the slope, which slowly gave a view of the extent of the killing as you approached from the top, and what it must have been like then, surrounded by the dead, to have been forced to the ground.

The tranquility was broken by the sound of shooting.

Guinean troops were fighting Taylor just beyond Sprigg's Payne, which they had captured the night before we went there.

General Dogonyaro, the unbuckled strap of his steel helmet swinging casually beneath his chin, strode back to his personnel carrier. The Nigerians we were with did not want to see more. They wanted us to leave immediately, so we drove back down to the airfield terminal building, where the control tower was a burned shell and the bullet-riddled bodies of light aircraft lay scattered on the tarmac.

We drove back toward the city, through streets over which Ecomog had only tenuous control. AFL troops, who had regained their former territory in Sinkor thanks to Ecomog having pushed Taylor back, occasionally appeared in jeeps or taxis. I could hardly look at them. I don't know whether it was fear or disgust. As we drove back toward the center of the city, Chris Otulana, the Nigerian major assigned to the press, told the driver of the personnel carrier we were traveling in, to stop.

On the left was a church.

Old clothes lay in the mud of the forecourt, which was surrounded by a wall and railings and an iron fence that stood open, one hinge broken. We walked into the forecourt, and then up the steps and into the building, whose wooden door was open.

The floor of Saint Peter's rippled with maggots. Bodies had shriveled, leaving only piles of rotting clothes on the floor. Contorted skeletons lay huddled beneath the pews. Others were piled up in a dark corner beside the altar. Up some narrow stairs, entangled bodies on the choir balcony testified to vain attempts at escape. Limbs dangled from the broken windows, the limbs of those killed while trying to flee the terror. In the classrooms next door, used as dormitories, bodies were rotting into their mattresses, and clothes clung to the skeletons of young children.

I shivered with terror. This was a monument to Samuel Doe, the leader and statesman who had drunk orange juice with the American ambassador, walked in the White House rose garden with Ronald Reagan, chatted with the Pope, and nursed thoughts of going to Oxford University for intellectual stimulation. There was nothing really to say, no conclusions to be drawn. Saint Peter's church was the reality.

Shooting broke out on the road outside the church. There stood Michael Tilly, the leader of the government death squad. I remembered him from the one time I had seen him before, in Monrovia back in June. Tilly leapt down from his Korando jeep. He was followed by around fifty of his men, all well armed, well equipped, young, their heads wrapped in bandanas decorated with cowry shells, charms dangling on rope around their necks.

"What are you white men doin'?" Tilly yelled at us. General Dogonyaro had driven on when we stopped at the church. Only Otulana and two other Nigerians were with us. "You're just actors," Tilly yelled, implying that we were pretending to be something we were not, pretending that we were journalists when in fact we were spies. Tilly's men surrounded us and the

Nigerian vehicle. They knew what we had seen, and there is no doubt that many of them had been at Saint Peter's church that night in July. Tilly himself was certainly there. But, like all the cowards of the AFL, whose experience of war was confined to killing unarmed civilians and preferably women and children, Tilly and his gang of murderers were frightened of real soldiers (which the foreign troops, away from home, had become, at least for the first days and weeks of their adventure in Liberia). Otulana calmed him with a few words and told him that we were with Ecomog, and after a few minutes we simply drove away.

As the perpetrators of Rwanda's genocide were forced to flee across the
border into neighboring Tanzania in the face of the RPF advance, they
left behind them the weapons with which they had perpetrated their
crimes, Rusumo, Rwanda, May 1994 (photo: Mark Huband)

President Mobutu Sese Seko of Zaire, whose corrupt and brutal rule over the country at the heart of central Africa has its legacy in the instability and poverty which dominates the region, N'sele, Zaire, November 1991 (photo: Mark Huband)

Patrice Lumumba became prime minister of The Congo at independence in 1960, and his short term in office rapidly became subsumed by the Cold War conflict between the United States and the USSR. (photo: AP Photo/Christine Nesbitt)

Sadiq el-Mahdi, the former prime minister of Sudan and grandson of the Mahdi who created Africa's first Islamic state in the late-nineteenth century, has been a player at the heart of the country's political scene for four decades, Omdurman, Sudan, 1993 (photo: Mark Huband)

Hassan el-Tourabi, the architect of Sudan's political Islamization project for much of the 1990s, saw his influence wane as the military-religious coalition started to fragment and Sudan's international isolation began to take its toll, Khartoum, Sudan, 1997, (photo: Mark Huband)

Blaise Compaore, President of Burkina Faso, has supported rebel factions led by Charles Taylor in Liberia and Foday Sankoh in Sierra Leone, thereby fuelling wars which have left both countries devastated, Abidjan, Côte d'Ivoire, 1993 (photo: Mark Huband)

Hunger and poverty have been the result of Sudan's 20-year civil war, which has turned the south of the country into a wasteland in which more than one million people have died since 1981, Southern Sudan, 1994 (photo: Jim Stephens)

Upon his release from 37 years in Robben Island prison, Nelson Mandela became the face of an Africa looking for hope and a new beginning, Abidjan, Côte d'Ivoire, 1992 (photo: Mark Huband)

Col. Muammar Gadaffi, the Libyan leader, backed African rebel groups throughout the 1980s and has since turned his back on his Arab neighbors and sought a great role in African affairs, Tripoli, Libya, 1999 (photo: Mark Huband)

Gen. Ibrahim Babangida, Nigeria's military ruler, left Nigeria in a political crisis when faltering steps to democracy led quickly to more military dictatorship, Bamako, Mail, 1990 (photo: Mark Huband)

Jonas Savimbi, leader of Angola's UNITA rebel movement, whose backing by the United States turned the country's civil war into Africa's largest Cold War military conflict. (photo: AP photo/Sasa Kralj)

As pro-democracy movements rapidly emerged across the continent in 1990, Kenyans took the streets to demand an end to the ruling Kanu party's grip on political power, Nairobi, Kenya, 1992 (photo: Jim Stephens)

PART THREE

Blood of the Ancestors

T HE 1990S WERE THE MOST significant period of political
change in Africa since the early 1960s. The end of one-party rule,
and the challenge that democracy posed to former single-party
rulers, revealed as much about the relationship between the traditional and
modern African political systems, as about the appropriateness of Western-
style democracy to the Africa of the 1990s and beyond. The decade has been
one in which dictators have sought to wrench the continent up by its roots,
to exploit its vulnerabilities as a means of setting enemies against each other
and thus to ensure their own survival. In doing so, politicians such as Juvenal
Habyarimana in Rwanda, Mobutu Sese Seko in Zaire, and Daniel arap Moi
in Kenya sought to prove both that democracy would fuel tribalism and that
their own continued presence as heads of state was essential, if the stability
of the nation state was to be maintained. Their readiness to sabotage the stability of their own countries by using their countries' tribal makeup as a political tool is the major proof of their betrayal of all the authority they sought
to draw upon. Their actions starkly exposed the urgent need to revolutionize
African government and made clear the importance and urgency of
strengthening the fledgling democracies that have been established, slowly
and painfully, in the past decade.

The "modernization" of government will fail, however, if it is not inspired
by and reflective of broad social change and development, out of which a
new form of rule may naturally emerge. Thus, the delicate process of marrying the traditional and the new, the known and the unknown, has dominated

the process of change undertaken during the past decade. As African countries seek to grapple with the task of building something durable upon the decrepit foundations bequeathed them by the stagnant Cold War years, tribal identity, tradition, and the continent's cultural riches have played a vital role. But it is the abuse of tradition, the enflaming of hatred, and the illegitimacy of leadership that have thus far ensured that this richness has been used to bring poverty, violence, and death.

8

MYTHS, CHIEFS, AND CHURCHES

Rwanda

WAITERS POURED DRINKS behind the glass doors of the lounge bar. The hairdresser made appointments, while chatting to her friend who ran the tourist clothes shop next door. The Belgian chef walked across the redecorated hotel lobby in his white uniform, nodding and smiling. "It's been a long time since you were last here," he told me. A year beforehand, on 11 April 1994, I had seen him and the hotel manager leave without saying good-bye. The lobby had been where terror hung in the air like ice. People had stood in the lobby, so weakened by terror that they could only walk with a drifting, wavelike step. There was a Yugoslavian woman with her Tutsi husband. He was a small, young man. He wore a brown, zip-up jacket and had thick spectacles. For days he never spoke. His fear had made him dumb. He only watched, barely moving his eyes, for fear he might catch the gaze of one of the government spies lurking in the lobby waiting to take people away to murder them on the road outside.

Blood had oozed onto the road from government lorries fueled with petrol provided by the Red Cross, as they drove by to deliver the bodies slung inside to mass graves. On 13 April I watched them haul six people out of a car there and shoot them on the roadside. The following day the French troops who had been sent to Kigali to evacuate foreigners and the Belgian troops who were already there as part of the United Nations Assistance Mission to Rwanda (Unamir), withdrew after evacuating 1,361 foreign nationals. Then the world closed its eyes to Rwanda.

Now, a year later, two men were drinking Primus beer in the red light of the bar of Kigali's Hotel Isimbi. Traffic outside died down as the sun set. There were voices lingering in the street on the other side of the hotel's ill-fitting curtains. The market round the corner was quiet. I felt as though I were walking on the dead I had watched dragged to slaughter a year beforehand, when I had arrived in Kigali three days after the genocide started. Now I made my way alone through the empty town at night. The people to whom the streets belonged were all dead.

Augustin Bizimana, the defense minister and co-author of the genocide, along with Lieutenant Colonel Theoneste Bagasora, had been sitting in the lobby of Kigali's Diplomat Hotel in early May 1994 when I had asked them if they knew about the killings in the backyard of the Hotel Isimbi. It had happened almost within sight of Bagasora's office. It had happened in broad daylight. It had happened in the city that he at that time claimed to control. He smiled, and said that if there had been a massacre we would have seen it. The militia who had barred us from the site earlier had gone by the time we arrived. There was only blood to see. The bodies of two Rwandan UN employees and six children had been taken away. A year later I looked out at the yard from my room at the Isimbi. I had not seen the yard from that angle before. Then I remembered when I had last been there.

In Rwamagana, east of Kigali, a woman in her thirties, wearing an elaborate hairpiece and a long, shiny blue dress, was sitting on a verandah staring silently into the distance. Her dress, her hairpiece, and her long, mournful face were made almost invisible by her sad, staring eyes. "They killed everybody," said Alexis, with whom I was traveling, of the woman's family. "They killed everybody. Mother. Father. Grandmother. Grandfather. All dead. All gone. All gone. All gone." I could see his breathing rise and fall, as he sat beneath the iron roof of the restaurant, waiting for grilled chicken, chips, salad, and beer.

Ash was still blowing through the church's metal windows, melted by the fire that the Rwandan Patriotic Front (RPF) lit to burn the bodies I had seen at Rukara a year beforehand. In Rwanda there are scores of similar churches. All monuments to horror. The birdsong in the forest of pines surrounding Rukara church was the same as it had been. The breeze blew. The flies buzzed. Then, RPF troops had occasionally ridden quickly by on bicycles. Nobody had stopped or looked. Bees had made a massive nest above the door of the church. Piles of cow dung littered the floor from which the dead had been cleared, leaving only their stains and juice and blood to dry on the concrete.

During the two days of slaughter at Rukara, 12–13 April 1994, Britain's permanent representative to the UN argued that the UN should adopt the role of "political facilitator" in Rwanda. This assumed that discussion was possible with those who were hacking the heads, legs, arms, and genitals off Rwanda's victims. All but the UN's African members—notably Nigeria, Ghana, Togo and Senegal, which called for an expanded UN force to stop the genocide—said Rwanda was undergoing a civil war between the RPF and the government. This was done so as to allow the UN to consider taking on the role of mediator and to introduce the prospect of a ceasefire. It was one of the more grotesque foreign responses to the genocide in Rwanda, where the issue of the civil war was insignificant beside that of the genocide.

"I only live with sadness," said Leoncia Mukandayambaje. Her baby daughter had saved her, one of only eight people who survived the massacre at Nyarubuye Catholic Mission, deep in the hills of eastern Rwanda. When the killing started, Sylvestre Gacumbitsi assured the public that as the local *burgomestre*, or mayor, he would ensure their safety. He gave those who were frightened a pass to allow them free passage to Nyarubuye church. Having gathered everybody there, he had no problem finding those he wanted to kill. He sent the militia to Nyarubuye, and they slaughtered 2,620 people on 15 April 1994. The militia chased their victims out of the nave of the fine brick church into the courtyard. They raped ten of the women. The women were still lying there a year later, with their underwear around the knees of their parched skeletons. Leoncia was saved by the daughter she held onto. The militia hacked at the baby so much that its blood covered Leoncia, and the militia assumed both mother and daughter were dead. The baby was dead. "I only live with sadness," Leoncia muttered, from despair, remorse, and deep, deep guilt.

The night Leoncia's daughter died the UN Security Council met in New York. U.S. representative Madeleine Albright said the U.S. might approve the scaling-down of the UN force in Rwanda, rather than its complete withdrawal. While Nyarubuye shook to the screams of the dying, Albright made a show of taking out her cell phone during the meeting and calling U.S. secretary of state Warren Christopher to see if he agreed to what she was portraying as a U.S. concession. But when the night was through, the Security Council had still failed to make a decision. "Let us say with great humility, I failed," UN secretary-general Boutros Boutros-Ghali admitted on 26 May. "It's a scandal. I am the first one to say it, and I am ready to repeat it. It is a failure not only for the United Nations but also for the international community, and all of us are responsible. It is genocide."

A Thousand Hills, A Thousand Shadows

The greatest mistake this government could make would be to suppress the Mututsi caste. Such a revolution would lead the country directly to anarchy and to hateful anti-European communism. . . . We will have no better, more active and more intelligent chiefs than the Batutsi. They are the ones best suited to understand progress and the ones the population likes best. The government must work mainly with them.[1]

As much as in Burundi, colonial interference with the existing social structure in Rwanda created the conditions for the instability of the system that emerged as a consequence of the colonial presence. Alain Destexhe makes the problem plain:

> When the evolutionary and racial theories were in vogue at the beginning of [the twentieth-century],[2] the phenomena of different social class was interpreted in racial terms and contributed to this habit of compartmentalizing Rwandan society. Power was in the hands of the Tutsi pastoralists and hard labor was the lot of the agriculturalists, the "Hutu negroes" and the Twa. In reality the division of the tasks was never that rigid and occasionally a less well-off Tutsi cattle owner might agree to marry his daughter to a rich Hutu farmer. As a result, the term "Tutsi" became synonymous with a rise in social position.[3]

The colonialists' decision to favor the Tutsi was felt in the administration, in the provision of military assistance to Tutsi in their conquest of independent Hutu areas during the early colonial period, and in the education system. "Thus, in short, if the categories of Hutu and Tutsi were not actually invented by the colonizers, the policies practiced by the Germans and Belgians only served to exacerbate them. They played an essential role in creating an ethnic split and ensured that the important feeling of belonging to an ethnic group was fueled by ethnic, indeed racial hatred."[4] Scholars widely accept that "it was the colonial era that served to transform a complex status hierarchy into a simplified ethnic antagonism—a hierarchy in which, apparently, the subdivision among the Tutsi became less significant."[5] What they are essentially saying is that the "mythico-history" of both Burundi and Rwanda, which were ruled as one, under the name Ruanda-Urundi, by the Belgian authorities until 1962, was created out of this colonial strategy of ruling through those perceived as the most appropriate agents of rule—the Tutsi.

The system of kingship that existed in both countries prior to colonialism certainly had its own iniquities. But was it more unjust than those to be found contemporaneously in other countries? Were the Ashanti more just? Were the rulers of precolonial Nigeria, where the British colonial authorities also introduced a system of indirect rule through traditional leaders, more unjust? Above all, was the system of rule in precolonial times responsible for creating the tension between those subject to that system? If yes, then why is it that only during the postcolonial era has there been violence in Rwanda on the scale suffered in 1959–1963, and later in 1973? There is no record of mass killing in Rwanda prior to colonial rule on the scale of 1959 and after independence. This cannot be put down to poor record keeping.

The use of mass slaughter as a political tool, of genocide as a policy, does not emerge as a part of the precolonial historical memory of Rwandans, where single clans included Hutu, Tutsi, and Twa, where armies brought all three groups together to fight common enemies, and where pre-Christian religious practice was similar in all three.[6] Only by the time the traditional, undoubtedly oppressive but nevertheless functional system of precolonial rule had been fully dismantled and the prospect of independence[7] had become imminent, did what had then become the two rivals for power turn upon each other. "Competition for political power—and not the 'old African problem of tribalism'—served to bifurcate the populations of Rwanda and Burundi into two opposing categories, Hutu and Tutsi, and to render other social divisions less meaningful and less powerful. The exclusive predominance of the ethnic bifurcation was at this level a markedly recent political phenomenon."[8]

Variety within precolonial Rwanda was perhaps the major source of its stability. A degree of intermarriage, the potential for movement within the class system, as well as the identification of Hutu and Tutsi as social classes rather than ethnic identities, created an atmosphere that was far less rigid than that which prevailed in the wake of the introduction of colonial definitions based on supposed ethnic differences. The question of who is a Hutu and who is a Tutsi has had a variety of responses at different points in history. Prior to the process of centralization by the Tutsi monarchy under the *Mwame*, or king, Kigeri Rwabugiri, between 1860 and 1895, Hutu and Tutsi even appear to have lacked the hierarchical dimension the labels came to imply. Only when the relationship between the central authority—the monarch—and the provinces became more pronounced, with the process of centralization, did the polarization begin:

> The state building efforts of Rwabugiri heightened awareness of ethnic differences. . . . [Lines] of distinction were altered and sharpened, as the categories of Hutu and Tuutsi[9] assumed new hierarchical overtones associated with proximity to the central court—proximity to power. Later, when the political arena widened and the intensity of political activity increased, these classifications became increasingly stratified and rigidified. More than simply conveying the connotation of cultural difference from Tuutsi, Hutu identity came to be associated with and eventually defined by inferior status.[10]

Catharine Newbury's work, based on research in the early 1970s in the Kinyaga commune of Rwanda's extreme southwest, portrays precolonial and early colonial Rwanda as an emergent nation state in which the process of political centralization created divisions that came to be ordered along hierarchical lines:

> Tuutsi and Hutu became political labels; "ethnicity," such as it was, came to assume a political importance, determining a person's life chances and relations with the authorities. With the establishment of European colonial rule in the country, ethnic categories came to be even more rigidly defined, while the disadvantages of being Hutu and the advantages of being Tuutsi increased significantly. Passing from one ethnic category to the other was not impossible, but over time it became exceedingly difficult and, consequently, very rare.[11]

What is clear from Newbury's analysis is that the emergence of rigid boundaries between Tutsi and Hutu is relatively recent. She essentially rejects the view that a functional relationship existed between Hutu and Tutsi, and instead stresses the inequality practiced by the Tutsi rulers of precolonial and colonial Rwanda, as an explanation for the eventual overthrow of Tutsi dominance in 1959, prior to independence. However, the question remains as to whether *ethnicity* is the key to understanding the political process of centralization that began in 1860 and continued under German and Belgian colonial rule, which heightened the inequities of Rwandan society.

The Hutu extremist view expressed vociferously prior to independence and ever since is that *ethnic* difference has been the cause of conflict between Hutu and Tutsi ever since the two groups had first come into contact with each other. The theory draws heavily on the view that the Tutsi arrived from the Horn of Africa and proceeded to carve out an ethnic empire to the east of the Great Lakes. But even though Newbury regards the eventual Hutu overthrow of Tutsi power as a response to "oppression created by clientship and policies of control-control [that] fostered the growth of political consciousness and pan-Hutu ethnic solidarity,"[12] she recognizes that the phenomenon of conflict between the two emerged much more recently, when patterns of rule and patron-client relations changed in the late nineteenth century. Ethnic difference—much blurred by intermarriage and mobility over centuries between what had been class rather than ethnic groups—never appears to have been of sufficient weight in itself to have bred the "ideology of extermination."

Centralization, of the kind that exacerbated the tension between Hutu and Tutsi, was vital to the evolution of colonial rule. Despite its relatively small size, Rwanda's unity as a single state was only fully established in 1931, with the incorporation of all the chiefdoms into the colonial-monarchical state. Although centralization had been taking place before German colonizers arrived in 1897, it was the continuation of this process and the further transformation of the key *social* division—between Hutu and Tutsi—into an *ethnic* division by the Germans and their Belgian successors, that marked the cataclysmic shift:

What is vital for our purpose of understanding the reasons for the tragic split which led to the present Rwandese ultra-violence is the fact that at the time it was a *centre versus periphery*[13] affair and not one of Tutsi versus Hutu. If the Kings chiefly agents in this [centralization] process were mostly (but not all) Tutsi, their "victims" in the newly "controlled" situation were both Tutsi and Hutu, and they were defined by their geographical location. And it was worse—in a way—that because [of] the Tutsi and Hutu categories not being the hard unchanging identities which many commentators have purported them to be, many of the newly integrated elites were co-opted by the monarchy in order to turn them into faithful servants of the new order. It is essential to keep this process in mind in order to understand the transformation which took place in Rwanda between 1860 and 1931 and which directly gave birth to its modern society—and its most intractable problems.[14]

The consolidation of Tutsi power and the evolution of Belgian colonial rule reached a watershed in 1931, with the accession to the monarchy of Mutara III Rudahigwa. Central to his incorporation into Belgian plans was his conversion to Christianity. From the mid-1920s, the benefits of conversion had been used to lure Rwandans to the Catholic Church. "A necessary prerequisite for membership of the elite of the new Rwanda the Belgians were creating was to become a Christian."[15] As advisers, as long-term residents, as the only Europeans with knowledge—often fluent—of the Kinyarwanda language, missionaries thus secured enormous influence over both indigenous Rwandan society and the practice of colonial rule. Belgian preference for the Tutsi was reflected in the educational opportunities of Hutu and Tutsi, the latter generally securing between 50 and 75 percent of places in schools and colleges, while comprising only around 15 percent of the population.

The impact of the church as a social element—as a provider of education and therefore the qualifications to rule, as an institution in which one's involvement was a mark of social position—was as marked as its impact on traditional belief systems was inadequate and destructive. The exploitative nature of colonialism clashed morally with the teachings of the Christian missionaries who were part of the colonial baggage. Genuine acceptance of the Christian God was complicated by colonial forced control, heavy taxes, and the indignity of control imposed by the white man. Conversion from the traditional Kubandwa religion to Catholicism barely helped overcome the colonial anomaly, as in return for submission to the colonial power, its institutions, and its religion the converts were subject simply to more entrenched colonization. Salvation for their converts was not the purpose of missionaries to Rwanda. Their clear aim was to strengthen colonization through indirect rule and Tutsi domination. Wrenched vigorously from long-established traditions during a mere fifteen years of dramatic change between 1916 and 1931, Rwandans saw their country transformed into an ethnic battleground for which nothing in their real history—as opposed to the *mythico-history* of Tutsi supremacy, which the Belgians, the church, and the Tutsi elite propagated widely—had prepared them. Catholicism, meanwhile, "since it was all things to all men, [could] not have any real healing power when faced with the deepening ethnic gap which the Belgian authorities kept digging."[16]

The ambiguities of colonialism, as well as the irreversible damage done to Rwandan society by the indigenous elite's complicity in allowing the emergence of the *ethnic* division as a vital element in its retention of power, then began to emerge. Coupled with this process, Belgian preference for the Tutsi can be seen as having been a trick by the colonial power. The Tutsi became too powerful, having swelled the ranks of the priesthood and been the first to soak up the anticolonial sentiment that emerged throughout Europe's empires after World War II. Meanwhile, the economic relationship between the largely Hutu Rwandan masses and the Tutsi elite and their Belgian masters also became less manageable, owing largely to the fact of centralized power having heightened individual enterprise as a consequence of regional power structures having been dismantled.[17] After 1945, the Belgians were forced to choose between an increasingly powerful Tutsi elite, which began to threaten their rule altogether, and a Hutu majority that had grown in economic importance under colonialism and evolved its own middle class despite its lack of political power. A broadening of the local administration during the 1950s to include local councilors appointed by the Tutsi chiefs failed to accommodate the growing political consciousness of either group.

As pressure for an end to colonial rule increased, so the lack of preparedness of the established power structure for such a shift in Rwanda became ever clearer. The response was an abrupt about-turn by the Belgian colonial administration, as it was forced to tailor its plans for independence to fit the reality it had foisted upon its colonial subjects. It would have seemed hypocritical to grant independence in a way that kept in power an elite that had, at the behest of the colonial administration, done the colonial master's bidding. Such a move would scarcely have met the aspirations for popular independence of anticolonialists in both Europe and Africa, and would have appeared neocolonialist. Thus, it was the majority that must be seen to benefit from such a move—that is, the Hutu majority. The shift intensified the rivalry between the "tribes." The groundwork was laid, as "the democratic principle of majority rule was cited as justification for the removal of the Tutsi from their previous positions of influence; a complete reversal of previous policy. The Hutu became the 'good guys' who 'have been dominated for so long by the Tutsi,' and the Belgians now expressed sympathy for the cause of the suppressed masses."[18] Thus, the *tribes* (which three generations beforehand had been social classes incorporated into an undoubtedly unjust but functional system) were defined in moral terms as oppressor and oppressed in order to salve the European conscience, in a manner that laid the foundation for the *ethnic* conflict that was soon to follow.

Liberated by their newfound favor with the Belgians, the Hutu in 1959 rose up against the Tutsi authorities. By the time independence finally arrived in 1962, 20,000 Tutsi had been killed, while the Belgian authorities generally turned a blind eye to the slaughter. By 1964, there were 336,000 Tutsi refugees in neighboring countries, a figure which had risen to around 700,000 by 1973, owing both to renewed violence and to reproduction within the established refugee population.[19] Vigorously practicing a policy of tribal quotas, which held that the Tutsi comprised 9 percent of the population[20] and could therefore have only an equivalent number of educational places and government posts, the Hutu majority secured total domination of the government under the Rwandan republic's first president, the Hutu tribalist Gregoire Kayibanda (1961–1973).

WAR AND WORDS

The manufacture of myths has marked the history of Rwandan politics since the first days of colonialism. The need of the colonialists to justify decisions in the early years of imperial injustice—their actions dressed up in the clothes of righteousness to disguise an undignified scramble for territory motivated by greed—made them unable, or at least certainly unwilling to preserve the historic society they found in Rwanda. Rwanda's experience was perhaps the first, and certainly one of the most destructive uses of pure power by the Western world, with the intention of manufacturing the past through propaganda, manipulation, and force, as a means of creating suitable foundations upon which to build the colonial future. Belgium was first attracted by the fine, cultured traits of the "noble" Tutsi. Then it was attracted by the rights and passions of the Hutu. The shift, together with the hypocrisy that lay at its heart, when fueled by propaganda, manipulation, and force, was dynamite.

Of course, the Tutsi and the Hutu were not passive. Having been defined by the Belgians as *ethnic* groups with histories and interests to match, they issued their own propaganda, manipulated opinion with skill, and were ready to fall back onto the use of force. Accordingly, a new version of reality was created, first under Kayibanda, and even more stridently under Major General Juvenal Habyarimana after he killed Kayibanda and seized power for the northern Hutu in 1973. The version created during the 1980s was that, unlike many of its neighbors, Rwanda was calm, stable, and subject to an extraordinary degree of cohesion. The success of this myth owed much to a "carefully-controlled machinery of hypocrisy, with the church playing the role of Chief Engineer."[21] The version of reality that sustained the Hutu regime until 1990 depended upon ongoing, skillfully discreet, and always deadly brutality toward the regime's detractors—both Tutsi and southern

Hutu—within the country, as well as sporadic reminders that control and vigilance were vital if the country were not to be overrun by the *Inyenzi*,[22] the armed Tutsi groups who had attacked from exile in 1961–1966.

That Habyarimana's northern Hutu had created an elite that excluded southern Hutu from power to an extent was almost as prejudicial as the exclusion of the Tutsi was ongoing proof of the fallacy of the tribal or ethnic revolution. Nevertheless, that fallacy, presented as fact, played an essential role in Rwanda's foreign relations. In supporting Habyarimana, the West was not supporting the leader of a once repressed majority, but merely bolstering autocracy centering on the power of a presidential family, a family that fell increasingly under the influence of Habyarimana's wife, Agathe Kanzinga.

The "revolution" of 1959, which saw Tutsi power terminated, was allowed to be regarded as such in part because the expulsion of Rwanda's Tutsi was never condemned by the outside world. Rwanda, like Liberia, Congo-Brazzaville, Togo, and other countries, benefited from an unofficial postcolonial rule practiced by Western countries. If Belgium, in need of cleansing its conscience after creating and supporting Tutsi supremacy and then shifting favor to the Hutu, did not complain about Habyarimana, then the rest of the world would remain silent. If France were not complaining about Gnassingbe Eyadema in Togo or Denis Sassou-Nguessou in Congo, then other countries would accede to the state of play. If the United States—in its role as superpower rather than former colonial power—was not complaining about Samuel Doe in Liberia or Mobutu in Zaire, then who among the other Western powers would dare to criticize them? Just as the colonial powers sought territory, so these same postcolonial states sought zones of influence. It was rare they trod upon each other's toes.

Meanwhile, until 1990, up to one million Rwandans were forced to live outside their country, as a direct consequence of a government policy of ethnic cleansing that compares in terms of numbers and motivation with the mass departure of the Jews from Nazi Germany after 1932. Western acquiescence in Rwanda's ethnic cleansing, in the interests of the need to portray political decisions as honorable and historical interpretations as consistent, is the single most catastrophic consequence of the self-delusion the West persisted in believing, as it accepted the deceitful *version of reality* that history appeared to make it necessary to accept with regard to Rwanda. Right up to the day the last Tutsi was killed in the spring of 1994, exactly a century after the first German, Count von Gotzen, arrived in Rwanda, reality was juggled by foreigners.

It is no surprise that the question of what Rwanda really is lies at the heart of the war that marked the beginning of the end of the Rwandan Hutu's bloody rise to power and the exposure of their 1959 "revolution" as a tool in the pursuit of genocide. It is also no surprise that, since taking power, the exiled Tutsi have had little that is good to say about Western countries that barely acknowledged the existence of their diaspora during three decades of exile. On 1 October 1990, the consequences of the Hutu revolution finally rebounded on Rwanda, when the victims of the revolution crossed the border from their Ugandan exile and invaded.

The idea of a return to Rwanda had not always been central to the exiles' aims. However, their involvement in the armed invasion of Uganda led by Yoweri Museveni, as well as the consequent part they played in the suppression of armed opposition to Museveni's National Resistance Army (NRA) in 1986–1989, had brought them enemies in Uganda.[23] In 1986, when Museveni captured Kampala, 3,000 of his 14,000 NRA fighters were Banyarwanda refugees from Rwanda. By 1989, they numbered around 8,000 in the by then 100,000-strong NRA. Increasingly, however, "President Museveni found the Banyarwanda presence in the army a stumbling-block in his efforts at negotiating some sort of peace with the eastern and northern insurgents. His negotiating partners . . . remained particularly hostile to the presence of 'those foreigners' in the NRA."[24] Museveni began to isolate the Banyarwanda, removing the Banyarwanda major general Fred Rwigyema from his post as NRA commander in chief and defense minister in the NRA government. Consequent to their increasingly difficult position in Uganda, the exiled Rwandans developed a strategy of nevertheless retaining their strong presence within the NRA. This strategy would allow them to shift a ready-made army into Rwanda when it was decided that the time was right to leave Uganda altogether and return to the land from which they had come.

By the time the exiles—organized as the Rwandan Patriotic Front (RPF)—launched their invasion, Rwanda itself was faced with growing political instability. The details of the invasion have been well documented.[25] A central question surrounding the invasion, the government's response to it, and the reaction of foreign countries, is whether it marked the "return of the Tutsi," or whether it was in fact one aspect of a broader Rwandan response to the growing political bankruptcy of the Habyarimana regime, as it sought to grapple with the increasing inappropriateness of a political culture rooted in tribalism, dictatorship, fear, and myth. More is perhaps revealed of the exiles' motivation by the details of the peace agreement it eventually signed with the government, on 4 August 1993, than by the conduct of the conflict that gripped Rwanda from October 1990. The peace process begun at Arusha, Tanzania, on 12 July 1992, took more than one year to create the final text of a peace agreement. A ceasefire was called on 14 July. "The end result [of the negotiations] was celebrated among participants as the framework for a 'new order' providing a comprehensive agreement that went beyond the traditional *settlement* of conflict, for the agreement made real inroads into resolving some of the underlying tensions which had sparked the civil war."[26]

The war itself had fostered a climate of political extremism within the country, which had starkly polarized opinion within the Hutu population. While the RPF, which was essentially a military machine, was able to present its case and demands with minimal reference to external factors, the government was forced to juggle a growing variety of political opinions. The regime had not only to negotiate an end to the military conflict, but to do so on terms that would satisfy its democratic opposition, while also avoiding any conflict with extremist Hutu, notably the Coalition pour la défense de la république (CDR: Coalition for the Defense of the Republic). The CDR had been created by Habyarimana in 1992, in part as a means of giving the impression that by comparison with such extremists, his ruling Mouvement Républicain Nationale pour la Démocratie et le Développement (MRNDD: Republican National Movement for Democracy and Development) was relatively moderate.

The MRNDD had adopted the word *democracy* in its name on 28 April 1991, when Habyarimana announced the creation of a multiparty state in Rwanda. Twelve opposition parties had emerged within six months of the announcement. Of these, however, seven were created by Habyarimana as a way of creating a sham democracy. Of the remaining five,[27] several were then infiltrated by progovernment extremists, creating internal factions whose essential point of division was their stance for or against the tone and direction of the peace talks with the RPF then taking place in Arusha:

> The invasion of Rwanda by the RPF/A[28] crystallized a process that had slowly been developing prior to this invasion. On the surface, the regime was bending to accommodate the internal opposition and the threats from the invading RPF. But this only reinforced the sense that extremism was the only force that the regime could employ in order to save itself from falling. . . . The result was that at the time of the RPF/A invasion of the country, erroneous signals regarding the enemy of Rwanda (*inyangarwanda*) had been sent. A mistaken identification of the problem of Rwanda was made when the regime of Habyarimana pointed an accusing finger at the Batutsi as the greatest enemy of the country.[29]

This rather understated explanation of Habyarimana's strategy tends to underestimate his clear wish to deliberately send "erroneous" signals. But the writers' point that the true nature of the crisis had been subject to "mistaken identification" is vital. The key point is the nature of the regime in place. By 1990 it was subject to pressure from Hutu favoring political liberalization, who were apparently no longer ready to accept that the regime was a necessary guarantor of the 1959 revolution. Even though the deliberate policy of anti-Tutsi discrimination had done its work over three decades in the schools, the army, the administration, and elsewhere, other factors were coming into play by the time of the RPF invasion:

[From] 1968 to the mid 1980s, the threat of refugee (Batutsi) invasion had greatly decreased. Hutu extremism, which had increased when there was the threat from the Batutsi, was for some time contained. . . . The majority of the party's strong men were men and women from Habyarimana's family in the north . . . who, in their attempts to consolidate their regime, turned to region-alism as their instrument of political control and cultivated an image of people in the south as the enemy.[30]

What is clear from this analysis is that the Habyarimana regime felt a compulsive need to oppress and manipulate, in order to remain in power. The *ethnic* card was the strongest; but without a Tutsi threat the regime turned on other Hutu, while Tutsi who had remained in Rwanda were gen-erally left alone, allowed to engage in commerce on the understanding that they would not aspire to political office.

The RPF invasion ought, if the government's political creed had contin-ued to enjoy credibility, to have inspired a united Hutu uprising against the invaders. But it did not. Instead, it intensified broad demands among Hutu for political liberalization, while polarizing Hutu opinion between moder-ates, extremists, and the government. Thirty-one years after the 1959 revo-lution, it was not *ethnicity* that drove popular opinion. Ethnicity was a card for leaders to play when they had nothing more tangible to offer, a factor that allowed the government to foster the atmosphere of extremism. Thanks to the colonial creation of Rwandan *ethnicity*, Rwanda's leaders had this card close to hand. However, by 1991, the emergence of opposition political par-ties revealed the key political division of the country in the 1980s as being regional rather than ethnic, between northern Hutu, from the Ruhengeri area of Habyarimana and his wife, and southern Hutu, who had been the backbone of the Kayibanda regime Habyarimana had deposed. Nkiko Nsengimana of the MDR (Mouvement Démocratique Républicain) opposi-tion party, who sought to press for a settlement to Rwanda's profound crisis by reforming the political structure while retaining the rights of the "socio-logical majority,"[31] gave me his picture of the situation in 1994:

Democracy in Rwanda started with the war. It was a catalyst. That's not to ex-cuse the war. But we said that the war came because of the political system we had. The war was conducted in a very secret way. It emerged because the dicta-torial regime had eliminated the financial and economic elite. The regime had done everything it could to eliminate them. But it couldn't explain why there was a war in a country that was growing economically. There was corruption, and an economic crisis from 1979. 1990 was the peak of the crisis, when the younger generation no longer talked about having a future. Access to land was another issue. The dictators couldn't carry out reforms on their own. They had to enlarge the social elite.

If we now overcome the impasse it's because there's a need to share political power. The political parties haven't had time to properly develop their ideologies. They have been too quick to have access to power. Within six months of being created they were being given ministries. Power here isn't understood in terms of political conciliation. There's no chance of sharing with adversaries. That's why we are at an impasse. The democratic culture isn't strong.[32]

Determination to dilute the exclusive nature of the regime was an important element in the growth of domestic political opposition. However, the opposition's tradition of exclusiveness and the determination with which it pursued its discrimination against the Tutsi, as if they were not real Rwandans, were intensified in response to the RPF invasion. The exiled Tutsi had indeed become outsiders, having been abroad for thirty years, speaking English rather than French, and having been exposed to the anticolonial ideas of Yoweri Museveni and the NRA. True, the RPF was not dominated only by exiled Tutsi; it contained Hutu politicians and military officers who had fallen out with Habyarimana. But the RPF had also come to represent a different political tradition from that which Habyarimana, encouraged by France and others, had created and preserved in Rwanda. Paul Kagame of the RPF put it this way:

There must be some things put in place first, as prerequisites, in particular national unity. If people are divided ethnically, then you can't have the multiparty system. There's no system of democracy that can work when people have their tribe written in their identity card. We were forced into a system of multipartyism before this issue of national unity had been dealt with. First, we are committed to the unity of the Banyarwanda, and we will see what they choose. We are not opposed to multipartyism. We want democracy, whether it's multiparty or not.[33]

Kagame, military leader of the RPF and now president of Rwanda, had by early 1994 seen the RPF secure much of what it wanted at the Arusha peace talks. He then watched as the Rwandan government sought to ignite ethnic tension and violence and engender extremism within the factions of the opposition political parties that it had bought off.

The Arusha accord included agreement on the creation of a broad-based transitional government, which was to stay in power for no longer than twenty-two months, at the end of which there would be multiparty elections. The powers of the president were reduced to those of a figurehead, whereas real power lay with the prime minister and the council of ministers. However, considerable power was also allotted to a Transitional National Assembly (TNA), which had the power to censure the government. The RPF succeeded in excluding the extremist CDR from the transitional institutions, and it also secured five seats in the council of ministers, achieving parity with the ruling MRNDD, while also securing eleven seats in the TNA, also on a par with the ruling party. The RPF, apparent representative of an exiled population that, anyway, only comprised between 9 percent (officially) and 14 percent (in fact) of the population, had thereby secured a degree of recognition that either way appeared disproportionate to its actual support. Meanwhile, trust had not emerged from the Arusha process, despite the length of the process and the familiarity the two sides had built up during their discussions. Justin Mugenzi, a pro-Hutu extremist, described the situation to me in a way that clearly exposed the Hutu extremists' perspective:

> There's a Tutsi consciousness. There's a belonging to an ethnic consciousness in their minds, which stops them from living with other Rwandese in harmony. Partly it's because they look to the past with regrets—their past power. They try to cultivate their ethnic group pride. This is why all along, through the centuries they have refused to mix with the Hutus. Otherwise how do you explain the fact that you still manage to spot them? They have consciously refused to integrate. The Hutus have a greater readiness to integrate and forget, as long as the Tutsis don't behave in a revolting manner.[34]

The views of extremist politicians, such as those of Justin Mugenzi, leader of the pro-Hutu extremist wing of the Parti Libérale, ignore the thirty years of Tutsi exile and project an image of the Hutu governments after 1959 as if they had sought reconciliation as a basis of government policy. These two issues are central to the propaganda diffused by the Habyarimana government and its supporters: The Tutsi have not changed, and the Hutu are seeking reconciliation. Neither was true. The political agenda, rather than the supposed *tribal* agenda, of the RPF was in fact what the government most feared, because of the break with the undemocratic past that it represented. Equally, neither Kayibanda nor Habyarimana can be said to have actively sought to create a permanent framework for peaceful coexistence. Hutu rights—interpreted to mean the right of the Hutu majority to monopolize power and education—were at the heart of the government structure, institutionalized, and based on ethnic quotas that, though not always strictly enforced, were generally adhered to. For a government dependent on this for its survival, it was necessary to promote the atmosphere of distrust, despite more than a year of negotiations that ought to have diluted it. Again Mugenzi's version makes the problem clear:

> As we come closer to integration of the RPF, one sees that there's an unseen and unsaid element behind the RPF mind. I won't venture to comment on their true mind or explain their behavior, but I would only tend to think that the present

176   THE SKULL BENEATH THE SKIN

situation shows that the RPF represents a grouping of those refugees who just
want to return to power. Irrespective of what you would call the reconciliation.
That is an empty word now, given the way they are trying to snatch the essentials
of power . . . When Arusha was done it was under a general atmosphere. People
were intending to build up a kind of contract: These people had suffered a lot
and lived outside. Now they are back. They have learned lessons. They will
bring their experience and we will share. . . . And we had the confidence that
these RPF people would bring this kind of experience. And this created the confidence that something could be built. Now, with the Burundi situation, people
are saying: Be careful, because the Tutsis may come with their guns.[35]

Although the RPF may have appeared more coherent than the government side during the discussions in Arusha, and certainly secured much of
what it wanted in terms of political representation and its incorporation into
the national army, it remained the case that behind the supposed extreme
discipline of the RPF, the political debate within the exiled Tutsi population
had barely begun. The reemergence of the Tutsi onto the Rwandan political
stage after thirty years in exile did not simply mark the arrival of a hitherto
isolated section of the population. It heralded the arrival of a group whose
ideas were, at least in their ideal form, a radical alternative to the highly conservative, tribal politics that Rwanda's leaders had portrayed as a revolution
during the previous thirty years. Of the RPF leadership that had grown up in
Uganda, Gerard Prunier writes:

All of them had imbibed a sort of mildly populist post-Maoist political philosophy adapted to the context of Uganda's politico-tribal wars. The lesson they
had derived from these violent and confused years was ambiguous. On the one
hand, tribalism was theoretically considered an absolute evil and "progressives"
were supposed to fight it relentlessly; seeing over and over again how absolutely destructive African tribal conflicts could be had strengthened their determination to avoid them. But they had realized at the time that without a
solidly trustworthy tribal core and attendant network the new "revolutionary"
power which came to replace the "primitive tribalists" of old would in practice
be blind and dangerously exposed. . . . Their political ideal was Yoweri Museveni, who had finally brought peace to a troubled land . . . [and] had been able
to combine a nationalist approach rejecting "gross tribalism" with the security
of a tribally-safe political inner-core.[36]

Kagame's skepticism of multipartyism stemmed in part from his exposure
to the experiences of Uganda, where Museveni has attempted to establish a
"non-party" democracy. But it also stemmed from the growing awareness of
the extent to which Habyarimana was intent upon manipulating multipartyism to secure his own position, by infiltrating the opposition. Kagame said:

The situation in Burundi proves that there's some logic in the fact that the multi-party system creates some problems for our African countries. It really strengthens the divisions, because in the rush for power people are ready to play on any divisions, on ethnicity, on religion. If you rush into elections the winner takes everything and you get back to the same questions. First you have to politicize the population. They have to understand what the process means to them. The whole thing is a disaster if it's not mainly generated from within the countries.[37]

By January 1994, when Kagame was speaking, what had been "generated from within" the country was the Arusha accord. On paper it promised power sharing, an end to three decades—possibly eight decades—of discrimination, a complete reversal of roles by the once all-powerful presidency and the prime minister, as well as a breadth of popular representation that even gave a voice to extremists. In practice, the Arusha accord was undermined by having been signed by a Rwandan president who intended to use it as a tool to pursue the very same goals that had created the war and the need for a peace agreement in the first place. Kagame understood this:

Habyarimana's motivation stems from the fact that the Arusha agreement reduces his powers. It's a struggle now, seeing his powers being trimmed down, and he is trying to solve this by creating camps within the other parties. He is operating like somebody who doesn't care about the consequences. He has committed a lot of crimes against the population. People may come up and hold him responsible for what he did during his regime. He plans on anything.[38]

As Prunier writes, "President Habyarimana had consented to sign the Arusha peace agreement not as a genuine gesture marking the turning-over of a new political leaf and the beginning of democratization in Rwanda, but as a tactical move calculated to buy time, shore-up the contradictions of the various segments of the opposition and look good in the eyes of the foreign donors."[39] What, then, was his purpose in buying time?

"KILL THE PEOPLE, BURN DOWN THE HOUSES"

The regime, in particular the senior officers of the Forces Armées Rwandaises (FAR), could only advance in the Arusha negotiations at a pace that allowed the concessions made there to be simultaneously compensated for by instigating increasingly elaborate plans for extremism to prevail covertly. The regime was rotten, safeguarding the guiding principle of northern Hutu supremacy, while at the same time failing to present even any credible defense of its own tribalism. The drastic alterations to Rwanda's system of government, as approved and signed at Arusha, marked a negotiated end to the values of the 1959 revolution. The poverty of the revolution, its ideals and purpose, were exposed for what they were—an excuse for government based on prejudice, a government that used prejudice to trick the population into believing it had brought salvation. Those who had created Rwanda's famed stability were themselves the causes of its undoing, of an explosion of evil on a scale never before seen in Africa.

At the heart of the inner core of extremists opposed to any concession to the RPF along the lines of the agreement reached at Arusha, was the *Clan de Madame*, the group of family members and close associates grouped around Agathe Kanzinga, wife of President Habyarimana.[40] In 1993 the senior ranks of the FAR had been reorganized to diminish the influence of extremists,[41] leading to the enforced retirement of several members of the Clan de Madame, including some of her own family members, and consequently leading to the rise in importance to the extremist cause of those officers who had retained their posts. Simultaneously, the armed power within the regime started to shift, away from within the ranks of the army and toward the armed militias, the MRNDD-associated militia, called the *Interahamwe*, and the CDR-associated *Impuzamugambi*. Although the political role of the extremist CDR had been contested at Arusha by the RPF, the armed militias remained officially secret, despite the results of their activities being widely known. As one deserter later told me:

> We were trained as death squads. We did military training day and night. During the day we trained in the camp. At night we trained in the country. In 1992 we did our first killing. Trouble started in Kigali and spread to the countryside. In January 1993 we killed Tutsi from the Bagogwe clan in Ruhengeri. We were seventy. It took a month. We killed 10,000 people. There were people there who saw the interahamwe killing, and then they started to kill their neighbors. When it was over we returned to the Camp Mukamira in Ruhengeri.
>
> We stayed there for one week. There were some who had been trapped by the Tutsis. We found them, but some had been killed. Then we went back to Kanombe [barracks outside Kigali]. Two weeks later we were sent military equipment—machetes, grenades, spears. Then we were sent to Bugosera, north of the capital, to the military camp, Camp Gako. After two days we were sent into the population. We did the same things. We killed at least 5,000 people. There we killed anybody who seemed Tutsi. After that we went back to the camp, to hide it from the population that it was us who had killed people. The aim was to blame the RPF.[42]

Janvier Afrika, who chose this pseudonym to preserve his anonymity when I interviewed him, was the son of a Rwandan diplomat, who had spent much of his life up to the age of fourteen in China, where his father had been first counselor at the Rwandan embassy. In 1984 he returned to Rwanda and worked for Sabena, the Belgian airline. He struck up close ties with the security services, passing on information that he thought might be useful to various branches of the regime. In 1989 he started working at the presidency and supplied information to the *Service centrale de renseignements* (Central Information Service).

> We trained people who could create trouble in the country. The president had certain people who would go into the communes and make contact with the chiefs and establish who was opposed to the president. Habyarimana created the Interahamwe and gave them military training. He used these people. He gave them money to buy beer and drugs. I was in that group myself. I had the contact with the superiors, the really strong men. One was Theonest Bagasora, who is the cousin of Habyarimana.[43]

Colonel Theoneste Bagasora, one of the Clan de Madame, had been the commandant of Camp Colonel Mayuya at Kanombe, outside Kigali, and then became cabinet director at the ministry of defense. According to Afrika, there were also presidential guards at the camp who worked with the Interahamwe and another group under Bagasora nicknamed the *krapp*. Several of those later removed from senior army ranks, including Colonel Laurent Serubugu and Colonel Pierre-Celestin Rwagafilita, Agathe Kanzinga's brother, were usually present and involved in the training, Afrika said.

> I was called by Joseph Habyambere, the *prefet* of Gikongoro. He worked with us to cause the trouble in the country. In February 1992 he encouraged us to burn down the houses of people who were not supporters of Habyarimana. He wasn't able to be with us all the time. He gave us petrol to burn down houses in Gikongoro. In May 1992 we organized demonstrations in towns. We did that to see who came to the demonstrations and who didn't.[44]

Members of the Interahamwe were paid 20,000 Rwandan francs per month, a large amount, and were fed and provided with beer. A Kigali hotel, the Tam Tam, was effectively made over to them, where they could sign their names and say the Interahamwe was paying the bills:

> We weren't organized like a military. Each group had a chief. There was a president—Robert Kajuga.[45] He is a Tutsi, but he was favored by the president because he had betrayed his Tutsi tribe. The presidential guard was looking for the political leaders, while the interahamwe was looking for the Tutsi population.
>
> We had two French military officers who trained the interahamwe. A lot of other interahamwe were sent for training in Egypt. The last group to come back from Egypt trained others, along with the presidential guard. The French military taught us how to catch people. There was a major at the Affichier Centrale, a military camp where people were tortured. That was where the

French military office was. I saw the French military show the interahamwe how to throw knives at the enemy, and how to assemble and disassemble guns. It was the French who showed us how to do this. We went to Mont Kigali with the French, where we had firearms training. We didn't know how to use the arms which had been brought from France. So the French military were obliged to show us, along with the Rwandan soldiers. Even the interahamwe didn't know early on what their real role was. We thought we were going to be military. We didn't then know what we were [ultimately] being trained for.[46]

On 1 September 1992, thirty-five leaders of the Interahamwe met at a house they had been given in the Kigali district of Lemera. According to Afrika, President Habyarimana, Agathe Kanzinga, and Colonel Bagasora were all at the meeting. Habyarimana told the meeting that it was necessary to identify all the politicians who were no longer supporting him and whom it was therefore necessary to regard as favoring the RPF. Agathe Kanzinga voiced her own wish to identify women opposed to the regime and offered advice on how to neutralize opposition among women. However, it was at this same meeting that Habyarimana decided to identify people among the ranks of the militia and army who had themselves turned against the strategy of killing, which had by then been ongoing for almost one year. Four people—three army officers and Janvier Afrika—were identified as having turned against the slaughter, which had by then claimed up to 30,000 lives. "Habyarimana said that we four were against the plan and that we could become opposition and become RPF. I tried to escape but I was caught and imprisoned until 22 February 1994. I was told that the interahamwe had started killing the opposition and that my name was on the list."[47] Janvier Afrika was spirited out of Kigali, where he had been held in the presidential palace under house arrest, by his own contacts within the regime.

Tension in the city had mounted to an unbearable level by January 1994. Demonstrations were marked by intense aggression. At a road junction near the UN headquarters[48] a group of fifty supporters of the extremist CDR had gathered to chant slogans and brandish sticks at the small UN vehicle in which I was traveling on the road north to the RPF base at Mulindi. Their tone, their aggression and manner, had none of the excitement and sense of purpose that dominated political rallies I had seen elsewhere on the continent during the previous four years of political evolution. Even at that time, on 8 January 1994, three months before they were to lead the genocide that identified these very people as the most evil in Rwanda's history, it was possible to detect from their behavior that they did not share the purposes of political campaigners elsewhere. They chased the UN vehicle, which was being followed by another carrying four armed UN soldiers. There was a sense that nothing would deter them.

"Democracy has aggravated tension, because it has led to everybody try-ing to form their groups. Now, people kill for ten francs. There's no value on life. People do politics to fill their stomachs," Charles Ntampaka, the secre-tary general of the Rwandan Association of Jurists, told me two days later.[49] "If there's no political will for integration, it will never happen. People don't understand democracy. And the regime is very content that nobody under-stands what democracy is. The only way to change things is if politics is based on the majority of ideas based on a program, rather than the ethnic majority." But the lead from the government never came, while even less po-litical individuals such as Ntampaka criticized the political representation ac-corded to the RPF at Arusha as being disproportionate to the constituency it represented. Of course his solution to the problem was not the same as the government's:

> The only way of ending all this is by creating an *état de droits*.[50] It's true that there's a definite ethnic problem. But the ethnic problem only arises when there's a change in the control of power. The ethnic problem is one. But the big problem is economic. Rich against poor. And the rich encouraging the poor to fight. I can't say that the ethnic problem is the most important one.

Led by the government, Rwanda's professional class, its academics, its thinkers, writers, journalists, and teachers, could not envisage a time when the Hutu majority would not enjoy a guaranteed monopoly of power derived from its demographic superiority. Their anxieties and prejudices intensified in October 1993, with the brutal killing of neighboring Burundi's first demo-cratically elected president, the Hutu Melchior Ndadaye. His death caused uproar in Rwanda, and led to many of the extremist movements condemning the moves toward democracy, owing to the brutality of the Tutsi it was por-trayed as revealing. Democratic change, ultimately forced upon the Rwan-dan regime by way of the concessions it was forced to make at Arusha, had only shallow roots among the population as a whole, cowering as it was in an atmosphere created by years of scare-mongering, propaganda, educational indoctrination, and a selective version of history. By early 1994, the main op-position parties were divided into pro- or anti-Habyarimana factions, those in his favor having been largely bought off by financial inducements or cabi-net posts. The scene was set long before the genocide, owing in part to the combination of failure, ill-will, and sabotage which meant the Arusha accord was signed—at least on the government side—by a head of state who had in fact prepared the way for a catastrophe from which he hoped to emerge with his power intact.

The UN convoy, in which I was traveling to Mulindi in January 1994, left Kigali behind. Camps dotted the hillsides to the north of the city. These were the homes of Hutu displaced by the war when the RPF invaded in

1990, forcing them to flee south. The hills rolled into the distance in an apparently endless wave of green slopes, some fallow but most neatly cultivated into strips of planted red earth and bearing the fruits of the labor of Rwanda's industrious farmers. After several hours we stopped at a FAR checkpoint that marked the ceasefire line between government- and RPF-held territory. A few miles further on was another checkpoint, manned by RPF soldiers. An hour or so later we veered off the road and up a gravel track into the hills and came to a halt among the wooden huts of a disused tea estate. This was Mulindi, headquarters of the RPF. The hills around were coated in a thick layer of tea bushes, which had been left to grow until what had once been a productive plantation had instead become a sea of lush, rambling green billowing out across the valley.

Since the Arusha discussions the RPF had withdrawn its forces to the north of the country from the positions thirty kilometers outside Kigali to which they had reached during the fighting. A small contingent of RPF troops had also been billeted in the city, to guard their officials at the CND, a building on the edge of Kigali that had housed the Conseil National du Développement, but that had now become the RPF headquarters in the city. But it was at Mulindi, less then ten kilometers south of Rwanda's border with Uganda, that Paul Kagame retained his headquarters. In a small wooden house with a verandah, from which the view overlooked the tea-covered valley, the RPF military leader attempted to cite examples of history and demographic arithmetic as a means of deferring reflection on what was clearly about to happen.

> The specific question Habyarimana has been able to play on is the ethnic one, even though it's not the biggest problem. It's not as big a problem as regionalism. Today, he tries to champion the views of the Hutu majority. But he doesn't really draw support from the majority of the Hutu. He has about 25 percent of the Hutu. He saw multipartyism as a way of undermining the RPF war. But this led to other groups within the country trying to exploit the situation, for example among the southern [Hutu] who were wanting to overthrow Habyarimana and end northern dominance.[51]

Four months later, on 8 April 1994, I was there again, among the same tea-clad hills. Water a foot deep sloshed around inside bunkers and trenches, where young RPF troops cowered as they waited for incoming missiles being fired from the government barracks at Byumba. "Vite, vite," said the RPF commander, wearing a fighter pilot's cloth helmet as he spoke into a crackling radio. The gunners emerged. An 81mm mortar shell was dropped into the mouth of a launcher. "Fire." The shell slid inside and with a crack shot through the air. On a track behind the RPF line, columns of fighters trudged through deep mud, bringing more ammunition for the mortar firers and an antiaircraft battery, from which shells gushed out across the valley. Strewn across what was once a football field lay green-painted ammunition boxes with their destination clearly marked: Kampala, Uganda. Their lethal contents were listed: "Parts of Sprays," "Spare Parts for Rock Drill," "Parts of Typewriter," while among the empty boxes lay the torn-out pages of a Kinyarwanda hymn book.

"The whole war front is active. Getting to Kigali depends on the resistance we meet. But at the moment our forward forces are thirty-five kilometers from the city," said Patrick Mazimpaka, the RPF's first vice chairman.[52] The UN had abandoned its checkpoints within the demilitarized zone. On the evening of 6 April, President Habyarimana had been killed when the presidential jet carrying him and President Cyprien Ntaryamira of Burundi—Melchior Ndadaye's successor—was shot down as it approached Kigali airport. Both presidents and the three-man crew were killed. Immediately the slaughter that Habyarimana, Agathe Kanzinga, Bagasora, and the others had planned was unleashed. From Kigali's defense ministry, over the extremist RTLMC radio, by word of mouth, in orders from the *burgomestre*, among the cells of the Interahamwe and impuzamugambi militias across the country, the word went out; now was the time to kill.

9

Genocide

Entebbe disappeared behind us. The bright, lush grassland gave way to the swirling gray currents of Lake Victoria. The enormous Ilyushin screeched up into the towering white clouds that billowed over the vastness of Central Africa, while the Russian crew slugged vodka from a seemingly endless supply of bottles buried somewhere in the cavernous belly of the transport plane. The roads to Kigali were blocked, and the aircraft was being used by the United Nations to transport food to the city. The crew agreed to take us, a small group of journalists, after we had left the RPF base at Mulindi and traveled back into Uganda, in search of another way of reaching the Rwandan capital. It was 10 April, four days after the death of President Habyarimana. Reports from Kigali told of a sudden eruption of violence within an hour of the presidential aircraft crashing. The UN office in the city, headquarters of the Unamir military, political, and humanitarian units charged with overseeing the implementation of the Arusha accord, became the major source of information,[1] as its officials rapidly became spectators and commentators on events in which the UN military element was neither equipped nor mandated to intervene.

What was to become, within three months, the most intense period of slaughter at any time in the twentieth century anywhere in the world, with more people killed per day than even during the Nazi Holocaust, spawned a succession of further grotesque injustices, as the truth of what was taking place was twisted by politicians and media who either failed to grasp the enormity of the crime, or who indeed wished to manipulate it for personal or political ends. Rwanda was the crime that everybody saw, heard, and even smelt, but that the world, in full view of the raw and horrifying truth, did nothing to stop.

For much of those three months of slaughter, the world in fact chose not to know. Most reporters left Rwanda after the first few days, leaving the country to its ghastly fate, just as the UN did when it pulled out 90 percent of its troops. Failing to understand that real knowledge of the situation on the ground was vital to making informed decisions as to how the world should react, the media departed shaking their heads. They would wait for the inevitable day when they would be able to feed off a supply of stories issued by international relief agencies who would, inevitably, arrive at some point and take the bloody ruins of Rwanda in hand, while feeding the world tales of how funds were required for those suffering. The media would—and did—transform the story they had missed through their own failings into another story; the lost story of the biggest genocide of the century was neatly replaced by a tale more familiar and easy to tell—that of millions of refugees fleeing war-torn Rwanda. The media knew how to handle refugees; sympathy was automatic, the language of sympathy well rehearsed, and the set-piece roles of the star reporters well known. So, having failed to report the genocide, they turned the world's sympathy to those fleeing. It was deemed necessary that they be seen to be fleeing a war, and that they should be helped. Had those same media considered it worth reporting what actually took place in Rwanda in April–July, they would not have been able to say that it was a war from which the people were fleeing. There was barely any war in Rwanda. There was a genocide that nobody had done anything to stop. But there was no war. And those running away, for whom the aid agencies sought to create sympathy, were those who had committed the crimes. Meanwhile, by the United Nations, for France, for the United States, for the distant news desks of London, Washington, and elsewhere, it was deemed necessary to call it war, because then the worldwide inaction could seem more justifiable.

Thus, those fleeing became refugees from a war, and the shorthand notes and camera angles thrust images of the war's victims into the developed world's living rooms. Because sympathy was what was dutifully invoked, the fact that those fleeing were the guilty rather than the innocent was a little too much for the developed world to understand. Relief organizations would have found it impossible to raise funds to feed, clothe, and administer health care to the vast crowd of mass murderers who flocked into Tanzania and Zaire. The debate over whether these people should be saved, in view of the horrendous crimes they had committed in Rwanda, was a debate that was all but forbidden.

As a journalist, I was ashamed that despite weeks of reporting from Rwanda, in the face of extraordinary resistance from discouraging and uninterested editors, I had failed to drive the message home that Western public opinion had been deceived by the omissions, ineptitude, and self-censorship of politicians, analysts, relief agencies, and decisionmakers in the media. Editors in far-off Western capitals failed as dramatically as the United Nations in their task of explaining and encouraging public opinion to respond. The media failed, the politicians failed, the world closed its eyes, and so Rwanda died.

"Patience has been one of our distinguishing characteristics," the RPF's Theogene Rudasingwa told me before I left Mulindi for Entebbe.[2] "We don't think that a military solution is a final solution. We believe in a negotiated and peaceful solution. If we are to fight again it's not that we wish to negate the peace agreement," he said. But he knew that the plans by extremists within the Rwandan government to attack both the Tutsi and Hutu political opposition were well advanced long before 6 April. The UN also knew well in advance. On 11 January, the commander of the Unamir force in Kigali, Major General Romeo Dallaire, sent a cable to his superiors at the UN in New York in which he confirmed the existence of many of the plans detailed to me by Janvier Afrika, as well as the existence of arms caches to be used by the extremist militia. The purpose of the Interahamwe was known to UN member states almost four months before the killing started. While the scale of what took place was impossible to predict, the extremist backlash against the RPF's successful negotiation of its way into power through the Arusha peace process had long been expected. As Rudasingwa told me, the peace process had exposed the extremism of the government and set it along the path it considered the only route to survival:

> In trying to achieve their own survival, the Presidential Guard won't stop at anything. It's definitely a continuation of the policy. Whatever we do from here will strengthen the position of the RPF. Because finally the dictatorship has lost its mask, because it has finally shown it only represents the constituency of killers.
>
> If you look at the list of the people who have been killed, it contains more Hutus than Tutsis. The character of the violence is attaining a more national outlook. It shows you that the people who are portraying it as straight ethnic [violence] are wrong. . . . And given the chaos in the country, there's a need to move pretty fast. We must take military action, given the fact the situation is not improving. It's deepening. . . . We are absolutely opposed to foreign military intervention. We had it right from the beginning of this conflict. It was foreign influence that has created the military establishment that is now doing this fighting.[3]

Deep suspicion, knowledge of their enemy, and the legacy of a life lived as refugees motivated the RPF leadership. Within hours of the killing starting, the RPF was talking of "lists" of victims, a direct reference to the planning and organization that it was variously assumed or known had gone into what was taking place. "We put the battalion in Kigali in good faith.[4] We don't intend to be a sacrificial lamb. It's not because we failed to give peace a chance. We don't sing songs. We fight with Kalashnikovs," said Patrick Mazimpaka, the RPF's first vice chairman.[5] The RPF regarded the UN as having irreparably damaged its role as a potential arbiter by, as the RPF saw it, failing to condemn the creation of a new government in the wake of Habyarimana's death. Those who had probably been behind Habyarimana's assassination formed this government on 8 April, and several of them were certainly responsible for launching the wave of killings, as Mazimpaka made clear.

> The government was put in place by the UN. It's an illegitimate government. The RPF will have to reconsider its relationship with the UN. There's no ceasefire signed. That was disinformation by the UN. We believe that the behavior of the UN mission has been less than acceptable, although we have not been prepared to talk about it. They have helped Habyarimana's government. Now they have said they have negotiated a government. But that's not in their mandate. We are keeping Arusha alive, and on that basis we are challenging this new government.[6]

Just as the agenda of those who were now directing the slaughter in Kigali and elsewhere was being determined by military officers, militia leaders, and the members of the Clan De Madame who had successfully obscured their identity and real purpose from the UN until the weeks prior to the genocide, so the military machinery of the RPF remained intact and ready to respond to a breakdown during the period preceding the explosion of violence. The Arusha accord was an agreement that overturned much that Rwanda had become during the fifty years that had preceded it. For a document to have the power to instigate such changes, when not preceded by the outright military victory of one side, would indeed have been a remarkable success.

It is fair to say that the extremist elements within, or influential upon, the Rwandan government, saw the Arusha process in part as a smokescreen and in part an opportunity to juggle power within their own political cabal by establishing exactly who would accord the Tutsi a substantial political role and who would not. This latter process led ultimately to the decision to assassinate Habyarimana. Despite his certain role in the creation of the militias who later led the genocide, the extremists within his regime perhaps did not regard him as a sure guarantor against loss of power. Although no definitive explanation of who shot down the aircraft has yet been established, the most likely explanation is that Hutu extremists who considered that he had capitulated to RPF demands carried it out.[7] For the Arusha accord to have been fully implemented would have been remarkable. The weight of history suggested that catastrophe, rather than a pacific transition to democracy, was always more likely. When the activities of the militias became known to the UN in January 1994, it appeared almost certain. When the killing started, on 6 April, the only thing which had until then been difficult to predict was the exact date, and with better Unamir military intelligence even this would probably have been possible to establish in advance.

April Is the Cruelest Month

French paratroopers strolled along inside the perimeter fence of Kigali's Gregoire Kayibanda international airport. The modernist architecture of the terminal building, dominated by a sweeping roof, large windows, and bright yellow bilingual French and Kinyarwanda signs directing passengers to arrivals, departures, customs, and passport control, seemed frozen in time. Nobody was leaving, nobody arriving. The formalities of statehood had been transformed into weapons of slaughter. Nobody could leave, as all had become either killers or victims. Rwanda's false stability, nurtured by obsessive political control, and permitted by self-delusion and foreign complicity, had become a void. The airport echoed only with the occasional sound of military boots, while outside military vehicles sped across the runway. Soldiers—French and Rwandan—eyed the gathering rainclouds, their neat uniforms, maroon berets set at jaunty angles, sophisticated weaponry held at the ready, all adding to an illusion of purposefulness. The elements of authority were there, in their outward appearance. Rwanda's presidential guard patrolled the external perimeter, the French paratroopers the internal perimeter. All was arranged. France had sent 190 paratroopers to Rwanda on 9 April, to oversee the evacuation of 1,500 Belgian, 650 French, and 258 American and other foreign nationals.

The morning I arrived, 10 April, Belgium sent 250 soldiers for the same purpose. All was activity. There was a semblance of order. I drove toward the center of the city in a military truck driven by a French soldier. The French had been lent the trucks by the Rwandan army, which had relaunched its war with the RPF garrison at the CND, while the militias turned on the civilians. We drove fast in a convoy, along the narrow, winding roads that rise over the low hills surrounding the center of the city. At the base of a hill from where the road leads up to the Antoine de Saint-Exupéry French school, where foreign evacuees were gathering, traffic lights slung on a cable across the road changed from red to amber to green. On the roadside lay body after body after body, strewn across the pavements, on wasteland, dumped, exhibited, discarded. The early victims of an orchestrated, predestined slaughter. Bursts of mortar, rocket, and machine-gun fire had stopped Unamir employees from reaching the airport from their headquarters on the other side of the city to be evacuated on the aircraft which had brought us from Entebbe. But at the school, the French troops loaded 68 foreigners into the trucks and transported them back to the airport, from which they took off amid heavy shooting. The daylight faded in the mid-afternoon. The last flight of the day flew into the evening sky. The expressionless faces of the presidential guard patrolling the perimeter watched another door close on Rwanda.

By then, on the fifth night of the slaughter, they and their militia allies had wiped out Rwanda's fledgling opposition political class. The prime minister, Agathe Uwilingiyimana, had been murdered within hours of Habyarimana's aircraft being brought down on the edge of the airport runway where the presidential guard patrol was now standing. Killed with her, by first being tricked by the presidential guard into handing over their weapons and then having their throats cut, had been ten Belgian Unamir soldiers, provided to her as a personal protection unit.

As the violence exploded, Belgian officers were the least restrained in their assessment of what was taking place and who was behind it. Belgian officers in Kigali disputed Rwandan army allegations that the RPF was responsible for the assassination of Habyarimana, saying they had seen rockets fired from the Kanombe military base at the plane carrying the two presidents on 6 April. "The French say that the RPF launched the attack on the president's plane, because they are working with the government forces. But I think it's highly unlikely that it was the RPF who did it," Captain Bruno Vandriessche, commander of the Belgian army unit at the airport, told me at his base.[8] The Belgian theory was the first to suggest the president died in a coup d'etat, one that had the initial effect of dividing loyalties within the various branches of the Rwandan armed forces. The commander of the presidential guard, Colonel Mpiranya, was among the plotters, according to Vandriessche.[9] The guard subsequently clashed with the Rwandan army,[10] until the RPF decision to lead an all-out assault on the government forces—the guard and the militia—who had become the foot soldiers of the genocide. Then, in the interests of unity, the three strands of the military were reconciled. With internal concord within the killing machine reestablished, the ultimate purpose was reasserted. Prunier summarizes the situation well:

> Although the pogrom was clearly focused on liberal politicians and other democrats, the victims were not only well-known people. The lists were long, detailed and open to extension. Tutsi were killed simply because they were Tutsi, i.e. ontological *ibyitso*, "accomplices" of the RPF, and this even in the case of people who had absolutely no sympathy with the guerrillas. Hutu who were either members or simply sympathizers of democratic opposition parties were also killed because their opposition to "the democratic majority"[11] had turned them into objective *ibyitso*, no better than Tutsi. Several journalists were killed because they had written too freely about corruption among senior officials. Many priests and nuns were killed because they tried to stop militiamen killing others. Some well-dressed people, or people who spoke good French, or peo-

ple who owned a car and were not known MRND(D)[12] supporters were killed
simply because these marks of social distinction made them natural suspects
for holding liberal opinions.[13]

Early next morning, 11 April, the French troops took a back road into Kigali from the airport, passing through the center of the city, where soldiers
and gangs of youths brandishing machetes manned roadblocks on streets
where piles of mutilated corpses lay in heaps, disposed of like refuse. Heavy
fighting had broken out between the government and RPF forces overnight,
along a line that had effectively cut the Unamir headquarters off from the
airport. The muddy back road passed between small houses and huts. Outside one lay the bodies of two newly killed men sprawled in the muddy
courtyard. At the French school, French troops lay on the roof with guns
trained on the deserted road outside, while the names of evacuees were read
out in the courtyard below. A mud road led up a hill on the other side of the
valley, which was overlooked from the school. The road was littered with
bodies. Halfway up the hill lay a pile of corpses. From nearby houses
women, old and young, were casually led to the pile and forced to sit down
on it. Men with clubs then beat the dead and dying bodies that surrounded
the women as they sat, screaming, pleading for their lives. Suddenly the men
turned on the women. They beat them until they no longer moved, then
went to find more people to kill, within view of the school where the evacuees packed their children, pet dogs, teddy bears, and suitcases into the
trucks lent to them by Rwanda's army.

The evacuation convoy returned along the back road to the airport. As we
passed among the shacks and houses, we saw people alongside the road up
ahead. The convoy slowed beside a young woman who was being pushed and
dragged along the road by a young man carrying a machete. He pulled at her
clothes, as she looked at the foreign soldiers in the desperate, terrified hope
that they could save her from the murder she knew was fast approaching. But
the French troops did not move. "It's not our mandate," said one, leaning
against his jeep as he watched the condemned woman, the driving rain
splashing at his maroon beret. Further on, where there had been the bodies
of two murdered men when the convoy had passed on its way from the airport earlier, the body of a woman and two more men lay with the two already dead, their eyes wide open. The woman had had one of her legs cut
off. On the other side of the road the bodies of three men lay with fresh
wounds. Watching the convoy were the killers—young men, two women
with clubs, old men, and children. Close to one body stood a man wearing
neat office clothes and carrying a clipboard, perhaps—though I cannot believe I saw it—ticking off names on a list. Beside him was a well-armed government soldier, spectating without expression from where he stood in his
smart uniform.

Colonel Theoneste Bagasora sat behind his desk as if it were another working day. His office in the defense ministry was simple—a desk whereon lay some papers and three chairs facing it, where I sat with two colleagues. There were few guards outside. The place was tranquil. "You can go anywhere you like,"[14] Bagasora told us. "You're quite safe. No harm will come to you." During those first days, there was little certainty what specific role people such as he were playing in what was taking place. Nor was there any way of knowing what was taking place outside Kigali, as there was little movement in the country, and so no way of knowing for sure the scale of what was happening. Colonel Bagasora gave us a copy of his visiting card, having written our three names on it, as a kind of accreditation. He signed it and stamped it, and we were free to go wherever we wanted. We even shook hands. I think he even smiled as we said goodbye. So now we had a ticket to watch.

We left the defense ministry, a group of single-story buildings beneath trees, and walked back down the hill to the Hôtel des Mille Collines. The corridors were silent, hundreds of people hiding behind doors that never opened, inside rooms from which no sound ever came. There in the lobby was the Tutsi man with his Yugoslavian wife, whose tale is recounted in the previous chapter. He silent, she wandering from group to group of the people who milled around the lobby waiting for something to happen. He never catching anybody's eye, she in a state of calm panic, as she pleaded her case with strangers who could nothing for her. He standing still, while she tried to save him from the soldiers on the other side of the glass door, who would take him away if only they could. She remained in a trancelike state of terror for three days, knowing what was likely to happen, knowing that he and possibly she herself were likely to be killed, as the deaths of foreigners married to Tutsis had been reported.

Watching the fear, watching the horror. I walked further down the hill from the hotel, to a large church that overlooked the city. A gutter a foot wide ran the length of the church. The murdered bodies of two women lay in it beside the tall gate into the compound. Inside, the lawn had become home to hundreds of families. In the church, children were drawing pictures of the Holy Family, which the nuns stuck up on the walls of the cavernous redbrick nave. Under every pew, a family had made its home. The altar was slung with drying clothes. The nuns tried to remain calm and jolly, smiling, complimenting the children on their drawings. When I walked outside, the body of a man had been slung into the gutter close to those of the two women. Men at a checkpoint behind the church manned by soldiers and civilians glared at me, but let me pass.

I walked down toward the French embassy, but was told it was closed. Then I went to the residence of the Papal Nuncio, but he was not available. The streets were empty. I walked back up the hill to the office of the International Committee of the Red Cross (ICRC). The staff had no time to talk. The fear that pervaded the city was heightened in the ICRC. Behind the building a clinic had been established, and then beds added for the wounded. Médecins Sans Frontières (Doctors Without Borders), the French aid agency, had been providing emergency assistance at Kigali hospital until two days beforehand. The entire MSF team had been evacuated on 10 April, after all the Tutsis receiving care had been slaughtered in the tents pitched for them outside the hospital. This left only the ICRC to provide care. Guarding the gate to the clinic behind the ICRC building were Rwandan soldiers, assessing who went in and out. The ICRC staff was simply waiting for the soldiers to go inside to pull out the Tutsis who had managed to find their way into the clinic.

It was late afternoon by the time I left the clinic to walk back to the Hôtel des Mille Collines. A truck drove past on the steep road outside the ICRC office. Blood poured from its slightly open flap as it ascended the hill, and bodies shifted inside. The truck was from the department responsible for refuse collection in the city. The men in the cab wore their cleansing department uniforms.

Major General Romeo Dallaire, the head of the Unamir peacekeeping mission, had just arrived at the hotel. He told the few reporters still there that his troops might remain in Rwanda to oversee a ceasefire, which he hoped had been arranged between the RPF and the government. Asked if the UN force planned to protect civilians in the city and elsewhere, he said: "What we would like to do is expand our capabilities to provide that opportunity of assistance. We have been looking and trying to find the means by which the two sides would be prepared to face each other. The difficulty has been one side not recognizing the other's government," he said, referring to the non-recognition by the RPF of the junta set up by Bagasora and other planners of the genocide in the immediate aftermath of Habyarimana's death.[15] "But if we see another three weeks of being cooped up and seeing them pound each other, then I have got to seriously assess the effectiveness of keeping the troops here," Dallaire said. He was as aghast at what was taking place as everybody else, despite having received and passed on warnings as early as January, four months beforehand, that plans were being laid for violence. The Yugoslavian woman remained close to him as he spoke. She appealed to him, explaining the situation her husband was in. They spoke quietly with each other, she not wanting to be seen by the Rwandan soldiers outside on the street. Then I saw him leave, with the Yugoslavian woman and her husband in his car.

Dallaire stayed on in Rwanda. But on 21 April the UN Security Council voted unanimously to withdraw all but 270 of its 2,500 Unamir troops. The pullout coincided with reports that the killing had spread to most areas of the country. The UN High Commissioner for Refugees announced, with a horrifying accuracy made possible only by a well-planned genocide in which nonparticipants were able to play a spectator role, that 16,870 people had been killed in nine villages around Cyangugu, in the southwest.

Condemnation of the UN's desertion was swift but ineffective. Meanwhile, the difficulty in comprehending the enormity of the crime being committed in Rwanda was matched during those first weeks by misinformation about what was really going on in the country. Despite the complicity and occasional involvement of the Rwandan army, as well as the organizational role played by Rwandan army officers in the genocide, most of the killers were civilians armed with machetes, knives, and clubs, against which a well-armed UN force could have been effective. The Rwandan army itself, preoccupied by the advance of the RPF, would not have been able to effectively oppose an aggressive UN force. But after the debacle of the UN and U.S. intervention in Somalia the previous year, there was little appetite for a UN role in Rwanda. Consequently the slaughter was wrongly portrayed as an armed conflict between the two sides in Rwanda's civil war, into which the UN would necessarily have to step if it were to have become involved. This was a deceit. The civilian slaughter had been going on for days before major battles erupted between the RPF and the government army in Kigali.

The ferocity of the violence blinded the UN to its potential military role. Instead, it concentrated upon bringing the two "warring" sides together for peace talks, even though neither the RPF nor the Rwandan army was involved in the real violence, which was at that time being perpetrated by the civilian militias against defenseless civilians.

On 30 April the UN secretary-general Boutros Boutros-Ghali made a belated appeal for more UN troops to be sent, only to be met with a refusal by the UN Security Council. Boutros-Ghali had said there was "strong evidence of preparations for further massacres of civilians in the city of Kigali. This humanitarian catastrophe demands urgent action."[16] All the council would do was issue a long statement condemning the "slaughter of innocent civilians," call for an arms embargo on the warring factions, and have its president, the New Zealand foreign minister Colin Keating, request that Boutros-Ghali "flesh out his proposal and provide some concept of operation" before council members could make a decision.

SPECTATORS OF HORROR

Nobody remembered the girl with no name. There was nobody left to remember her. She sat in silence on the floor of the church in Byumba, northeastern Rwanda. Others spoke of their nightmares. Each was different, but also the same. A few kilometers north of Byumba a line of women and children wound slowly along the road. Most had come from Kigali, and had been barely prepared for the three-day walk. The center of Byumba was completely deserted. The shops were stripped bare of goods. It was a ghost town. A hospital had been set up behind the church, which had been the target in the gun sights of the RPF when I had watched them pounding the town with mortar shells three weeks beforehand. MSF, some Italian surgeons, and a team of Rwandan doctors and nurses, who had been displaced, were working there. The smell was of antiseptic and urine, while the homeless and terrified refugees sat on the church steps huddled in the rain. Children of five or six were among the injured. And the girl, alone. Too shocked even to talk. Mute with shock. No one knew her name, nor where she came from, nor where she would go.

We drove slowly through the deep, lush green fields bulging with overgrown tea in the valley that led away from the RPF headquarters at Mulindi, north of Byumba. We drove for half the day, 30 April, along dirt roads through land deserted by the government and the militias as the RPF advanced through the country, until we reached a tarmac road beside Lake Muhazi. The length of the shoreline where the gray water lapped the reeds and mud was strewn with half-submerged bodies, shifting slightly as a breeze swept the surface of the lake. We stopped in a small house at Gahini, and then drove through woodland along a soft mud road to Rukara, a church and mission run by foreign nuns.

The early evening sunlight flickered through the forest, exposing piles of corpses dumped beneath the trees. The church overlooked a wide, open space. A water tap dripped onto a bloody dress hidden in the shrubbery. A tabby cat trotted silently out of a room with broken windows. Inside, a bloody sheen had spread across the floor, which could not be seen for bodies. Children lay as if sleeping on mats beside their mothers. The faces were fading. A baby's legs were splayed out, like those of any child lying on its back. A skull grinned. Outside, a whistling bird flew by, swooping from its perch on the large white cross that dominates the courtyard of the mission. The hum of bees filled the stinking vegetable garden as the sun began to set over the forest, which hung like a gloomy curtain around the cluster of buildings. The people who had died there were cooking when the killers came. The charcoal was still fresh, the cooking pots upturned. Branches for fuel lay half torn from trees, as if they were being collected just before the death squad arrived. The fingers of a whitened hand clawed at the steps of the altar inside the church. Pews lay scattered, broken, twisted around the bodies on the mats where the people had slept. Outside the building, two armed and uniformed members of the RPF sped by on bicycles, holding their noses, passing without looking.

"I hid with my daughter among the bodies they left behind after the gendarmes had come with the Interahamwe. We hid there until they had gone. I think they thought we were dead, so they left us," said Therese Uwiligyamana, as she walked by the church.[17] Another survivor, Agathe Nsengimira, clung to the baby that she managed to save when she fled: "There were so many of them, with their weapons. They came during the day to my home near Rwamapanga. All the village was out of their houses. They knew where the Tutsis lived, on top of the hill. I ran with my baby, but my young boy was left behind. I didn't see him. He was running, but I lost him. I could see them killing the people near the houses. But I lost my boy."[18]

That day, 250,000 people had crossed from Rwanda into Tanzania. Among the other records the horror of Rwanda's genocide was to give the world, other than the slaughter reaching the fastest rate of killing of the twentieth century,[19] the crossing of the Rusumo Falls bridge into Tanzania was the largest crossing of its kind by a group of people in a single day. The following day, 150,000 more Rwandans followed them. They fled the advancing RPF, which the following day, 1 May, reached the eastern border with Tanzania.

It was night when we reached Gahini again. There was the occasional sound of shooting ringing out in the darkness. The RPF officers in whose house we stayed would not explain why. They just grinned and talked about other things. The war, the clashes between the RPF and the government, were too far away to be heard from here. The militias were not active there, most of them apparently having fled. We never knew what the shots were, and the RPF troops accompanying us were giving no explanations, preferring instead to talk politics.

"Hutu means *servant* in Kinyarwanda," Captain Diogene Mudenge elaborated, in the dim candlelight of the sitting room where we ate beans.[20] "Somebody with lots of cows had the right to have servants. Tutsi meant rich. In the 1950s and 1960s these differences became the politics, and the Hutu and Tutsi became ethnic groups. But it's contested, the theory that the Tutsis came from Ethiopia," he went on.

> The Tutsis have some similarities to the Nilotic peoples, like the Maasai. But the history of Rwanda is still being researched. But the colonialists divided the population. Hutu and Tutsi are in fact all Bantu, not Nilotic. There are no signs which distinguish the different groups, in terms of the way of life. You can't any longer find a two-meter Tutsi. The significance of the difference between Hutu and Tutsi is something purely economic. Between the peasants there's no problem. In the bars you'll find the Hutu and the Tutsi will share the same calabash. We don't work on the basis of ethnicity. We don't keep any statistics. There is no ethnicity. There are hypotheses but no proof.

It was remarkable, this ability of the RPF to talk, while outside, across the country, on every hill, the most evil things were happening. Just as the killers were methodical in their program, so the RPF knew exactly what it was bound to do.

The scale of the horror was not betrayed by the sounds—save perhaps the occasional gunshot—which it would seem to require. Rwanda's horror was conducted with quiet stealth. The RPF responded with similar stealth—until clashes brought armies into direct confrontation. Then the government troops tended to flee, in the face of the determination of the RPF to decimate their military opponents.

Sleeping in a house nearby was a Belgian farmer, Marcel Gerin, and his Mexican wife Gloria, who had been discovered by the RPF the day before, after they had spent twenty days living on the grasslands of their wildlife ranch in eastern Rwanda. They were planning to leave Rwanda for Belgium where, as he had been born in the former Belgian Congo and left for Rwanda when Congo was plunged into civil war in 1960, he had no family. When the violence had started, they had tried to prevent the militia from murdering their Tutsi employees. Eventually they were forced to desert their house and disappear into the game park they had established, wherein lived zebras, topi, hippopotamuses, and impala:

> During the day we could get food from the garden. When the night came we would climb up into the trees because of the hippos. In the daytime I had my hunting rifles. I could keep a watch on the situation. But it was a matter of days. There were about 500 extremists. They were a mass. They went through the population, and whatever wasn't pleasant to their eyes they just killed off. The children. They threw them in the lake. They tied their hands, and put grass in their mouths, and threw them in the lake to drown. I saw it. They said we would go the same way. I survived because I was armed. We just tried to avoid all contact. To make ourselves very small. One day I was patrolling and I stopped when I saw some movement in the bushes. I was surrounded by men in uniform who I had barely noticed. It was the rebels, who brought us here yesterday.[21]

We left Gahini for the east early the next morning. On the shore of Lake Muhazi a young boy stood alone, filling a yellow plastic watering can with water, a few yards from the slowly turning body of a man, which lay face down. We passed brick-built houses torn apart by fire or grenades, families lying dead in the yards, roadside villages ransacked, drifting groups of survivors lighting fires under the driving rain. A woman in a red T-shirt stood at the door of a mud and grass hut. She was the only person there. All the other huts were empty. A sign marked the road to the Akagera National Park, and then Ranch Mpanga, where Marcel and Gloria Gerin had hidden for twenty days. The route climbed up hills and passed through woods, and we followed it as if following in the path of a hurricane that had moved ahead of us, leaving selective devastation: some houses looted, others with their doors closed;

some yards filled with the bodies of families, others with sunflowers bending slightly in the wind.

The road passed through the eerie silence of a deserted hillside refugee camp of grass-covered huts to which people had fled from the RPF during the 1990–1993 war. The grass hovels were all deserted, the gaping holes of their dark entrances like a heap of open mouths, on a hillside that had been stripped of its trees by the people who had lived there. At Gatare the Karibu Bar has been destroyed. At Kivehe an old man lay dead on the roadside. At Nyakavambi dogs were rooting among the trash. At Rwanteru a frightened boy of six or seven wandered alone along the roadside, hot, wide-eyed, lost. Outside Kayanzi, the road was littered with clothes, abandoned cattle chewing the grass, bags, pots, buckets, shoes, pineapples, sacks of ripe maize, beans, and stores lay round abandoned fires. But the people had gone. Not a single person was left, only discarded identity cards, Bibles, and letters unsent blowing in the breeze. At Rusumo, at the entrance to the border village, there was the stink of a rotting body wafting from a maize field. The refugees had piled up their weapons on a bend in the road just before it descended the hill to the border post they had crossed two days beforehand. Thousands of machetes, knives, daggers, kitchen utensils, hacksaws, and spears lay piled in a heap, some still stained with blood. Among them were discarded identity cards, all left by people now perhaps frightened of what might happen to them if it were known who they were once they crossed into Tanzania to the town of Ngara, where the world's relief agencies were waiting to feed the fleeing killers at Benaco, claimant of another world record—that of being the world's largest refugee camp.[22] At the bottom of the hill was the frontier. From the elegant bridge across the narrow gorge marking the border, through which the Kagera River passes, Tanzanian border guards counted as another bleached and bloated body plunged down Rusumo Falls. They pointed at a cluster of bodies that had become entangled in weeds on the Tanzanian side. "It's Habyarimana's gift to the president of Tanzania," one said.[23]

An Army on the Move

The RPF had advanced rapidly from their northern base at Mulindi, not just to the eastern border but also toward Kigali from the eastern side. A column of RPF troops was also advancing on foot from Mulindi to the north of the city, to reinforce the troops who had been besieged there ever since the violence had erupted. By 2 May, the RPF troops sent to the eastern side of Kigali had the city in their sights. Major Philbert Rwigamba led us up a steep mud track that passed through thick forest. We had left Rusumo and driven back west toward Kigali. He talked about his years in the National Resistance Army, the force that had brought Yoweri Museveni to power in

Uganda in 1986, which many Tutsi exiles in Uganda had joined. "The NRA brought us up. Most of us trained with the NRA. In 1982, Obote massacred many Rwandans, and chased them from Uganda. We asked ourselves: where can we go? So, we went to the bush to fight Obote, and we had the same goal as the NRA. Even though eventually we stole guns and deserted the NRA after they took over, we remain friends," he said, referring to the RPF's theft of guns from the Ugandan force of which they had been part, which allowed them to launch their invasion of Rwanda in 1990.[24]

He led us into a small village, Kabuga, on the summit of the hill, where a few people watched as the line of troops filed past without acknowledging them. Major Rwigamba stopped to talk with them. They said Kabuga had been a stronghold of the Interahamwe. On 6 April they had heard the missile that had brought down Habyarimana's aircraft, as Kigali was just over the hill. When the killing started some of the villagers, Hutus and Tutsis, had tried to take refuge in Gasagarawa village nearby. The army had sent a helicopter to bomb them, said one survivor, Faustin Nsengimana.[25]

> All of the people there were exterminated. They said that the Hutu and the Tutsi who were not in the MRNDD would be exterminated. The *burgomestre* tried to prevent the killing. He organized a meeting and told the people not to kill. He was accused by the interahamwe of sympathizing with the RPF. He fled, and the Hutus who didn't support the killing were killed. We knew some of the killers. The village chief of Kabuga, Leonard Mwongereza, led them. There's one survivor.

We reached the other side of the hill and walked through vegetable plots beside deserted homes, where French beans had ripened but been left unpicked. From the top of the hill we watched a UN aircraft swoop down low at the last minute as it prepared to land at Kigali airport two miles away. RPF forces were being relieved by fresh troops. The tired, quiet column of troops, carrying hoes, guns, umbrellas, ammunition boxes, and multicolored scarves, paced steadily away from the front-line trenches. Shafts of sunlight poured through black thunderclouds and onto the lush, green valley. "We have divided the country into two. We haven't lost any ground in Kigali since the campaign started," Major Rwigamba said. "The massacres. . . . It's the whole country. Not just the city. It's too much. It's too much. If they don't stop the massacres. Our target isn't the city. The city is where all this started. But now we realize it's going on in the whole country. So we will go through the whole country. We are trying to move fast," he said, peering through binoculars at Kanombe barracks beside the airport, home to the presidential guard.

We spent that night, 2 May, in Kibungo. We had passed General Dallaire, the UN military commander, on the road near Rwamagana. He was on his way to meet Paul Kagame. "My mandate was peacekeeping. We're trying to stop massacres. The question now is: What should we be doing? We are also in negotiations to make a neutral territory." Dallaire said, as he stared out from within his white UN Toyota Land Cruiser, protected by his bulletproof vest, hidden inside his camouflage, looking and sounding like a man on the verge of despair, as the stark reality he was witnessing failed to move the institution he represented into action.[26] He drove off for his meeting. A few minutes later, Kagame drove past in the same direction. Patrick Mazimpaka, the first RPF vice president and effective political leader, stopped to discuss the emerging rationale behind UN thinking.

> If it's an intervention force, and Boutros-Ghali thinks that this is about Hutu and Tutsi killing each other, then that would not be solving the problem, because it is the government killing civilians. It would be based on the wrong premise and would be doing the wrong job. We think Dallaire is giving correct reports [to the UN], but the [UN] secretariat doesn't want to hear this. It's the same reason why the UN Security Council refuses to use the word genocide. They didn't want to blame the previous regime. France was one of them that didn't want to. It is a matter of refusing to accept the correct analysis.[27]

The same point continued to be made by the RPF, as the pattern of killing emerged. At a press conference in Nairobi a few weeks later, Theogene Rudasingwa, the RPF military second in command, said: "Contrary to some reports that we continue to see, the killings in Rwanda are not ethnic killings. There are not massacres being fought out by either ethnic group. The killings that are taking place are political killings."[28] The RPF leadership saw the slaughter as an attempt by the ruling elite to retain power, as politically motivated, rather than having the purely ethnic motive of genocide.

We were given an abandoned bungalow in Kibungo, opposite the building in which Dallaire and Kagame were meeting. The bungalow smelled of decay, but inside nothing had been upset or broken. Water came through the taps, but the nauseating smell deterred anybody from using it. Darkness fell. Dallaire left in the night. Kagame drove away some time later, and we met him midmorning at Rusumo, the border post. He was sitting on a chair on the verandah of the border post, just above the gorge over which the bridge arched. He condemned the UN, and in particular the way the French government had manipulated opinion in New York to move it against the RPF, a topic that had dominated his meeting with Dallaire the previous night:

> I could only notice that there was little understanding of how to solve the problem. In the first place [Dallaire] was the one who suggested pulling the [UN] forces out. Finding the same man turning around and saying they should have a massive deployment . . . to save nobody, anyway. All those who are still

alive may be killed in the next few days. They don't understand the problems at all. [Dallaire] isn't well advised, or he is influenced by people who are the cause of the problem. An intervention by a big force would be irrelevant and useless in this situation, and would only add up to more problems.

Somebody must answer for this killing. Unfortunately, in the past, the international community has . . . failed to condemn such people. There are some people who simply don't want to talk the truth. The French didn't want to call the killings genocide. And when the French were still operating with the government, they were manning roadblocks at which they demanded identity cards which showed peoples' ethnic background.

There was little concern by the international community for the suffering of the people of Rwanda. This became more apparent when people began blaming us for taking up arms and fighting the government. This shows the double standards. We are trying to intervene and save as many people as possible. We are not able to cover the whole country. But what we have done is much better than anybody else could have done, and much better than what an intervention force could do. . . . I think that the ultimate victory of the RPF is the best solution, because it makes people get to understand that they can't just be there all the time depriving people of their lives. There isn't much to be gained by talking.[29]

Dallaire had made many suggestions during his meeting with Kagame, but the RPF knew it was alone if it wanted to stop the massacres. Once again it was isolated, just as its main supporters and foot soldiers had been isolated throughout much of the three decades they had spent in exile. Their identity had evolved into an organization dominated by bespectacled intellectuals leading a force of quietly confident foot soldiers wearing Wellington boots and smart uniforms, which always seemed to be neatly pressed. There were said to be as many as four hundred PhDs within RPF ranks at that time, setting the tone of a force combining a frosty coldness with a disarming honesty.

We drove west toward Kigali, guided by the "minders," who barely let us out of their sight and were the guardians of a creed of strict discipline. Passing an abandoned truck by the roadside, our driver said he wanted to take off a wheel to replace a punctured spare tire. "No, you can't just take it," said our minder, Anthony Kabano. "You have to seek permission." We drove to a nearby RPF checkpoint, where the driver talked for some time with the checkpoint commander, who eventually gave his assent. We then drove back to the bus. "Now, we have permission, and you can take the tire," said Anthony, pompously but correctly, concerned about righteousness and discipline, as the stink of rotting corpses along the roadside lingered in the air. The corpses had not been there when we had passed the day before. Who killed them? Anthony would not say.

We stopped in Rwamagana. Dazed patients wandered around the yard of the Fontanas hospital, where the smell of the dead, the dying, and the injured wafted from the wards. "We had taken refuge on a hill with hundreds of other people near Bichumbi," said Agnes Nyamahore, whose hand and left leg were wrapped in dirty, blood-soaked bandages.[30] "When the militia came, many people put up resistance using bows, arrows, and stones. They attacked us for three days. Then they sent for assistance from the army, and the army came with guns and grenades and killed many people. The attacks were all organized by the chief of the district, Juvenal Rugambarara. And he was with Karakezi and Kahano Mugabo," she said, referring to her neighbors. She said she saw them, along with the army, under the direction of the chief, kill her other neighbors.

In the hospital, most survivors were able to identify by name at least some of the death squads. "We saw people who were visibly under the orders of others," said Frederick Rubwejanga, the Roman Catholic bishop of Rwamagana.[31] He had visited the barracks close to his diocese headquarters, to ask for military protection for himself and the priests after the killings started.

When I went into the office I found the commanding officer, Colonel Anselme Mkuriyekubona, talking about tactics with the local head of the MRNDD and Cyasa Habimana, who was known as the interahamwe chief. He was the one who killed a priest, Michael Nsengiyumra, as he was taking an injured man to the hospital. A lieutenant, Mihigo, came to our church and said he would protect myself and seven priests. He left, leaving in command one of his men, who immediately said to me that he could only guard two of the priests and asked me which ones should be allowed to live. I said all of them must be allowed to live. Then he shot Father Elisée Mpongano. Mpongano had had a gun, and he had shot some of the militia when they tried to attack his church a few days beforehand. I think he killed one of them.

By 7 May, the RPF had advanced to the perimeter at one end of Kigali airport. The area on the city side of the airport, as well as the Kanombe barracks, had been depleted of troops as the RPF advanced. The government had meanwhile fled to a town near Gitarama, thirty miles south of Kigali. I drove with Anthony Kabano to the edge of the airport and reached a group of buildings, across from which was the road I knew led into Kigali. The RPF positions, marked by trenches intended to protect its troops stationed in the city since before the crisis erupted on 6 April, were almost within sight. The remains of the government army were nowhere to be seen. In the face of Anthony's stiff resistance, I told him I would continue into Kigali, across a front line which in fact seemed nonexistent and which appeared to have been deserted. A group of journalists then appeared from the city, and we drove together up the hill away from the airport, into the silent, empty, late afternoon streets of Kigali.

The Face of Hate

"Usually the Tutsis look just like . . . you." Lieutenant Wenceslas of Rwanda's Gendarmerie Nationale pointed at me. "They are tall, and have long, straight noses. But I don't know any of them. . . . I don't know any Tutsis. None of them have ever been my friends. Not one. Never."[32] He was standing in the lobby of the Hotel Diplomat in the heart of Kigali. The hotel had become the military headquarters of the self-appointed government since its departure for Gitarama. "We have tried. . . . We are trying to calm the population. We really don't know who killed Agathe Uwilingiyimana, the prime minister, and, you know, well, the civilians are very angry." He was a bad liar. Everybody knew the presidential guard had slaughtered the prime minister and her family on 6 April. Did he admit that there were elements within the armed forces responsible for the killings? "No. No. It was the militias. The civilians. They have nothing to do with the army," he said. But who are the militias? "The interahamwe and the impuzamugambi." And who are their leaders? "Well, their president is Robert Kajuka."

Kajuka had held regular meetings with UN officials once it became clear that the worst people in the city were the only ones worth talking to if the UN wanted to save lives. On 3 May, the UN had had to abandon an attempt to rescue the 300 people, mostly Tutsis, still cowering inside the Mille Collines hotel. A crowd wielding machetes had ordered the evacuees out of the buses and surrounded their UN-escorted convoy. Two were slashed with machetes through the bus windows, and the UN troops were forced to return the entire convoy to the hotel. On 12 May the hotel manager had threatened to throw his guests out, because they had not paid their bills. Robert Kajuka was then asked by the UN to allow the hotel occupants to leave under UN escort.

On 13 May he stood outside the Hotel Diplomat, fumbling with the six-inch blade he wore strapped in a sheath on his hip. He was tall; his eyelids drooped slightly over his large eyes. He was a Tutsi, who had joined the Hutu extremist cause. He smiled pleasantly as the UN force commander, General Dallaire, shook his hand and treated him with the painful civility thought necessary to discourage the death squads he controlled from butchering more people. He, Lieutenant Wenceslas, and other senior officers of the Rwandan army disappeared into a side room of the Hotel Diplomat to discuss the fate of the innocents in the Mille Collines. Dallaire emerged and left.

Kajuka assured me, "You can get around everywhere. We're going to help you circulate everywhere in the country, to see what has been going on, to see what has happened."[33] Instead of discussing the activities of the murderous men and women under his influence, he preferred to talk about his shock at the eruption of popular anger:

> I'm shocked, certainly. There's a war here. There are people who have created problems. For me it's the RPF who have created the problems . . . the violence. It's the RPF who are attacking the country. They say that they are Rwandans, but they are attacking the country. And when they attack the country it's the population that takes the consequences.
>
> To defend the country there are regular soldiers. The RPF aren't regular soldiers. It's not the military. It's the population who are angry. We want peace. We want dialogue with the RPF. Because they say they are Rwandans. We will discuss. We will settle our problems.
>
> We need the UN. It's for that reason that General Dallaire has come to meet us. We are very happy with Unamir because they help us . . . they try to help us . . . to give us peace in the country . . . to help the population find peace. We're ready to defend our country. We are here. We're not going to attack Uganda. Because Uganda is the RPF. But if Uganda and the RPF keep on attacking us we are going to fight. We're going to stay in Kigali. Whether or not we're awaiting an attack, we're going to remain in Kigali. There's no problem.[34]

The UN had been talking to all sides in Kigali, in an effort to negotiate safe passage for the handful of people to whom its few remaining troops had some degree of access. The government in Gitarama had proved not only its illegitimacy, by the way it assumed power, but also its ineffectiveness as an interlocutor with the UN. UN officials knew the civilian officials within it were either lying when they said they would attempt to arrange for those in the Mille Collines to leave, or were being sidelined by the real power, which lay in the hands of the military-militia "coordinating group" that was masterminding the genocide. "The government can't effectively control any of the other entities," Abdul Kabia, the Unamir executive director, told me in his office at the Unamir headquarters on the other side of the city, beyond the trenches that marked the frontline, which white UN cars were alone able to cross.[35]

> We have been talking to everybody: to the army chief, the gendarmerie chief, and the prime minister. We have not been talking to the coordinating group. They're extremist Hutus. So that's why when the army told us we could take the people from the Mille Collines, we were stopped by the militia. The army gave us permission. But some of the army told the militia. They worked together to stop the evacuation. We are now working with the militias, because we realize that getting through the barricades, it's not enough to have the permission of the government.

Thus the murderers controlled the city and the UN operation, whose officials and 275 troops were powerless to do anything but accommodate the genocide, in the pathetic hope that by doing so they could save a few lives out of the million lost. Such was their impotence that even the inflammatory propaganda broadcast by Rwandan radio stations continued to poison the airwaves, just as the slaughter had poisoned the land.

"We are trying to inform people of that which is the reality. We are always trying to find verifiable information," said George Ruggiu, a Belgian-Italian employed on a six-month contract to coordinate the radio's extremist broadcasts, which were used to inform militia gangs where they should go to find more victims.[36] The Radio Libre des Mille Collines, created by the CDR militia when Radio Rwanda came to be regarded by the extremist tendencies as too liberal, broadcast from Kigali radio station throughout the genocide. Its content and advisory role undoubtedly played a vital role in launching the genocide as a countrywide slaughter. Ruggiu carried a gun and covered his face when I tried to take his photograph when I saw him at the Hotel Diplomat. "I never travel with the army. That would be dangerous," he said, inexplicably. But he didn't seem to need the army, as the militia to whom he was answerable was clearly in charge.

That afternoon, 14 May, I went with the former French minister for humanitarian affairs Bernard Kouchner to the radio station. Since 6 April, French military and political officials determined to oppose the English-speaking RPF, against whom France had fought during the 1990–1993 war, had discouraged the UN from intervention in Rwanda, by promoting the view that the conflict was a civil war, rather than a genocide being perpetrated by the very people alongside whom France had fought when the RPF invaded Rwanda in 1990. With memories of the U.S. and UN debacle in Somalia the year before still strong, the prospect of intervening in a civil war could not be sold to any Western public opinion. But as Kouchner, the only foreign politician to visit Kigali during the genocide, seated himself in the studio of the Rwandan radio studio, another voice was heard.

The interviewer, expecting further French complicity in the outrageous attempts at manipulating world opinion about what was taking place in Rwanda, sat stunned as Kouchner condemned Rwanda's army, militias, military leaders, and extremist politicians on live radio for perpetrating a genocide that politicians in Paris refused to say was even taking place. "It's one of the greatest crimes in the history of humanity. It's not a crisis like others," he told his interviewer, who sat in silence beneath a wall calendar depicting a photograph of Habyarimana standing beside General Dallaire. "It is a genocide. The whole world is appalled. Rwanda's friends, like France, are saying: Lay down your arms. Barbarism doesn't enhance the dignity of your country. This genocide . . . it is inadmissible at the end of this century. It's unacceptable to other Africans."[37] It was a commendable performance, there in the heart of the genocide. But the only people listening were the criminals, and the appeal fell on deaf ears.

Outside, in the sinister streets of the empty capital, soldiers guarding the radio station stared blankly at Kouchner as he left. Next day, Kouchner and I drove south in a UN convoy to Gitarama, seat of the murderous junta. As we left the city, the road passed through a narrow gorge. There, the convoy came under heavy gunfire from a hillside to the right. The UN drivers accelerated, and the road opened out to a wide valley. Every half-mile there were checkpoints. At Bunda, just beyond the city limit to the south, people were pushing heavily laden bicycles as they fled. Roadside shacks were deserted. Kigali's frightened poor gathered at a checkpoint manned by crazed boys armed with machetes. Women sat on the roadside, wondering which way to go, feeding their children with sugar cane. We drove between treeless hillsides, the woodlands having been ripped up for firewood, leaving slopes covered in stumps. There were fires burning with smoke billowing into the cold, damp air. A smiling boy was selling bananas beside the road, near a man who had found the time to wash his car, while a woman walked past carrying a baby in one hand and an eight-inch blade in the other. A few farmers were working the hillside, but otherwise the fields were deserted. We stopped at another checkpoint at Kamonyi, where a teenage boy with a three-foot sword in an animal-skin scabbard was in charge of a group of boys who were drinking beer and had stick grenades jammed inside their belts.

On the hillside above the checkpoint, 120,000 people were living among the desolation and the smoke, having fled Kigali as the RPF advanced. "The situation is very bad. We are not eating anything. We are looking for food, but there is none," said Festus Byaruhango.[38] He had walked for two days to reach Kamonyi and had arrived three days beforehand. "You see the situation. The Tutsis want to rule. But we want to share power. There were Tutsis in my village. They're dead now. There are many who died. There were about 1,500 in my commune. Almost all of them are dead. I killed some myself, before I came here." As a reward for killing the enemy, the Hutus were starving. If hunger did not kill them, then perhaps the RPF would.

The interim government had installed itself just outside Gitarama, at Muvambi, in a training center. A small helicopter, an Alouette of the kind I had seen bombing parts of Kigali when the violence had first erupted five weeks beforehand, was parked on an overgrown football field. The low wooden huts and grassy patches crisscrossed with concrete paths were filled with government officials, going about the business of genocide. Here were the men who had masterminded Rwanda's horror, sitting behind desks, speaking on handheld radios, giving orders, writing memoranda. I hated them. The businesslike atmosphere of this evil operation, run by people so soaked in blood, was so repellent that it was impossible not to simply want to attack them.

"We have done everything we can to pacify the areas under our control. The massacres are now more or less over, and people are returning to work," said Jean Kambanda, prime minister in the government.[39] He was sweating nervously, and peered into space through the thick lenses of his spectacles. He seemed barely to be seeing whom he was talking to, as he clearly found it difficult to look into anybody's eyes. He was lying. The massacres were continuing in the south of the country, in which the militia and army still had control. He pretended the government was ready to have a meaningful dialogue with the RPF, though he knew it was a false claim, as the government had no right to even consider itself worthy of dialogue owing to the role it was playing in organizing the slaughter. He went on:

> The population are trained to defend themselves, and have the military training to defend themselves against attacks by the RPF in the communes. The RPF had placed soldiers in every commune secretly. The population was unarmed, and then they rose up spontaneously. . . . For us the conflict is essentially ethnic. If we don't resolve the situation on that basis, we never will. All other issues are superficial.
>
> Why did people reach that ferocity of violence? Because they thought that the RPF were going to win the war. The majority could be governed by a minority. That's what explains the violence. It's possible that [the violence] was organized. But how can one explain why the whole population was involved? There were perhaps elements that were organized. But how could it happen spontaneously, all over the country?[40]

There was no shame, no remorse, nothing but evil. He even pretended he did not know who had killed Agathe Uwilingyamana, saying that perhaps a conflict between the Unamir troops guarding her and the Rwandan army was to blame. I asked him how many Tutsis there were in the interim government of which he was head. He said he did not know because "I have never asked." He blamed the RPF for having sparked the violence by its refusal to allow the extremist CDR into the government created at Arusha. It was revealing that he did not cite the death of Habyarimana as the cause of the violence, but the political events that preceded the president's death. According to him, the exclusion of the CDR

> explains the massacres. In all the accords, the main problem was not solved. That is the problem of ethnicity, and the sharing of power between the two ethnic groups. If we don't have a balance between the tribes, the war will continue. It's not a war between the parties, but a war between the two tribes. To resolve the ethnic problem it's necessary to recognize that problem. The RPF doesn't accept that there's a problem. The ethnic problem is for me the only problem.

Standing on the grass outside Kambanda's office was Colonel Theoneste Bagasora, the defense ministry *chef de cabinet* (cabinet chief), who had given me the assurances in early April that I could indeed be a spectator of the events he had been planning and that had then begun to unfold. His face was as devoid of expression as Kambanda's. "In Rwanda we have three tribes. The RPF, which attacked, is considered the army of the Tutsi minority. There was a small war on every hill,"[41] he said, perhaps taking the line offered to the UN by the French government, that Rwanda was a war into which the UN could step if it sought to become embroiled, and not a genocide in which the civilian population could be confronted if the UN had decided to send a well-armed military force.

I asked him why the people—mainly Tutsi—hiding in Kigali's Mille Collines hotel had been attacked, even though the government had given the UN assurances that they could be escorted to safety.

> The role of the Gendarmerie Nationale is to defend everybody. The people in the Hotel Mille Collines are guarded by the gendarmerie. You can't give orders that would be carried out by everybody in the same way. The UN arrived at the hotel. Then they arrived at the blockade of the civil defense. They had not been warned in advance. A principle job of the government is leading the people. But eccentric people exist everywhere. It's an ethnic war.

He spoke in a tone devoid of feeling, apparently intent only upon diminishing in the eyes of the outside world the horror of what was taking place, perhaps in order to ensure that there was no real likelihood of the UN or anybody else stepping in to halt his and other's plans for Rwanda. Spreading the blame seemed also to be the purpose of Theodore Sindikabwabo, the interim president. He sat, smartly dressed, in a room, wearing a large gold ring that seemed to match two large gold teeth that shone when he spoke. He was a pediatrician before joining the murderous junta. "We have demanded that the population remains calm. We have condemned all the massacres," he lied.[42] "After the death of the president, there was a great shock among the population. There were confrontations on both sides. We will pursue the law." I left the room in disgust.

A few miles away, at the Virgin Immaculata Catholic Mission in Kabgayi, on the other side of Gitarama, around 15,000 Tutsis were sheltering. It was night they feared most. "They have come every night," said a teenage boy, Jean-Luc Mbarushinana. "They look for young people, or civilized, educated people, and take them outside. The teachers and administrators are the people they want. And the students. They want the people who are intelligent, and demand their identity cards." He fell silent as a gendarme strode over to a crowd gathered around a boy, aged ten, with a shorn head and starving face who had a five-inch gash across the top of his head. "It hap-

pened yesterday morning," whispered a man, Felicien Twagiramungu, pointing to the boy whose bewildered eyes were set in a face of fear, as the gendarme who perhaps would soon kill him stood listening nearby. "He went to
find water, because there's hardly any here. He saw some military and they
attacked him. We thought he was dead, but instead he came back badly injured. It happened just outside the church." A crowd gathered around us
where we talked. "How do the soldiers outside treat you?" I asked. "They
have taken twenty-eight people away from here, at night, in the past week,"
said a woman. "No, it's thirty people now," said another. How could we leave
these people here? The fear of their known fate clung to them. They drifted
toward death as their last days slipped away behind them, with us perhaps as
their last witnesses, driving away, back to Kigali in our convoy.

We came under fire again at the same point as that where we had been targeted by the RPF on the journey south. The shots were clearly aimed at us and
exploded in the dirt within feet of where the driver made the mistake of stop-
ping our car, the last in the convoy, while the other four cars sped on to safety.
We ran for cover and cowered in a ditch under a hail of 50-calibre machine
gun and antiaircraft fire. Kouchner, the UN press liaison officer, Mokhtar Gueye, four UN soldiers, a photographer, Steve Lehman, and I lay in the ditch
behind a low mud wall. Appeals by the convoy commander, Colonel Isoa
Tikoca, for the UN headquarters to radio the RPF base in Kigali to request a
ceasefire, were ignored for nearly an hour. Gueye was almost hit as he crossed
a small gap in the roadside wall to reach the Tunisian UN soldiers who had returned under heavy fire in an armored personnel carrier to retrieve us.

The reason for the barrage was a mystery. The UN cars were clearly
marked, and while we lay in the ditch a group of women fled along the road
with loads on their heads, without being fired on. Then a minibus carrying
civilians sped past, with machine gun fire bouncing onto the road behind it.
The white UN APC (American Policy Center) roared through the hail of
bullets that exploded in red flames onto the road. We reached Kigali, horri-
fied by a day spent witnessing cruelty and evil and despair, and ending in violence and danger. We were just spectators, whose efforts, through newspaper
reports, photographs, Kouchner's radio broadcast, and talks with the gang of
murderers at the camp outside Gitarama, failed to make any difference. The
faces of fear in Kabgayi had, by the time it got dark, probably become fewer,
with more screams piercing the silence, before the silence itself enwrapped
the terrified people as they awaited their turn.

"I LIVE ONLY WITH SADNESS"

The road dipped into thick bush as it sloped down into the northwestern
lakeland. Endless plains rose high in the distance, where lush hillsides
formed the horizon's curve against the late afternoon sky. We had stopped

briefly at Kirundo, where the road passed through the town on the way to Burundi's northwestern border with Rwanda. The atmosphere of the town was dominated by the slow, drifting step of the people who had survived the horrors of Burundi the previous October. An old man with no hands wandered through the somber streets. A young man with a scar from an old wound across his entire face beat a stick against his thin, wobbly legs. He had survived last October by lying among the corpses of a massacre in a house south of the town. We drove on, toward the southern finger of Lake Cohoha, past the scenes of the previous year's massacres, villages torn apart by killing, where people walked slowly among the grinding poverty of their mud-brick huts to the lush green fields.

"We are wanting to see the way things go in Rwanda. We are sorry for the suffering there," said Severin Mugenzi, where he sat in Kirundo's La Bagatelle café.[43] "We are sorry." He had seen it, just like all Burundians. It was a part of life among the hills, the breathtakingly beautiful hills, which rose up on the far shore of the lake, and faded into a purple evening, as we listened to the crickets from the verandah of the wooden hut we stayed in at Yaranda, a mission station just above the clear mirror of dark water.

The RPF met us as we crossed the border at Gasenyi the following day, 26 May. The sight of their familiar uniforms was the proof that their advance had reached the southwest tip of Rwanda. We had had no idea who would be on this side, until the Burundian soldiers at the border post told us the RPF had arrived some days beforehand. With their usual preoccupation with protocol and control, the Rwandans told us we would have to be accompanied. But we had no space, and they had no car, so we drove first a few miles north, then west, to Ngenda. We wanted to see how far they had reached westwards, toward Gitarama and the seat of the provisional government at Muvambi.

The homes of Ngenda were arranged neatly on either side of a long patch of grass. We talked to people in shops who, in seemingly inexplicable contrast to the victims in the towns in the north and east, seemed relatively unaffected by the violence stalking the rest of the country. Then we began to understand why. A man who had been a refugee in Burundi after the massacres in Rwanda had started told us: "We were protected by the Burundi military while we were in Burundi. We came through here to reach Burundi. The Burundi military came here into Rwanda to find people who needed to be protected. They protected us. It was Tutsi with Tutsi. We are brothers. They came to protect us. There were 20 Burundians who came to find us."[44] It had not seemed possible that soldiers from Burundi's Tutsi-dominated army would venture into Rwanda in this way. Several other people in the small town said the Burundians had crossed the border and escorted Tutsis back to the frontier and into Burundi. "But before, when the killing was happening, there were Burundian soldiers who came to help us," another refugee said.

"We came through [Ngenda]. There were about 20 Burundian [soldiers] who came to protect us and they accompanied about 2,000 people."

I was never able to ascertain whether the Burundian protection was carried out with or without the knowledge of Burundi's government. But the readiness of the Burundian soldiers to risk a conflagration explained why they had managed to escort Rwandans—both Hutu and Tutsi—to areas throughout the border area, where they lived as refugees in grass huts covered with plastic sheets provided by the United Nations. I later learned that 4,000 refugees were living on the surrounding hillsides around Kirundo, in small enclaves on the edge of town. Upon seizing Ngenda, they had turned the town into what an RPF soldier there called a "reception center" for refugees they had visited in Burundi, in order to encourage them to return, which the Tutsis appeared ready to do.

The road ended close to Ngenda. The RPF had captured a strategic bridge west of the town the previous week. Civilians trapped at the Rwabusoro Bridge across the Akanyaru River, fled to the other side. Government forces, who had lost twenty miles of ground in two days, blew up the bridge as they retreated. The battlefield beside the bridge was strewn with the bodies of rotting animals and the clothes, suitcases, pots, and Bibles of fleeing Hutus. Downstream, rebel troops in black Wellington boots opened multicolored umbrellas to fend off the driving rain as they wobbled across the river in rope-pulled barges, clambered up the bank, and strode into swampy meadows on the other side to make their way toward the front.

The RPF soldiers refused to let us move west with them, so we returned, close to the border post at which we had crossed from Burundi, and drove north through hamlets and villages, all but deserted, the most recent conquests of the RPF, the most recent victims of the *genocideurs*. Among eucalyptus trees, swamp, and savannah on the eastern side, was Nyamata. In the church there was blood on the altar. There was blood on the white drapes behind it. There was blood on the pulpit, and outside was an enormous mound of earth, a grave to—some said—5,000 people. There was blood beneath every pew. Blood on the walls. Would the smell ever go away?

"We took refuge in the swamp and hid under the papyrus," said Annonciata Umupfasoni.[45] She was sitting with outstretched legs on a mattress on the floor of a dormitory beside the church, gently rocking her six-year-old daughter, Harriet Niweburiza, in her arms:

We took refuge in a swamp, and hid under the papyrus. The interahamwe caught us there. They cut me with a machete and spears. They came and spat in our eyes and cut us and hurled abuse. They attacked us, and then they left us five days ago, because the time for them to kill was over. My eldest daughter ran away, and they caught her and killed her. My husband was caught, and he is dead. My child here is scared. She can't speak anymore. When she tries to speak she only asks where her brother and sisters are. When she sees me putting on rags or bad clothes, she asks me, "Where did you put your clothes?" I comfort her. I tell her, "Don't get worried. Things will be normal." But all the children are traumatized. Whenever somebody bangs the door, you see them running to their mothers for protection. But one of my arms was cut, and my leg was cut. I'm completely incapacitated, so I don't know how I will look after my girl.

Evariste Bapfakurera, a trader in the town and a member of the ruling MRNDD political party, led the killers of Nyamata. He and others organized the militia and drew up lists of who would be killed, Annonciata and others in the church dormitory said. The others included Vincent Karerangabo, a school inspector, and the *burgomestre*, Bernard Gatanazi. The killing went on from 6 April until 21 May, when the RPF forced the militia to flee. It was not clear where the killers had gone, whether to Tanzania to the east, or west toward Gitarama.

Next day, rocking slowly backward and forward where he sat on a chair on the verandah of a wooden house outside Nyamata, we saw Colonel Alexis Kanyarangwe, the RPF chairman, and the most senior Hutu in the largely Tutsi organization. He wore a peaked workman's cap and a well-worn suit. Between 1968 and 1973 he had been the head of Rwanda's security and intelligence service, and had subsequently been minister of the interior and minister of public works. But he had fled Rwanda in 1980, after being implicated in a coup attempt. His decision to join the RPF had never been easy to explain, as he had not been part of the Tutsi diaspora, and had played important roles in the tribalist and dictatorial system of government, until it had suited him to leave. The RPF had nevertheless seen the advantage of including a high-profile Hutu in its leadership, and gave him the symbolic post of chairman, which accorded him status, though little power compared to that of the vice chairman and, after 1990, military leader, Paul Kagame.

"The people who started the RPF were Tutsi. But little by little the organization was enlarged. We must move towards the idea of national identity, away from Hutu and Tutsi. There are no differences between Hutu and Tutsi," said Kanyarangwe.[46] In that desolate land, that blood-soaked hell, the political force of genocide seemed to have no match from any other quarter. To an outsider at that moment, what did it matter what kind of distinction there was between Hutu and Tutsi? Nothing he said, nothing anybody had said on either side in the previous two months, had come close to recognizing the profound truth. Neither the UN nor the United States had referred to genocide, for fear that it would create some legal obligation to intervene. Genocide had been denied by Rwanda's churches, which were so riddled with evil and hypocrisy that a horrendously high number of clergy had slipped apparently easily into the political camps from which their religious conviction had in any case emerged.

Genocide was what was taking place in Rwanda, and few people who were aware of it around the world were ready to say that genocide was and is an absolute, not an extreme form of tribal war. Its context, its planning, its eruption, all are forged within the political parameters of rotten states, which are in the vast majority in the post–Cold War world. But once it erupts, genocide becomes a way of life. The act of slaughter, the blood on the altar of Nyamata church, the blood beneath the pews, the blood on the stone floor, the blood on the drapes and the curtains, cannot ultimately be explained by Hutu and Tutsi fighting each other for the hills and valleys of Rwanda. The blood was that of humanity, and the failure of humanity to intervene was less a mark of informed political decisionmaking than a sign of humanity's cowardly reluctance to intervene when that human urge to kill erupts. But as he rocked slowly on his chair, Alexis Kanyarangwe seemed to have no sense that Rwanda was in fact not a battlefield between rival perceptions of history and politics, but instead humanity's latest Armageddon. "We find ourselves in a situation that has been programmed by the authorities. Perhaps the question should be: Were people involved voluntarily? We think not. If you tell somebody to kill, he will kill. It's the people who gave the orders. They are the people who are responsible for developing a policy of massacres and killing."

Rwanda's victims of mass killing, exclusion, prejudice, and expulsion have borne the weight of humanity's extremes. The response of the Tutsi has been rigid and full of determination, with rarely a reference to the deeper aspects of the horrors that have been visited upon them. They have sought their solace in political programs intended to deny the extremists the opportunity to use their devastating tools. During the hundred or so days of genocide in April–June 1994, the RPF rarely referred to the profound issues of humanity's evil, preferring instead to target their fire on the bankruptcy of the regime they were intending to overthrow. For the RPF leadership, the overthrow of the regime was the only goal. Rarely were they seen to be sidetracked by deeper reflection on the implications for the country of what Rwandans were doing to each other. Evil would be overcome by careful military planning, ruthless determination, and rigid control of the territory they occupied. Seen from this pragmatic perspective, there was no sense of good versus evil; the battle was between a regime that had become politically bankrupt and a diaspora that intended to ride to power on the back of this bankruptcy. Liberation would not entail making any promises about the future. It was rarely the case, during many hours I spent talking with Rwandans while the genocide raged, that there was any sense of the future.

We followed the northern road, which traced Rwanda's eastern border with Tanzania. The emptiness of one of the most densely populated countries on earth was vividly illustrated by the emptiness of the villages and isolated roadside homes we passed. Everybody had fled somewhere, Hutu,

Tutsi, moderate, extremist—everybody seemed to have gone from that region of flatlands, swamp, and savannah. The complexity of the slaughter, the targeting of the victims, had poisoned the veins of the entire country. Nobody had been spared, it seemed. "There were some whites who were protecting us at the Ecole Technique in Kicikiru. After the whites left the militia came with government soldiers and started firing at us," said Cecile Uwamwezi, as we stood talking beside the road at Kicikiru.[47]

> When they started firing everybody started to stampede. I hid in a house just behind the school with my children. Then I got out of the hiding and took my children. I was prepared for anything to happen. I went back to my home. Then the interahamwe came and looked at me. They said they would come and kill me even if I was a Hutu. I'm not a Hutu, but I was married to one. I don't know where my husband is. But I have my children. Three. One girl and two boys. I don't think my husband joined the interahamwe. I know his character. I don't think he could join the militia. When we were in our house my nine-year-old boy went to fetch milk for drinking, and on the way he met the interahamwe, and they realized that we were still in the house. They came with him and said they would kill me if I didn't give them money. I gave them 10,000 francs and they left. . . . The interahamwe had a technique: Whenever a Hutu man was married to a Tutsi woman, they would take the wife and then tell the Hutu husband, "Your wife is dead and now you must join the interahamwe and kill other Tutsis."

The road crossed a long causeway, which carried it over swamps where the tortured shapes of gnarled trees were reflected in the still, dark water. We passed through villages on the other side, where the road turned east, then north, then east toward Kabuga and Kigali. The hot afternoon sun shone through the trees, beneath which Paul Kagame was leaning against a Land Rover, arms folded, as if waiting for us, though there had been no way of planning any meeting with him in advance. He told us the RPF was less than five miles from Gitarama, and would begin an assault on the remaining RGF-held areas of Kigali within three days. That day, 28 May, the UN evacuated 690 people from the city, including 400 Hutus from the football stadium controlled by the RPF. A total of 290 Tutsis were also escorted from the Mille Collines Hotel. The same day, as the RPF took control of the eastern side of the city and drove the government forces out of the city center, the first UN transport aircraft arrived at the by then RPF-held airport, carrying food supplies. At the same time, the RPF told the UN it could dispatch a UN force of 2,500 troops, to oversee the distribution of humanitarian aid. The RPF rejected UN plans for a force of 5,500. By the end of May there was no purpose in sending more UN troops—there was nobody left for them to protect.

So complete had been the UN's betrayal of Rwanda and the insistence of the United States, France, and other states that the country be left to die, and so completely had Rwanda been left to its horrifying fate, that the seeds of the United Nation's broader sense of failure in Africa—a sense of failure that started with the unraveling of its peace plan in Angola, followed by the catastrophic failure in Somalia—took firm root. The rival agendas of the Security Council's permanent members in particular exposed the absence of a global vision for what was supposed to be a global organization. "I think they simply don't understand what is going on. [Even though] they have been here long enough [to understand]," said Kagame of the UN, aware nevertheless that the UN could do little more than defer to the strategies of its most influential members.[48]

Mitterrand I think knows more about ethnic conflicts than myself. Some people have wanted to simplify the conflict in Rwanda. They have failed to see that there are political problems. They have been involved in everything bad. Whether they did it before or after 6 April doesn't matter. It contributed to the situation now. There has been information that the French have provided arms through Zaire. But investigations won't stop them doing this. They never stopped when we complained before.

The aim is to pacify as many parts of the country as possible. The dilemma is that the [military] advance might put more people at risk. The best alternative will be to stop the massacres. But this hasn't been achieved; so the remaining option is to take the whole country by force. . . . There are some things we do that are not necessarily what we want to do. There are some things we do because other people want us to do them. We are going to give a try to things that other people want us to try.

Kagame's quiet anger, his resentment of the outside world, which had for thirty years largely ignored Rwanda, erupted during the weeks of slaughter. "There are several problems: southern Hutus are having problems with northern Hutus. Some of the people who have been coming over [to RPF territory] are southern Hutus," said Kagame. Explaining such complexities was difficult; expecting the outside world to break free of rigid and simplistic explanations was asking for too much. The individual testimonies of victims and perpetrators are the only real source of truth. The testimonies alone reveal the political and apolitical motives, the absence of motives for some, and the nature of the motives of others:

I killed one person and we were related. I killed my brother—same mother, same father. When I reached him, the people told me, "Why don't you do this?" There were some militia with grenades and machetes. The militia said that both me and my brother were in the Parti Libérale. My brother was already injured, and they told me to finish him. I killed him with a stick. On the head. The militia told me to follow them. But I escaped and found my wife and children dead. I'm a Tutsi.[49]

The testimony of Joseph Bukwavu shows how the slaughter could happen from neither political nor tribal motives, simply by contagion. Why was he not killed? Was it because he killed, and thus earned his own survival? He was still a Tutsi, whether he had killed other Tutsi or not. For the outside world, understanding Rwanda as it tore itself apart became too great a challenge, leaving real analysis to those involved in the conflict, or to powerless outsiders. "The conflicts are indeed about power. The *Garde Presidentielle*, which began the massacres, and the militias that rapidly joined in, are defending northern Hutu supremacy," was the blunt assessment of *Africa Confidential* in May 1994.[50] The way I would sum it up is that this "tribal conflict" was less a clash of blood ties than a power struggle in which a variety of agendas converged.

"I killed five people, five men. Both Hutu and Tutsi. I used a machete. The people were brought to us to be killed in the compound. The second time they were brought to be killed they were shot by soldiers," said Felicien Turatsinze.[51] He had been captured by the RPF, and was sitting with a group of twenty or more men and women in the compound of a house in Kabuga, a few miles from Kigali. His victims were political enemies, but as with many of the killers, his story was full of contradictions:

I was forced to do it. We were living in harmony with these people. I'm telling the truth. The people we were doing it to. I was in the interahamwe. I joined three days before the killing started. We were trained by administrators. I was trained how to use machetes. I was trained for one week. I killed my first person two days after Habyarimana died. Some soldiers said that if I didn't kill then I would be killed too. I wasn't interahamwe at first. I was Parti Libérale—the Mugenzi faction.

Why would he have joined the Interahamwe prior to the killings, engaged in the training, and shared its clear intent, if he had not shared the purpose of its leaders? Fear played a role. Fear of all sides perhaps. Not to join the ranks of the killers would have exposed him to the accusation of sympathy with the other side. Even so, the Mugenzi faction of the Parti Libérale had made its anti-Tutsi sentiments clear for months.[52] Other contradictions, which involved the link between the armed militias and the political parties by which they were supposed to have been formed, also became apparent: "I was in the interahamwe. But I was in the PSD (Parti Sociale Démocrate: Social Democrat Party), and never in the MRNDD or CDR. They forced people in other parties to join the interahamwe. We were forced," said Julienne Mukanyarwaya.[53]

I was captured from the village and instructed to kill people. The ones I killed were opposed to the MRNDD. I killed three. Three men. I knew them. They were Icyoribera, Kamonyo, and Gacyeri. They were my neighbors.

It was very sad to me. But I didn't have any alternative, because the government soldiers were behind me with guns. I lost my child. When I refused to kill, the government soldiers banged the gun on my child and she died. She was one and a half months.

All the people who were involved never did it on their own. They were all forced to do it. It wasn't easy to convince people to kill. The fact that the government soldiers were always at the back to shoot them if they didn't do it. The driving force of all this was that the leadership just instructed us to do this.

Sitting on the ground, with their heads bowed, watched by the RPF, the group sought to offer proof that they were coerced. There was no defiance. Their clothes still bore the blood of their victims. Considering the planning, the foresight, and the popular wave of slaughter upon which Rwanda on that day, 28 May, was still riding, the excuses offered by these men and women for the horrors they had perpetrated appeared all the more pathetic. The colonialists' history of nobles and peasants, of revolutions driven by Christian convictions, of kings and princes overthrown by the righteous and freedom-loving masses—all this had been reduced to what it really was—a mass murder by impoverished peasants, who had no more dignity than animals, left to sit in a muddy courtyard offering feeble excuses for what sometimes appeared to be their pathetic weakness rather than diabolic evil. "I beat two women and one man to death. I was forced by the *burgomestre* and the army to beat them to death," said Justin Mbongata.[54] He went on, like the others:

The councilors showed us how to kill and where to kill. We started killing during the day. On April 13. The first person I killed was a man. I killed him with a stick. I beat him. We were chasing them in the bush. I was with some other people. I know the man I killed. He was Emmanuel. I used to see him just around the place. The man was a peasant. He had eight children. Some were my age. We used to meet and play sometimes. I killed their father because we were instructed to do that. I couldn't run away. I had nowhere to run. I killed Tutsi, but I also killed Hutu.

I don't feel good about what I did. I don't sleep properly. I think a lot when I'm sleeping. What I did wasn't good. But because of the government we were forced to it. I would like to ask for mercy. I don't feel I should be killed myself. What I did—I am asking for mercy. I did it unconsciously. The RPF has treated me properly—we eat twice a day. I don't expect anything apart from getting mercy. I expect to be killed all the time.

10

The Spit of the Toad

Zaire, Kenya, and the Abuse of Tradition

> This mosaic of tribes and cultures, linked by a general wish to live together, to form a nation united by the cement of the republic, holds close to its heart the aim of national cohesion and an advanced notion of citizenship.[1]

MARRYING THE IDEAL OF STATEHOOD with the reality of an often fractured mosaic of tribes and cultures is a challenge few of Africa's leaders have met. The historical truth is hopelessly enmeshed in genuinely old traditions shaped by the vicissitudes of oral transmission, invented traditions, and *mythico-history*.[2] "This tribalism that was a genuine product of African diversity but also an invented weapon of self-defense, became a potent factor in opening the route to nationalism," writes Basil Davidson of the tribal unions and associations that evolved in the early years of the twentieth century.[3] "Their nature, of course, meant that they were destined to become divisive of national unities. They would then play the role, after independence, of opposing 'tribe' to 'nation'. But that was still to the future." The nationalist political creed that ultimately succeeded in ridding Africa of European domination clearly revealed the imperative of achieving freedom. But it did not create a workable ethos for the building of independent states. However, as Davidson states bluntly, ultimate responsibility for these problems rests with the colonizers:

> At the same time it needs to be recalled that any informed "looking ahead" was difficult or impossible if only because, to the very last, colonial governments in all the empires hugged closely to their chests whatever sound information their administrative files might contain. They camouflaged their social and economic problems with clouds of condescending propaganda. Or they simply denied that these problems existed. . . . [They] generally behaved as though every arrangement for decolonization must be expected in any case to end in tears.[4]

The failure to distribute the fruits of independence beyond the political elites of many African countries, dominated the Cold War period. Occasionally this was by default, but usually it was by design. Since the end of the Cold War, the shift that has taken place in much of Africa has involved the emergence of two political trends, one propagated by tribalists seeking to create multiparty systems based upon the distribution of political power in a manner reflecting the national tribal complexion, and the other marked by a resurgence of various forms of nationalism. Within both tribalist and nationalist camps there are moderates and extremists, but broadly speaking the post–Cold War decade has been dominated by a confrontation between individuals determined to identify themselves as vital to the tradition of exclusion of other tribes from power—ultimately as a means of assuring their place within the structure—and those seeking to strengthen institutions through which they may wield more effective power on a national basis.

Neither side in this evolving confrontation has been noticeably successful. "In fact, ethno-political conflicts since the end of the Cold War are a continuation of a trend that began as early as the 1960s. It is a manifestation of the enduring tension between states that want to consolidate and expand their power, and ethnic groups that want to defend and promote their collective identity and interests," write Abiodun Alao and Funmi Olonisakin.[5] They are correct to point out that the character of postcolonial rivalry has endured into the post–Cold War period. But their assertion that the tension is between the state and particular ethnic groups is far less certain. It is more accurate to say that in the period after the Cold War, rivalry exists between the ethnic groups who have control of the levers of state power and those who do not.

Attempts to resolve the crisis of political isolation by promoting multiparty political systems since the end of the Cold War are thus the most significant recent shift in the political complexion of many African countries. Prior to multipartyism, the failure of traditional political systems to transform themselves so that they could function effectively on the national level was derived in large part from the exclusivity that lay at their heart. While the system of chiefly power and influence by elders remained workable on a local level in many countries of the continent, it has not generally been successfully adapted to incorporate the aspirations of rival hierarchies from other tribes, within the context of the nation and nationwide institutions. Even so, the continued rigidity of most of Africa's political systems—ten years or more after the clamor for political change started to bear fruit—should not be regarded as a sign of caution on the part of responsible incumbent national leaders keen to avoid a rupture along tribal or communal lines. It is more a sign of their determination to cling to as much power as they can.

The real task facing those in favor of democratization has been to consolidate the split with the extremist camps and strengthen the institutions necessary to bolster the democratic process. The issue of tribalism has receded where the promise of institutional reform, intended to lead to democratization, has gained ground. The slowly waning power of ethnic sentiment has generally been given renewed force only when extremist politicians sought to do so. In Burundi, for example, the Tutsi extremists' argument centered on the claim that a Hutu government implied the "institutionalization of the tyranny of an ethnic majority."[6] In fact, the electoral voting patterns during that first multiparty contest in 1993 were not so clear-cut, as Hutu and Tutsi did not vote unfailingly for their supposed ethnic party interests. "The leveling of the political playing field made possible the rapid expansion of cross-ethnic alliances in several crucial sectors of civil society," Lemarchand writes.[7]

In their study, Alao and Olonisakin emphasize the historical and geopolitical context in which ethnic conflict has erupted in the post–Cold War period. Their study is intended to assess whether the end of the Cold War was itself responsible for a resurgence in ethnic or other tensions, which had lain either dormant or repressed by the conditions imposed by the superpower conflict. They largely ignore the more cynical question of whether political leaders deliberately exacerbate tensions as a means of securing political advantage, and so they avoid the vital issue of political opportunism. This is unfortunate, since the use of ethnic tension as a political tool is central to any analysis of the political reality of the continent. The readiness of many leaders—from Moi in Kenya to Mobutu in Zaire—to deliberately exacerbate differences goes much further toward explaining why violence erupts than does mere reference to *traditional* rivalry.

The analysis in the preceding chapters of the evolution of the violence in Rwanda is intended to show where the historical root of such rivalry lay, and later how it was provoked in a premeditated and planned way. The genocide was ultimately an extreme measure taken with the aim of retaining power for the northern Rwandan Hutu military-political elite. It was the scale of the genocide that distinguished it from other mass killings. But Rwanda's government was not alone in retaining in its armory the political tools necessary to enflame nascent or dormant ethnic tensions, or to create them where they did not exist. More than one of the rotting political systems that multiparty democracy sought to replace in the 1990s was equipped with the tools by which demagoguery, violence, and murder on a significant scale could play a part in forging the process of political reform. Rwanda was the extreme, but the motivation and means that lay behind it were far from unique.

"BETWEEN A BROTHER AND A FRIEND"[8]

At night the city outskirts were ablaze with fires on the stretches of rubbish tip wasteland alongside the boulevards, warming the homeless, the abandoned, the hungry. Men sat with their heads bowed in cupped hands, silhouettes around fires that would die before the sun came up. It was the dry season. The mosquitoes hovered in languid swarms, waiting, like everybody else, for the dawn. As Kinshasa ground along in hopeless desperation, money was worth less by the day, petrol queues stretched along the roads of both the poor and the smart suburbs, and the country at the heart of Africa moved steadily toward collapse. It was the summer of 1991. Nobody else left the Ethiopian Airlines flight when it landed at 3 A.M. at Ndjili airport en route from Abidjan to Nairobi. The crew looked at me strangely as I left the comfort of the aircraft and descended the steps leading to the seemingly deserted airport on the edge of a collapsing state. I heard the aircraft take off behind me, as I stepped cautiously into the arms of Zairian officialdom, but was left to wander through the near-sleeping terminal with little trouble, waking a man in passport control and asking him to stamp the elaborate visa the ambassador in my home city of Abidjan had, after a discussion verging on interrogation, sold to me.

A welter of expectations initially dominated that first visit to Zaire. It seemed that it was here that much of Africa's post–Cold War future ought to be settled. It was here, if anywhere on the continent, that a successful transition to democracy would provide a model for other states. A successful change in Zaire, where the political maneuvering of the Cold War had—as in Liberia, Somalia, and Angola—been at its most invidious, appeared to have the potential to drag its twelve neighbors along with it, in a manner and on a scale that really had the potential for engineering a genuinely continent-wide shift. But these expectations were the hopes of a young reporter at that time unfamiliar with the nature of power, the character of rule, and the depth of depravity into which Zaire had, by that early morning of 24 July 1991, sunk.

Already at that time, the game President Mobutu was intent upon playing with his opponents was to lay the foundation for the disappearance of Zaire altogether. Zaire no longer exists. Clearly its name has gone forever, with the creation of the Democratic Republic of Congo (DRC). More significant, however, is the probability that when the current conflict wracking Central

Africa is resolved, the geographic identity of Zaire, as well as the inheritance of the DRC, will no longer resemble the borders inherited from the Belgian Congo at independence in 1960.

Population pressure in Rwanda and Burundi, the anarchy prevailing along the Zaire-Angola border, the breakdown of order in the Central African Republic, and the impact of the civil war in southern Sudan, all these have created pressures that are likely to tear at the very structure of the country. Mobutu's total identification of the Zairian state with himself as the all-powerful ruler made it impossible for any successor to occupy a role like his at the heart of the system he created. There could never have been a transfer of power, owing to the highly specific nature of the power it would have been necessary to transfer.

For Mobutu, resisting the pressure for democracy, and with it the pressure for inclusion from political aspirants beyond his coterie of tribal allies, lay at the heart of his strategy following his declaration of a multiparty system on 24 April 1990. For two years, 1990–1992, he played cat and mouse with the opposition, succeeding in his ultimate purpose of creating a stalemate. But the stalemate, from which he intended to emerge the sole power broker, was his downfall. As Zairians lost heart, his opponents were easily infected by the call to arms of Laurent Kabila and his Ugandan and Rwandan backers, after the transformation of Central Africa's political landscape following the genocide in Rwanda. The catastrophe of the genocide and the massive shifts of population it had created had exposed the leadership of the group of countries infected by the genocide as being destructive and immoral. Mobutu, an ally of Juvenal Habyarimana, was the most vulnerable, as disgust with the genocide and all those associated with its perpetrators spread. More than anywhere else in Africa, the walls came tumbling down in Zaire, as the isolation Mobutu had secured for Zaire collapsed and the state fell prey to the structural weakness he had deliberately maintained as his guarantee against domestic threats to his rule.

The political map of Mobutu's Zaire bore little or no comparison with that which had existed prior to the arrival of the Belgian colonizers. Even so, as Young and Turner explain, during the colonial twilight of the 1950s,

> since political parties were not permitted, candidates were thrown back on the organizational resources of the assorted voluntary associations that were tolerated; of these, only the ethnic organizations provided political communications capable of linking the numerically small elites, who provided the candidate pool, and the mass, whose adult male component was to be permitted to vote. . . . Conflict polarized around a largely novel set of urban ethnic self-identifications, which had gradually taken form in the postwar years [after 1945].[9]

The elections heralding the independence of Congo in 1960 were hurriedly organized in three months. The 250 political parties barely had time to establish a nationwide presence, let alone develop nationwide strategies and political platforms that were truly national. Young and Turner discuss the issue:

> The fears and insecurities engendered by the tumultuous electoral campaign, confirmed by the disorders which emerged immediately following independence, created a political environment saturated by ethnicity. . . . Mass perceptions, . . . traumatized by the guerrilla theatre of the elections, continued to find the ethnic meanings politicized by the parties to be the surest guide to political understanding.
>
> Ethnicity, used as a guide to political behavior, appeared to serve the instrumental needs of both leader and follower. Politicians required an electorally demonstrable following to accede to the power and status (and ultimately the class position) attached to high office; no comparably effective avenue to clientele building was open. For the mass, torn between momentary hopes of unimaginable abundance and fears of calamities that might lurk in a suddenly unpredictable future, security seemed to lie in vesting trust in affinity.[10]

The crisis of 1960–1965, which led to Mobutu coming to power, was ultimately a response to the political impasse created by a mixture of the ethnopolitics of the post-independence period and the foreign Cold War interests and strategies of the United States, Belgium, and France.[11] Mobutu's rule, during his pursuit of "authentic Congolese nationalism" in 1967–1971, sought to diminish tribal loyalties by forcing the disappearance of the locally based institutions in which regional loyalties could be influential and replacing them with national structures controlled by the central authority. But just as the institutionalized weakness of the administrative structure, which was retained as a security against internal insurrection, was ultimately a cause of Mobutu's downfall when it proved unable to defend the country from external threat, so the adoption of Zairian *authenticité*, in 1971, and *Mobutism* or *Zairianization*, inaugurated in 1973–1974 as a political creed, served to undermine the credibility of a national consciousness. As Mwabila Malela writes:

> Ethnic consciousness became accentuated by the policy labeled Zairianization, inaugurated in 1973. . . . As a result of this policy . . . a middle class appeared, essentially composed of "Zairian businessmen," while at the same time a "national bourgeoisie" became reinforced; to a growing degree, the latter based itself upon the group consciousness of the various ethnic communities to which its members belonged.

A new type of class alliance founded on ethnic solidarity thus took the place of worker solidarity and consciousness of material conditions. . . . It was, in fact, an alliance within which there occurred a kind of chain of clientalization, internal to the ethnic group, whose final object was to hoist the wealthy members of the ethnic group into the proximity of political power, so that the "interests" of the ethnic group and geographic region might be protected.[12]

The creed *was* Mobutu, and Mobutu was a product of his ethnic and, more specifically, his regional background in Equateur province. Thus, "the growing public perception of the hegemonic inner group, regionally recruited, has focused growing resentment on Equateurians," Young and Turner wrote in the early 1980s, of the social elite originating from Mobutu's region of *Haute-Zaire*. Language played a key role in personalizing the regime and undermining the pursuit of nationhood. The use of Lingala, the language of Equateur spoken by Mobutu, in national discourse emphasized the process of projecting traditions specific to one region onto the national stage, and thereby sidelining other linguistic traditions, notably Kikongo, the equally widely spoken Tshiluba, and the even more widely spoken Kiswahili.

Although the regime sought in the 1970s to use regional rather than ethnic bases for various forms of affirmative action intended to facilitate fairer access to education and other services, the centralization of political power on Kinshasa, the primacy of Lingala in the army and an ultimately failed attempt in 1974 to declare it the national language, as well as the control Equateurians enjoyed over state finances, cemented the process of exclusion from power. As Kabuya Lumuna, a sociologist at Kinshasa University and a political adviser to Mobutu in the mid-1990s, said:

The essence of the political system in Zaire is tribalism. In the national mentality the return to the village from the city is regarded as a negative thing: a place to where people are banished when they are punished. There's richness to the tribal identity.

The political debate is between federalism and centralism. The fact that France is not a federal state is very destructive for us. We have grown up being made to believe that federalism is regressive. This means that there is a lack of respect for differences because of this centralism.[13]

To strengthen its exclusivity, the regime evolved internal manners and traditions that drew heavily on its linguistic "tradition," created its mystique, and asserted its power. Such measures were influenced by, consciously or not, the colonial inheritance. In a revealing study of the Belgian colonialists' use of Kiswahili as a lever of political power in the southern Congolese province of Katanga (later renamed Shaba, though now renamed Katanga), Johannes Fabian writes:

> Maintaining such power was the foremost concern in policies regarding Swahili in Katanga. . . . From the point of view of the colonial administration and of industrial-commercial interests in Katanga, Swahili was above all a means to implement certain labour policies. . . . [It] is important to see that the promotion of Swahili was prompted by ideological, political concerns; that the primacy of ideology prevented authors of language manuals from appreciating the actual linguistic situation that existed when they began their work (around 1920); and that self-imposed limitations to describe only what was of "practical use" further widened the gap between linguistic reality and descriptive codification.[14]

The emergence of political opposition to Mobutu cannot be reduced to ethnic rivalry. Undoubtedly the growth of resentment, anger, and loathing against Mobutu and his regime during the 1980s included criticisms of those from Equateur who had participated in robbing the country of its potential owing to their positions within the presidential entourage. However, the practice of power had tarred many non-Equateurians with the brush of corruption. Shabaians, Kasaians, and many others had all been in government throughout Mobutu's rule and been exposed to and benefited from his kleptocracy. In this way, Mobutu had secured a lever to control all those who would perhaps later defy him. But in the 1990s, Mobutu's strategy for dealing with political opposition was dominated by a reversion to playing the tribal card, which his earlier "unifying" political creeds had sought to make disappear.

On a warm July morning in 1991,[15] tens of thousands of Zairians flocked to a Kinshasa football stadium to witness what on the surface appeared to be a turning point in the political evolution of Zaire. The Union Sacrée, the Sacred Union of 148 opposition parties, had ignored the government's refusal to authorize their rally. For a morning, as spectators clung high on the metalwork towering over the stadium to support the floodlights, and dancers and musicians filled the pitch with flamboyant music and vivid color, it appeared that the gathering presented the spectacle of something much more formidable than just a significant political rally. Reclining in the shade of the stadium's covered terrace were the leaders of the opposition, ranging from Etienne Tshisekedi, to the former prime minister, Kengo wa Dondo, from Nguza Karl-i-Bond, the former foreign minister and prime minister, to Joseph Ileo, a minister in the government of Patrice Lumumba in 1960. It appeared that a common purpose—that of ridding the country of Mobutu—had created the potential to avert Young and Turner's prediction that "a return to full-scale political competition would remobilize ethnicity"[16] (a claim made with the condition however, that it would not be the "sole determinant of alignments.")[17]

After the sudden disappearance of the state-run buses from the streets of Kinshasa, the crowd had defied the regime's efforts at diminishing the attendance level and arrived on foot. The rally was the last before the scheduled opening of Zaire's national political conference, which was due to open the following day, 30 July. Few, even at the rally, had expected it to start on time, as the opposition had rejected the composition of the delegate's list, which had been packed with members of the ruling Popular Movement of the Revolution (MPR) party.

The success of the opposition depended upon the national conference securing real administrative power, including over the army. This would mean depriving Mobutu of control over the institutions of repression that had sustained him since the 1960s. "We have to come out of the conference a different country. We can't do anything in the economic field until we change the political field," Nguza Karl-i-Bond told me the next day.[18] But despite unity on the issue of ejecting Mobutu, there were differences over what should be done in the interim. Even though Karl-i-Bond was the Sacred Union's candidate for the presidency, he accepted Mobutu's retention of the position during the political interim. Tshisekedi, the Union's prime ministerial candidate, wanted Mobutu arrested or forced to leave the country. By the time the conference finally opened on 7 August, these differences had not been resolved. Instead, the conference was accorded "sovereign" status by the then prime minister, Mulumba Lukodji, and remained packed with MPR supporters, whose presence was intended to ensure that its sovereign powers were exercised in the interests of the incumbent ruler.

The character of the conference reflected the concentration of power in Kinshasa, with all its implications for the country and the imbalance between regional and ethnic groups. Mobutu sought to deflect challenges to his power by working steadily to exacerbate the tensions within the opposition alliance. Invoking the very powers the national conference sought to strip him of, Mobutu offered the premiership to Tshisekedi in July, only to have the offer rejected on the grounds that the national conference was alone capable of nominating a prime minister.

Riots in September 1991, led by unpaid soldiers, brought the downfall of Lukodji and forced Mobutu to accept Tshisekedi's appointment to the premiership on the opposition's terms, or so Tshisekedi thought. Following a highly symbolic 30 September meeting with Mobutu at Kinshasa's Palais de Marbre,[19] their first in three years, Tshisekedi believed the president had accepted that the national conference had the power to nominate the defense minister, thus taking a significant step toward diminishing Mobutu's own power and that of the cabal of Equateurians who had held the power of Zaire in their hands for three decades. The real shift had perhaps started. A curfew imposed after the September riots was lifted. Tshisekedi left the meeting saying that he would respect the demands of the national conference. He said the meeting had been carried out with a sense of responsibility and that control of the army would pass to the national conference, once it resumed discussions following a period of suspension. But within a day Mobutu had demanded he retain the power to nominate key ministerial posts, including defense.

Mobutu's determination to retain control of the army was less due to any clear evidence that it could act as a guarantor of any kind of stability during the transition, than to the fact that ceding its control to the opposition would boost Tshisekedi's campaign to demystify the president. But even if an opposition defense minister had been appointed, he would only have held symbolic control over the army, owing to the real loyalty of its senior officers remaining with Mobutu. General Singa Boyenge made the situation clear:

> The generals see their chief as being the head of state. [The prime minister] couldn't replace the army chiefs, because he would court a conflict with Mobutu. The reason for the army generals remaining faithful to Mobutu is because they're all from his tribe, the Ngbandi. All the other tribes are sidelined. Among the lower ranks there are other tribes, but they are marginalized. Money is also the thing that keeps the generals faithful. He gives them money. But tribalism is more profound.[20]

Nevertheless, the determination of the opposition to draw upon the discontent of the lower ranks, the unpaid, impoverished foot soldiers who had led the rioting in September, could have led to a wedge being driven between the tribal elite and the rank and file. As General Singa, a former head of the state intelligence service, the SNIP, as well as a former defense minister, said: "The lower ranks are incapable of reacting to the inequalities within the army. Mobutu has concentrated all the army resources in Kinshasa. For the riots of 1991, the military knew about it beforehand. It was a reaction to the situation within the army. The army sees Tshisekedi as acceptable. It doesn't matter to the FAZ whether it is one person or another who is leading, even though Mobutu has ousted most Asians from the army."[21]

Mobutu had to retain the myth of his own invincibility. To do so required imagery, even if the image was derived from unstable or even nonexistent foundations and a well-established political practice of abusing the tradition of power broking, which he derived from his self-appointed image as "father-chief."[22] The opportunity to reassert his mythological status arose a month after the frosty meeting at the Palais de Marbre. On 21 October, Mobutu told his supporters: "The chief is the chief. He is the eagle who flies high and cannot be touched by the spit of the toad."

The irreconcilable positions of Mobutu and Tshisekedi led to Mobutu demanding the dismissal of the UDPS leader as prime minister and his replacement by another candidate. The political crisis was deepened furthermore by Nguza Karl-i-Bond's announcement on 21 October that he was breaking ranks with the Sacred Union. Three weeks beforehand, Karl-i-Bond had told me: "In the face of the total absence of authority, the Sacred Union has created a crisis government, and has decided that Etienne Tshisekedi will form a government of national salvation. In the event of this, we demand the sacking of the heads of the national conference, and their replacement with a Catholic priest."[23] Years earlier, Karl-i-Bond had written of his first Council of Ministers meeting as foreign minister under Mobutu, in the late 1960s; he had related how the president had clearly defined the responsibilities of the political class, the *hommes d'état* (men of state), as they were known, by telling the gathered ministers: "A *man of state* is one who knows to guard the secrets. If we decide today to kill somebody for reasons of state, it must remain between us."[24] In his memoir, Karl-i-Bond later wrote:

> Nothing is possible in Zaire without Mobutu. He created Zaire. He fathered the Zairian people. He grew the trees and the plants. He brings rain and good weather. You don't go to the toilet without the authorization of *Le Guide*. Zairians would be nothing without him. Mobutu has obligations to nobody, but everybody has obligations to him. As he said to me on August 13, 1977, in front of three witnesses: "Nguz', there's nothing I have to do for you; on the contrary, I have made you whatever you are."[25]

Nevertheless, just as Karl-i-Bond had once been an imprisoned opponent sentenced to death and had later returned to being a Mobutu confidante, so in the fall of 1991 he was gone once more, back into the Mobutu fold, the truest picture of the political chameleon. Four days later, on the overcast morning of 1 November, Mobutu reasserted his role of *Maréchal*[26] as well as head of state after dismissing Tshisekedi and, on 25 October, appointing Bernardin Mungul Diaka in his place.

At a meeting of the Sacred Union earlier that week, Mungul had applauded the opposition's decision to reappoint Tshisekedi to the post, even though Mobutu had just sacked him. But then within days, Mungul had followed the example of Nguza Karl-i-Bond and slipped back into the Mobutu camp. For much of the previous thirty years Mungul had practiced the same political game, veering sharply from one political stand to another, twice falling out with Mobutu and twice returning to the fold. In 1980 he had fled Zaire as minister of education, after being accused of stealing funds from his department. He returned only after the granting of an amnesty to exiles, after which he became an enthusiastic activist in the ruling MPR.

The embattled political class gathered in a large, low hall at the *Domaine Presidentielle*, the sprawling presidential estate at N'sele, fifteen miles down river from Kinshasa. A plantation, delineated by a tangled barbed wire fence and a rusting sign that read "British-American Tobacco," ran along one side of the road. Green hillsides rolled off into the distance, covered with trees.

The decay of Kinshasa was left behind. A ramshackle café with the bright reds and yellows of its furniture chipped and fading was open but empty on the right, a few yards from an entrance gateway arching over a road on the left. A group of soldiers lounged on broken chairs beneath the arch and waved visitors through, along a road that wound past a Chinese-style summerhouse and into the heart of the domain of the Maréchal.

In the hall, a windowless block of concrete, a large stage ran the length of one wall. Two gilded thrones whose arms were carved with winged lions had been placed at opposite ends. A dais had been raised just above floor level, upon a carpet whose dramatic colors climaxed at one end in the vast woven head of a leopard. At the entrance to the hall, and surrounding the stage, exceptionally tall members of the Presidential Guard carried swords and wore tall busbies, evoking the atmosphere of the court of the czars of prerevolutionary Russia. Mobutu appeared, proceeding to his gilded throne, resplendent in white military uniform, complete with a sash and the scepter of the Maréchal of the Republic. Beside him was his wife, Bobi Ladawa, equally resplendent in a long silky gown, who took her place on the throne opposite Mobutu.

Mobutu's appearance in such surroundings, the attempt to reassert the good old days of total power, total fear, total mystification, heightened the sense of tension. "Now he finds that sharing is to lose. So, behind the scenes, he is trying to take power back,"[27] Kengo wa Dondo, the former and future prime minister, told me later:

> He loves power. Above all. When I was prime minister, he didn't like discussion. But you understand a lot from him. But I wasn't head of the government. He was. He can't see himself sharing the power with somebody that he hasn't nominated. His conception hasn't changed since democracy arrived. Mobutu explains it to himself very easily: One chief governs. The chief is surrounded by advisers. He consults his college of advisers on decisions. He does consult. But people like him never believe that they take the wrong decision. Mobutu is a man who is very influenced, but he has his opinions. The last word is always his.[28]

Kengo's previous experience within the government gave him a useful insight into how Mobutu was handling the process of power broking in this time of change. Steadily, the presidential entourage lost all the people who had initially promoted a peaceful transition, as the president began to surround himself with people who, as Kengo said, accepted the view that while everybody else should change, Mobutu should be allowed to remain the same. From the perspective of those who had seen both sides of Zaire's political character, the logic of this position was perhaps clear. As Kengo said, "I don't like to criticize [Mobutu]. We didn't have the courage to leave the regime. Can Mobutu take responsibility for yesterday? No, because we were with him. We have no political culture, except for a twenty-seven-year dictatorship. People are now seeing that democracy is bringing problems."[29]

Mobutu addressed the gathering, thanking the absent diplomatic corps, which had boycotted the installation of a government it regarded as illegitimate. Then began the theatrical process of installing the government, which Diaka claimed was 40 percent drawn from the opposition, a figure Tshisekedi vigorously denied. Each member of the new cabinet approached the floor-level dais to sign a large book, in which was listed the result of the deal making of the previous few days. A pen lay on the register, but instead of using it, one minister took his own from the breast pocket of his *abacost*[30] in an apparently symbolic gesture, whose significance perhaps only Mobutu could decipher. Then, after signing their names, the new ministers bowed first to Mobutu and then to his wife, before returning to their seats. Noticeable within the ministerial lineup was the new interior minister, Midao Bahati, who had a plaster covering a wound on his head. According to his wife, Bahati had been kidnapped two nights earlier and driven round Kinshasa by Mobutu agents intent on persuading him to accept his ministerial post. His wife pleaded for assistance at the French embassy and was refused. When she returned home, Bahati had been returned by his kidnappers and had decided to accept the job!

Two days after the inauguration, the chief fancied he was once again the eagle flying high above the toads. Youthful soldiers were patrolling Mobutu's ship, the *Kamanyola*, like ants, loading pump-action shotguns off the deck and into the back of a rusting Mercedes. In the distance, against a gray sky filled with the sound of flapping flags, children swooped, yelling, down the bright red plastic slide in the playground of the Domaine Presidentielle. Albert-Henri Buisine, a French businessman nicknamed "The Cook," who had been given a role as a fixer who dabbled rather ineptly in the area of protocol under the title of *chef de la maison civile* (head of the household), lowered himself from his black and gold bullet-proof Jeep Cherokee and led the way into the luxurious, refurbished Belgian colonial riverboat upon which Mobutu had made his Kinshasa home. Below deck, in a dining room, the table was set for a breakfast of omelettes, coffee, and charcuterie. Daisies in pots on each table were wilting in the air-conditioning. Landscape photographs hung on the walls. The cups and saucers and bright, copper-plated teaspoons were stamped with the national emblem—a leopard's head—and the words *Justice, Paix, Travail* (Justice, Peace, Work). A poor joke, in a country where justice was barely imagined, peace merely the product of weakness and poverty, work an activity that the thieving regime had turned into a crime, as honesty was rewarded with isolation, jail, and sometimes death. A French police movie was playing loudly on a large television in the corner of the paneled room, gunshots echoing.

Soldiers, young and armed, with the Hebrew insignia of their Israeli instructors stitched to their uniforms, wandered past the portholes. Buisine, tired eyes underlined by sagging bags, scuttled along the deck. "I came here twenty-one years ago from Europe. It was all by chance really, that I came here. I have hotels, hunting grounds, and investment in tourism. But it was only by chance I found myself doing this."[31] After breakfast, Mobutu appeared from his cabin at the end of the deck wearing a shiny green and brown abacost. Tall and portly, he wore pointed black slip-on shoes that were the fashion in the 1950s. Cane in hand, leopard-skin hat on head, he sat on a rose-colored sofa shaped like an oyster shell, and prepared to go through the daily routine of defending his place in history. The rapid clatter of the *Kamanyola*'s engine rumbled through the vessel as he took questions, and the gathering distance from the shore of the Zaire River steadily emphasized the fact that all aboard were in his hands. He half smiled, as he looked through the heavy-rimmed spectacles that are part of his myth.

"But is there, Mr. President, a difference between the myth and reality of Mobutism?" he was asked. "The world thinks I do things rather bizarrely. But I really can't answer that."[32] "Do you think that the era of the big African leaders is coming to an end?" "Well, that is very difficult to say. I believe that is very difficult to say." "How many of your famous leopard-skin hats do you have?" "Ah, well, I have seven. They were made in Paris." The *Kamanyola*'s engine rumbled steadily, as he strode out onto the deck and took his place at the rail. The riverboat edged its way toward a small village. Fishermen in canoes waved, people on a passing barge waved and cheered. The president waved in a grand gesture with his cane. It was rumored that everybody who waved when the president passed was paid a little later by the agents driving the speedboats accompanying the *Kamanyola*.

We drew closer to the village where everybody was cheering, a national flag flying, and four soldiers standing to attention. "It's all spontaneous," said Buisine. The presidential cane arched across the sky, the ship's horn sounded. "Do you go far on your boat, Mr. President?" "Why yes, of course. It is the fastest boat on the river. I have the fastest boat on the river. It is three days to Kisangani on the *Kamanyola*. It takes other people two weeks. But I have the fastest boat on the river," he said, as if it was some surprise that nobody in Zaire had a boat faster than his.

"Listen to them. You know what they are saying to me—"Yamukolo Oleki Bango," which means, "You are the strongest, you will suppress everybody else." I find my legitimacy with the people. Legitimacy is that," he said, pointing his cane at the waving fisherman and the villagers, "the little people. Kinshasa is not the Republic of Zaire." "But is Zaire like Zambia?" The question unnerved him. "Is the result confirmed yet?" "Yes. Kaunda has lost." "So, it is confirmed." He turned away and bowed his head as if at a funeral, though time would show that he had no intention of following Kaunda off center stage of the African political scene. After thirty minutes he bade farewell and disappeared, and the *Kamanyola* returned to its berth near the playground at the estate, where scuba divers every day checked beneath the landing stage for bombs. Mobutu was said to have slept on board every night since the opposition began to bite in 1990, leading the people of Kinshasa to call him *le voisin*, "the neighbor," because he no longer shared the mainland with them.

The Cat and the Mouse

Vital to Mobutu's success at manipulation and the continued assertion of his role as arbiter—the eagle flying high above the toads—was the readiness of erstwhile opponents to be lured back into his camp. Infinitely more important in this process than Mungul Diaka was Nguza Karl-i-Bond. Speaking of his previous returns to Mobutu's government, in the 1980s after he had been pardoned and had a 1977 death sentence imposed upon him removed, Karl-i-Bond told me in July of 1991:

> It's like a cat chasing mice. To save themselves, the mice select somebody to become the friend of the cat, so that others can know when he is coming. But there's a chance the cat might turn against that mouse. I was that mouse, and I was condemned to death in 1977. Now there's democracy, and the cat doesn't scratch anymore, as he has no claws and no teeth.[33]

Complicity in the strengthening of a corrupt and brutal regime goes far beyond the coterie of immediate beneficiaries gathered around the ruler. Systems spread, and draw in distant adherents and advocates, who themselves never see the spider at the heart of the web, but through hearsay are given the vague promise of some crumbs from the high table at a distant point in the future. First appointed foreign minister in 1972–1974, Karl-i-Bond had later, as the director the MPR political bureau in 1974–1977, defended the introduction of authenticité in 1975 when the political program was introduced to parliament. His role as foreign minister and later as prime minister was clearly active rather than passive. This active role was his downfall when on 14 September 1977 he was sentenced to death for high treason, accused of playing a role in the Shaba uprising. Perhaps of more political significance than the death sentence was its commutation by Mobutu two days later, followed by Karl-i-Bond's sudden release from prison the following July, his reappointment to the post of foreign minister in March 1979, and then his appointment as prime minister in 1980, followed by his loss of office in 1981, when he was sacked. The cat and the mouse were at play again.

"The opposition is made up of opportunists. They all worked with Mobutu at one time or another," said Father Jose Mpundu, priest of St. Paul's Catholic Church on the edge of the Kinshasa suburb of Limete.[34] The tall brick tower of the church rose out of the slums. A tall double gate entering onto a sandy courtyard squeaked open to break the evening calm. The doorbell had a small cage around it, with a padlock to prevent it from being stolen. Father Mpundu never expected to be living here, taking mass in the small church but living outside the Church hierarchy, which had isolated him when he began to criticize the Mobutu government and denounce those behind Zaire's catastrophe.

> I hope there isn't a trial of Mobutu. Because if there were, it would mean we would have to try all Zairians. Have the Filipinos or the Liberians benefited from the deaths of those leaders, or from the death of Ceaucescou in Romania? It is we, the people, who create dictators, and in Africa we believe that the chief is the chief because he is rich. If he's not rich, then we don't see him as a chief. So they get rich any way they can. It's the same with the Church. People give the Church money, even though they have little themselves. The mentality is such that they continue to enrich the rich.[35]

Mobutu's failure to control Zaire's transition away from Mobutism in the 1990s was derived as much from the institutions with which he had repressed the country and its people for twenty-five years as it was from his capacity to manipulate tradition. "There's a political conscience within the army. For twenty years they haven't revolted. But now they have had enough,"[36] Kabuya Lumuna had told me after the army-led rioting of September 1991. "But why did they loot certain ministries? Because there is a political conscience. Mobutu knows that the army wouldn't shoot on the public. In that way the government is weak. The soldiers see the cause of change as being as much theirs as that of the people," he argued. Doubtful of unequivocal support from the army, Mobutu saw his ultimate means of survival as being derived from his self-appointed role of father-chief. "The essence of the political system in Zaire is tribalism. . . . There's a richness to the tribal identity," Kabuya Lumuna had said. For Mobutu the reassertion of this "richness," its manipulation to halt progress toward democracy, depended upon co-opting the opportunists condemned by—among others—Father Mpundu. In so doing, Mobutu's use of the tribal exposed the limitations on the modern aspects of dictatorial power—the military and security services—and highlighted the aspects of his power derived from this "tribal identity."

On 23 November 1991, Mobutu achieved what he had long intended, by definitively splitting the Sacred Union of opposition parties. That day, Nguza Karl-i-Bond was expelled from the union, along with his UFERI party. The expulsion resulted from Karl-i-Bond's offer to Mobutu to stand as an interim prime minister during a transition to democracy. His offer defied the union's policy, already under strain following Mobutu's appointment of Mungul Diaka, since the union had firmly asserted that only Etienne Tshisekedi could occupy this post. Following Diaka's appointment, Tshisekedi became an alternative prime minister at the head of an alternative cabinet, from which Karl-i-Bond had been excluded after a damaging argument between the two party leaders. The split had been long awaited by Mobutu. Karl-i-Bond was then appointed prime minister by Mobutu, thereby creating two governments. Mobutu sought to strengthen Karl-i-Bond and thereby neutralize the opposition. On 17 April 1992, however, the national conference reconvened after a three-month suspension, and declared its own sovereign status, in direct defiance of Karl-i-Bond's instruction that it should not attempt to take over the running of the country. The conference decision undermined Karl-i-Bond rather than Mobutu, as the president had already acceded to its demand for sovereign powers and preferred to manipulate its decisions rather than halt it altogether. Meanwhile, Mobutu was ultimately prepared to sacrifice Karl-i-Bond if it meant he could retain the presidency. Whereas Karl-i-Bond had ultimately to rely on a popular mandate to save his political career, Mobutu still had the card of the father-chief to play.

"Nguza [Karl-i-Bond] has no position. It's the West which gave him too much importance," Kengo wa Dondo told me in October of 1992.[37] The former prime minister, who had also been the state prosecutor who had led the case which had resulted in Karl-i-Bond being sentenced to death in 1977, had insights into the course followed by Karl-i-Bond, owing in part to having first been at the heart of the Mobutu government, then joining the opposition, and then in 1994 rejoining Mobutu as prime minister.

Nguza was not the strongest against Mobutu in the Sacred Union. Mobutu is in the process of setting Nguza against Tshisekedi. . . . If I was close to Mobutu I would tell him not to put obstacles in front of Tshisekedi, because if Tshisekedi fails then he will be *mystifier*, just like Mobutu was *mystifier*. The people are impatient to harvest the fruits quickly. Nguza is afraid of Mobutu. But he knows Mobutu. Mobutu needs Nguza because Nguza is a puppet. The night before Tshisekedi accepted the prime ministership, Nguza had accepted the post.[38]

The night Dondo refers to, when Tshisekedi was once again appointed to the premiership, had come on 17 August 1992. The national conference insisted that Tshisekedi become premier. In July, Mobutu had ceded control of the gendarmerie and Garde Civile to the then prime minister, Karl-i-Bond. When Tshisekedi became prime minister three weeks later, Mobutu appointed Karl-i-Bond as minister of state at the presidency, charged essentially with operating to thwart Tshisekedi's attempts to gain power over all the security forces and the economy for the national conference. Karl-i-Bond's first act was to return to his home province of Shaba—the former and future Katanga—and announce that it would not accept the authority of the Tshisekedi government. This was followed on August 23 with an announcement by Zaire's exiled Katangese secessionist movement that their loyalty lay with Karl-i-Bond and that they would not accept the authority of the

Tshisekedi government, led as it was by a Luba from the central Zairian province of Kasai. The so-called Katanga Gendarmes, the force, led by Karl-i-Bond's late uncle Moïse Tshombe, that had split Zaire in 1960 and reattempted secession when they invaded the province from Angola in 1977 and 1978, said they were awaiting Karl-i-Bond's orders to return to Zaire.

"We left the village because the Katangese burned our house. We went to the military camp. There we had a bit of security. But then the military chased us out of the camp. We went to another military camp five kilometers from Likasi. The Katangese Gendarmes didn't assure our security. So we came here until we can get to Kasai."³⁹ Mashala Kabumba was peering out anxiously from a grass-covered hovel made from the twisted branches of a tree, built hurriedly on the roadside between Likasi and Lubumbashi, Shaba's main towns, in the extreme south of Zaire and 900 miles from Kinshasa. She told me that the local authority commissioner in Likasi, Kitanika Mwenda, had asked the army to push her, her family, and the twenty other Kasaian families living there, out of their shantytown by the end of that day. He had threatened to burn any houses by 5 P.M. if they didn't leave. In a schoolyard along a quiet street bulging with jacaranda trees in Likasi, 8,000 families hid behind the low brick walls awaiting a decision on their fate. They said the Katanga Gendarmes had attacked them. Classes were closed. The displaced people had nothing, except a burning desire to believe that if they returned to Kasai they would be safe.

Official figures revealed that by 20 September, a month after the changes in Kinshasa, 648 houses had been burned to the ground in the area around Likasi, where five camps for the displaced were then established. Around 10,000 people, of a total 40,000 displaced by the violence, were said to be wanting to leave for Kasai, while of 27,000 Angolan refugees who had been in Shaba since 1984 at the town of Dilolo, 3,000 had left for Angola after the 1992 election there. "Everything started with the political problems. Everything started with Nguza, when he was sacked as prime minister. From that moment it started," said Choni Claude Mwana, president of the refugee commission in Likasi.⁴⁰ He went on:

> He came here and brought all his brothers together, including the tribal chiefs, and formed a youth organization. They were formed from what? They have training camps. There were demonstrations. The militia started to attack the Kasaians in the towns and villages. They finally arrived at Likasi. All the villages were occupied by Katangese. The Kasaians' possessions were taken and some houses were burned. Even yesterday there was a house burned.
>
> People did live together. So just Kasaian houses were burned in villages. It was the Katangese Luba who attacked the Kasaian Luba. They led the Lunda, who were also involved in the attacks.

The history of the Luba during the Belgian colonial period had been dominated by Belgian importation of labor to Katanga from Kasai. A community of Luba already lived in the predominantly Lunda province of Katanga before the fresh influx of Luba from Kasai took place in the early part of the century. The new arrivals were employed in administrative positions in the mining activities developed by the Belgians in Katanga. The indigenous Lunda, as well as the Luba who had been long established in Katanga, always portrayed themselves as having been the disadvantaged residents of the province, victims of the Belgians' alleged preference for the Kasaian Luba, whose favored position depended upon the colonial authority. "We lived in harmony before the Nguza statement," said Mwana. "It's a problem created by Nguza. When Nguza realized he was failing, he looked for another route. Mobutu wants to divide Luba and Lunda, because unless he does so, he won't be able to stay in power. He has created it in order to then calm it down and play the role of peacemaker, which can help him stay in power."[41]

Central to Karl-i-Bond's strategy of destabilizing Shaba in this effort to hamper the consolidation of power by the Tshisekedi government was the role played by Gabriel Kyungu wa Kumwanza, the governor of Shaba. Like Karl-i-Bond a formerly outspoken critic of Mobutu, as well as having been an associate of Tshisekedi, Kyungu leapt readily aboard the Mobutu bandwagon when it appeared that Tshisekedi's dominant role within opposition politics created the possibility that Mobutu's opponents would be denied the fruits of their opposition to Mobutu. "Kyungu organized the anti-Luba clashes. He drove around Lubumbashi in his car encouraging people, and then didn't give any time to the inquiry[42] into the troubles," said Jacques Kote Tshilembe, provincial director of Tshisekedi's UDPS party in Shaba, and himself a Lunda from Shaba.[43] "The troubles in Shaba benefited Mobutu because it allows him to discredit the change as a whole, with regard to multipartyism," he said.

Kyungu sought to portray resurgent Katangese sentiment and its manifestation as an anti-Kasaian protest as emanating from the historical relationship between the two groups originated under colonialism, rather than as reflecting a real political divergence symbolized in the distant villas of Kinshasa by the split between Karl-i-Bond and Tshisekedi. As was normal and acceptable within the political vocabulary of Zaire, Kyungu was scathing about Mobutu, even though he was playing a political game in Shaba that Mobutu supported because it undermined Tshisekedi's grip on the opposition in Kinshasa.

But the question remained as to how the strategy then being employed in Shaba was linked to the aims of the Shabaian political class with regard to their national ambitions. "The desire for secession is total among the population, because the Katangese have been misunderstood. But now the leaders

are different. They want to see Katanga remain in the country under federalism," Kyungu told me, late one evening in the red-carpeted residence in
Lubumbashi of the governor of Shaba.[44] He went on:

> Tshisekedi newspapers said I said inflammatory things. The Kasaians of
> Tshisekedi's tribe were the provocative elements who provoked the fury. The
> Katangese no longer accept the Kasaians here. Their presence is an insult. In
> Katanga there's no general movement. There's just one tribe against another.
> Nguza [Karl-i-Bond] is the only man who can really say he controls an entire
> province. Nguza can do what he likes here.

Both Karl-i-Bond and Kyungu opted to believe that Mobutu genuinely
favored not only the rise of multipartyism but also moves toward federalism.
This assumption exposed above all the absence of a sense of responsibility on
the part of the leadership in Shaba. Federalism was an empty promise made
to garner popular support in Shaba. In fact, Mobutu had never made any
commitment to it. Karl-i-Bond had sufficient knowledge of Mobutu to know
that he was being used by the president for his own ends, and yet he was prepared to create havoc in Shaba for Mobutu's goals. Why did Karl-i-Bond go
along with such a strategy, when Mobutu was so unlikely to deliver on the
promises Karl-i-Bond sold to the Katangese in Shaba, and when he himself
knew that his very "return" to Shaba following his dismissal from the premiership in August 1992 was in itself an admission that his political career
was at an end? The answer seems clear. In that desperate and unprincipled
political climate, all means were to be used. Mobutu had always imposed his
will on the political life of the country, in the interests of centralization, with
little heed paid to the sentiments emerging on the local level, and this tendency to ignore local sentiments was as natural to the opposition as it was to
the regime. In such a climate, the people were merely to be used as pawns in
the game of cat and mouse, to use a metaphor with which Karl-i-Bond often
described his relationship with Mobutu—with Mobutu as cat.

The strategy used by Karl-i-Bond had irreparably damaged the process toward multipartyism in Shaba, encouraging many former members of Mobutu's
ruling MPR who had defected to Karl-i-Bond's UFERI party in 1990–1991 to
return to the MPR and thereby reverse an apparent trend toward political pluralism. The strategy had dashed any remaining optimism that there could be a
steady transition toward a new political dispensation. There was real reason to
be disappointed by the sabotage of progress toward real democracy, a sabotage
that had exposed the ruthlessness of incumbent politicians.

The aspirations of the people, though clearly impossible to generalize,
were less complicated than those of the politicians claiming to lead them.
The politics of Zaire had to be seen on two levels—the political maneuvering of the elite, driven by the raw hunger for personal power, and the aspira-

tions of the people, driven by the raw need to break the cycle of poverty. By 1990, most of Zaire's opposition politicians had, understandably, developed personal obsessions with Mobutu. Popular opinion was generally less dominated by the politics of the presidential court, and more by the daily need to survive. Thus, while bringing out the egoism of the political class, multipartyism had brought out the rationalism of the people.

As one example on the local level of political preference superseding tribal considerations, the traditional chief of Shaba, Mwant Yav Kawel, was sacked from his position in August 1992, after he had declared his support for Tshisekedi. Kawel was from the smaller Mpande tribe in Shaba, from which was also drawn the bulk of the local gendarmerie. His decision was a serious threat to Karl-i-Bond, whose UFERI party's youth wing threatened to attack the chief on 7 August. Kawel summoned the gendarmerie, who were attacked with stones by the youths. The following day they attacked the chief's house, forcing him to flee to Likasi with forty of his colleagues. The cynical use of an invented or at least dormant tribal tension exposed more about the bankruptcy of experienced political operators and their failure to meet Zaire's pressing needs with dynamic and appropriate solutions, than it did about the social reality of the country itself, as Jacques Kote Tshilembe of the UDPS made clear: "The difference between now and the 1960s: people have fled because of the violence. Now there is political maturity. Tribal clashes only happen when somebody encourages them. The real reason for the whole thing is that Mobutu can't tolerate multipartyism."[45]

THE LION AND THE COCKEREL

The battle between the eagle and the toad, the cat and the mouse, in Mobutu's Zaire was ultimately a battle for control of a nation that was unlikely to survive in any recognizable form beyond the lifespan of the man who had created it. The institutional and institutionalized weakness of Zaire was the built-in guarantee of the country's fall once Mobutu was no longer at the helm, as much as it was Mobutu's own guarantee of survival while he remained in charge. Perhaps Mobutu never intended for Zaire to outlast him? It would be consistent with the disdain and arrogance with which he viewed a country he saw it as his right to plunder that he would want it to disappear with him. However, it is really unnecessary to pose such questions as to the vision of men such as Mobutu. His demystification during his own lifetime raises the question of whether he was ever so mysterious as to have earned the right to undergo such a process. Mobutu was ultimately a master criminal, who poisoned a country after tearing the flesh from its bones.

The weakness he perpetuated in Zaire as a means of ensuring his survival was balanced by the strategic importance of the country at the heart of Africa. At its burial in the autumn of 1997, Zaire was a sick giant. Geography had ordained that Zaire was important. But after twenty-seven years, Mobutu had added nothing more to this importance than notoriety, despite the country's potential. During the "era of Zaire," the smaller states of Benin, Sierra Leone, and Cameroon had contributed more to African academia than had Zaire, while Kenya and Côte d'Ivoire had used their relatively limited resources to develop greater levels of economic sophistication, despite their being a fraction of the size of Zaire. Of the larger African countries, Nigeria had meanwhile become one of a handful of countries in sub-Saharan Africa other than South Africa to establish an internal dynamic that, despite its serious shortcomings, went a long way toward creating a sense of nationhood. Even Zaire's famed popular musicians relied on the facilities and marketing skills offered them in Belgium and France, rather than on an indigenous music industry. In short, Zaire was a disappointment, not just for Zairians but for Africa as a whole.

Mobutu's failure to create a durable political ethos in Zaire was most clearly exposed by his own readiness to subvert the big ideas he had promoted in the 1960s and 1970s—*authenticité* and *Mobutism*—in the interests of his own political survival. The stark revelation of this readiness, seen in his encouragement of ethnic rivalry in Shaba, was as much a sign of his political bankruptcy as that of Karl-i-Bond. For any regime faced with a similar absence of credibility, the strategy of division can only be an effective tool to intimidate opposition and enhance ruling party authority if it draws upon *genuine* ethnic tensions. Mobutu ultimately failed in his attempts. But while the eagle was dodging the spit of the toad and the cat was chasing the mouse beneath the rain clouds of Zaire, the cockerel and the lion were chasing each other across the hills and valleys of Kenya, where President Daniel arap Moi had launched a much more sophisticated strategy to foment ethnic rivalry. With the resources of a stronger state than those of Zaire to draw upon, Moi did not have to contend with the accusation that he was reversing previous policies of national unity by voicing calls for a tribally based provincial federalism—*majimboism*—that amounted to ethnic cleansing.

Unlike Mobutu, Moi had rarely voiced any clear idea of how he envisaged Kenya developing. As a man without ideas, Moi could not be said to have either promoted or rejected particular political philosophies. He did, however, ultimately mirror Mobutu in his basic instinct, which was to place his own political survival above that of the nation he was supposed to lead. Like Mobutu, Moi enjoyed the complicity of a political class that was vulnerable to ethnic rivalry, both within the ruling Kenya African National Union (KANU) party, and among and within the opposition parties that emerged after the legalization of political opposition in Kenya on 10 December 1991.

The battle between the cockerel—symbol of KANU—and the lion—that of the Forum for the Restoration of Democracy (FORD), the first opposition party to be registered—was as dirty as that in Zaire. Moi lacked the military background of Mobutu. Whereas, prior to multipartyism, Mobutu had traditionally depended upon weakening all potential forms of resistance to himself as a means of neutralizing opposition and in particular ensuring the ultimate loyalty of the security forces from which his power was drawn, Moi brought with him a more sinister and desperate array of lethal weapons with which to divide Kenya and secure his survival. As a civilian, he could not hope to prolong his presidency by using the threat of military power to assert his primacy in the way Mobutu had. Instead, he employed the security forces to maintain a highly partisan version of law and order, within the parameters set by the ruling party's policy of fostering tribal violence.

It is notable that, although Moi lacked all the outward charisma of the tribal *father-chief*, developed so devotedly by Mobutu over almost three decades, he was nevertheless able to reach into the heart of the tribal complex and use it more effectively than Mobutu. Moi could set the tribes off against each other in order to create fear, neutralize his political critics, and split the parties ranged against him. His aim, like Mobutu's, was to heighten divisions within the country and reap the political capital. Mobutu, vain and obsessed with power, sought to secure his future by attempting to be viewed as a monarch. Moi's ambitions were far less grand, which is perhaps why Mobutu ultimately failed and Moi's strategy worked.

Kenya's shift to multiparty politics in late 1991 emerged as a result of the most intense pressure exerted on any of the one-party states of sub-Saharan Africa by domestic opposition, foreign governments, and multilateral financial donors. But Moi's corrupt, brutal, and discredited administration was not just facing the winds of post–Cold War political change when it succumbed to this pressure. The need for political change in Kenya was more firmly rooted in the domestic political situation. The murder of the foreign minister, Robert Ouko, on 16 February 1990, had led to an explosion of vitriol directed at Moi's government. Ouko had been about to submit a report on government corruption before his death. High on the list of those expected to be exposed by his revelations was the minister for energy, Nicholas Biwott. In an inquiry by a detective from the London Metropolitan Police, John Troon, Biwott was identified as the prime suspect in Ouko's murder. Troon's uncompromising revelations eventually forced Moi to demote Biwott, then sack him, then, on 26 November 1991, arrest him. Moi simultaneously suspended an official inquiry into Ouko's death, and to this day the guilty have never been tried.

Biwott had emerged as one of the most powerful members of the government in the mid-1980s and succeeded in using his largely ill-gotten wealth and hard-line opposition to outspoken churchmen and liberal lawyers as a means of securing a key position within the inner circle of ministers surrounding Moi. As significant was the fact that coming from Moi's Kalenjin tribe, he represented ethnic loyalty for a president whose tribe was small and in need of strengthening. It was Biwott who first articulated KANU's response to the gathering pressures on the government to allow political change, by initiating the call for majimboism in October 1991, when he encouraged the Kalenjin of the Rift Valley to seize land from tribes regarded as interlopers on their territory, namely the Kikuyu from central Kenya and the Luo from the west. "Beset by calls for multi-party democracy and for the disclosure of their land deals and business interests, Biwott and his colleagues deliberately began to incite Kalenjin fears about their future in a Kenya without Moi as president."[46]

Coming as it did at a time of tremendous upheaval in Kenyan politics, during which the ability of the state to endure the pressures being exerted upon it was severely tested, the revival of a long defunct majimboist political program as a means of attempting to steer political change confused and destabilized the transition to democracy. The tribalist rhetoric appeared to confound all that Kenya had sought to become since independence. "After independence there was a determination not to be a 'native', as this was a colonial definition. Instead, people wanted to appear 'Kenyan,'" said George Kamwesa, a deputy secretary general of the National Council of Churches of Kenya (NCCK).[47]

Under heavy pressure from foreign donors to create a more accountable and less corrupt government, Moi routinely portrayed the changes through which Kenya was being forced as being the result of a neocolonial attitude on the part of the United States and other Western countries. To an extent he had grounds for making this claim, as Kenya was undoubtedly subject to pressures that these same Western governments would themselves have denounced as meddling in the internal affairs of another state, if the excesses of the Moi government had been easier to ignore. Moi and KANU appeared isolated, in the world and within their own country. The policy of majimboism, which evolved out of this deserved isolation, was an extreme attempt to deny this isolation, to turn the tide rather than ride the wave. As George Kamwesa told me, it was not based on the real situation:

> National exposure in the past has led to extensive intermarriage. It's not possible to unwind all that. When you raise the issue of majimboism, you are actually trying to erase the purpose of the church and the community.
>
> The things that are happening are part and parcel of change, in a very ugly form. . . . I don't think it's really the idea of the old tradition versus the new tradition. The people who are advocating change have all been in the old system. It's not as if it's only the lawyers. The old guard is there.[48]

For KANU, the need to create a tribal alliance to ensure its political survival was much more stark than it was in Mobutu's Zaire. The isolation of Kenya's Kikuyus from political power since the early 1980s, the corruption and brutality of the Moi government, the disproportionate influence of a small tribe—the Kalenjin—over the affairs of state and particularly the awarding of business contracts, all had driven a wedge between the cabal of decisionmakers and the mass of the people on all social levels. Throughout the early 1990s, Moi was also regularly involved in attempting to settle disputes within the Kalenjin, where there was long held resentment of his own rise from within the relatively small Tugen subgroup. Majimboism was in part intended to rally all Kalenjin behind Moi. The death of Robert Ouko, the most prominent Luo—Kenya's third largest tribe after the Kikuyu and the Luhya—in government at that time, together with the political isolation of the Kikuyu, created the risk for Moi of a Kikuyu-Luo opposition alliance, which had the potential to oust KANU in a fair election.

KANU's support base in the Rift Valley, derived from the Kalenjin, Masai, Samburu, and Turkana tribes, amounted to only 15 percent of the population and controlled only 35 seats in the 200-seat national assembly.[49] Consolidation of this support was vital for KANU, though it would only bring electoral success if it was accompanied by concerted efforts to lure political opponents into the KANU fold with financial inducements, while also using all the state's means to intimidate the political opposition. In the Rift Valley, this strategy meant creating bands of Maasai and Kalenjin *moran* (warriors), whose task was to force "settlers" from other parts of Kenya to swear allegiance to Moi and KANU. On the national level, the strategy split KANU itself, as KANU supporters and KANU's Kikuyu and Luo members of parliament foresaw the dramatic loss of all Luo and Kikuyu support. Some Masai supporters were themselves opposed to the strategy, notably John Keen, a KANU M.P. and former minister of state in the Office of the President, who defected to the newly formed Democratic Party. "Most KANU leaders, however, did not understand the changing political environment. Leaders of the *majimbo* campaign remained determined to push ahead, whatever the political cost, with their search for the chimera of Kalenjin self-rule."[50]

The successful rebirth of multipartyism in Kenya[51] was dependent upon overcoming, at least temporarily, the tribal loyalties that had determined the previous experiences with multipartyism in 1960–1964 and 1966–1969. The genesis of FORD lay in a deliberate attempt to create a tribal alliance within the leadership, based on the realization that the formidable power of KANU would be difficult to confront, unless there was a united attempt to do so.[52] But throughout 1992, as the elections planned for the end of the year approached, this alliance rapidly collapsed, and, as the most comprehensive analysis of the emergence of Kenya's multiparty system in the twentieth century states:

As the personal rivalries within FORD's leadership became more and more vituperative, the party's factional struggles and its leaders came to resemble KANU's more and more, rather than exemplifying a new political order that

could solve the nation's problems. FORD was ceasing to be a credible alternative government and becoming no more than a vehicle for protest votes. The
conflict also made it likely that voting in most areas would be determined by
ethnic rivalries and local issues and loyalties, rather than by national political
issues and the parties' policy manifestos.[53]

In reality, there was little alternative to the tribal nature of the opposition
alliance. Such an alliance reflected the reality of Kenyan society. Politically,
however, its potential for success was limited by the contradiction between
the tribal character of the opposition alliance and the supposedly national
outlook of the party platform. The opposition wanted to use its tribal power
to seize control, while simultaneously decrying the conduct of the Moi government for the tribal favoritism it practiced. Even so, FORD leaders did
not shy away from acknowledging that the legacy of one-party rule necessitated such a strategy. "If you have Matiba as the FORD candidate, then Moi
will win without even winning the elections, because if you have Kibaki and
Matiba, you have two Kikuyus against Moi," said Paul Muite, who became
FORD's vice-presidential candidate in 1992, referring to the FORD leader
Kenneth Matiba and the Democratic Party (DP) leader Mwai Kibaki.[54] His
summary shows the complexity of the problem:

> The majority of people vote on tribal lines. It's because of the one-party sys-
> tem, in which dictators surround themselves with their own tribe. This is be-
> cause of insecurity. Therefore, the majority of people are reminded of their
> own ethnicity. In the initial years of multipartyism, the people will look to their
> own ethnic group for protection. And there are very few people who will be
> able to see beyond that.
>   The Luos [the second largest group] will not vote for either Matiba or
> Kibaki, because they will feel that they have marginalized their candidate,
> Jaramogi [Oginga Odinga]. So the Luo will go back to Moi. The Luhya [the
> third largest group] will feel that Masinde Muliro and Martin Shikuku have
> been sidelined. So the Luhya in Western Province will go back to Moi. Moi
> will publicize this as a vote of confidence in the one-party system.
>   I think it's crucial to forge ethnic alliances as the only way of having a party
> which has a wider base and can dislodge KANU. Only then can we start to
> confront the ethnic issues facing the country.[55]

The threat of a split in FORD increased as the party approached a delegate's conference on 5–6 September 1992, at which the presidential candidate would be selected. The rift manifested itself as a personal battle between Matiba and Oginga Odinga. Their differences centered on the
process of selecting the candidate, with Odinga insisting that party members

elect delegates throughout the country to select a candidate, while Matiba demanded a direct secret ballot of all party members. Both sides in the dispute conducted their campaigns against the other along lines that revealed their need to maintain one tribal alliance or another. Odinga, a respected veteran of Luo politics, could not hope to win an election if he split with Matiba, a Kikuyu, unless he found another Kikuyu with whom to ally himself. Consequently, Odinga entered into secret talks with Mwai Kibaki, the DP leader, also a Kikuyu.

The Odinga faction within FORD saw itself as presenting a real alternative to the voters, by offering a presidential candidate—Odinga—who was not a Kikuyu and did not depend upon the uncertain alliance of smaller tribes that bolstered Moi. Matiba's critics within FORD, even those among his natural supporters, were doubtful that a member of his Kikuyu tribe could take power, owing to the strong memories of the domination of the dictatorial Jomo Kenyatta, Kenya's Kikuyu founding president. "The country isn't ready for another Kikuyu president, so they won't vote for Matiba," Raila Odinga, a member of the FORD executive committee and Oginga Odinga's son, told me.[56] "People want fundamental change, and they don't see Matiba and his clique as capable." The dispute was partially settled when Oginga Odinga was selected as the FORD candidate at the September conference. Matiba refused to attend, saying he would conduct his own selection procedure.

The rift within FORD led to the party splitting in October 1992, heralding the creation of FORD-Asili led by Matiba and FORD-Kenya led by Oginga Odinga. Their attempts to balance tribal loyalties and potential voting patterns, as a means of creating a formidable opposition to KANU, allowed Moi and the extremists within the ruling party to portray both FORD parties as essentially alliances that had failed to attract the support of the Kalenjin and other traditional tribal supporters of KANU. In the climate of fear and anxiety, fostered by Moi's own self-fulfilling prophesy that multipartyism would breed tribalism, extremist ministers and KANU party officials accelerated their efforts to promote the ethnic cleansing of the Rift Valley in order to secure it as an "exclusive KANU zone."[57]

"The president has in his own way been trying to bring his prophecies true. The Kalenjin themselves have openly said that they have been paid to do what they are doing," a church pastor told me in Kitale, the western town at the center of government-inspired clashes in 1992.[58] He continued:

> The gains for Moi from the clashes: to cover up the things that he has done. He has been trying to bring about a sort of emergency, many times. He would like to eliminate all the people who know about these matters. There's corruption, and mass killings. In a state of emergency he would be able to protect himself from disclosures. The problem isn't localized.

The pastor claimed that Moi's plans were not working, because the church had early on exposed his intention. Rifts within Kenya's opposition parties throughout 1992 meant that they were ineffectual in contending with the issue of the clashes. The most effective critical voices in the political arena were KANU parliamentarians from the Luo and Kikuyu tribes who feared that their party's strategy of violence would lose them personal support at the election. Of course, there were KANU politicians who genuinely condemned the policy and used parliamentary privilege to identify Nicholas Biwott as the architect of the clashes. It was the Anglican and Catholic churches, however, who were the most uncompromising in their condemnation of the violence, and they unambiguously blamed the government and the security forces for planning and perpetuating it. In April 1992, the National Council of Churches of Kenya (NCCK) issued a report:

> These clashes were and are politically motivated . . . to achieve through violence what was not achieved in the political platform, i.e. forcing *majimboism* on the Kenyan people. Here the strategy being to create a situation on the ground for a possible political bargain in the debate about the system of government in future Kenya. Obviously one of the consequences of the clashes is slowing down of the current democratization process. With the clashes, energies and focus have been redirected and ethnicity has become an important factor in the political debate.[59]

The NCCK report catapulted the issue of the clashes and, in particular, the government's role in the clashes, into the full glare of public scrutiny. Two months later, after the speaker of parliament had four times prevented debate on the issue of the clashes, a parliamentary committee was established to look into the violence. The committee of thirteen parliamentarians, all of them from the ruling KANU party that was at that time still the sole party in parliament, delivered an even bigger shock than that of the NCCK. The Kiliku[60] committee's 238-page report, issued in September 1992, three months before the election, named Nicholas Biwott and other KANU hardliners as being the instigators of the violence. The report went further by concluding that its evidence revealed that "warriors" had been paid by the politicians to kill rival tribes in the Rift Valley and further afield: "[Our evidence] indicates that the fighters were on hire and were paid large sums ranging from Kshs.500 for safe return from the clash front, Kshs.1,000 to Kshs.2,000 for killing one person or burning a grass-thatched house and Kshs.10,000 per permanent house burnt."[61]

High on a windswept plain on the western edge of the Rift Valley, Mark Mereng was grazing his sheep, close to the deserted ruins of the village of Kolongolo in the area of Trans-Nzoia. The village had been deserted in 1991. "When the people ran away, we moved the grazing into the area. The people left when the clashes started. We have lived with these people, and they only left when the clashes started. I am not happy that people have left, but I am happy to be able to graze," he said, admitting that the attack, which had led to the local people leaving, had been launched by his fellow Pokot tribesmen.[62] The village, a trading center in which Luhyas had owned most of the shops, was deserted. The Pokot, a subgroup of the Kalenjin who had attacked on 24 December 1991, had not taken over the shops and businesses. The attack had more than halved the population, reducing it from 12,000 to 5,000. "Now, I can't take the Pokot to be friends. They are my enemies. In my lifetime I don't think I will ever live with the Pokot. The Pokot children will never play with us," said eleven-year old-Isaac Baraza, whose parents and seven brothers and sisters fled that night, when Pokot from the neighboring district attacked, burned their houses, and forced them to leave.[63]

In the shadow of Mount Elgon, clustered at the base of the mountain slopes where the rough ground meets the lush farmland, was Endebess Camp, ten miles west of Kitale. Small huts covered in plastic sheets had been erected in neat lines, when the people living there had arrived after fleeing from their homes at several nearby farms that had been attacked on 26 December 1991. Endebess was at one point home to 8,000 people, though 6,000 of these eventually found shelter elsewhere. In mid-1993, the security forces emptied the entire camp forcibly, after the local council had said it wanted the land back. "It was the Saboat who attacked us," said Paul Kibate, who had fled to Endebess on 27 December 1991, from Mango Farm, a small holding nearby which had subsequently been occupied by the Sabaot, a subgroup of the Kalenjin, and been renamed Mosop.[64]

> They came during the day with guns, and some of them in uniform. They shot two people, and we fled and came here. I can't go back, because they are saying I took my farm from them. But I bought it in 1988 from Wandera, a Luhya like me. And he had bought it from a white man called Stamp. Now, I have to stay here, because I have nowhere to go. I can't go back. They have guns. They would kill me. And we can't get guns, because the government won't allow us. We don't want war.

The argument of extremists like Nicholas Biwott and William ole Ntimana, a Maasai M.P. and KANU's minister for local government, that the Rift Valley was the patrimony of the Kalenjin, Maasai, and related tribes prior to the arrival of European settlers, and that it should therefore be returned to its original owners, was a spurious, unproven argument. "Even at independence there were areas of the Rift Valley which were not earmarked for a particular community," said George Kamwesa of the NCCK.[65] "The land clashes don't have their root in land changes after independence, as shown by the fact that the clashes have not been going on since independence. It's only explicable in terms of the events of the past few years." The realization among the clergy, lawyers groups, opposition parties, and other organizations that the Kenyan government was effectively mounting a low-level insurgency against sections of its own population was deeply shocking. Kenya had always known political violence, but for the government to behave in this way and to face the wrath of its own more moderate members for doing so was rare.

The deep anxiety and fear that had grown throughout the country in response to the violence in 1991–1992 intensified in early 1993, when it was realized that the ethnic cleansing intended by Moi, Biwott, and others was not going to stop with the re-election of Moi and KANU at the 29 December 1992 poll. The purpose seemed much greater than simply winning an election.

"There's an incident every night. Last week, on one day, there were twenty houses set on fire. There's a new development, which is that most of the houses which are burned were evacuated a long time beforehand."[66] Father Peter Elun'gata, a priest at Burnt Forest Catholic Church in Uasin Gishu district 150 miles north of Nairobi, peered warily into the darkness when I knocked on the door of his small bungalow well after dark late on an April evening in 1993. He invited me into his spartan home and shared the *ugali* and beef he had been eating in front of the single illuminated bar of an electric fire. It was quiet and cold, and the rain, which had been threatening to fall all day, began to spatter at the window.

The election, which had seen the divided opposition disappoint the people by allowing Moi and KANU to return to office with a small but workable majority, had come and gone. With it had gone the hope of profound change. In Burnt Forest, the hopes had been intense, the suffering dreadful, the violence a nightmare. In the run-up to the election, 20,000 people had been living in the church compound, though they had since left. The experience in the area, where Kalenjin traders had bought and sold goods from Kikuyus ever since independence, was the most severe example of the post-election punishment by the Kalenjin against those in areas that had not returned KANU candidates to parliament. Later that year, on 2 September 1993, the government declared Burnt Forest and two other areas[67] to be "security operation zones," in which a form of martial law was imposed by troops of the General Services Unit (GSU).[68] The three zones were closed to outsiders. Prior to the creation of the zones, groups of between 200 and 300 moran warriors, armed with spears and poisoned arrows, had launched attacks on Kikuyus and others in Burnt Forest. After the zones had been created, the attacks continued, and they spread to other Kikuyu communities in the Rift Valley, notably around the town of Narok. In the gloom of his home in Burnt Forest, Father Elun'gata smiled wearily, his brow wrinkled with anxiety, as he tried to find some solace in an increasingly desperate situation:

We thought the clashes were a response to the multipartyism situation. But as it has happened since the election, we realize it is an attempt to create federalism and majimboism. Land is not the issue, as this area was not originally Kalenjin. The Kalenjins prefer to stay on their own. Once you develop a relationship with them, they are trusting. Since independence, the Kalenjins have been doing business in Burnt Forest. But since the clashes, this has stopped completely. Some Kalenjins speak Kikuyu, showing how well they were established. There's been a lot of talk about oathing[69] among the Kalenjin. The Kalenjin have to be cleansed of their oaths before they can stop targeting their enemies.

Now, there's a new tactic that is unfolding. The Kalenjin are sent in to provoke. The government will use it as if it is some kind of an uprising. When the Kikuyus resist, the GSU is sent in. The Kikuyus have been able to organize their security by staying together after they have been displaced.

The church is finding it difficult to bring Christians from the different tribes together. The Kalenjins don't come to church when there are Kikuyus. They are afraid they might be victimized.[70]

THE TWILIGHT OF THE HELMSMEN

The amalgam of traditions that created the character of single-party rule in much of sub-Saharan Africa, from the 1960s until the early 1990s, owes more to political opportunism than it does to faith in the chiefly practices of the precolonial past. Olushola Isinkaiye analyzed the situation in 1990, just as Africa was about to embark on a decade of profound political change and upheaval:

The conception of the power of the traditional ruler or chief in virtually all of Africa, his supposed fatherly role and his holding of power for benevolent communitarian ends, has been interpreted to mean and to sanction the absolutist rule observed in many presidential regimes of the parliamentary genre. . . . The general tendency has been to ignore or abandon the democratic values inherent in the traditional African political systems.

[The] general tendency in African presidencies . . . is towards monarchism, either rationalized purely by *raison d'état* or legitimated by traditional myths. This has led to the emergence of what may be qualified as the "monarchical state" that obeys two contradictory logics: one that is modern, and the other that is traditional. The attempt to resolve the contradictions inherent in this curious hybrid appears therefore to underlie the perversion of traditional principles of government in modern presidential systems.[71]

The issue is a highly complex one, owing in part to the variety of systems that have emerged in African countries since independence, especially since 1990. The purpose of this chapter has been to highlight the efforts by two

African leaders to foster disharmony by inventing tradition, as a means of determining the course of their respective countries' shift toward a more "modern" system of government. Isinkaiye perhaps confuses the issue, by associating tradition with the idea of the monarchical state and modernity with the shift toward democracy, when earlier he had spoken of the "democratic values" inherent in African tradition. This apparent confusion is extremely revealing. It reveals the extent to which the real experience of states under the domination of the father-chiefs, the "Helmsmen," the "Guides" of modern Africa, has itself served over time to lead to the forgetting of aspects of tradition that did not suit their personal vision of statehood. Such democracy as there had perhaps once been was the first tradition to be dispensed with, closely followed by responsible rule and accountability.

Even though multiparty politics has produced political parties and cross-party alliances that identify strongly with one tribe or another in a variety of African countries, in at least these two key instances of tribal violence during the early years of political reform, the violence was not a natural consequence of that reform. As with Rwanda, the violence in Kenya was planned and deliberate. It was not a spontaneous outburst of traditional rivalry. The Kenyan violence would not have been possible, if those responsible for it had not had the organizational infrastructure of the modern state to hand. There, the use of traditional weapons—spears, and bows and arrows—was of no real significance, and certainly has no bearing on whether the violence was traditional in nature.

This use of violence, as well as the attempt to dub it *tribal* as a means of creating the kind of fear that dampens enthusiasm for political liberalization, broadly had the opposite effect to that which its perpetrators had intended. It is a major sign of the ongoing crisis in African leadership that men like Moi have survived, despite their lack of respectability or credibility.[72] This absence of credibility is total, from the perspective of both the traditional expectations held of the father-chief and the modern expectations of a national head of state. Viewing experience through the eyes of his character Ikem, the Nigerian writer Chinua Achebe reflected in *Anthills of the Savannah* on the condition of his country, and perhaps others, when he wrote in 1987:

> The prime failure of this government . . . can't be the massive corruption, though its scale and pervasiveness are truly intolerable; it isn't the subservience to foreign manipulation, degrading as it is; it isn't even this second-class, hand-me-down capitalism, ludicrous and doomed; nor is it the damnable shooting of striking railway workers and demonstrating students and the banning thereafter of independent unions and cooperatives. It is the failure of our rulers to re-establish vital inner links with the poor and dispossessed of this country, with the bruised heart that throbs painfully at the core of the nation's being.[73]

PART FOUR

New World, Old Order

T HE END OF THE COLD WAR in Africa may be the moment at which the *African* history of Africa is about to begin again. The colonialist legacy has been buried, in particular by the experience of France in Rwanda, while the interventionist Cold War legacy has been buried by the near total disappearance of any importance most of Africa may once have had for the United States. After more than a century, foreign domination and meddling have perhaps now come to an end. Determined to bury their own ghosts, however, the Cold War victors regarded the 1990s as a chance to have one last fling with the continent, under the guise of the "New World Order." The scale of this last burst of activity betrayed the opportunism and ineptitude lying at the heart of the destructive Cold War relationship. For reasons that will remain unspoken until the West steels itself and admits that its relationship with Africa is at heart based on a mixture of vanity, bullying, and ignorance, this final engagement was a disaster, as has been shown by the failure to address the conflict in Sudan, the catastrophe of the U.S.-led intervention in Somalia, and the soul-searching the Rwandan genocide forced upon France.

On the global stage, the end of the Cold War has left the world fractured rather than united. Internal differences within nation states, suppressed during the superpower conflict, inevitably burst into the open when that conflict came to an end. The emptiness of the promises of the Cold War, the one-sidedness of the deal the conflict represented, the absence of any kind of peace dividend for those countries that had actually suffered mortal damage,

249

all soon became obvious. As the proxy wars became civil wars, the truth became clear, that not only was the "New *World* Order" a misnomer owing to its limited applicability, but also it represented much the same desire to impose order from the outside as had the old order of the Cold War.

The United States is now faced with an internal debate about how best to conduct itself as the single most influential state in the world. One theorist argues, "The puppeteer has to accommodate the recalcitrant desires, doubts, and objections of the puppets-turned-actors. That is the arena every leader must enter. Until America's leaders address the American people and other nations with that kind of respect, attention and persuasion, we shall lack foreign policy leadership of any sort."[1] Even among more conservative thinkers, doubts about how the United States has handled its primacy in the post–Cold War period have been loudly voiced, as Samuel Huntington, one of the most influential American social scientists, makes clear:

> In the unipolar moment at the end of the Cold War and the collapse of the Soviet Union, the United States was often able to impose its will on other countries. That moment has passed. The two principal tools of coercion that the United States now attempts to use are economic sanctions and military intervention. Sanctions work, however, only when other countries also support them, and that is decreasingly the case. Hence, the United States either applies them unilaterally to the detriment of its economic interests and relations with its allies, or it does not enforce them, in which case they become symbols of American weakness.[2]

The limitations of influence have been exposed, though Britain's long-term commitment to rebuilding Sierra Leone is perhaps one sign that an "ethical" foreign policy in a former colony can provide the basis for beneficial ties. In general, however, it has become ever clearer that foreign influence among superpower former client states in Africa was dependent entirely upon close ties with ruling elites, rather than any form of broader links. The United States has little influence among the populations of Africa, despite the economic success of the United States being the object of envy in much of the developing world. This harsh reality was most brutally exposed when 19,000 U.S. Marines arrived in Somalia in December 1992 with a mission to save the people of state formerly allied to Washington as a Cold War client, and the state they were supposed to save ultimately rejected their efforts.

These limitations are not confined to the U.S. relationship with Africa. France is regarded with immense ambivalence among the populations of its former colonies, dependent as it has been upon close ties with leaders rather on any genuine rapport with the led. The 1990s saw France forced to accept that Africa could no longer be used as a lever which, by using its claim to be able to "deliver the African vote" at the United Nations and the assertion that *la francophonie* was a major global force, it could use to heighten its own importance on the world stage. France's century-old rivalry with English-speaking Africa died on the battlefields of Central Africa, as its old allies died or fell from power and its efforts to "save" Rwanda failed. Out of this old rivalry may now have been born real cooperation between Britain and France, and the rivalry of which Britain was barely conscious, but which France wore on its sleeve, may have reached an end.

Meanwhile, the new order into which Africa has itself emerged has brought with it ideological and, in particular, religious beliefs that are certain to become key determinants of the future direction of the continent. Islam has taken root way beyond the historic regions of North Africa and the Sahel, in a manner symbolic both of the rejection of a century of imposition of Western values, and of a growing need to find a new source of spiritual equilibrium. The challenge to the outside world—and in particular to the countries of the West seeking to assert a global role and a global presence—is to rid itself of the assumption prevailing in the early 1990s that years of contact with Africa equipped it with even a basic knowledge of the continent's affairs.

11

"ROGUE" STATES AND RADICALS

The United States and Sudan

PLUMES OF SMOKE FROM BURNING incense curled into the hazy blue-gray afternoon sky, as the magnificent red blaze of the sun cast the shadows of singers and dancers onto the harsh rock and sand of the graveyard.[3] Dry, gnarled trees stood motionless in front of the conical dome of the saint's *qubba*, or tomb. Roughly hewn, white-painted stones marked the graves. Lines of men, bareheaded, dressed in fine white cotton robes, called *jelabias*, filed between the graves toward the incense-burner. The raging sun burned the land, and the men shielded their eyes as they gathered in an ever growing circle on the plain, leaving an open space in their center. The slow setting of the sun dictated the timing of the ritual, which slowly gathered pace on the edge of Omdurman, one of the three cities that, divided by the confluence of the Blue and White Niles, form the Sudanese capital—Khartoum, Khartoum North, and Omdurman. The rivers, the desert, and the ritual marked the confluence of cultures and religious practices through which Sudan has evolved, by way of dramatic phases of history, in the face of invasions and the conflict of ideologies, which have both enriched and devastated its land and people.

Sudan is a crossroads of civilizations, where a rich cultural heritage has imposed a great weight upon the course of change. New ideas have been forced to coexist with what has been inherited from the past and have constantly been manipulated by a political elite with an enduring attachment to power. Religion has shaped the course of Sudanese politics, directly or indirectly, since the collapse of Ottoman power and the eruption of revolt in 1881, led by Muhammad Ahmad ibn 'Abdallah. In June of that year, he dispatched a series of letters to the rulers and administrators of Sudan declaring that he was the Mahdi, the expected messiah. A century later, the religious root of political life remains firmly entrenched. Since it seized power in a 1989 coup d'etat, the Sudanese government has attempted to create an Islamic state in which policy is inextricably linked to the mechanism of government. Although the *sharia*, the code of law based on the Koran, has had some impact on Sudanese life, Africa's largest country has become an international pariah rather than a model for other developing Islamic countries to follow, a "rogue" state rather than a respected Islamic society.

Sudan has presented a challenge to the West and to African and conservative Islamic states, both as a political and military opponent of Western influence, and as a religious and social experiment. It has been condemned in part because it is weak and easy to condemn without fear of the consequences, and in part because of the frustration in the West at having failed to achieve a substantive dialogue with the Islamic world, a failure that has exposed an increasingly dangerous flaw in the global outlook and foreign policies of the world's most powerful states. Western countries have relied upon their dictatorial allies among Islamic countries to use brute force rather than persuasion to dilute the message of political Islam.

For its part, the West—and the United States in particular—has pursued a policy of isolating Sudan, which has largely failed to dilute the dictatorialism of the current regime, while also failing to show any genuine understanding of what it is that drives Sudanese politics and lies behind the events of the past decade. Only as the fading of the short-lived New World Order became obvious has the ineffectiveness of the such isolation emerged, as Samuel P. Huntington among others made clear when he wrote in 1999:

> American officials seem peculiarly blind to the fact that often the more the United States attacks a foreign leader, the more his popularity soars among his countrymen who applaud him for standing tall against the greatest power on earth. The demonizing of leaders has so far failed to shorten their tenure in office. . . . Indeed, the best way for a dictator of a small country to prolong his tenure in power may be to provoke the United States into denouncing him as the leader of a "rogue regime" and a threat to world peace.[4]

These multiple failures have served to worsen the plight of the Sudanese population in both north and south. More broadly, they have also seriously undermined the post–Cold War assertion that a New World Order could be created on the basis not only of mutual respect, but also of real understanding of the world's cultural and religious diversity, notably on the part of the Western architects of that new order.

Although political instability, poverty, and war in developing countries have hindered the expansion of the new order, perhaps the greatest single challenge to global acceptance of the new, post–Cold War, Western-led order, has been political Islam. The catastrophic violence in Israel and Palestine that erupted in October 2000, the collapse of the Middle East peace process, and the election of the contemptible Ariel Sharon as Israel's prime minister have fully exposed the unraveling of U.S. policy in the region in which political Islam is strongest. The inability of the United States to convince the Arab side in the conflict that it could play the role of honest broker had been obvious to the Palestinian masses for years and has since been accepted by U.S. policymakers themselves. It finally became impossible to hide when the U.S. could no longer conceal the fact that its policy never incorporated a sincere acknowledgment of the historic grievance felt by Palestinians over the issue of land, and of the power of religion and the significance of the Palestinian claim—and thereby that of all Arabs and Muslims—to control of the Islamic holy sites of Jerusalem. The exposure of Western diplomatic weakness in the face of the violence was not only a turning point in the process of finding a peaceful solution to the Palestinian-Israeli conflict, but the final proof, if more were needed, that the West had only the most superficial understanding of the political-religious character of the broader Islamic world.

The multifaceted north-south conflict that has wracked Sudan in phases since independence in 1956 is a microcosm—albeit on a vast scale—of many of the religious, racial, and political battles that face much of the rest of the African continent. These battles are certain to dominate its future history, as Islam expands, and the sorry condition of post-independence sub-Saharan Africa leads to an inevitably decisive break with the quasi-colonial attachments of the past forty years, including the attachment to Christianity. Increasingly, the search for solutions to the continent's dire economic and social condition will come to be articulated in anti-Western sentiment, with blame increasingly being laid at the doors of Western financial donors, governments, and political liberals. As much as questions of faith and ideology have been prominent in the conflict, history, tradition, and a drive for modernity have also presented conflicting visions of what the Sudan of the twenty-first century should be. A conviction of the failure of the Western model is the major element in the new thinking, and it will become even stronger.

The original, though now discredited, foundation of the past century of Sudan's political and religious history is the tradition of Mahdism. The Koran foresees the arrival of a restorer of faith just before the Day of Judgment:

> And (Jesus) shall be
> A sign (for the coming
> Of) the Hour (Of Judgment):
> Therefore have no doubt

About the (Hour), but
Follow ye Me: this
Is a Straight Way.⁵

Muhammad Ahmad "was the 'leader', thrown up by the times, of a pecu-
liar type of Sudanese nationalism. Lying behind his emergence was a very real
and unwavering belief in his divine call—a belief which exercised a com-
pelling influence on others."⁶ Mahdism catapulted Sufi mysticism and vener-
ation of an inspired leader into the political arena of late nineteenth-century
Sudan, an arena in which Muhammad Ahmad played a role from an early age.

The 1881 Mahdist revolt against Anglo-Egyptian influence in Sudan was
a remarkable attempt to create an Islamic state. By the time of independence, on 1 January 1956, Sudan's political life was dominated by the political ambitions of Sayyid 'Abd al-Rahman al-Mahdi, the son of the Mahdi,
ambitions that, after 1945, he had channeled into his newly established
Umma Party, led by his son Sayyid Siddiq al-Mahdi. This creation of a party
by heirs of the Mahdi stoked fears of the creation of a new Mahdist state,
particularly within the Khatmiyya Sufi religious order led by Sayyid 'Ali al-
Mirghani, whose ancestor's close ties with Egypt had played a key role during the Ottoman period before the Mahdist revolt and who after the revolt
channeled their political ambitions into the Democratic Unionist Party
(DUP). Together, "the sectarian leaders retained the keys to political
strength."⁷

Civilian rule lasted until 17 November 1958, when Major General
Ibrahim Abboud led an army coup, largely in response to the chaotic and unworkable civilian coalition government that had failed to address Sudan's severe economic and social problems. Sayyid 'Abd al-Rahman al-Mahdi died
in 1961. His religious-political role was split between his brother, Saayid al-
Hadi, who became the leader of the Ansar sect founded by the Mahdi, and
his son, Sadiq al-Mahdi, who became leader of the Umma Party. Also
emerging as political forces during this period were the Communist Party
and the Muslim Brotherhood, the latter led by a law lecturer at Khartoum
University, Hassan el-Tourabi, who went on to found the National Islamic
Front (NIF) in the mid-1970s.

As potent as the machinations of the northern-based political parties in
Khartoum, however, was the growing political activity of the southern Sudanese. After 1922, the British had effectively barred northern and southern
Sudanese—effectively Arab and African—from each other's essentially tribal
areas, proclaiming the south an officially closed area. The aim of the British
was to incorporate the south into its East and Central Africa policy. Even before independence, southern consciousness, particularly heightened by the
south's almost routine exclusion from the negotiations that led to the final
settlement of the terms of independence, was emerging. In 1955 a battalion

of southern troops had refused to open fire on striking southern workers, and following their mutiny they had gone underground to form the nucleus of what became known as the Anya Nya movement, named after a poisonous plant that grew in Kordofan province. In 1964 they reemerged as a focus of southern opposition, attacking the southern town of Wau, and taking the government by such surprise that it eventually fell from power. For the following five years, government fell into the hands of a succession of coalitions, led from July 1966 to May 1967 by Sadiq al-Mahdi as prime minister. In May 1969 the civilians were once again sidelined when Colonel Gaafar Nimeiri seized power in a bloodless coup. But Nimeiri's pursuit of large-scale development programs, as well as the introduction of Islamic-oriented policies in the justice system, neither alleviated the widespread poverty of the country nor appeased the civilian and religious political establishments.

The worsening political and military crisis in the south, with the outbreak in 1981 of a full secessionist war by the Sudan Peoples' Liberation Movement (SPLM), and the unceasing economic hardship in the north combined to bring down Nimeiri in a 1985 military coup. Civilian rule was restored in 1986, with Sadiq al-Mahdi as prime minister, although the war in the south remained the key factor in ensuring the continued instability of the government. In 1989, el-Tourabi was appointed deputy prime minister to al-Mahdi, an appointment which, given the NIF's strong support for sharia within a unified Sudan, was unlikely to appease the SPLM. The rebel force succeeded in gathering cross-tribal support from the largely non-Muslim south, from Christians and animists, while asserting as its key demand the end of Muslim dominance. War raged in the south, and al-Mahdi was overthrown in yet another bloodless coup, on 30 June 1989, by army officers led by Brigadier Omar Hassan el-Bashir, whose stated objective was to bring an end to the war.

"I do believe there's a revival in all the Islamic world. There's a renaissance of Islam. But we don't meddle in the internal affairs of other Muslim countries, because we don't want others meddling in our affairs. There is a renaissance of Islam, and these countries are retarding this. But we believe eventually that our view will be triumphant."[8] President el-Bashir sat serenely on a grand armchair in a large office on the upper floor of a nondescript concrete government building off a tree-lined street on the edge of Khartoum. It was late December 1993. "In Sudan there is a freedom of creativity, and everything is open to debate."

El-Bashir had forged an alliance with el-Tourabi's National Islamic Front soon after seizing power. In 1991 the military government began introducing elements of sharia into policy. "Our guiding principles are constant and have nothing to do with the conflict in southern Sudan or the economic situation," el-Bashir told me. "On the contrary, we know that these guiding principles address many of the grievances that have led to the conflict. When you try applying Islamic ideas, it could be that there are points of convergence between Islamic thinkers, and differences as well. You find different points of view, to the extreme right and the extreme left. Our way is mediation."

"Mediation" in Sudan, since the 1989 coup, and more specifically since the launch of the Islamization program in 1991, has been dominated by the lessons gleaned from the political failures of the country's post-independence history. It has also been heavily influenced by the weakness of a political system dominated by the religious-political elite that had drawn its power from the Ansar and Khatmiyya religious orders established during precolonial times. "Our most serious problem in Sudan since independence has been the search for stable government. We have had a formal democracy ruled by tribal families. Then a military dictator [Nimeiri]. Because there's now a religious spirit, the military can't rule the government," Hassan el-Tourabi told me.[9]

> You can't have democracy without basing it on the spirit of the people. Throughout Africa there are parties, but they are tribal actually. And Islam is based on democracy. In the new Sudan there is no following of the [religious] sects and their relevant political parties. Revolutions run against the old order, and people don't join those sects anymore. People worked for them for the hereafter. But now people know that in the hereafter they don't get anything for working for these people.

El-Tourabi's rejection of the old order dominated by the Ansar-Umma and Khatmiyya-DUP religious-political groupings, as well as his alliance with a section of the army in which political Islam had a strong root, set him on an extremely isolated path—isolated both from his numerous domestic political opponents and from other countries of the Islamic world, which were intensely suspicious of Islamic fundamentalist government. Sudan's policy was not something its architects felt the need to conceal, despite the consequences for their relations with the countries that fell within Khartoum's spotlight in the early 1990s: "Some countries are more wary of us than others," said Ghazi Salah Eddin Atabani, Sudan's minister of state for foreign affairs until 1996.[10]

> For example, Saudi Arabia is a corrupt system which corrupts Islam. It's decadent. It represses women, and can't accept these changing, modernist ideas. At the same time, they are not providing an Islamic government. The problem for the royal family there now is their relevance. They don't have the right mindset, nor will they accept new ideas because they are so corrupt. . . . The role we are playing is one relating to the revivalist model, which is what makes Sudan central to the revivalist model. The Islamic model is considered incomplete until its political component is implemented. So, it's the first time that a revivalist movement has been both fundamentalist in the way it perceives things and views life, while at the same time being a modernist movement.

The determination to strengthen the policy and its effectiveness within Sudan, as well as bolster its influence outside the country, had, by 1995, inspired a rare degree of coordination in opposing Sudan between the often fractious countries of East Africa and the Horn, within which Sudan's influence was being felt. Vital to these efforts was a growing determination on the part of the United States to actively confront Sudan's ambitions. To this end it placed Sudan in 1992 on its list of states allegedly sponsoring international terrorism, to enhance the effectiveness of regional opposition to Khartoum. As one U.S. regional strategist said at the time: "You do what you need to do, and we will help them[the neighboring countries]. But it's a very dangerous game. Something has to be done to change the course of Sudan's policies. If they don't change their internal policies, their human rights policies, then they're digging their own grave. This is just one step short of saying that we will provide the bullet."[11]

ALL THE WORLD'S A STAGE

Rusted metal sheets welded into a five-foot sculpture of an iron fist stood red-hot as the heat rose to 104 degrees in the garden of the Hamas militia office, hidden in a maze of sandy streets on the edge of Khartoum. Neat coils of barbed wire topped an iron fence surrounding the Palestinian group's two-story building, where the children of the diaspora played beneath giant-size currency notes of their nonexistent state, encased in plastic on the wall as the backing for clocks whose three hands ticked in the red, green, and black of the Palestinian flag. Security was tight, the soft drinks were warm, and Mounir Said, the representative of the Palestinian Hamas Islamic Resistance Movement, brushed away the flies that droned incessantly in the hot building.

We talked about Sudan, and its role as a haven for organizations like Hamas, whose rejection of the Oslo peace accord with Israel[12] was bringing it into direct conflict with the Palestinian Liberation Organization (PLO), as the PLO sought to patch up a deal on the future of Palestine before the chance was lost. Said told me, "We have an Islamic project. Sudan has the same project, and we are going to carry out this project in all Islamic countries."[13]

> We feel about Sudan the same that they feel about us. We respect one another. Arabic countries are going through a difficult time now, and the rulers of the Arabic countries are not in touch with their people. In Khartoum we lecture in the schools and universities, and mount exhibitions to show what Hamas is doing, to make people know that we are still struggling against the occupation of Palestine by the Israelis.

Part of the unspoken terms that Hamas agreed to before it established itself in Khartoum was that it would not carry out its operations outside Palestine. The same had generally been the case with other organizations with a presence in Khartoum throughout the early and mid-1990s. Lebanese Hizbollah, the Abu Nidal Group, the Popular Front for the Liberation of Palestine, the Algerian Islamic Salvation Front (FIS), and others visited Sudan, usually for conferences of the Popular Arab and Islamic Conference (PAIC), the platform from which el-Tourabi sought to assert his influence on the Islamic world, until it was effectively dissolved in the late 1990s. The Khartoum government had discouraged activities by these groups within Sudan—against foreign embassies, for example—which would complicate its own relations with the countries involved. "We are a wise movement," observed Said.

> We know that Israel is a very strong power, and that we Islamic people are not in a strong position. So we are creating good relations with all Arabic countries, by carrying out our operations only in Palestine. We never do anything outside Palestine. We don't have many important targets outside Palestine. The Israelis have many important things outside Palestine. We have been talking about not taking the war outside Palestine. But if they want us to take it outside Palestine, then we will. We have told the Israelis this. Also, there's no need for those of us in Sudan or Iran to be fighters. So there's no problem for us to live above ground rather than underground. But we will take the war outside Palestine if they want us to.

In the early 1990s, Sudan became preoccupied by the deteriorating situation in Somalia, and came to regard it as offering fertile ground for the spread of its influence in the Horn of Africa. It viewed the growing U.S. military presence there in 1992–1993 as intended to create a buffer against its Islamic agenda. "We saw [the UN intervention in Somalia] as the imposition of the way the U.S. wanted things to be, and it has used the UN to do this," said Baha Al-Din Hanafi, director of the political department of the Sudanese president's office during the early 1990s.[14]

> They see a dramatic change coming in the whole area, along Islamic lines. They see what happened in Sudan and what was about to happen in Algeria. So they want to be prepared for it if it happens. They want to be able to influence. They want to stop what they like to call Islamic fundamentalism spreading. Most of the friends of the U.S.—Egypt, Saudi Arabia, Tunisia—are in trouble. When you look closely at the senior foreign policy advisers in the U.S., they see this era as a clash of cultures. They are looking for another ism.

The extent to which Sudan developed a detailed strategy for armed intervention in Somalia is open to question, and it has been the subject of highly partisan accounts with little supporting evidence other than claims by individuals on one side or the other. Offering no eyewitness or documentary evidence from the anti-Sudan side, Yossef Bodansky, in his influential book *Bin Laden: The Man Who Declared War on America*, asserts: "The Islamists' decision to fight the U.S. forces [in Somalia] was determined by the Iranian-Sudanese strategy. The tenets of this strategy were clearly outlined in the Islamist analysis of U.S. intervention. Islamists throughout the Middle East elucidated the perception of threat and the expediency of action as perceived by Khartoum and Tehran."[15]

Bodansky writes that the key players in these activities were Hassan el-Tourabi and the dissident Saudi Islamist, Osama Bin Laden, who had led Arab fighters in the U.S.-backed Afghan Mujahideen in their fight against the Soviet Union in the late 1980s, and who lived in Sudan from 1992 to 1996, after leaving Afghanistan. Bin Laden, Bodansky says, was instrumental in establishing training camps for Somali Islamists in various parts of the region and in setting up front companies through which funds could be channeled to these groups. "The mission was to 'turn Somalia into a trap and quagmire for the U.S. forces through a guerrilla war against them',"[16] Bodansky quotes an unidentified source as saying.

Using this network, el-Tourabi determined a political agenda for the Sudanese-backed groups, collectively called the Somali Islamic Union Party (SIUP), created as "an umbrella for a few Islamist organizations with clan or tribal loyalties, as the main vehicle for Iranian-Sudanese operations, including the insertion of expert terrorists," Bodansky writes.[17] On 9 December 1992 the U.S. assistant secretary of state for African affairs, Herman Cohen, arrived in Khartoum, ostensibly to warn President Omar Hassan el-Bashir against interfering with U.S. military operations in Somalia, operations that constituted the first—and last—post–Cold War *humanitarian intervention* by the United States. The mission had been launched at 3 A.M. that day, when an advance party of bewildered U.S. Special Forces troops emerged out of the Indian Ocean surf and landed on the beach at Mogadishu, in the glare of the waiting media. The U.S. presence was regarded in Khartoum as part of a grander post–Cold War design, ultimately intended to create a buffer against el-Tourabi's regional ambitions, which extended from Egypt to Uganda, from Chad to Kenya.

Although there is no doubt el-Tourabi had major ambitions for the Horn of Africa and beyond, the assessments of writers such as Bodansky have a tendency to make neat connections between all the enemies of the United States in a manner that is often belied by the facts on the ground and thus likely to inspire responses derived more from paranoia and grand conspiracy theories than rational assessments of what is likely in reality. Prominent among Bodansky's claims was one that, because of his role as director of the U.S. Congressional Task Force on Terrorism and Unconventional Warfare, he was able to have an unfortunate influence on U.S. thinking: "The major escalation of the fighting in Mogadishu that took place in fall 1993 was the implementation of the long-term plan decided on by Tehran and Khartoum."[18]

This is a gross oversimplification of the situation. Aside from the fact that the violence was the culmination of many weeks of provocation and bad decisionmaking in Somalia, the main Somali faction fighting the U.S. troops at that time—that led by Mohamed Farah Aideed—had condemned the role of Islamists in Somalia. Aideed had told me in September 1992 that "an Islamic group known as *al-Itihad* is in the [Somali] town of Merka, and they are equipping themselves to take over the country. They have a connection with outside countries, and they are receiving money and military equipment and buying weapons."[19] Despite the use of a variety of Islamic slogans, Aideed and his closest advisors routinely condemned Islamists, and were particularly virulent in their condemnation of the introduction by rival faction leaders of sharia law in several areas of the country. Nevertheless, Bodansky asserts that in 1992 a "[Pakistani and Iranian-trained] militia force allocated for East Africa including six companies and three battalions manned by 3,000 troops from Yemen, Algeria, Somalia and Kenya, [fought] in Somalia alongside the forces of General Muhammad Farrah Aidid against Ali Mahdi Muhammad's forces."[20] It is unfortunate that he does not provide a source for this significant claim, which suggests that Aideed was criticizing the presence of foreign-backed Islamists while simultaneously benefiting from their services. He also overlooks the fact that Pakistani UN troops in Somalia were key victims of Aideed's attacks.

Bodansky goes on to assert that Ayman al-Zawahiri, an Egyptian Islamist and a close associate of Bin Laden, was present in Somalia in October 1993, when the fighting between the UN forces and General Aideed's supporters escalated and when "there was no longer any doubt that the escalation of the fighting . . . was a result of the long-term plan decided on by Tehran and Khartoum to use the 'Islamic International,' all the Islamic forces, in a major operation intended to transform Mogadishu into a 'second Kabul' or a 'second Beirut' for the Americans."[21] Bodansky asserts that Arab "Afghans" who had fought with the Afghan Mujahideen, assisted by Iraqis, fought at the front line in the Mogadishu battle of 3 October 1993, which left eighteen U.S. troops dead and heralded the U.S. abandonment of the Somalia operation. "Aidid's people, both militiamen and civilians, were introduced in huge numbers in time to create the enraged mob and join the onslaught, as well as take casualties and the blame,"[22] Bodansky asserts. Such a claim is one of the more extreme in his account and is only serious due to the influence it may have had on the flawed decisionmaking that deepened the UN-U.S. Somalia quagmire.

Fundamental to the problems faced by the UN and the U.S. in Somalia was the fact of Somali distrust of outsiders. Iranians, Sudanese, and others were on the receiving end of Somali xenophobia, as much as Pakistanis,

Americans, and Kenyans. Bodansky's assertions, based—it appears from his book—on not a single visit to Somalia or any interviews with Somalis who might have given some substance to his claims, ignore the character of the country and the impact of this character on the events of 1992–1993. This omission is a serious one, and it is symbolic of the ineptitude that has marked much Western foreign policy since the end of the Cold War. The failure to understand the nature of the problems to which the theory of humanitarian intervention was being applied was a major flaw in the practical application of the New World Order. Osama Bin Laden himself made this clear in August 1996, when he issued a statement declaring jihad against American forces in Saudi Arabia, in which he said:

> Your greatest scandal was in Somalia where, after huge media propaganda over many months regarding American power in the light of the fall of the cold war, and American leadership in the "New World Order," you deployed tens of thousands of troops in an international force, amongst them being 28 thousand American troops, to Somalia.
>
> Nevertheless, after a few small confrontations, where scores of your soldiers were killed and an American pilot was dragged through the streets of Mogadishu, you departed in defeat and humiliation with your dead and injured troops. . . . It became clear as to the extent of your inabilities and weakness. In fact, the image of your defeat in the three Muslim cities of Beirut, Aden and Mogadishu brought joy to a Muslim's heart and delight to those who believe."[23]

Meanwhile, clearly emboldened by whatever role Sudan had actually played in Somalia, Hassan el-Tourabi sought to continue on his path toward becoming the leading Islamist in the region. "The challenge now is the neighborhood. To the east, the south and to the north. It's obvious that some international forces are seeking to undermine the Sudan," he told me.[24] Throughout the mid-1990s, Sudan sought to become a catalyst for regional political upheaval. "I saw the Eritrean opposition in Khartoum. They held security meetings with the NIF, which has given them financial support, vehicles and weapons," said Mohamed Ahamed Abdelgadir al-Arabab, a former Sudanese state minister who fled the country in 1995, and had been directly involved in the establishment of military training camps for foreign groups.[25]

> They established training camps for the Eritreans at Kassala and Gedaref, and in the Markheatt mountains near Omdurman, where there was a terrorist military training camp for several nationalities, and another at Jebel Awliyaa in the south of Khartoum. Other camps were at Al-Gash River in Darfur, the eastern mountains of southern Kordofan, in Senaar state, the Mazmun mountains, the Kardus forest, and in the far north. All of these areas have military training camps for foreign extremists, as well as housing the Sudanese [Popular De-

fence Forces]. At Hajyosif there's a camp for a regiment that has been specifically trained for the assassination of politicians. There are also 400 teenagers
there, who have been trained for the killing of domestic opposition leaders and
non-NIF people. By 2002 they will have executed their entire plan: the secret
plan of the NIF, and the PAIC, is to become the leader of world Islam. The
PAIC will support the extremists throughout the world, to allow them to seize
power in their own countries, to change governments and replace them with
Islamic groups. They are planning to do this in Eritrea, Somalia, Ethiopia,
Chad and Niger, and elsewhere. There are ten countries in all.

Al-Arabab had been the head of the Sennar state security council, in
which role he had been instrumental in preparing the military camps for
training. He had been under pressure to join the NIF, but had resisted.
Meanwhile, the government had found willing recruits in the border areas to
the east, particularly among the Eritrean refugees who had been living in Sudan for up to thirty years. Among the movements to which Sudan had provided weapons was *al-jihad al-islamiyya*, Islamic Jihad.

"Our al-jihad al-islamiyya movement was founded in 1990, and it's very powerful inside Eritrea. The aim is the liberation of Eritrea, and the domination of
Islamic morals. Now, we have fighters inside Eritrea, and after victory they will
establish the Islamic government," Idriss Mohamed Idriss explained, sitting inside a large grass-walled and grass-roofed hut whose walls were hung with colored cloth, at the Kashm el-Girba refugee camp in Sudan's north-eastern
desert.[26] The Eritrean government had demanded that Sudan prevent Eritrean
dissidents using the camps as a base for their activities. But the calls were ignored
throughout 1995 and well into 1996. Four Eritrean organizations—not all of
them Islamist—were said by the refugees at Kashm el-Girba to be operating inside Eritrea. "The Eritrean Muslims have been strongly influenced by the way in
which Sudanese Islam has been practiced since 1989," said Sheikh Mohamed
Ismael Ali.[27] "Because Sudan is ruled by an Islamic government, we feel secure,
and that Islam has a new life here."

But within a year that apparent security had been shattered, and the border area around the camp had become a war zone. The National Democratic
Alliance (NDA), an Eritrea-based Sudanese opposition force largely comprised of northern Sudanese Muslims opposed to the government in Khartoum, began attacks in the border area in early 1997. These attacks were coordinated with a renewed campaign in the south by the Sudan Peoples'
Liberation Movement (SPLM), led by John Garang. The government in
Khartoum was being squeezed. The training camps in the east had been
closed, and the government took steps to try and appease its critics. In 1996,
the Saudi Arabians used their influence with the United States to demand
and achieve the expulsion of Osama Bin Laden—their most outspoken
critic—and his return to Afghanistan. The government then sought to repair

its relations with foreign donors, by agreeing to a series of measures that would prevent an increase in the repayment of arrears of its debt to the International Monetary Fund. It then began putting out feelers to Egypt, in an effort to repair the damage done by accusations that it had harbored the assassins involved in an attempt to kill President Hosni Mubarak in Addis Ababa in 1995.

NEW WORLD: ORDER AND DISORDER

Trapped by a mixture of poor intelligence gathering[28] and personal prejudice, U.S. policy in the Islamic world broadly—and in Sudan as one stark example—has failed to respond to a relatively rapid evolution that has taken place within political Islam. To date, U.S. policy has largely relied upon the existence of a divided Muslim world, centered in the Middle East. U.S. support for Israel, the U.S. manipulation of Arab allies for the purposes of strengthening Israel, the connivance of the Western media in bolstering the racist stereotype of the Arab world and its relations with and attitude toward Israel, all have been made possible by the atmosphere of turmoil that Israeli military superiority, U.S. impunity in its policing of the "rogue states" of the Middle East, and the illegitimacy of all Arab leaders in democratic terms have together fostered in the region. These elements have allowed political Islam to do some of its work, giving voice to a politicized religion way beyond the theatre of the Middle East and the specificities of the Arab-Israeli conflict.

Vital to developing an appropriate response to the political changes within the Islamic states is an understanding of the domestic conditions that brought these changes. In 1997, Hassan el-Tourabi had told me: "If most of society becomes like me, that will be my success." Within two years he was in the political wilderness, and in March 2001 he was jailed in Khartoum after seeking an accommodation with John Garang's forces in the south. In northern Sudan, pressure for change has emerged, as the personalities controlling the political life of the country have found the accommodation sustaining their military-political alliance failing to produce solutions to the pressing problems facing the country: the devastating war in the south, the armed opposition of Muslim northerners based in Eritrea, and the impact of Sudan's isolation by African, Arab, and Western countries. The strains within the military-religious alliance had intensified the disaffection among natural supporters of el-Tourabi, many of whom had remained passive during the early years of the regime but had then joined the chorus of voices critical both of the evolving style of government and the paucity of its achievements.

As Abel Aleir, a respected southerner who was twice vice president of Sudan, wrote in 1990: "The real participants in any talks for a settlement of the problems are those political organizations which are effective decision-makers in the country."[29] He continued:

As 1988 drew to a close it was generally realized in the Northern Sudan that unless the civil war was brought to an end through a just political settlement, standards of living would continue to sink as commodity prices soared, more taxes were levied and socio-economic development programs were curbed, in order to raise the necessary resources to prosecute the war.[30]

More than a decade later, exactly the same conditions prevail. But instead of seeking a solution that addresses the causes of the war, the U.S. government in particular has been lured into supporting those it sees as its natural allies—the nominally Christian, black Africans of the south—in a fight against a "Muslim north" that is in fact deeply divided on issues of religion, politics, and race. As Aleir wrote in 1990,

> [Non-Moslems] are not alone in their rejection of a theocratic constitution. A large number of Moslem Sudanese of informed opinion, who are devoutly religious, support the non-Moslem on this subject.
>   The issue of religion is real and could lead to failure of any attempts to reach a settlement unless it is dropped altogether.[31]

Following the 1992–1993 debacle in Somalia the United States was in no mood to engage in any meaningful way in African affairs. Madeleine Albright's heartless refusal to bolster the UN force in Rwanda during the genocide in the spring of 1994 proved as much. When, in May 1994, President Clinton appointed Melissa Wells as special representative to Sudan, with a brief to assist regional efforts at finding a permanent peace agreement to the southern war, it was an initiative that was bound to achieve zero results, owing to the anti-Khartoum bias of the regional peace effort. That effort—coordinated under the auspices of the Inter-Governmental Authority on Drought and Development (IGADD)—was dominated by Kenya and other generally corrupt, anti-democratic, and seriously flawed mostly non-Muslim regimes highly suspicious of Khartoum and traditionally the Cold War allies of the United States.

A potentially far better U.S. initiative would have been to encourage Muslim states in North Africa—with Egypt the obvious priority—to seek to engage Sudan and encourage it to compromise. However, during the 1992–1995 period, when poor U.S.-Sudanese relations were cemented, the United States considered "internationalizing" the situation in Sudan by exerting pressure with and through Sudan's neighbors to force a policy shift in the country.[32] Hardly surprising that the IGADD initiative, intended to end the war, was regarded with suspicion in Khartoum, and was thus undermined by this secondary strategy of attempted regional coordination against Khartoum. In 1995, the United States further undermined its potential diplomatic role by donating $20 million to Uganda, earmarked for "improving security" and thus effectively given to buy weapons that few doubted would be bound for the SPLM led by John Garang in its war against Khartoum.

U.S. policy toward Sudan throughout the mid-1990s was dominated by exasperation with the Sudanese government in general and Hassan el-Tourabi—the presumed power behind el-Bashir—in particular. El-Tourabi was generally suspicious of U.S. motives. "The failure of U.S. policy toward Sudan to achieve its primary objective was virtually foreordained, in view of the kind and extent of the differences between the U.S. and Sudanese governments,"[33] wrote Donald Petterson, U.S. ambassador to Sudan in 1992–1995. The United States, which has rarely established its foreign policy positions on the basis of genuine respect for the kinds of variety it has encountered in cultural environments at odds with the American mainstream, was never likely to shift opinion within the Islamic government. It was therefore never likely to play the post–Cold War role it sought, as the founder of a New World Order. It missed the chance, and the belligerent, often dishonest, violent, and intolerant military-religious regime it encountered in Khartoum presented a challenge that U.S. policymakers failed to meet, leaving them frustrated and—ultimately—vengeful.

American frustration at the refusal of Sudan to succumb to diplomatic pressure, following closely on the heels of the U.S. and UN failure in Somalia and the general condemnation of its failure to take action against those committing the genocide in Rwanda, was compounded by the gathering perception that a New World Order founded on democracy and free market economics was unlikely to take root in Africa for years to come. In 1996 the U.S. embassy in Khartoum was effectively closed, a move that left U.S. policymakers largely unable to follow political developments accurately. Consequently, U.S. policy failed to keep pace with the changes in the country. Little that the United States has said with regard to Sudan since 1996 reflects any kind of recognition or understanding of how the political life of the country has evolved. Most glaring was the failure to acknowledge that, far from being dominated by the reputedly all-powerful Hassan el-Tourabi, the political life of Khartoum was subject to a much greater internal variety and pressure, and the government was not the immutable junta it was portrayed as being.

"Since the last election, which made him president, Bashir has distanced himself from Dr. Tourabi," said Osman Khalid Mudawi, a Khartoum lawyer and founder member of the National Islamic Front (NIF).[34] He continued:

> Tourabi had great influence in the early years. He was practically the only voice. But he has used up his political capital. Over the years he has antagonized his political base. Now he has very little influence on decisions. There is a preponderance of evidence that Bashir is firmly in power and is calling the shots. People

learn from their mistakes. Tourabi unnecessarily antagonized people by making them afraid of nonexistent dangers, making threats that weren't there. He didn't project the right image. He has a love affair with the media. The Tourabi I knew in the past was a very different person. Why this change? I have no answer. Tourabi is no longer an asset, but is the greatest liability to Sudan, and I think the president knows it.

Mudawi was clear that the evolving situation had manifested itself in growing tension between el-Tourabi and President el-Bashir, a tension that had left the two men not on speaking terms on several occasions. It has since manifested itself in the political conflict over the role of the National Congress (NC), the political party established by el-Tourabi, when a new constitution was passed that allowed the creation of opposition political parties for the first time since the army seized power in 1989. It had been asserted that all ministers must be members of the party, and that the NC should have the power to dismiss ministers who performed badly. These claims to power were rejected, and even the party's leading members rejected the idea of the NC becoming essentially the party of the state. "Sudan is trapped. The agenda is concentrated on survival strategies not long-term policies," said Hassan Maki Muhammed, an influential university professor and member of the consultative council of the NC.[35]

To make long-term policies we would have to have a stronger position and build institutions. For the past six to seven years this government has just passed from crisis to crisis. From pressure to pressure. From test to test. These people in government, after ten years, have discovered that the survival of Sudan itself depends upon [them] changing [their] policies.

I think that the role of Tourabi is diminishing because there are only twenty-four hours in the day. He is fed up and has started to withdraw. He has many many problems from the government, from insiders and outsiders. I think Tourabi himself talks about the failures. He has the courage to admit them.

The war in the south is the main cause of the change in the government's direction. If it hadn't been for the religious propaganda of jihad, the government wouldn't have lasted the ten years it has been in power. In fact it's been a success in keeping them in power. It's an unwinnable war, but it's working.[36]

The momentum of this political shift was seriously threatened when, on 20 August 1998, the United States launched a cruise missile attack on the al-Shifa pharmaceutical factory on the outskirts of Khartoum. The United States claimed that the factory was associated with Osama Bin Laden and was being used to produce precursors for the manufacture of chemical weapons. The attack took place simultaneously with an even more dramatic bombardment of Bin Laden's base at Khowst in Afghanistan, which was struck by seventy cruise missiles. Both attacks were the U.S. response to allegations that Bin Laden had masterminded the devastating bombings of U.S. embassies in Nairobi and Dar es Salaam on 7 August 1998, in which 263 people, most of them Kenyans and Tanzanians, were killed.

The attack on the al-Shifa factory exposed an uncontrollable vengefulness on the part of U.S. military planners. Two embassies had been attacked, so two targets had to be hit in response. Within three weeks of the embassy bombings, four people had been arrested and accused of responsibility. Pakistani police arrested two, a Saudi and a Sudanese, on 29 August 1998 at Torkum, the Pakistani-Afghan border post at the western end of the Khyber Pass. The principal suspect, Mohammed Sadiq Odeh, had been flown to the United States from Pakistan the week beforehand, after being captured by Pakistani authorities. Odeh had identified Bin Laden as the mastermind of the bombings when he had appeared in court in New York the previous day, and had named Bin Laden's al-Qaeda organization as having arranged the bombings.

After the attack on the factory, a crowd attacked the British embassy in Khartoum, leaving gashes and holes in the brickwork. A few days later, the foreign staff of the embassy was evacuated. The British, the close ally of the United States, had not been given advance warning of the attack on the factory, though they pretended they had known.[37] The cruise missiles that struck the factory had been undetected by Sudanese radar, because of a power cut at Khartoum airport, site of the only radar in the country.[38] Other European diplomats who knew the al-Shifa factory quickly condemned the attack itself. "On the basis of what we know of the factory and the evidence we have been given by the U.S. so far, there is no reason to believe that the U.S. knew what was going on inside that factory, other than with regard to its function as a major supplier of pharmaceuticals," one European diplomat told me in Khartoum. "Nor is there any evidence that the factory had links with Bin Laden. This robust support by other governments for the U.S. action was frankly very stupid,"[39] he said.

Diplomats in Khartoum took seriously the Sudanese sense of grievance at the attack, largely because there was a strong sense at the time—and subsequently—that Sudan was changing its political direction and might have been diverted from this shift by the U.S. aggression. The attack was viewed by both Sudanese officials and diplomats as having been directed at Sudan itself, rather than Bin Laden. "The U.S. says it has destroyed Bin Laden's infrastructure. The fact is that the aggression has destroyed only the infrastructure of Sudan," said Ghazi Salah Eddin, who had become the government spokesman by the time of the attack.[40] "The factory is a private facility owned by people who have links to Gulf countries who have problems with Bin Laden," he said, implying that the factory owners were not sympathetic to Bin Laden's campaign against U.S. influence in the Islamic world.

To Sudan's chagrin, Arab states only condemned the attack four days after it had happened; such was their keenness to prevent Khartoum using anti-U.S. public opinion elsewhere in the region as a lever by which to diminish its own isolation. "Should we approve or should we reject it?" the Egyptian foreign minister Amr Moussa said in the immediate aftermath of the attacks.[41] "Why should we? Why should we use this language of black and white? We are absolutely against terrorism. We called for the [UN] Security Council to take the necessary steps and meet for an international summit [against terrorism]. So our position is very clear."

Nothing was really clear, however, least of all how the UN Security Council could allow the attack on Sudan without insisting on seeing and making public the evidence to justify it. Ultimately, concerns that the bombing might end whatever moves toward a new political direction the Sudanese government may have started as el-Tourabi's influence receded, did not materialize. El-Tourabi appeared not to have the energy to capitalize on such a blatant and apparently unjustifiable attack by his movement's archenemy. Speaking in his house near Khartoum airport late one evening, he seemed almost resigned to his eclipse when he said with obvious bitterness:

> I don't mean much myself, personally. If religious values are spreading I don't have to be in government. People are haunted sometimes by ghosts. There's a renaissance of the Islamic spirit. People don't know much about Islam. In Islam we don't believe in the concentration of religious power. That's why I supported Omar Bashir. Islam cannot come to power except by force, because the West wouldn't allow it. All things being equal, they hate me because I'm a Muslim.[42]

A COLD WAR

The steady exposure of how ineffectual the rigid U.S. policy of isolating Sudan had become was impossible to prevent after the bombing of al-Shifa. Up to that point, intense U.S. criticism of the Islamist-led government had failed to change Sudan's policies or create the conditions for the regime's downfall. Despite suspicions in the past among some Arab leaders that Sudan was indeed a security concern, by the late 1990s it was no longer regarded by these states—notably Egypt—nor even by Islamist political organizations themselves, as a major player on the Islamist political scene. Ties between Cairo and Khartoum are now much improved, as are relations with Algeria, Tunisia, and Saudi Arabia, which had previously harbored suspicions of the Khartoum government.

But the diminution of Sudan's apparent threat to its neighbors did not change U.S. policy, and Sudan's obvious weakness has since exposed how inappropriate U.S. policy has been. A key player in this rigidity was Susan Rice, U.S. assistant secretary of state for African affairs in the second Clinton administration, and prior to holding this post an advisor to the U.S. National Security Council. U.S. diplomats and intelligence officers regard her views as having strongly influenced the formulation of U.S. policy. In September 1999, in a characteristically myopic assessment of the complex situation in Sudan, composed in response to the Khartoum government's efforts at retrieving some of its nonexistent credibility, Rice wrote:

> A quick glimpse within Sudan's borders . . . reveals a world of famine, slavery, torture, religious persecution, rape, massacres, pillage and looting. The Sudanese population and the world community should not be taken in by the new government rhetoric.
>
> Sudan has been engulfed by a brutal civil war since 1983. For years southern rebels have fought for a democratic, secular Sudan that would guarantee equal rights for those southern Sudanese who have been treated as second-class citizens for too long.
>
> The Sudanese regime, which displaced a democratically elected government in 1989, has engaged in a policy to divide and destroy the people of the predominantly Christian and animist south. It uses terror against civilians as a weapon of choice and pits different ethnic groups against each other, resulting in southern factional fighting that has complicated the overall situation.[43]

Rice's loathing of the government in Khartoum blinded her to the fact that all sides in the war had been equally guilty of human rights abuses—the SPLM effectively enslaved women to their cause, while looting and the use of hunger as a weapon in the SPLA armory as well as the killing of tribal opponents by both the Dinka-dominated SPLA and the Nuer-dominated breakaway faction led by Riek Mechar, were routine throughout the 1990s. Taking sides on the basis of such issues was not going to contribute to finding the negotiated settlement to the conflict which was and remains the only potentially fruitful course of action. Khartoum's assertion that the United States, as well as the IGADD states, were biased, remained most clearly seen as credible in the statements made by Susan Rice. The break-up of the SPLM into the Garang and Mechar factions in 1991 did not improve respect for human rights among the southern rebels, despite this being a stated aim of the faction led by Mechar.[44]

Rice, as the key U.S. policymaker on Sudan in recent years, has concentrated on criticizing the *results* of the war—the violence, abuses, and hunger—as if such an approach would precipitate a shift in strategy by the warring parties of a kind that could address the fundamental *causes* of the conflict. This approach has created only frustration for the United States, as well as exposing poor diplomatic skills on the U.S. side. Just as the United States has failed in its role as an honest broker in the Arab-Israeli conflict, owing to the U.S. bias in favor of the Israeli side, so it has failed to use its considerable potential weight to address the complex and important issues raised by the Sudanese conflict, whose resolution is essential if eastern Africa and the Horn are to enjoy peace and development. Rice's treatise on these issues continues: "If the Khartoum government were serious about fulfilling its expressed commitments, it could demonstrate as much by taking a number of steps. It could begin by negotiating seriously in the peace process, which it has consistently acted to undermine thus far."[45]

An historical perspective on the process of attempting to negotiate an end to the conflict can only be fully informed if, again, the failure of *all* sides to negotiate with full sincerity is recognized, as for example in Abel Aleir's important book—*Southern Sudan: Too Many Agreements Dishonoured*. Part of the apparent intractability of the conflict lies in the distrust that is both cause and effect of the conflict, and certainly a reason behind its longevity. Any diplomatic effort must accept that the conflict has deep historical roots, and that, even though public statements by the different sides may be exposed as insincere when subject to scrutiny, lying behind these words are genuine positions—understanding of which is likely to bring more fruitful diplomacy than anything the U.S. policy under Susan Rice managed to achieve.

Recognition of the failure of beating the Khartoum government with a stick has been a slow process, and in 1999 the non-governmental organizations, whose efforts to feed those affected by the war have placed them at the center of the conflict on a daily basis, began to try to speed the process up. In October 1999, CARE, the international relief agency, began to openly criticize the U.S. government view, which saw "Sudan primarily through an anti-terrorist lens," as Peter Bell, president of CARE USA, put it.[46] "The only way we could really provide support for these cycles of famine and humanitarian emergencies was if we worked on the root cause of these crises, which is the war. . . . We want the U.S. to look at Sudan through a humanitarian lens, making the achievement of a just peace its primary objective in dealing with Sudan." The implication was a serious one, as it clearly suggested that the concern over human rights issues, about which the U.S. government had made considerable noise, was in fact not the main motive behind U.S. policy. Jimmy Carter, the former U.S. president, supported the need for a shift in that policy bluntly: "[The] United States government has a policy of trying to overthrow the government in Sudan. So whenever there's a peace initiative, unfortunately our government puts up whatever obstruction it can."[47]

A series of efforts by Sudan in the middle and late 1990s to escape its pariah status revealed the hostility of the United States. According to a senior Sudanese diplomat, Sudanese and U.S. intelligence officials and diplomats met secretly as early as 1996, to discuss basic U.S. preconditions for the normalization of ties. The United States at that point demanded—and achieved—the expulsion from Sudan of Osama Bin Laden. The United States also demanded the closure of the al-Makhtiar training camp, which was at that time thought to be used for training foreign terrorists, as well as the opening for inspection of other military camps. Sudan was also told to deny entry to individuals regarded as close to militant organizations. According to a former senior CIA officer with extensive knowledge of Sudan, the al-Makhtiar camp was opened to the FBI for inspection.[48] After Islamic militants attempted to assassinate President Hosni Mubarak of Egypt in 1995, visa restrictions for all Arabs entering Sudan became tighter. In 1996, after Saudi Arabia and the United States rejected Sudanese suggestions that it was better to keep Bin Laden under surveillance in Sudan, the Saudi was advised to leave on the grounds that Sudan could not guarantee his safety. Mahdi Ibrahim, Sudan's ambassador to the United States until 1997, then led secret discussions with the FBI regarding the opening of an FBI antiterrorist office in Khartoum. But immediately after these secret contacts, the U.S. State Department barred the FBI from opening an office in Khartoum, according to the same former CIA officer.

The election of the second Clinton administration led to Sudan making even more public and assertive attempts to mend relations with the United States. Ali Osman Taha, the foreign minister, wrote to Madeleine Albright, the U.S. Secretary of State, to list the measures Sudan had taken in response to international criticism. "Sudan's previously open borders have been replaced by a system of entry visas to prevent exploitation of Sudanese soil for terrorist purposes. Persons suspected of terrorism have been removed from the country."[49] He offered freedom of movement to a U.S. mission to investigate whether Sudan was harboring or training terrorists, while supporting U.S. mediation in the disputes between Ethiopia and Eritrea, and "United States mediation between the Government of Sudan and John Garang to end the war in the south coupled with a guarantee of any negotiated settlement."

Albright's reply, sent three months later, dismissed the measures taken by the government as if they added up to nothing. "The United States government looks to your government to take substantial, concrete steps to ensure that Sudan does not serve as a haven for international terrorists," Albright wrote.[50] Taha's assertion that this demand had already been met, and the ongoing fact that the United States had never once provided evidence of Sudanese involvement in international terrorism since the country's inclusion on the U.S. list of alleged state sponsors of terrorism, made Albright's dismissal all the more unproductive. It was clear that whatever Khartoum did, it would be inadequate. Her letter was also in part a response to a letter of 16 February 1993, from President el-Bashir to President Clinton, in which el-

Bashir said much the same as Taha in his letter to Albright. Clinton did not reply.

U.S. rejection of Sudan's efforts on the political level led to attempts by Khartoum to establish ties with the United States through intelligence and security links. On 12 September and 5 December 1997, David Williams, assistant special agent of the Federal Bureau of Investigation Middle East and North Africa department, met with Mahdi Ibrahim, Sudan's ambassador to Washington. On 2 May 1998, Lieutenant General Gutbi el-Mahdi, the director general of Sudan's External Security Bureau (ESB), wrote to Williams "to express my sincere desire to start contacts and cooperation between our service and the FBI."[51] The ESB chief also invited Williams to visit Sudan. On 24 June 1998, Williams replied by saying: "Unfortunately, I am not currently in a position to accept your kind invitation. I am hopeful that future circumstances might allow me to visit with you in Khartoum and to extend a reciprocal invitation for you to visit us here in the United States."[52]

Despite this rejection, Sudanese officials retained sporadic contacts with the FBI. On 6 August 1998, two days after the bombing of the U.S. embassies in Kenya and Tanzania, two Pakistani nationals, Sayyid Nazir Abbass and Sayyid Iskandar Sayyid, arrived in Khartoum from Nairobi. They attempted to rent an apartment close to the closed U.S. embassy in Khartoum. Suspicious Sudanese officials arrested them and, through a European intermediary who allowed them to maintain contact with U.S. intelligence officials in Cairo, informed the FBI that they were being held on suspicion of involvement in the embassy bombings. Yahia Babiker, the deputy secretary general of Sudan's intelligence service, believed the two men to have been an advance team sent to organize the bombing of the U.S. embassy in Khartoum.[53] However, the FBI rejected Sudan's offer to make the two men available for interview, and they were then handed over to Pakistan's intelligence service, the Inter-Services Intelligence, and allowed to travel back—as it happened—to Afghanistan.

"The Sudanese did everything the U.S. asked for, and they expected there would be some sort of signal from Washington in return. But nothing came," said the former CIA officer. Other U.S. officials believe the rigid U.S. opposition to Sudan's government meant that relative moderates within that government were weakened, allowing hardliners to take control. "The problem for the moderates was that the U.S. didn't sufficiently respond. There were moderates in Sudan who wanted to meet legitimate U.S. concerns," said a senior U.S. official with intimate knowledge of Sudan.[54]

If it is true, as the preceding evidence suggests, that on specific issues Sudan had sought to end its isolation by meeting U.S. demands on security-related issues—many of which had lain at the heart of the policy pursued by el-Tourabi and which had been the raison d'être of the Islamist government in the early 1990s—this was in part a mark of the weakness of the Sudanese government. Whatever the reason behind the government's attempts, in

1999 they laid the foundations for a new kind of relationship. Yahia Babiker himself told me in October 1999:

> We are not going to compromise with everything in order to please the Americans. They are not ready to be pleased. But we are willing to be very cooperative at all levels, and we are ready to talk to anybody and to listen to their concerns. If they are sincere then so are we. There are many important security issues—drug trafficking, terrorism, money laundering. And, though we won't be running after them, we are ready to cooperate with the Americans in all these areas.
>
> We suggested to the U.S. that if they wanted to send some FBI delegates to check for themselves what was going in the camps, and even if they wanted them to be stationed in Khartoum as part of their embassy, we would not object.[55]

Ignorance rather than sound policymaking has been the basis of many U.S. decisions regarding Sudan. The bombing of the al-Shifa pharmaceutical factory was the starkest example. An investigation into the ownership and function of the factory, compiled for the owner by the London office of Kroll Associates, a reputable investigative agency, revealed that there was no link with Bin Laden and that the factory was not being used to produce elements for use in chemical weapons. The absence of evidence to substantiate the U.S. accusation against Sudan with regard to the factory was part of a pattern. When Sudan was placed on the U.S. government list of state sponsors of terrorism in 1992, no evidence was offered to support the decision. Nor has Sudan subsequently been found guilty of involvement in terrorist acts, despite retaining ties with groups such as Palestinian Hamas.

Until the beginning of the twenty-first century, U.S. policy has been to beat Sudan as a human rights abuser at home and a supporter of terrorism abroad. That policy is heavily influenced by lobby groups, notably the highly conservative Zurich-based Christian Solidarity International (CSI), which has condemned Sudan's government for human rights abuses. The UN Children's Fund in 1999 condemned the practice of slavery, which it said is rife in Sudan. All sides in the civil war, including the main southern secessionist faction, the Sudan Peoples' Liberation Army (SPLA), have been accused of abuses throughout the conflict. CSI accuses the Sudanese government of encouraging slavery. However, many human rights organizations refute CSI claims, saying that the war has created the conditions in which a tradition of abduction, abuse, and slavery has reemerged. In June 1999, the UN Committee on Non-Governmental Organizations withdrew CSI's status as an observer, on the grounds that it did not fit the criteria of a nongovernmental organization. Four months later, the UN Economic and Social Council (Ecosoc) did the same.

Over time, U.S. policy on Sudan has failed to accept the reality of the country with which it is dealing. Susan Rice, in her tenure as assistant secretary for African affairs, made no contribution to ending the north-south war, which lies at the heart of Sudan's problems and which long predates the arrival of the current regime in Khartoum. Rarely have "revelations" about slavery and other gross human rights abuses had any impact on the conduct of the conflict. The failure to use diplomacy, to promote genuine dialogue, to accept the fact that Sudan—both north and south—is a vast, complex, badly administered country that requires constant engagement, has appeared deliberate. The appointment in August 1999 of a U.S. special envoy to monitor human rights and humanitarian aid in Sudan, former member of Congress and chairman of the congressional subcommittee on Africa Harry Johnston, was initially regarded with suspicion in Khartoum. However, southerners saw it as a sign that the United States may have accepted that the war is the root cause of the decades-old political instability, of the appalling human rights abuses, and the humanitarian catastrophe, and that these issues cannot be solved separately. Such an acceptance has perhaps marked a shift in U.S. thinking, away from a readiness to line up with one side against the other in the belief that a cultural-religious conflict can be won by force of arms, and toward a view that Sudan represents a chance to realize a dialogue of major significance, which could become a blueprint for interfaith and interracial dialogue elsewhere.

12

The Mogadishu Line

The United Nations and Somalia

THEY HUDDLED BENEATH the rusting wrecks of army trucks abandoned by fleeing soldiers. They drew their rotting rags around them as they crouched around the embers of a fire. The dying children of Baidoa dragged their fading bodies along the sandy streets of a town engulfed faintly by the soft cries of the hungry. A tall boy eased himself painfully down onto a lorry tire lying beside the road. His legs twisted awkwardly. His bare shoulders stretched beneath skin caked in mud and dust. He slowly twisted his wasted body until he was half lying, half crouching on the tire. Barely moving, he fingered the sandy ground. The owner of the Bikiin restaurant stared out across the street. Militiamen passed in a heavily armed Land Cruiser, a mounted machine gun jutting out across the camouflage-painted bonnet. Two boys ran past, one carrying a model machine gun made from twisted metal, the other with one carved from wood. They yelled and laughed as they chased each other.

Meat and pancakes were cooking in the Bikiin restaurant. The owner said he bought his rice for 120,000 Somali shillings a sack and went all the way to Mogadishu to get it. Outside the restaurant, donkey carts passed laden with the rice sacks. The rice market was thriving. A lorry blocked the main market street. Tiny dying children stared blankly, as they shuffled aimlessly through the throng of adult legs, patient donkeys, stalls selling packets of salt, neat piles of stock cubes, pans, and cooking spoons. Sandaled feet skirted around exhausted, rag-wrapped bodies lying curled in the sand.

"There are homeless. There are starving. Some people care. Other people don't," said Chris Giannou, a surgeon with the International Committee of the Red Cross Flying Surgeons Team.[1] He stubbed out a cigarette in the room next to the operating theatre, his plastic apron smeared with blood. He had operated on forty-nine people in Baidoa hospital since his team had arrived eight days earlier. All his patients had been suffering from gunshot wounds, and one from a bomb blast. The fighting in and around Baidoa, between the retreating army of the deposed president Mohamed Siad Barre and forces of the United Somali Congress-Somali National Alliance (USC-SNA) of General Mohamed Farah Aideed, had stopped three months earlier. The injured were seeking treatment for three- and four-month-old wounds. Battles had shattered the lives of the living as much as the dead. Barre's troops had slaughtered the animals they couldn't steal and burned the villages as they fled. The blackened ruins of deserted homes lined the road from Mogadishu to Baidoa. Displaced families coming out of the bush wandered toward the town, toward Mogadishu, toward food.

"Twelve people died here last night. Come and see. Come and see them," said Isak Ali Ibrahim. He led me through the parched ruins of Sooqxolaha animal market, where he was handing out meals of rice provided by the ICRC. Roofless rooms stood round a small courtyard with a dry well. Faces stared through frameless windows. Old dying men leaned against the mud walls. Sooqxolaha had no medicine. The infirmary—roofless, bare, no door—was where the people who could not move were laid. A loose sheet of corrugated iron was picked up by the wind and clattered onto the roof of the mortuary. The dead were lined up on the mud floor to be washed.

Outside I could see, from every dark, panelless window, from every doorway, down every street in the town, the skeletal, rag-draped people staring as they wandered starving among the rubble. Baidoa had become a camp where dead bodies were as much a part of the rubble as the homes destroyed by the civil war. The back streets were silent. Children whose age and sex were impossible to identify, drifted around, too weak to beg or speak or react to anything. Upon the fire-charred bricks of a ruined building the dead body of a young man lay spread-eagled. On the main road to the hospital an old man lay dead, clutching a walking stick. Beside him lay another old man. He was dead, too. A hand reached out from beneath a colorful shawl, just a hand held out for whatever might be placed in it by whoever was passing. But the people who were passing were dying too.

Two U.S. Air Force Hercules transport aircraft, which on 28 August 1992 had begun an emergency airlift of food into Baidoa and other famine-stricken Somali towns, had been greeted at the town's airfield by local politicians, their accompanying gunmen, and a handful of demonstrators carrying signs in English and Arabic saying, "Foreign Army No, Food Yes." Abdi Warsame Isak, the local warlord whose Somali National Movement (SNM) was aligned with General Aideed, welcomed the U.S. food airlift but said that *his* fighters should be left to arrange security for relief food, not a United Nations force, which it had at that time been proposed would be sent to protect the aid shipments. "It will be too much having thousands of foreign troops," Warsame said on the runway. "In Baidoa, the security is improving, it is getting better." Just before the U.S. planes landed, carrying nineteen tons of maize flour, a gun battle in the town had left one man dead. Soon after, an argument at the airfield's entrance saw two teenage gunmen arguing, the barrels of their AK-47 rifles inches from their faces.

Somalia's disintegration from a tenuously united nation state into a war-torn patchwork of rival fiefdoms controlled by clan chiefs—chiefs who had rarely in the past reverted to the violent means that erupted in the early 1990s—is still today in 2001 the most vivid example in Africa, and perhaps the world, of the devastation bequeathed to developing countries by the end of the Cold War and the end of superpower political interest. With that conflict having reached its end as the USSR stumbled and crumbled, dictators throughout Africa who had clung to power by promoting the strategic importance of their impoverished states in the eyes of the Eastern and Western power blocs, found their former backers departing amid lukewarm calls for improvements in human rights, economic reforms, and political liberalization.

In Somalia even these calls barely surfaced. The end of the Cold War in Somalia was marked by the last remaining U.S. officials throwing the keys to the embassy to the local staff, before they themselves escaped the advance of General Aideed's forces as the civil war reached the doors of the presidential palace in January 1991. By mid-1992, the entire country was reliant on foreign food aid brought into ports and across isolated land borders. The Red Cross alone was feeding 700,000 people at camps throughout the country, camps where at least one-fifth of the population was by then dying every day. The north and south of the country were equally devastated. Even in the southern, well-irrigated farming region along the Shabeelle River people were dying, despite the fields overflowing with crops. A year beforehand, the country had been largely self-sufficient in food. But with the collapse of the Barre regime and the emergence of warlordism, control of food supplies became the major political tool for local rulers.

The politics of hunger and plenty lay at the heart of the starvation. Bouts of extreme hunger and the hardship of the nomadic existence that lay at the heart of Somalia's social fabric had been ever-present aspects of life. Within three years of Mohamed Siad Barre's seizure of power in a 1969 coup d'etat, Somalia was faced with the most severe drought in its history. At their height, famine relief camps housed over 250,000 people. Barre took advantage of the regime's links with the USSR to ease the plight of famine victims, by using Soviet aircraft to carry out an airlift of 140,000 people who were relocated to less affected areas. This measure resulted in a relatively low estimated death toll of 18,000.

The use of Soviet military personnel and aircraft during the 1972 famine heralded a massive increase in Somalia's reliance on the USSR, leading to the Soviet development of the northern port of Berbera, the provision of enormous supplies of Soviet weaponry, and the arrival of 6,000 Soviet military advisors, whose presence thrust Somalia into the regional theatre of the global superpower conflict. Chief among the regional conflicts was Somalia's claim to parts of the Ogaden region of Ethiopia, ceded to Ethiopia by Britain in 1954, where many Somali Ogadenis continue to live today. Heightened nationalism following Somalia's independence from Britain and Italy in 1960 had brought the Ogaden issue to the fore. In 1977 Lieutenant Colonel Mengistu Haile Mariam seized power in Ethiopia. Soviet influence in that country increased after Mengistu announced his intention to steer a Marxist political path and expelled the U.S. personnel, who had established close ties with the ousted imperial regime of Haile Selassi.

This shift across the border increased pressure in Somalia to grab territory in the Ogaden. Barre secured a promise of $300 million in financial assistance from Saudi Arabia with which to buy arms for the Ogaden campaign, though on condition that he reestablish closer ties with the West. In 1977 he expelled the Soviet military advisers in the hope of securing Western aid for the war. In July 1977, the United States told the Somali government that it had decided in principle to provide Somalia with military assistance. However, the principle remained just that when the Carter administration discovered belatedly that Somali troops had invaded the Ogaden. Then, at the end of November, six weeks after it had cut off military aid to Somalia, the USSR began a $1 billion airlift of arms and 17,000 Cuban troops to assist the Mengistu regime in Ethiopia in its fight against the Somali-backed Western Somali Liberation Front (WSLF) in the Ogaden.

It took the United States until March 1978 to begin a review of its position on providing arms to Barre. The Africa Bureau of the U.S. State Department, which had been resurrected by Carter in an effort to develop regionally appropriate "African solutions to African problems"—in contrast to the global Cold War theatrics of previous U.S. presidents—nevertheless regarded Barre with immense suspicion and saw him as the aggressor in the Ogaden war, despite the rapid shift toward Moscow being conducted by Ethiopia. Carter was under pressure, following the rise to power of a Marxist government in Afghanistan in 1978 and the emergence of a variety of potential East-West flash points in Africa. By the end of 1979, after the seizure of the U.S. embassy in Tehran following the overthrow of the shah of Iran, it was the case that, "[although] the strategic situation in the Horn of Africa may have remained fundamentally unaltered, U.S. policy in the entire north-west quadrant of the Indian Ocean—north-east Africa, the Arabian Peninsula, the Persian Gulf, and South Asia—now became linked perceptually to the Iranian crisis and the looming Soviet threat."[2]

The Soviet invasion of Afghanistan in December 1979 finally ended any U.S. doubts as to whether a closer relationship with Somalia would be beneficial, and the United States sought to establish access to military facilities in Kenya, Oman, and Somalia.

> The risk of encouraging Somali military ventures in the Ogaden by supplying arms was now outweighed by broader strategic considerations. Somalia's cooperation was deemed necessary to implement the Carter Doctrine, announced by the president in his January 23, 1980, State of the Union address: "Any attempt by any outside force to gain control of the Persian Gulf region will be regarded as an assault on the vital interests of the United States of America and such an assault will be repelled by any means necessary, including military force."[3]

In return for U.S. access to the Soviet-built airfield of Berbera, Somalia was to receive $45 million of "security assistance"—far less than Barre had demanded, but all the United States was prepared to provide to an "ally" of whom it remained suspicious. To place the U.S. assistance in perspective, Italy sold Somalia $410 million worth of the total $580 million of arms it bought between 1979–1983, while China provided $50 million worth. Somalia was the region's fifth largest recipient of U.S. military assistance, after Diego Garcia, Egypt, Oman, and Kenya.[4]

The Carter administration was meanwhile moving away from the "African solutions to African problems" strategy, and looking for ways of countering the Soviet Union, with minimal concern over who would receive U.S. assistance in the process. "Virtually no one outside the Africa bureau wanted to examine the pros and cons of a Somali [air] base deal," according to Lefebvre.[5] Somalia's entry into the Western bloc was finally assured, however, only when it ended its territorial claims to parts of northern Kenya, where the government of Daniel arap Moi was regarded by the United States as an important ally in the Indian Ocean strategy. The Kenyan secessionist movement, the Northern Frontier District Liberation Front (NFDLF), nevertheless retained its offices in Mogadishu until 1991.

The U.S. arms shipments agreed to by Carter in 1979 did not arrive in Somalia until 1982, more than one year into the Reagan administration. The decision to finally airlift the weapons was triggered by the occupation of two Somali towns by Ethiopian-based Somali dissidents. "The Reagan administration's decision to airlift into Somalia was based on a belief that there was a radical plot to destabilize pro-Western governments in north-east Africa,"[6] in which a key player was perceived to be Colonel Muammar Gadaffi, the Libyan leader.

Washington's anxiety brought with it a rapid dissolution of the doubts that had slowed the pace of assistance under Carter. By contrast with the relatively small scale assistance during the 1979–1983 period, U.S. Security Assistance Program (SAP) aid to Somalia had by 1986 reached $266 million, the largest of its kind in sub-Saharan Africa, including $114 million in grant military assistance, in addition to U.S. guarantees for $172 million of foreign military sales (FMS) cash sales. In seven years—1979–1986—the United States provided $500 million worth of military resources to Barre.[7]

Barre's rapprochement with both superpowers was not only a denial by those powers of the realities of internal Somali politics, it was an act, at least on the part of the Western powers, of atrocious opportunism. Donald Petterson, U.S. ambassador to Mogadishu in 1978–1983, wrote with startling cynicism in 1985:

> During the four years I was in Somalia, I heard many predictions of Siad's imminent demise. These ignored his strengths, the lack of cohesion among his opponents, and the fact that within Somalia in recent years no person or faction had emerged as a realistic alternative to him.
>
> Looking at Somalia, let us bear in mind that all things are relative, and in the sphere of human rights the Siad government does not compare all that unfavorably with many other Third World governments. Consequently, although Siad's internal security and political freedoms policies have been a constraint on the kind and extent of the relationship that has evolved between the United States and Somalia, they never deterred the U.S. government from pursuing first closer ties and later the [military] access agreement [to Berbera]. Nor have they been such as to stimulate vehement opposition in this country [i.e. the United States] to what the current and previous administrations have set out to accomplish with respect to Somalia and the Horn of Africa.[8]

It was as if the fact of human rights abuses in other countries somehow made such abuses relatively acceptable in Somalia. Moreover, the calculation exposed how incapable U.S. policymakers were of recognizing the possibility of opposition emerging in the future, as well as of understanding what conditions might lead to the creation of such opposition and what impact it would have. Moreover, the arms the United States provided would inevitably be used to prevent that opposition from emerging and can only be regarded as having had that intent on the side, opposed as the United States was to Barre's foray into the Ogaden and his claims on northern Kenya. U.S. military assistance—if used in accordance with the agreement of ending the Ogaden aggression—could only have been used to violently quell domestic dissent. Ultimately, as proved to be the case by the end of the decade, the emergence of an armed opposition to Barre did not in fact discourage the United States from maintaining support for the regime, despite growing concern within the U.S. Congress that civilian opponents of the regime were being killed, imprisoned, and treated as fodder in the growing insurrectionist war Barre faced in the north of the country (which by 1991 spread south and overthrew him). The Bush administration in 1989 requested Congress to release $55.5 million of aid to Somalia that had been frozen in response to revelations of the Barre regime's human rights abuses. The aid was eventually released, but by then Somalia's disintegration into clan-based conflict had fully taken hold, as a consequence of Barre's exploitation and encouragement of clan rivalry throughout the 1980s, a tactic he had had the resources to pursue in part due to his access to foreign aid and weapons.

By then, however, Saddam Hussein had become the major post–Cold War foe of the United States in the region, the Soviet Union had withdrawn from Afghanistan and subsequently disintegrated, and Somalia lost any strategic importance it once had for the United States. Barre turned to Libya for military assistance, the Gaddafi regime having by 1988 become his major supplier of small arms. Libya was also thought to have provided Barre with napalm canisters, while the desperate regime also employed South African and Rhodesian mercenary pilots to bomb the opposition-held town of Hargeisa. By then, Barre's manipulation of Somalia's clans, and the centralization of power around himself and his Marehan clan and their allies, the Ogadenis and Dulbahante, had created the false unity reliant on dictatorship by which he had stored up the instability that exploded in the months that followed. This tripartite tribal alliance itself began to disintegrate, a measure of how catastrophic the political situation facing Somalia quickly became as the Cold War ended.

"Somalia is now reaping the harvest of the policy of divide and rule which President Siad Barre has wielded so effectively for a decade or more. But it is a policy that depends upon the skill of the individual at the top. Without Barre, or a figure of comparable talents, it is a policy which may be very hard to carry out," *Africa Confidential* reported in July 1987.[9] Where once there had been only a tradition of distrust between the Hawiye clan of General Aideed and Barre's Marehan, the enmity that erupted into war was something new. Moreover, the allies in the south of the country who had once united in opposition to Barre quickly turned against each other, and there was enmity between the Abgal clan of Ali Mahdi Mohamed—who had been elected interim president on 28 January 1991 by the opposition prior to the fall of Siad Barre—and the Habargidir clan of General Aideed, both of which were subclans of the Hawiye. Such a division was unprecedented in the history of the Hawiye, the biggest clan in the country.

On the north Mogadishu street that linked the hospital with Ali Mahdi's office, the bandits arrived at the crossroads everyday at around midday or at dusk. The policemen who had the courage to show their faces, disappeared. People ran along the hot pavement to the gates of the houses, which were slammed all along the street. The bandits strode across the street with

bazookas on their shoulders. They forced people out of their cars at gun-
point. Sometimes they blew the people up with bazookas, because there was
nobody to stop them. There was always shooting. It was normal. They shot.
And then they took away the cars. Usually there was a gun battle as they
drove away, the screech of brakes, people running.

Looking down from a rooftop in early September 1992, I could see them.
There were three old men who had dyed their beards with henna sitting under a flame tree in a garden. They were fumbling with rosaries as they said
their prayers, while other people were running in through the gate to their
garden. Outside on the street people in uniform were shooting at people
without uniforms. A Land Rover with rice had been apprehended by bandits
at the crossroads where two policemen had been standing only a few minutes
beforehand. A boy led a blind man across the street that had become the battlefield. Another boy with a bazooka on his shoulder pushed them both to
the side. A bandit—they were the ones without uniforms—sat behind the
wheel of the Land Rover and drove off with a roar. Somebody would have
eaten that night. Somebody else would have gone hungry.

Camel meat hung from hooks in a market along the then tranquil roadside. Among the stalls, in the shadows of the whitewashed walls, silent children wandered with faces as stretched and lean as the meat. They were hungry. There was food. They had no money. They didn't eat. They died, too
old to receive the relief organizations' rations of high-protein food given to
all those below the age of five. Before the war, sharks had lingered around
the slaughterhouse effluent pipe on the edge of north Mogadishu where the
camels were killed. The beach had been too dangerous for swimming. With
the war it had become safer. There was no electricity to pump the organs of
the dead animals out into the sea. So the sharks had gone elsewhere to feed,
and children could swim in the clear blue water. The vile stench and the rotting bones and hides not cleared because of the lack of power had not
stopped the herdsmen bringing their camels for slaughter. They arrived in
the evening. Herds of camels trotted over the sand dunes to the courtyard
surrounded by roofless sheds. The killing happened at dusk. By morning the
heaps of shining camel guts slithered under the weight of buzzing flies and
seabirds, which flocked to peck at the skulls and ribs that were strewn across
the blood-blackened concrete.

The sight of the camel herds trotting toward death on their great padded
feet, past the dome-shaped hovels of twigs and plastic sheets under which the
starving and the sick were dying, made looking at Somalia like looking at a
country through a kaleidoscope. Everything reflected upon everything else,
every image was the reverse of what appeared beside it; hunger and plenty,
strength and weakness, brutality and kindness—all these elements were
twisted by a terrifying centrifuge, a spiral propelling the entire country into an
abyss. Daily life was propelled by repulsion.

North Mogadishu, where the streets are sometimes difficult to identify because they are only rubble, was where Somalia's interim government was in power. Under A'i Mahdi Mohamed, it claimed control of a few square miles of the city, which had been carved up by the clans. The interim government was forming alliances with at least four other clans so that its influence could be extended to other parts of the country. But it claimed its real power was in north Mogadishu. Despite the claim, the street was blocked as I tried to get to an interview with Ali Mahdi. A gang of bandits had blocked it a few hundred yards from the president's office. The presidential army, wearing smartly pressed uniforms imported two months previously from the then West Germany, was guarding the nearby gate to the office. The bandits set up metal spikes on the road. Drivers turned away, knowing that if they approached the bandits their cars would be stolen. The presidential guards waited for the bandits to go away. They weren't going to fight.

FROM SIDESHOW TO PRIME TIME

By the silver light of a new moon in March 1995, the last contingents of foreign troops boarded their landing craft and slunk away into the darkness of the Indian Ocean, bringing to a desultory end one of the saddest chapters in the history of the United Nations. A week beforehand, 9,000 UN troops had been a postscript to international efforts to bring peace to Somalia, which had begun with the sending of 500 Pakistani troops under the UN flag in September 1992. The departure of the last foreign troops would barely have been noticed by the residents of Mogadishu, had the U.S. Navy not decided to wake the sleeping city by staging an off-shore son et lumière show from its battleships moored a few miles off the coast. The boom and whiz of flares and tracer bullets, apparently intended by the United States as the closing act of the inglorious Somali drama, was a wretched display of bravado that brought back memories of the bombing raids launched on Mogadishu in 1993.

The most incisive analyses of the UN's failure to bring peace to Somalia, after spending more than $3 billion and expending the lives of 132 peacekeeping troops and nearly ten times that many Somali lives, have come from the insiders who themselves became casualties of the fiasco when they dared to criticize. The former UN special representative to Somalia, Mohamed Sahnoun, wrote:

> The legacy of the Cold War is being felt in the ineptitude of the UN's structures and in the waste of its human resources. . . . The current system is not adapted to the post-Cold War international environment and routinely reacts to crisis through improvisation. This explains why there are so many delays and contradictions in the UN's response to crisis, for instance, its incapacity to respond earlier to the crisis in Somalia.

> The existing UN structures are not at all adapted to the requirements of the
> new era, especially in apprehending the whole problem of conflict between and
> within states. . . . The UN recruitment process does not necessarily respect the
> criteria of competence and experience. . . . Even less regard is given to the cri-
> terion of commitment.[10]

Sahnoun, who was forced to resign from his post in 1992, wrote in 1994.
While the UN's armor was being flown out of Mogadishu in 1995, American troops handed out leaflets telling Somalis that the Joint Task Force of
American and Italian troops sent to protect the departing UN troops intended no harm and were not, as Somalis seemed determined to believe,
about to occupy Somalia. Simultaneously, the iron fist in the velvet glove of
public relations was shown. Posters were strung to razor-wire around the
airport that adjoined the beach from which the last troops would leave,
telling Somalis, "Your presence is a threat to the Joint Task Force. If you
don't go, it's possible you will be wounded or killed. Don't enter this zone
and don't interfere with this operation of securing the withdrawal. The Task
Force has orders to use deadly force."

Orders from whom? Did anybody really know, and if they did, were those
orders appropriate, or being handed down by individuals who understood
the mess in which the world's most sophisticated armies had found themselves? In his book *Whatever Happened to Somalia: A Tale of Tragic Blunders*,
John Drysdale, a British former senior advisor to UNOSOM and, more sig-
nificantly, a fluent Somali speaker with a long experience of the country and
direct links to several of the faction leaders, wrote: "The bedrock of UN interests is to approach competing struggles in other people's countries with
neutrality. The U.S. State Department's interests are to ensure that their foreign policy objectives are paramount. An attempted convergence of these respective interests . . . has not always been helpful to Somalis. Dual interests
have made matters worse."[11] Even before the UNOSOM mission was catapulted into the media spotlight by the rapid U.S. military buildup, the role
of the UN in the post–Cold War world was the real source of the crisis into
which the 1992–1995 intervention in Somalia would plunge. The views of
one man were very clear on this issue, however:

> In these past months a conviction has grown, among nations large and small,
> that an opportunity has been regained to achieve the great objectives of the
> Charter—a United Nations capable of maintaining international peace and secu-
> rity, of securing justice and human rights and of promoting, in the words of the
> Charter, "social progress and better standards of life in larger freedom." This op-
> portunity must not be squandered. The Organization must never again be crip-
> pled as it was in the era that has now passed.[12]

Boutros Boutros-Ghali, the then UN secretary-general, envisioned the post–Cold War role of the UN as vital to securing the promises of decolonization—promises that the decolonized states of the developing world felt most acutely should be kept—, promises that the adversarial climate of the Cold War had undermined from the 1960s onwards. Central to his *Agenda for Peace*, first published in 1992 and then updated in 1995, Boutros-Ghali saw growing potential for UN involvement in preventive diplomacy, peacemaking, and peacekeeping, in part derived from his view that "the time of absolute and exclusive sovereignty has . . . passed; its theory was never matched by reality. It is the task of leaders of States today to understand this and to find a balance between the needs of good internal governance and the requirements of an ever more interdependent world."[13]

His vision was to be disappointed from the start, by the United States. It saw the end of the Cold War as a victory for itself, and for a handful of its key allies. The tensions that built up between the United States and the UN during the intervention in Somalia soon threw into doubt the motives for the U.S. involvement in the country. The tensions, lack of coordination, resentment, blame, along with the confusion in the chain of military command, which largely stemmed from the refusal of a highly skeptical U.S. military establishment to cede meaningful control of its troops to UN command, all undoubtedly contributed to the debacle. But it all began in a less sordid atmosphere. "Having pledged himself to reinforcing [the UN's] mission and placing it at the heart of the New World Order concept, [President] Bush could hardly afford to see it rendered impotent by the actions of a few rag-tag militias in Somalia," one analyst of Bush's foreign policy wrote.[14] But the reality for the UN was that as it sought to assert a new post–Cold War agenda under Boutros-Ghali, it failed to secure the resources—financial and material, for which the United States held the purse strings—to move even some way toward achieving these aims. Even as the *Agenda for Peace* was being published in 1992, the reality in Mogadishu exposed the dearth of commitment to the UN as a force in its own right with an agenda that reflected global needs rather than the ambitions for the "New World Order" of its most powerful members. "The UN are not in touch with the reality here. Their biggest mistake was to come late and then not do enough," was how the head of one relief organization echoed a widely held view in Mogadishu in August 1992. David Bassiouni, the representative of the UN's then newly created Department of Humanitarian Affairs, lamented the slow pace and lack of resources, which had crippled his own operations. "I'm supposed to be creating a database of projects under way. I'm supposed to provide air support to the aid agencies. I'm supposed to provide security for both the UN and other relief workers. The lack of resources means that I can't do any of these things. One feels that if this was not happening in Africa, I wouldn't be facing these problems," he said.[15]

Contradictory motives by the main participants were a key feature of this first post–Cold War humanitarian intervention, undertaken initially by the UN but soon swamped rather than sustained by the U.S. political and military establishments. In the run-up to the multinational UNITAF intervention of 8 December 1992, France was determined to secure a "peace meeting" between General Aideed and Ali Mahdi Mohamed on board a French naval ship, which would steam into Mogadishu harbor as a victory for French diplomacy over that of the United States. Meanwhile Italy, as southern Somalia's former colonial power, established links with the warlords outside the diplomacy of the UN, "and it was suspected that the Italians were tipping them off to UN military movements," Boutros Boutros-Ghali claimed.[16] Meanwhile, the United States under the soon-to-be-ousted George Bush, was seeking to create a New World Order, in the context of which a response to the crisis in Somalia and the United Nation's role there was essential.

Boutros-Ghali himself was meanwhile less than flattering about the richness of the pastoral nomadic life of Somalia, which he regarded as merely "a desperately poor, dry, hook-shaped country in the Horn of Africa with a recent history rich only in colonialism, hunger, disease, and weapons transferred from abroad as part of the cold war competition between the United States and the USSR."[17] The limitations of his attitude contrasted sharply with the broader and more incisive view of Said Samatar, a Somali and professor of African history at Rutgers University, who said of his compatriots:

> Except for the urban dwellers of the few coastal towns and the stretch of farming enclave between the Shabeelle (meaning Leopard) and Juba rivers, precolonial Somalia lived in a world of egalitarian anarchy, a world of camel husbandry and clan-families as liable to be at war with each other as to assemble under an acacia tree in order to exchange oral poetic contests that sometimes lasted for days. . . . [18]

As much as it became a political-military conflict, the war that the United States and UN fought with General Aideed in 1992–1993, was a cultural conflict. Essentially, it began because the cultural divide between the two sides was not bridged, and it was ultimately purposeless and unwinnable for the same reason. Boutros-Ghali, whose period as Egypt's minister of state for foreign affairs had rarely endeared him to those opposed to the dictators of the African continent, whom Egypt generally found itself supporting, oversaw the rise and fall of the three UN Somalia operations, called successively the United Nations Operation in Somalia or UNOSOM 1 (April–December 1992), the Unified Task Force or UNITAF (December 1992–May 1993), and UNOSOM 2 (May 1993–March 1995), the last of which was, on that moonlit night in March 1995, evacuated under the protection of a task force grandly called "United Shield," comprising troops from the United States, Britain, France, India, Italy, Malaysia, and Pakistan.

The "unity" of the victors of the Cold War had been given its greatest boost as the superpower conflict was winding down in the form of the alliance that had driven Saddam Hussein out of Kuwait; it was that unity Boutros-Ghali referred to when he said that "[The] United States believed it could also work against the warlords in Somalia."[19] Boutros-Ghali states clearly that he regarded the disarmament of the warring factions of Aideed and Ali Mahdi Mohamed as vital to the success of any foreign military intervention intended to safeguard food supplies. After the killing in Mogadishu of twenty-six Pakistani UN soldiers by General Aideed's militia on 5 June 1993, he became fully convinced of his view that "It was useless to try to solve the Somali crisis by negotiating with Aid[ee]d."[20] The absence of reasons to be optimistic about the value of negotiating with Aideed did not, however, stem from the absence of a need to do so.

Negotiations conducted by Mohamed Sahnoun in late 1992 had led to Aideed accepting the arrival of the first contingent of UN troops. Negotiations of a variety of different kinds with the militias on the ground, in Mogadishu and elsewhere, had led to scores of non-governmental organizations establishing a presence in Somalia and the provision of food and medical assistance. Negotiations had worked in the past. The only way in which the UNITAF mission and the UNOSOM 2 mission that followed it could have succeeded, without the loss of foreign lives by which that success was judged outside Somalia, would have been if they had been conducted fundamentally on the basis of negotiations with relevant Somali interlocutors, however brutal and greedy those warlords were.

The confusion surrounding the purpose of the UNITAF mission, as it moved beyond the safeguarding of food supplies and toward the "mission creep" that plunged the UN and the United States into a catastrophe, as the "Mogadishu Line" from humanitarian intervention into full-scale war was crossed, is made clear in the accounts of Boutros-Ghali. In his introduction to the official UN account of the Somalia operations[21] the former secretary-general writes:

> The general wording of the mandate in resolution 794 (1992), which made no specific reference to disarmament or demobilization and referred only to the establishment of a "secure environment" for humanitarian relief, was interpreted by the United States command of UNITAF to mean the securing of ports, airports, warehouses, feeding centers and roads to ensure the unimpeded delivery of relief supplies. The United States did not interpret the mandate as extending to the disarmament of armed gangs, the confiscation of heavy weapons or forceful action to stop outbreaks of interfactional fighting.[22]

However, in his own memoir, Boutros-Ghali relates how he told the UN Security Council and President Bush that "the first condition is that the Unified Task Force should take effective action to ensure that the heavy weapons of the factions are neutralized and brought under international control and that the irregular forces and groups are disarmed before the Unified Task Force sent on 8 December 1992 withdraws."[23] He clearly became more emboldened as time past, at one point implying simply that the mandate was not specific, then later saying that the United States simply failed to do what was appropriate. In fact, the United States had clearly had a hand in writing the mandate, as a member of the UN, and did not seek confrontation with the Somali factions. When the United States later launched a war against Aideed, its recognition of its failure to understand whom it was dealing with in Somalia was made clear. Had it disarmed the factions upon arrival in December 1992, rather than leaving it for more than six months, the bloodshed of July–October 1993 would perhaps never have happened.

Long after that war was over and the United States had left Somalia, history was rewritten to suit those within the United States who, though deeply involved in the planning and execution of the UN operation, insisted on reminding posterity's decisionmakers that "[the U.S.-led UNITAF operation] did not seek to disarm the militias; its primary interest was the securing of deliveries of international aid. In addition, it did not seek to marginalize or confront, but to take Somali political movements along on every move. UNOSOM II interpreted its mandate as not merely authorizing but requiring it to disarm the militias."[24] In a letter on 8 December 1992 to President Bush, Boutros-Ghali said, "without this [disarmament] I do not believe that it will be possible to establish the secure environment called for by the Security Council."[25] The letter led to John Bolton, the U.S. assistant secretary of state, accusing Boutros-Ghali of "trying to change the goalposts in the middle of a game."[26] The UN Security Council Resolution 794, passed on 3 December 1992, did indeed permit the UNITAF operation that succeeded UNOSOM 1 to use force to intervene under Chapter Seven of the UN Charter. But, in a devastating condemnation, Boutros-Ghali went on to describe the U.S. reaction to the situation:

> [The] Pentagon instantly announced that it had no intention of disarming the factions, and the Bush White House, then in its last days, did nothing to override this military reluctance to do the job right. . . . In my opinion, three critical steps were needed: disarming the warring groups; establishing a secure environment; and creating a workable division of labor between the U.S. and UN operations on the ground. The United States did not do any of the three.[27]

THE *GEEDKA* GIVES NO SHADE

Ali lay alone under the hot sun, as the sweating men hacked at the hard ground that would become his grave. All morning they had been digging the earth on the top of the dyke beside the riverbed. They had to chase away sightseers, who peered at Ali's body where it lay amid the buzzing flies. "This is the death people. Come and see. This is the death people," said Hassan Mahmud Mohammed, chairman of Bardera's relief committee.[28] He was appointed to the job when fighters of the Somali National Front faction seized Bardera two weeks before our interview, in mid-November 1993. The fighting led to relief flights being suspended and the withdrawal of all relief workers. By 29 November there were 258 bodies waiting to be buried. That was the death toll from the previous night. Sometimes the daily rate rose as high as 400. Ali's hole on the dyke was flanked by graves that stretched out of the town and into the scrub. The seasonal rains had started, and the dyke was becoming sodden. The earth would slip away, and the sightseers would be back to see the corpses exposed. "We are tired of digging. We think only of digging. We bury them on the top of the mound because the ground is softer on the top. We dig quickly. One day we buried 323 people," said Abdukader Yassin, the only doctor in Bardera—a doctor with no medicine.[29]

Bardera was trapped between a minefield to the west and the front line of fighting to the east. The Somali National Front, which then held the town, was led by General Mohammed Sayeed Hersi Morgan, son-in-law of the deposed dictator, Mohammed Siad Barre, and a man with a reputation for brutality that matched Barre's. SNF forces camped for four months in the hills west of Bardera waiting for General Aideed, who had his base there, to leave Bardera on a visit to Mogadishu. When he did, they marched in.

Aideed declared his aim of recapturing Bardera. When he lost the town, he told the United Nations that all the civilians had fled. This was a lie, intended to discourage the UN from sending food aid. The UN believed him for a few days, and the people of Bardera started to die. Then the UN realized they had been tricked. They had not expected Somali leaders to be that callous. The minefield, which was laid by the SNF when they were planning their siege of Bardera, had stopped relief agencies arriving by road from Kenya, making its 60,000 people entirely dependent upon flights. Meanwhile, the only activity in Bardera was grave digging. Beside the riverbed a woman lay sprawled on the hot ground waiting to be buried. Without saying anything, the gravedigger explained how she died. He just used his hands to point to his empty throat and empty belly. He pointed to the woman, then he pointed to the grave.

Children licked cornmeal from where it had spilt in the sand at Mulid camp, a mile outside Bardera. A man in a camouflage jacket chased them away with a stick. There were 11,000 people in the camp, and they were all starving. In hut after hut, baking under the scorching sun, drenched when the rains poured, people lay waiting to die or to bury the dead, in the parched earth where the *geedka*, the tree under which clan elders would in the past have sat to resolve their quarrels, gave no shade. The SNF, responsible for organizing the composition of the relief committee, had omitted one of the twenty-five local subclans from the committee, thereby depriving members of that subclan of their cut of the food automatically looted by the warlords. During the unloading of cooking oil and high protein Unimix, an aggrieved member of the excluded subclan fired a missile over the plane, and the missile exploded beside the runway. The plane immediately took off, and further relief flights were suspended.

Such horrors—the visible horrors, the greed and selfishness, the readiness to inflict suffering—made Somalia famous. When one was in the midst of it, it was often impossible to believe that it was real. The hunger, the killing, and the pain were too much to comprehend.

I looked out of the window of a cavernous Hercules transport aircraft as it lumbered down onto an airstrip 50 kilometers from Mogadishu. It was early August 1992, and my first morning in Somalia from my home in Kenya. Southern Air Transport (SAT), a front company for the CIA during the Cold War, leased the aircraft to the Save the Children Fund. SAT turned from spying to flying mercy missions to the hungry victims of conflicts in the former client states of the Cold War superpowers. They were mercy missions at a heavy price. To lease a plane cost $6,000. Mercy was lucrative. Hunger was money. It was cold on the runway. The propellers continued to spin. The planes could take off quickly if there was trouble. Somali porters unloaded sacks of food from the cargo hold and carried them to waiting lorries. The lorries, the porters, the armed guards to protect the food from other peoples' armed guards, the massively inflated petrol price, and the right to use the airport, all had to be negotiated with those Somalis who perpetuated their country's horror by insisting on their right to make money out of the devastation. These payments amounted to another $6,000 per flight. The foreign relief agencies paid. No choice. Profiteers from the hunger in Somalia ranked among the cruelest people in the world.

I stayed in a house owned by Somalia's most successful drug dealer, Osman Ato. He owned or had taken possession of many of the large houses in Mogadishu, and rented them to the relief agencies. He earned hundreds of thousands of dollars from the proceeds. He also controlled the import of the narcotic drug *qat* from Kenya. The gunmen and criminals who ran the country were usually high on qat when they slaughtered the innocents and stole food from the hungry. The gunmen drove around in armored "technicals," pick-ups mounted with recoilless rifles. Osman Ato owned these vehicles too. Before the war he had been the representative of the American oil company Conoco. Then Conoco's office was rented out to the American special envoy to Somalia, Robert Oakley. It had a large, landscaped garden and a tennis court, where U.S. officials played before the sun rose too high into the pale blue Somali sky.

By the early afternoon Osman Ato's speech was slurred. He invited his friends to his house, where they sat in an air-conditioned room, chewing *qat* and deciding on the country's future. I went there many times. We got along well. Even so, by late afternoon it was useless to expect much sense from him, because of the *qat*. He remained the richest man in the city, and one of the richest in the splintered and shattered country. He was somebody the UN and the United States were doing business with in pursuit of their international rescue mission.

The mission had begun in earnest on 9 December, when Oakley engineered a meeting between Aideed and Ali Mahdi Mohamed. They shook hands on Osman Ato's tennis court, and the media blitz began. In time for the arrival of the American marines, the American television network, NBC, brought in a staff of seventy-nine reporters and technicians. ABC rented a mansion from one of Osman Ato's rivals in the property business. The Save the Children Fund had wanted to rent the house to accommodate its staff, but ABC outbid them. Matching the outlay of ABC, CBS promised dollars in its search for an adviser on Somalia who could compensate for their reporters' ignorance. A journalist with experience of Somalia was paid $400 a day and allowed to spend up to $3,000 a day on logistical arrangements without having to justify the expenditure in advance. In less than three weeks, a CBS source said, the company spent $2.5 million on covering Somalia. Not to be outdone, CNN brought in six camera crews to record the arrival of U.S. Marines on the beach at Mogadishu on the night of 9 December. At a cost of $15,000 they rerouted a London-Nairobi Kenya Airways flight via Cyprus to pick up other members of their reporting team. A passenger airliner was chartered to fly to Mogadishu carrying lorry-loads of recording equipment and satellite facilities to establish a live link with CNN Center in Atlanta, Georgia.

The normally bright blue sky had remained gray for much of the day. By evening Mogadishu hummed only with generators. The vast, familiar expanse of the airport runway, the first sight in so many of my previous and subsequent visits to Somalia, opened out onto the ocean from which salvation was supposed to arrive. Dusk quickly turned to night, the sky cleared, and stars flooded the inky blackness. I wandered along the beach, away from the gathering throng of journalists, the high profile faces of the famous network anchormen seeking to be recognized, the regional Nairobi-based journalists prepared to see the impending invasion merely as one more chapter in the sorry history of the country, a country which to many of us had in the preceding months had become more familiar than home. Half a mile along the beach I walked onto the scrub and was immediately halted by a voice from nowhere. "Just walk away," I was told in the unmistakable tone of the U.S. military. "Just walk right away." While the world's media awaited "the landing," it had in fact already happened. And I was the first to know, too exhausted to care, too skeptical about what it would bring to feel any exuberance. "Sure," I replied. "Welcome to Somalia." But there was only silence.

In the early hours of the morning, the first Special Forces SEALS came ashore and fell into the hands of the assembled media circus. An advance party of about three dozen men, heavily armed and with their faces blackened, strode through the surf and into the dunes before spreading out along the beach where they stored ammunition and dug in among gorse bushes after being ferried ashore in inflatable dinghies. Television crews followed the bewildered soldiers as they tried to settle into positions facing the airport. "The operation stinks of arrogance," General Imtiaz Shaheen, the Pakistan head of the UN force that had arrived in Mogadishu weeks beforehand as a result of negotiations with Aideed, had told me earlier that day.[30] The split between the UN and the United States, between those with experience on the ground in Somalia and the "big picture" strategists of the New World Order, was widening. "All this bullshit about 80 per cent of food being looted and all that—it's all very well stage-managed by the United States. That's why there is no coordination with the UN or the relief agencies. This whole operation is a test case for future conflict resolution. It's as if the U.S. had a new vaccine they wanted to test. Now they have found an animal to test it on," Shaheen told me.[31]

Robert Oakley and the head of the U.S. military airlift to Somalia, Lieutenant General Frank Libutti, had that week held meetings lasting less than thirty minutes each with senior UN staff and relief organizations. More important to Oakley was having been able to negotiate with Aideed and Ali Mahdi to allow a safe arrival for the Marines. Both had agreed to the intervention—of course. They had no choice. But what they—and in particular Aideed—intended afterward would have to be seen to be believed. So confident was he—and with so little reason, had he only retained the same skepticism about the warlords as he claimed he had always had about Siad Barre when he had dealt with him as U.S. ambassador to Mogadishu—that Oakley two days before the military operation had told relief agencies they should pay off the Somalis who had guarded them for much of the previous year and replace them with the troops who were about to arrive. The agencies ignored him, instinctively aware that to do so would be to sever one of the vital sources of contact they had established with the remains of Somali society.

As dawn broke over Mogadishu following the landing, the full scale of the military operation became clear. The Marines had invaded an airfield that had been secured by Pakistani UN forces six weeks beforehand. By midday the airport was deemed safe. No shots had been fired. There was no enemy. It was a farce. The only violence took place when Marines bound and beat some unarmed Somalis sleeping in a hangar. They were bound with wire, until an incensed General Shaheen, on hand to see the spectacle, angrily ordered the

U.S. troops to release them. Meanwhile, the television network reporters spoke to their viewers as if they were in a dangerous war zone. But there was no danger. Everybody—soldiers, Marines, reporters, technicians, financiers—was pretending. At 3 P.M., the first relief flight appeared over the newly liberated airport. It was a UN World Food Program flight: the first for weeks to arrive at Mogadishu airport. It circled for over half an hour to give Paul Mitchell, the WFP man on the ground, time to ensure that all the television cameras were trained on the aircraft's WFP insignia. It landed. It slowly edged its way along the tarmac. It taxied for twenty minutes. It usually took five minutes to maneuver from the runway to the airport apron, but the UN had to get its publicity just like everybody else. Mitchell was heard saying with elation that he had secured more live television broadcasts for WFP than his "rival" UN agency, UNICEF, had been able to.

That first night after the fake invasion, the black, star-speckled sky hummed and buzzed. Until then the streets had been where the noise was—guns, arguments, car horns. Now, U.S. Marine Cobra attack helicopters buzzed across the city, two hundred feet up. They were painted black, invisible against the night sky, just traced across the darkness by their deafening sound. Then a flare would be launched, suspended in the darkness, and the helicopters would hover menacingly over streets and buildings doused in light as red as fire. It was an image of the future as portrayed in science fiction. It was the land of Blade Runner, the city of Robocop. Imagine a city wracked with crime, where villains career through the streets on camouflaged battlewagons, high on drugs, free to roam at will, extort money, slaughter their enemies. Then suddenly the "forces of good" discover a new weapon: night vision glasses to spot the bad guys. An old machine gun is fired by a desperado at the rotor blades, slashing the darkness. In return a missile is fired from the night sky. The crooks are blown to pieces. That was the reality of Mogadishu, complete with film cameras to record it all.

Media complicity in the shot-free invasion was an essential element for the mission to succeed. The Marines had to be the invincible forces of good, free of personal interest or hidden agendas. The display of military power was the insurance against failure. On the ground, the warlords and clan rivals had simply hidden their guns and awaited the departure of the white knights on a new mission. North of Mogadishu, at Baledoglay, silence had descended on the once top-secret air base where Siad Barre had housed his fleet of Soviet-supplied MiG fighters. The roof of the hangar and the glass panels of the massive doors had gone. The jet planes that once screamed across the sky in defense of the Barre regime were crippled and silent. The ground was strewn with user manuals in Chinese and Russian, walls were ripped apart where cables had been torn out by looters, the whistling of exotic birds echoed through the bare struts and beams. It was a museum commemorating the end of the Cold War.

First Lieutenant Robert Van Hoesen of the U.S. Army drove past in his Humvee to see the sights. His stars and stripes gleamed on the shoulder of his combat uniform. He was a conqueror driving across a silent airfield strewn with the debris of his Cold War enemy's military hardware. He stared at the MiGs, which, had things been different, might one day have set their gun sights on him. What did it feel like to be victorious? "Right now I'm just a soldier in the United States army. I don't get paid to think big thoughts like that. As a soldier it's kind of a shame to see these planes falling apart. It's the first time I've seen a MiG this close, and I can say that they're not as good as anything we've got," he said.[32] A few days later, he left for Baidoa.

Against a dark sky streaked with early morning red and green and inky blue, U.S. and French troops halted outside the town that had become a death camp. Donkey carts trundled past as the convoy of tanks, M1-A1 Abram fighting vehicles, and jeeps that made up the land-based armada prepared for another victorious entry into the horror. Two Marines mounted an enormous stars and stripes on the leading armored personnel carrier. "What did you say this place was called?" said a Marine as he leapt off a helicopter at Baidoa airstrip later that day. French foreign legionnaires lounged smoking on their vehicles as the U.S. troops strode onto the tarmac, guns at the ready, looking for the enemy. They fanned out across the airfield and took up combat positions, while the French, the press, and the U.S. troops who had arrived unopposed on that morning's convoy, watched the ritual.

Two-star general Wilhelm Charles, commander of the U.S. Marine forces in Somalia, left the airfield bound for Baidoa's Al-Amin orphanage, which President Bush also visited the following month. His convoy consisted of four Humvees and two armored personnel carriers. He strode into the orphanage in full battle dress, and a few sacks of rice were ritually handed over to the orphanage head, Abdu Nur Ali Hassan. The soldiers interrupted the children, who were chanting the Koran as the troops arrived. A new song replaced their chanting. Over and over again they repeated the line: "Welcome with open hands the American troops." A hundred journalists followed General Charles. They were staying at the Bikiin Motel on the edge of town. CNN spent $1,300 per day for armed protection, transport, and the right to pitch its tents in the hotel garden when there were no more rooms. "Frankly we'd have paid twice that if we'd been asked," said a CNN reporter. The satellite telephone at the CARE International office, which was within sight of the hotel, rang for the fifth time that morning. It was CNN calling from the hotel. A satellite phone call then cost $20 per minute. Relief workers and CNN reporters established that the CNN coverage cost more than the entire food relief operation mounted by CARE International in Baidoa, one of the numerous fantastical aspects of the intervention in Somalia that helped keep reality at bay.

So, was there another reality that was being missed, and that would prevent the Somalia of Marines, media, satellites telephones, and convoys of relief workers from making any real difference? At the heart of the crisis that engulfed the UN was that the intervention had started with a potent lie. The lie was the claim by the United Nations that, by December 1992, bandits were stealing 80 per cent of relief food in Somalia. President Bush used this figure, for which the UN World Food Program was initially responsible, as a reason for sending in the troops. UN officials, desperate for intervention, knew it was untrue but refrained from correcting it. The maximum figure for food looted was under 50 per cent, and most of that eventually reached the needy, the International Committee of the Red Cross (ICRC) maintained even at the time. By December 1992, many relief agencies held the view that, although there had been 350,000 deaths from starvation, hunger was diminishing. What Somalis needed was careful, sustainable relief. Instead they got a foreign invasion.

The invasion failed because the bandits had gone beyond stealing food. Their determination to grab power was much stronger than their desire to steal maize. But the foreign military presence reestablished the by then diminishing link between food and power. The question remained as to whether it was U.S. "arrogance," as General Shaheen had described it, which led to the military disaster, or whether the U.S.-led forces simply made bad soldiers when fighting people who were more passionate believers in their cause. If the theft of food was the *key* issue, then why—when growing supplies of foreign food aid meant there was no longer a shortage and therefore less of a food-power link, and long after the famine had stabilized "naturally" by killing off those who were most vulnerable—did insecurity continue to prevail in Mogadishu and elsewhere? The answer lay in the vengefulness of Boutros-Ghali, the failure of the U.S. military to respond adeptly to an ever changing situation, and the failure of the UN to address the crisis in Somalia at a pace that responded to the internal political reality, rather than foisting a blueprint for development on a society that few within the UN really understood.

"ROBOCOP' AND THE NOMAD

The airport had closed. We were cut off from the rest of the world. It was 11 June 1993. A week beforehand, Aideed had struck at the heart of the UN operation in two separate attacks, killing twenty-four Pakistani troops at Mogadishu's radio station and two at a feeding center on the city. The UN had told Aideed in advance that it intended to inspect the radio station for weapons. This plan had led to rumors among Aideed's supporters that the UN intended to take over the radio station itself. "If the United Nations did not respond, a dangerous precedent would be set, and other factions would assume that assaults against the United Nations could be carried out with impunity," was how Boutros-Ghali gauged the significance of the attack.[33] The UN Security

Council, deeming the attacks "part of a calculated and premeditated series of cease-fire violations" and "[the] Security Council, with the U.S. vote powerfully influential, unanimously adopted Resolution 837, authorizing me as secretary-general to take 'all necessary measures against all those responsible for the armed attacks . . . to secure the investigation of their actions and their arrest and detention for prosecution, trial and punishment.'"[34]

It is startling that a year later, when the UN report on the killing of the Pakistanis was published, its sentiments were the reverse, exposing the confusion by which UNOSOM 2 was consumed, and the desire of its single most important contributor and strategist—the United States—to have history remember Somalia as a UN rather than a U.S. crisis, one which departed from the virtues of the U.S.-led UNITAF and became embroiled as a result. The UN's 1994 report into the killings states:

> It was in this sudden atmosphere of tension that UNOSOM II suddenly decided to carry out its first ever inspection of SNA weapon sites including the highly sensitive Radio Mogadishu. It was effected against strong objections and warnings by the SNA who clearly considered them provocative. The size and military strength of the inspection teams left no doubt that UNOSOM II had decided to use force if necessary to impose its will.[35]

Reluctantly, I moved into the Hotel Sahafi, the "journalist hotel," and out of the rented house opposite Osman Ato's, from which most of the hospitable members of the Save the Children Fund who had been my hosts had been evacuated. The hotel, a multistory building on one corner of a key road junction in south Mogadishu, was dominated by its calm, smiling owner, Mohamed Jirdeh Hussein, a large man by Somali standards, whose business was not only providing a remarkable standard of service in the circumstances, but also remaining extremely well informed, both as an essential element in his own survival and as a vital source of considered opinions, which he was happy to pass on to the journalists he felt were genuinely interested in Somalia and Somalis. Preferring to find my own way in Somalia, which the constant company of other journalists was unlikely to foster, I rarely stayed at the hotel myself, but I spent hours talking with Jirdeh in a sitting room he had set aside for himself above the hotel dining room.

On 11 June, daybreak brought a summons from General Aideed. Beyond the hotel's steel gate, the convoys of pick-ups were parked ready to take their employers in the press under guard to Aideed's house three streets away. I walked. At a lean-to restaurant on the opposite side a few yards up the Afgoy Road, where you ate by winding long strands of spaghetti and meat around your fingers, the owner looked away as I passed, despite having served me lunch there in the company of Ato and other of Aideed's close circle many times in the past. Now was not the time to recognize the *gal*, the infidels, the invaders, the white men, the enemy. Further on, the sidewalk stalls were empty, and the street stretched ahead in an eerie silence, until a crossroads at which Afgoy Road met the street leading up a hill to Digfer hospital. Silent calm gave way to hostile suspicion, except on the part of the tall, distinguished policeman with silver gray hair; he remained at his post through the worst of Mogadishu's violence, and he waved at me as he directed the chaotic traffic of donkey carts, camel trains, and Land Cruisers with mounted machine guns.

I felt encouraged, as the scowling of the passers-by seemed diluted by the policeman's recognition that I was there, walking in the city as I liked to imagine he wanted everybody to feel they could. While the hundreds of UN personnel worked behind barbed wire and traveled at speed in their cars, and the foreign troops peered at Somalia through gun sights mounted on their barricades, at least I could walk around and feel that I was in the real Somalia. The policeman, I hoped, would step in if the boiling anger turned to violence behind me, as I turned my back on the crossroads crowd and made my way toward Aideed's house down a sandy side street cluttered with huge trucks and fleets of pick-ups carrying qat-chewing militiamen bristling with weaponry.

Aideed, dressed in his usual crisply ironed shirt, led his allies onto the terrace of his villa, and they sat in the morning sun beneath an explosion of bougainvillea. After raising his fist and, for the first time in public, using the rallying cry of Islamic fundamentalists, uttering the words "Allah akhbar, Allah akhbar" (God is great), he told the gathering of journalists, referring to the UN forces: "We don't wish to create difficulties for them, and we feel a special responsibility to preserve their safety, . . . but it's not the business of the UN or anybody else to appoint or remove leaders."[36] He called on the UN to send an "independent and impartial" team to establish who was responsible for the killing of the Pakistani soldiers, and he said he would accept their findings even if it meant his own arrest. Then, without a glance at the media, with no betrayal of any recognition of the journalists who had talked with him on numerous occasions before, he disappeared through a door at the end of the terrace and was gone.

In the early hours of 12 June the bombing started. Edging slowly like ghosts across a moonlit sky a few hours before dawn, U.S. Air Force AC-130 Specter gunships, equipped with computer-guided Howitzer guns, struck compounds on the western perimeter of the city where Aideed's forces were said by the UN to have stored weapons. The catastrophe into which the UN was being plunged was laid bare, as the thud of the weapons, attempting to blast the warlord into submission, resounded through the entire city. The human level of the conflict—the negotiations through checkpoints, the petty street-corner disputes, the neighborhood firefights, the territorial claims to desolate strips of land or ransacked buildings—was shattered as the United States acted, under the UN umbrella, in the futile belief that by making a louder noise than all the combatants they could somehow force their submission. The very mentality that had led to Somalis bringing their country to its knees was the mentality that assured the UN would fail. It could never succeed, and nobody at the time nor since ever put up a convincing argument to prove that the strategy of confrontation could work, or that it was somehow connected to the broader UN plan for national reconstruction. Sitting on the hotel roof in the warmth of that June dawn as the night sky flared with the blast of the weapons, fired in a spiral that drew ever closer with every shot to the point at which I was sitting beneath the stars, the only thing to feel was despair.

Missiles struck Radio Mogadishu, vengeance striking the scene of the killings. Dawn broke, and stepping out of the iron gate of the Sahafi hotel and into the city was truly like entering a nightmare in broad daylight. A war had begun, I was on neither side, a city and to some extent the country beyond it had become—as General Shaheen had told me six months beforehand—"an animal on which to test a new vaccine." Into the early afternoon, Cobra and Black Hawk helicopters attacked the white villas and compounds said to contain weapons, while occasionally scattering leaflets exhorting Somalis to surrender their weapons and believe the foreign troops meant no harm, as they circled above derelict buildings to flush out gunmen, while smoke belched from bombed sites.

Afgoy Road, the long route whose length is marked by much of the history of what happened in Somalia, echoed with the anger of crowds condemning the bombing, idolizing Aideed. I jumped onto the back of a pickup, whose driver made his way through a crowd at the crossroads, then continued past Benaadir hospital until he was stopped by a crowd that had tried to march toward the vast compound housing the UN operation at the end of the road. A barrage of machine-gun fire from a Pakistani UN post perched on the corner of a wall had stopped them. The crowd ran back. I wanted to get through, and the crowd barred the way until I promised to take a woman wounded in the barrage back to the hospital.

We drove on. Beside the road, lying wounded by a bullet that had passed right through her, a young woman lay dying. I picked her up. An American photographer I was with yelled at me. "Put her down. Put her down. Get out of the fucking picture." He wanted me to put her down so that he could have a picture of her where she lay, without the presence of another foreign witness to betray the fact that he had not stumbled on this victim alone. I ignored him, put her in the pick-up, and drove her to the hospital and carried her fragile body into the surgery. She died an hour later. I went back to the hotel when I saw my clothes were soaked in her blood. I threw the clothes away. The photographer I had been with later wrote an account of this incident, in which his own behavior was quietly forgotten.

The futility of the drama was overpowering, and I went to find Osman Ato, Aideed's financier, in the hope of learning that something might come of the stupidity. He had left his house with the tennis court. One of his drivers was there, and he said he would take me to where Ato was hiding from the onslaught. The helicopters skimmed overhead, the menacing cannon of the Cobra gunships shifting from right to left like the tongues of the beasts from which they took their name. They hovered a few hundred feet up, their cannon roaring, pumping blasts of venom, leaving puffs of smoke puncturing the turquoise sky. We wound through the sand of the back streets of Hodan district. The car windows were closed. The driver played Somali music on the tape recorder, the piercing voice of the singer, the impossibly low notes of the lute, straining like the last gasp of a dying world consumed by the forces surrounding it. Gunmen walked quickly through the streets, casting rapid glances at the car, seeing it belonged to Ato, and eyeing me suspiciously in the back. We crossed the waste ground near the stadium where Siad Barre had in long-gone days inspected his forces at military parades, then plunged into the maze of streets of Wardhiigley district.

Ato was lying on the cushions of an upper-floor apartment. We drank tea and chewed qat. He was angry. Gone was his faintly endearing look of perplexity, replaced by an aggression and anger that he felt more strongly than most of Aideed's henchmen, he having been more instrumental than most in facilitating the U.S. arrival the previous December, lending Oakley his house, and retaining his links with the United States through his oil company interests in Conoco. He was agitated, and asked me to put my notebook away. I wanted information, but he just wanted company. I was in his home, so we ate and drank tea. He was silenced only when a helicopter roared past the window. He knew they would come looking for him. "They may have the better weapons, but we have the better motivation," he said, cutting cake and handing it to me.

We talked until the afternoon light began to fade and I made to leave. He sent me out with another of his drivers. It was getting dark, and as we emerged from the warren of streets onto Afgoy Road, we were plunged into a wall of thick black smoke from burning tires thrown up as barricades the length of the road in defiance at the onslaught. A gunman held his rifle to the windscreen. The driver was calm. "Ato's car," he said. The gunman was joined by another, grasping a grenade in his hand. As we were about to drive off he let the grenade fall, and it rolled beneath the car. A ringing, screaming silence filled my ears as the driver pulled away into the black smoke, and through the rear window I saw the grenade rolling slightly from side to side where it lay unexploded on the sand of the street.

The barricades burned into the morning of 13 June. The bright calm was savagely broken by heavy machine-gun fire beside the hotel. I stood outside the gate with Alexander Joe, a brave colleague who was photographing Somalia's plight for Agence France Presse. Together we ran toward the Kilometer Four circle beside the hotel. Again the Pakistani forces had opened fire with 50-caliber machine guns, this time pumping bullets into a passing pick-up. The two of us stood alone on the hot road, the UN troops in a nearby building yelling at us to leave, a lake of blood seeping across the sandy street from the bodies that had tumbled from the pick-up as it careered away from the shooting. Fourteen bodies were taken to the city's Digfer and Benaadir hospitals after the UN troops opened fire. A crowd of fifty people had been approaching Kilometer Four at 11 A.M. Some people said shots had been fired at the Pakistanis from the crowd. I knelt down beside a boy of around twelve years who had fallen from the speeding car. The barrage had shot the top of his head away, leaving his brain deflated inside his skull. A man lay nearby with both his legs practically shot away. A woman lay screaming in agony, as the Pakistani troops on the nearby rooftop yelled at what had by then become a group of journalists to get off the street.

"Our rules of engagement are clear. We are authorized to shoot at armed gunmen even when they are in the crowds, because they are a threat to the soldiers. . . . We shoot at anyone who shoots at us," the commander of Pakistani troops in Somalia, Brigadier Ikram-ul-Hasan, told me later.[37] The dead and injured we carried away, and burning roadblocks instantaneously appeared on the Afgoy Road and other main streets, their fires being fed by men armed with Kalashnikovs and knives. I saw Aideed at Benaadir hospital. "I am very very much disappointed by the killing of the Somali people, which has been ordered by President Clinton. The Somali people are very much disappointed, and the world will realize now who is right and who is wrong," he told me.[38]

It was the last time I saw him. He had felt the target edging toward him. Two days beforehand a compound next to his house had been decimated by the precision bombing of the AC-130 Specters. Three days later, on 16 June, his home exploded in a barrage of bombing, and he became a fugitive. In the predawn hours the silhouette of the AC-130 edged across the sky at 2,000 feet, the awesome thud of its firepower resounding through the city, the aircraft's piercing spotlight cutting through the smoke and dust and casting the warlord's headquarters into a pool of light. As dawn broke Admiral Jonathon Howe, the UN special representative, declared Aideed a wanted man, issuing ludicrous "WANTED" posters written in Somali, a clue that the New World Order was little more than a clichéd version of the Wild West of Buffalo Bill and Doc Holliday.

Under cover of the predawn aerial bombing, UN ground troops from Italy, Morocco, and Pakistan had moved into southern Mogadishu and fought their way to Aideed's by then deserted house. Throughout the night, the UN troops battled with Aideed's gunmen, fierce street battles between the troops being punctuated by barrages of Tow missiles launched from Cobra helicopters and heavy machine guns mounted on UN armored personnel carriers. Somali snipers fired bursts at UN troops advancing down near-deserted streets strewn with the rubble from buildings and vehicles destroyed in the fighting.

Admiral Howe later that day described the military operation as a "total success. . . . It is time for General Aideed to be detained . . . in order to ensure the public safety."³⁹ But nobody knew when or to where the general had fled. The aura of invincibility that surrounded his once heavily guarded villa had evaporated with the departure of Aideed and his henchmen, leaving only a sinister silence on the sandy street, which betrayed the evidence of their rapid flight. The text of the speech Aideed had made at the press conference several days beforehand lay on a shelf in his bedroom. Beside it were nine copies of the Koran—new and barely opened hardback volumes. Other books lay with them: *Ivanhoe* by Sir Walter Scott, *Portraits of Chinese Women in Revolution* by Agnes Smedley, and a revised edition of the US Constitution. A handwritten note was still taped to the mirror and signed by the general. Called "The Timetable for a Hardworking Man," it detailed his day in curious chronological order: "1.30 lunch, 8.00 dinner, 7.30–8.00 breakfast, 9.00 sleep."

Outside the residence, Pakistani troops nervously edged their way along the street. "Salaam. Salaam. Bonjour," a unit of Moroccan soldiers said as they crouched on a sandy verge at the end of a street overlooking Mogadishu parade ground a mile or so away. A Moroccan army jeep sped around the corner under a torrent of machine-gun fire from the scrubland between the parade ground and the street. Then a Moroccan army truck pierced by bullets sped around the corner and screeched to a halt, its back covered in camouflage netting pulled away to reveal an antiaircraft gun. On the street Aideed's supporters set tires ablaze. "Down with America!" they yelled at the foreign troops, and to any passing foreigner a clear message was conveyed: "We will kill you."

A FIGHT TO THE FINISH

The battle that started with the killing of the Pakistani UN troops, on 5 June 1993, ended four months later, on 3 October. It was a golden late afternoon. I was sitting on the roof of the Save the Children Fund house close to the UN compound at the end of Afgoye Road farthest from the Sahafi Hotel. The call to prayer from a nearby mosque came to an end, and the empty sky suddenly rattled with the clatter of Black Hawk helicopters stationed a few hundred yards away. First one, then another buzzed across the city just above the tree line, troops dangling their legs from the open doors, some waiving as they crossed the city in the direction of Wardhiigley. Then there was silence. For a few hours nothing seemed to happen. After darkness had fallen, the man in charge of SCF's team of Somali drivers said there were injured people arriving at Digfer hospital. The hospital was running out of bandages and medicine. A major battle was being fought in Wardhiigley. Helicopters began to fly back toward the UN compound. We took a car full of medical equipment and drove through the darkness without the headlamps on to avoid being targeted, winding through the sandy back streets to Digfer. The hospital operating theatre was awash with blood, which sloshed around the floor while surgeons did emergency operations by candlelight, and children held bags of blood for the injured patients. Abdirazak Hassan Ali, the hospital director, nicknamed "Fuji," was tense. We talked briefly, saying there were hundreds of injured with bullet wounds. Where was the battle? I asked. "Olympic Hotel. People were attacked from the air and by ground troops. They're killing everybody. We have twenty dead just in this hospital," was all he would say.[40]

The driver of the car wanted to leave, and we made our way back to the house. Early next morning we drove out again, to the Olympic Hotel. The devastation that became the graveyard of the UN operation in Somalia, of the New World Order as George Bush had envisioned it, and sealed the fate of Rwanda when the decision was made by the UN at U.S. bidding six months later to abandon its people to genocide, lay along Hawlwadig Road. One burned-out UN armored personnel carrier lay close to another. A huge crowd filled the street. I got out of the car. Women, children, men raged against all enemies, yelling and screaming. I was led down a sandy path be-tween iron-roofed shanties, and there in a courtyard lay the fractured re-mains of a Black Hawk helicopter, which a group of men were attacking with axes. Children bounced on the rotor blades, rising from ground level high into the air. People talked, yelled, screamed, everybody talking at once, not excitedly but with venom, anger, and hatred. "There were six Americans in-side the helicopter. I saw it had been hit, and then it crashed down on six children who were coming out of the Koranic school," said Hassan Issa Ahmed, whose house faced the courtyard. "The Americans defended them-selves by opening fire on all sides. So people went into their homes to get their guns. We killed three of the Americans, and one of them ran away."[41]

I went back out onto the street. The crowd separated. Somebody was dragging a coiled strip of corrugated iron tied with a rope. It scraped on the ground. He stopped dragging it as he reached where I, the only non-Somali there, was standing. I watched. The rope binding the iron was cut and sprung open. Inside lay a badly beaten corpse, a white body dressed only in khaki military underwear. The driver, a member of Aideed's clan, a man with nothing to fear from the angry people, for the first time in the weeks and months I had known him, beckoned for us to leave. A while later some other journalists arrived. Photographs were taken, and transmitted around the world. America's adventure in Somalia was about to come to an end. We drove away, passed a boy hauling another naked corpse along the street, by a rope tied to its ankle.

One of the Americans who had not been killed when the helicopter crashed into Ahmed's courtyard was Mike Durant. After a week of sporadic fighting in the city, Durant became the focus of U.S. public attention. Early on the afternoon of 8 October an associate of Aideed I had first met on the day of Aideed's last press conference, Burhane Daalbaas, arrived at the villa I was staying in. I had seen him most days since that first meeting. We had toured the city in his car, which, like that of Ato, was recognized by the gunmen and allowed to pass unhindered. After Aideed had gone into hiding following the bombing of his house in 16 July, Burhane had tried to organize a meeting for me with the fugitive warlord. It had never worked out. But that afternoon he arrived and insisted that he had a good story for me. Initially I didn't believe him, and only when my friend and colleague, Stephen Smith of the French newspaper *Libération,* insisted that we take up his offer did we drive out of the compound and onto Afgoye Road.

Burhane said little. We left the main road and drove slowly past Digfer hospital and across the parade ground and wound through Hodan and Hawlwadaag. We stopped at a house, and another man, whom I recognized as Aideed's close confidante Abdi Qaaybdiid, sat down in the front seat. They talked quietly, and we then drove up to an iron gate, which was opened immediately from inside and then quickly closed. We got out and walked across a small courtyard hung with bedsheets drying on a washing line. We were shown into a corridor and then taken into a room where, lying on a single bed, we found Mike Durant. A brief television interview after he had been taken hostage had made his haggard, frightened face familiar. He lay on his back, staring at us with dark eyes, not moving. We asked Burhane to leave us so that he could speak freely, and we were left alone.

We talked with the pilot for less than one hour. As he spoke my mind wandered from the tiny detail of one man's painful capture, and the terror he described when his helicopter was brought down and he was eventually seized by a mob that had killed his fellow crew members, to the panoramic vastness of what was taking place in Somalia. His captivity, the battle that had ended so disastrously for the U.S. military, the realization that an entire foreign military intervention could be transformed by the capture of one American, all these elements echoed round that small room, with its bare concrete floor and varnished wooden bed. Two days later the United States did abandon the fight; it called for a political solution to Somalia's crisis, which would never come and was merely a pretext to end its military involvement there.

While the White House was wringing its hands, Durant fought off the nightmares. "I think I was dragged out of the helicopter by one of the crew. I think everyone was alive when we crashed. As soon as we crashed there was a lot of gunfire and we were trying to protect ourselves. The shooting went on for about twenty minutes. I couldn't move because of my leg and back injuries. And I was lying right beside the aircraft, so I couldn't see anybody. I could hear one of the crew chiefs. He was hurt very bad. I could hear him moaning."[42] His bloodshot eyes stared blankly, as the terror of his capture flashed through his mind.

Outside in the courtyard, a woman was hanging out washing, as her children chased each other with sticks.

We lay there on the ground beside the aircraft and I saw people coming out of tin shacks trying to get to us. I kept shooting at them, but then I ran out of ammunition. There was a large group of people. They grouped together on the other side of the aircraft, shooting. Then I heard the other crew saying: I'm hit. Then the people got to me and started to hit me. They pulled off my clothes and tied a rag around my head before dragging me out onto a main street. They held me up in the air. Some people would break through the crowd and hit me. But there were other people shouting at them, it seemed as if they wanted them to stop the beating.

After ten minutes I was put in a truck and driven away as people screamed at me. I was taken to a house and left for thirty minutes, by which time it was dark. I was taken to a second house where a Somali cameraman filmed me. They chained me up in a room. The chain was like a dog chain, with a small lock on it. In the morning somebody came when I was chained up. I saw the door open and the barrel of a gun—I think it was an AK-47—come round the door. I didn't see the gunman. He opened fire and then disappeared. The bullets hit the floor and I was hit by shrapnel that I had to pull out of my arm.

That night I was unchained and moved to another house. As they were moving me I thought I was going to be killed. On the way here we stopped at roadblocks where the people who were taking me had to explain to the gunmen what was going on. They gave me some spaghetti and milk and then left me in the car for about an hour and I thought: This is it. But instead they brought me here.

Each of the three mornings he had spent at the house by the time I saw him, he had been visited by a doctor to treat his broken right leg, facial injuries, and bullet wounds. On a bedside table were tablets, mineral water, and cotton wool. A newspaper lay on the narrow bed, and he fumbled with the controls of a small radio.

I have asked them a lot about what they intend to do with me. Initially they said they were trying to work a deal in exchange for twenty-four of their people who are held. I heard on the radio that that won't happen. It's not what I want to hear, but I understand it. The SNA want to show the world that they're not barbarians. Everybody wants it to calm down. People are angry because they see civilians getting killed. I don't think anyone who doesn't live here can understand what is going on here. I regret the rest of the crew. They don't have a chance to see their families again. They were the greatest Americans. Americans mean well. We did try to help. Things have gone wrong.

13

FRANCE, AFRICA, AND A PLACE CALLED FASHODA

All the problems we have had in French West Africa have
nothing to do with a desire for independence, but are rooted
in the rivalry between the French and British blocs. British
agents have fomented all our problems.

François Mitterrand

François Mitterrand, who expressed the sentiments cited above several years
before France granted independence to its African empire,[1] was probably the
last French president after the decolonization to be accorded the semi-
imperial status of his predecessors. Much as he would have liked to carry on
the tradition, his successor Jacques Chirac lacked the aura and substance that
would have accorded him a similar stature. However, times were changing
even while Mitterrand was still at the helm of the French Republic. On 7
February 1994, he led seven former French prime ministers and a former
French president on a procession which—unknown to all of them—marked
the twilight of the long period of their imperial influence in Africa and presaged an end to anglophone-francophone rivalry there.

The foundations of that rivalry had been laid on 17 September 1898,
when Jean-Baptiste Marchand, a French emissary charged with establishing
a French presence at Fashoda, 700 miles south of Khartoum, was forced to
abandon his mission when confronted by forces led by the British general

Kitchener, leading the khedival army of British, Egyptian, and Sudanese troops. The confrontation ended French plans for an empire stretching west to east across Africa and allowed the British to forge south and control a line from Egypt to South Africa. For France, thus was born the "Fashoda complex," which underlay French attitudes toward "Anglo-Saxon" ambitions in Africa for the next hundred years and strongly influenced the strategy of excluding the "Anglo-Saxons" from French areas of influence both before and after independence.

The Fashoda complex obsessed Mitterrand throughout his life, and it was in Yamoussoukro that he led the French establishment on what in retrospect was its last gasp. The official capital of Côte d'Ivoire, the birthplace of Felix Houphouët-Boigny, always shimmered in the hazy heat, rising out of the red earth and lush forest. The town was a grand scheme, a symbol of supremacy, an expression of both the vanity and insecurity of leadership. A warm wind brushed the palm trees lining the wide boulevards, neat lawns replaced the dense forest, and everywhere the fertility of the soil fed its riches into luxuriant flowers blooming in the gardens surrounding vast buildings constructed to reflect the images of the nationhood that Houphouët-Boigny asserted with passionate zeal and practiced with exemplary adeptness. Cool drinks were always served in the Maison des Hôtes, a huge marble hall open to the day within the vast walled presidential compound, in which the Ivorian president would bring together interlocutors from across the vast political landscape of Africa and beyond, to discuss economy, the war in Angola, the conflict in Liberia, and more. They would sit talking, content to see foreign journalists like me mingle with the grandees of African politics, a relaxed courtesy dominating the discourse, a sense that great decisions were being made lending the place an atmosphere of optimism and expectation.

But on 7 February 1994, the Maison des Hôtes was empty and silent, as the presidential guards donned their plumed helmets, brandished their sabers, and towered over the largest gathering of dignitaries Yamoussoukro had hosted since the day in 1990 when Pope John Paul II had consecrated the towering edifice of the basilica of Notre Dame de la Paix. It overshadows the town, with its vast dome whose colors change as the day progresses. That day, the open arms of its colonnades embraced the personalities whose adventures, plots, schemes, and programs had played so large a role in Africa's history since independence. Rarely had so many of the magnificent, mythical, terrible, and radical leaders of the continent gathered with such piety, in one place.

For France, the occasion was one to both lament and celebrate. It was a chance to dominate a visual feast, a chance to plot the future complexion of its foreign policy by determining the seating plan inside the vast building, which was filled with light filtered by thousands of feet of elaborate stained glass and which echoed to the glorious hymns of the choir. Houphouët-Boigny, the former minister in the French government of Charles de Gaulle, the founding president of West Africa's most stable country, the African ally who had lent France a major part of its global credibility by retaining close ties with Paris after independence and giving substance to *la francophonie*, the global group of former French colonies that France promoted as an alternative to the Commonwealth of former British colonies, was dead.

The traditional chiefs had until that moment, two months after *le vieux* (the old man) had died, only admitted to having heard that the president was in a bad way, so they had come to pay their respects. A delegation from the town of Katiola was told by the presidential spokesman: "Evidently your chief had a terrible toothache. We isolated him, in order to assure him the best possible care. But unfortunately the great baobab has fallen." The falling of the baobab was the closest Houphouët-Boigny's Baoule tribe was able to get to saying that the president was dead. Other delegations were told he had a bad foot and had retired to his room, but that since he had done so the same great African tree had tumbled to the ground. Solid gold bars littered the stage beneath a canopy sheltering the flag-draped coffin, which had lain in state surrounded by baskets overflowing with glittering gold staffs, by gold crowns, and by two gold thrones. The day of the funeral came, and eight senior military officers strained under the weight of the coffin as they carried the embalmed eighty-nine-year-old founding president from a gun carriage and into the basilica.

Mitterrand had been the last to arrive. His chartered Concorde had flown from Paris that morning and had circled over the town for more than an hour. His *intention* was to arrive last, and in particular to arrive in the basilica after Houphouët-Boigny's replacement as the doyen of the African presidents—Mobutu Sese Seko. Mitterrand did not like Mobutu, but protocol dictated that the most senior participants at the funeral would sit in the first row, a bowl of flowers symbolizing the late Ivorian leader; next to the bowl would be the president of France, then—if only to separate Mitterrand from Mobutu—the Ivorian prime minister, and then the Zairian president. The view of these maneuverings was a spectacle in itself, from where I sat on a balcony overlooking the proceedings. Mitterrand led the seven former French prime ministers and former president Valéry Giscard d'Estaing in an oddly arranged queue, Giscard d'Estaing striding alone, the former prime ministers in an advancing wall whose composition was intended to show that none was more important than the other, Mitterrand arriving last, like the emperor, prepared for the sake of reputation, image, and *la gloire* to keep the other 7,000 guests waiting.

After all, this was as much a French affair as an African one. As minister for French overseas territories in the early 1950s, as minister of justice and later president of France, Mitterrand had the accumulated experience and stature of an elder statesman, one who could assert French interests by portraying those interests as to the benefit of both France and its former colonies in Africa. His readiness to do so—and the sense that it was correct and acceptable to do so—was built both on the long-established practice in Paris of dictating to the dictators in command of former French colonies how they should behave in certain areas of diplomacy, economy, and political action, and the necessity of using both the myth and reality of this influence as a means of asserting France's role as a global power on the world stage during the Cold War.

For more than a century before Mitterrand became president, the role of France in Africa had seen a remarkable political consensus between the left and the right wings of French politics. The political class was united in the belief that a pronounced grip on African affairs was essential to the prestige of the French republic. "Sans l'Afrique, il n'y aura pas d'histoire de France au XXIème siècle."[2] (Without Africa, there will be no French history in the twenty-first century.) So Mitterrand wrote in 1957. Four decades later, at the Franco-African summit in Biarritz in November 1994, he told the gathering of leaders in the immediate aftermath of the Rwandan genocide: "La France ne serait plus tout a fait elle-même si elle renonçait a être présente en Afrique."[3] (France would no longer be itself at all, if it were to renounce its presence in Africa.) The sentiment ran across the French political spectrum, with numerous French leaders uttering what to many other heads of state might appear bizarre professions of affection for the African continent. Both Valéry Giscard d'Estaing and Jacques Chirac routinely poured praise; "Ah, j'aime l'Afrique" (I love Africa), they would say, as they headed off to hunt the continent's endangered wildlife, or accept the largesse and hospitality of some of its most brutal dictators. Chirac even went so far as to say on one occasion that "'depuis trente ans'" il n'a jamais pris une décision importante 'sans aller consulter Houphouët à Yamoussoukro.'"[4] (For thirty years, he had never taken an important decision without going to consult Houphouët in Yamoussoukro.)

Direct ties between the leaders of much of French-speaking Africa and the French presidency—which has continued to formulate Africa policy through the *cellule africaine* (Africa or department cell), while other foreign policy issues are handled by the foreign ministry—were long established by the time Mitterrand took up residence at the Elysée Palace in May 1981. The legacy of his predecessors was already visible on the continent. From the high-rise block in which I lived in Abidjan, capital of Côte d'Ivoire, two elegant bridges could be seen spanning the sweep of the Ebrie lagoon. One, Pont Houphouët-Boigny, was older. The other, the newer Pont Charles de Gaulle, swept traffic from the winding corniche across the water and on toward the airport along the Boulevard Giscard d'Estaing.

In the early 1990s, Ivorian government officials refused to speak any language other than French. Superficial aspects of French daily life were the norm—breakfast was a baguette, cars clogging the streets were often the latest Renaults or Peugeots from France. The major banks had large share-

holdings by French banks, French companies generally won building contracts, and the language of daily life was French. Take a flight on Air Afrique
to the Gabonese capital, Libreville, and seek a visa at the airport in 1990, and
the uniformed head of the airport police was a Frenchman, one of the large
number of French nationals living in Africa, who numbered 114,800 by
2001, among them 1,500 French government-paid advisers and experts, the
coopérants (cooperators). *La francophonie africaine* was real. It was not just a
political relationship, nor a nostalgic reminiscence of the days of the French
empire. It was profitable, in 1993 being the second largest market for French
exports after the European Union, with Africa as a whole by 1999 being the
destination of FF39.7 billion worth of French exports, and source of FF27.7
billion of its imports.[5]

It could be said of much of *la francophonie*, that France's former colonies in
Africa, which comprised half the countries of this linguistic bloc, "turned towards France because she was the only country which retained a policy reflecting an interest and friendship for a continent which seemed to have been
largely abandoned by the other powers."[6] Others argue that the prestige successive French governments earned as the self-styled guardian of African interests at world bodies such as the European Union and the United Nations
far outweighed any real benefits to African countries themselves. The sentiment behind this often self-styled role is readily expressed: "We are still convinced that we have links that are special with Africa. We know Africa. We
have africanists who have studied the continent. We still think we are the
best placed to understand the continent," said one former French ambassador who had served in senior posts on the continent, as recently as 2001.[7]

The politics of the Franco-African relationship, which had at its heart the
readiness of French governments of the right and the left to do business with
dictators such as Jean-Bedel Bokassa, Mobutu Sese Seko, Juvenal Habyarimana, and others, should be seen within the context of the end of European
global power after World War II, and its replacement by that of the United
States. France benefited from a certain "mystification" of the African rulers
who emerged in the 1960s. It was made to appear as if France's traditional
enemies—the "Anglo-Saxons," in the form of both the British and the
Americans—somehow lacked the adeptness and agility of French diplomats
in their dealings with the larger-than-life figures of African politics between
the end of the colonial period and the end of the Cold War.

The architect of the postcolonial ties, Jacques Foccart, had dominated
the construction of these ties from 1958 as an adviser to President de
Gaulle, as councilor for African affairs under President Pompidou in the
early 1970s, and—until his death in 1997—in a similar role during the premiership and later presidency of Jacques Chirac. Foccart's *gaullist* political
outlook, and his attitude toward the French role in foreign policy, were
clear, being dominated by the primacy of "l'indépendance nationale et pour

que la France maintienne son rang dans le monde"[8] (national indepen-dence, and the retention of France's place in the world.) For Foccart, the ca-pacity to pursue his ambitions depended upon the networks of influence that had been essential to the support of the French Resistance during World War II and that endured, notably within the Gaullist political party, Rassemblement du peuple français (RPF), beyond the defeat of Nazism. Much of the *reseau* (network) that had helped the French war effort, by re-taining support and supply networks for the Resistance from French colonies in Africa that had not been occupied by Nazi Germany, was trans-formed into the *"reseau Foccart."*[9]

In 1953, Foccart organized two extensive visits by de Gaulle to Africa. The visits stamped the general's seal on the continent, such that "Grâce a Foccart, les fidelités gaulliennes sur le continent, forgées a l'heure de l'épreuve, deviennent des points d'appui."[10] (Thanks to Foccart, support for Gaullism on the continent, forged during that difficult period, became all the more significant.) When Foccart became de Gaulle's *secrétaire-général de la Communauté*, which became known as secretary-general for African and Malgache affairs at the presidency in 1958, "il s'est familiarisé comme aucun élu n'aurait pu le faire avec l'appareil de l'Etat, ses rouage administratifs, ses serviteurs."[11] (He familiarized himself as no elected official had been able to do with the state apparatus, the wheels of the bureaucracy, and his under-lings.) Foccart's looming presence throughout the half-century during which France played a direct role in the affairs of its colonies, then of its former colonies, as well as in the French-speaking former Belgian colonies of Congo (later Zaire), Rwanda, and Burundi, gave a character to this involve-ment that was as imposing as that of the leaders of independent Africa with whom France began to deal in the early 1960s.

What has become clear only since such direct involvement diminished is that personality was really the sole foundation of the relationship. "It has never been the case that there was an 'Africa policy,'"[12] argued Antoine Glaser, editor of *La Lettre du Continent*, the leading French newsletter fol-lowing African affairs. The foundation of Foccart's interest in Africa was not an abiding interest in Africa in and of itself, but an obsession with France and its place in the world. Although there was an economic cost to the French treasury of providing monetary support for the CFA franc—the common currency of most of the former colonies, which was pegged to the French franc and which is now tied to the euro—as well as the cost of pro-viding technical assistance, the pay-off *to* France was much greater. "The policy was essentially 'Franco-Franco-African',," said Glaser. The policy was about France in Africa rather than the internal reality of Africa itself, the aim being to bolster African leaders who would give preference to French busi-ness interests, would treat French expatriates favorably, and would vote en bloc with France at the United Nations. The exposure in 1997 of a political slush fund based on the earnings in Gabon and Cameroon of the French state-owned Elf-Acquitaine oil company, before it was privatized in the late 1990s, has shown the extent to which French political power and Franco-African business interests were intimately linked. Rather than there being a "policy" at the heart of Franco-African relations, there was merely an "arrangement," as Glaser said: "The Anglo-Saxons looked for a Franco-African policy, but they couldn't find it because it didn't exist. For Foccart it was a question of placing people—of having people in place who would define French interests. The aim was to create an African who was like a typical Frenchman."[13]

Foccart was secretive throughout his life, and only toward the end of it did he emerge from the shadows in which he had deliberately hidden himself. The inherent weakness of a policy that is derived from the personal rather than institutional ties between those involved was not a concern to Foccart, as he revealed candidly in 1995 when he told one interviewer: "[Trente-cinq] ans après l'accession de nos anciennes colonies a l'indèpendance, il serait déraisonnable que la France reste le gendarme de l'Afrique. Nous n'y avons aucun intérêt." [14] (Thirty-five years after the independence of our former colonies, it would seem irrational for France to remain the policeman of Africa. We have no interests there.) Such realism has only found its way slowly and through a series of crises—of both action and of conscience—into the administration of French policy in Africa in the post–Cold War period.

While French companies, along with the thousands of coopérants, assisted in the establishment of the infrastructural and administrative capacity of francophone African countries during the Cold War, the Anglo-Saxons were largely content to let them get on with it. When the United States required the support of a francophone African leader, it usually managed to secure it by exercising the real weight of the superpower, while sensitive to the fact that Africa was not important enough to risk falling out with France over. Moreover, Cold War realities were such that French and U.S. interests were similar, in the face of the Soviet presence on the continent, even though the Franco-American rivalry was and remains just beneath—and sometimes above—the surface of the two countries' relations. Whatever the motives of the Anglo-Saxons, French opinion on all levels perceived the diplomatic and business success of French initiatives in francophone Africa as a result of a certain genius in foreign affairs—for which Foccart was the benchmark. The "rival" English-speaking world in fact regarded its lack of similar influence as the result of a lack of interest in opposing Paris's plans for Africa, rather than as any kind of diplomatic defeat. Thus was allowed to develop the view among the nevertheless small number of French policymakers who regarded Africa as important, that: "Ce qui est bon pour la France, n'est-il pas bon, par définition, pour l'Afrique?"[15] (Isn't what is good for France by definition good for Africa?)

Like the United States in Central America during the days of the Monroe Doctrine, France looked for threats to the status quo in Africa, as justification when required for a more assertive and overt interference in the affairs of the continent. By 1990 and the end of the Cold War, that "threat" came from the United States, and the English-speaking world generally:

> Structurally, with an interval of two generations between them, the United States and France found themselves in exactly opposing positions: the American superpower, having nothing to lose in the marginal areas of the world but everything to gain from their integration into the global economy, put France—a medium-sized power which was a "great" power only on the African level—on the defensive.[16]

The end of the Cold War thus obliged François Mitterrand to be seen to be *leading* the calls for single-party dictatorships in Africa to open up the door to political pluralism. Not to have done so would have left such calls to the Anglo-Saxons—calls that to the opponents of dictatorship would in fact have appeared more consistent than those of France, with its close ties to those dictators so fresh in people's minds. At the conference of French and African heads of state at La Baule, a town on the French coast, on 20 June 1990, Mitterrand announced: "Le vent de liberté qui a soufflé a l'Est devra inévitablement souffler un jour au direction du Sud. . . . Il n'y a pas de développement sans démocratie et il n'y a pas de démocratie sans développement."[17] (The wind of liberty that has blown in the east must inevitably blow one day in the direction of the south. . . . Without democracy there is no development and without development there is no democracy.) He went on: "La France liera tout son effort de contribution aux qui seront accomplis pour aller vers plus de liberté." (France will link all its assistance to those efforts which are made towards creating freedom.) His words apparently imposed a strict conditionality on further French aid.

Within a few years, however, the grand challenge presented by Mitterrand at La Baule had been watered down, if not diluted altogether. The enforced moves toward democracy, in response to the collapse of communism in Europe and the fall of the Berlin Wall, appeared increasingly inappropriate, as well as having failed entirely to win any sincere support within the political elites that constituted France's traditional allies in Africa. Rigged elections and other political charades took place, but all sides knew it was a farce. Moreover, for France, the logic of engaging only those African countries that had economic potential—a strategy then being promoted by the United States within the context of the post–Cold War New World Order—would simply have led to the marginalization of countries that were economic failures. For the most part, such countries were francophone; francophone African countries were divided by some into those that were "useful" and those that were "useless."[18]

To desert them in the name of economic imperatives would be to undermine the investment successive French governments had made in them since the first colonialists had arrived on "a mission to civilize" in the latter half of the nineteenth century. Thirty years or more after the emergence of independent states across the African continent, continued engagement barely drew upon a sound economic rationale, despite ongoing Franco-African trade.

Although it had less overt political import than Mitterrand's declaration at La Baule, a more dramatic redefinition of the French relationship with the *pré carré*, the "private domain" of France in Africa from which the Anglo-Saxons were excluded, came with the decision in 1993 to devalue the CFA franc by 50 percent. The decision again in part showed the extent to which Africa "policy" depended on personality rather than long-term strategy. Edouard Balladur, the rightist French prime minister during the left-right political cohabitation in the early years of the second Mitterrand presidency, was not part of the reseau, which drew much of its strength and until the 1970s much of its party finances from the gaullist links with Africa established under Foccart. "Balladur did not have an 'African mask,'" as Glaser put it. The upper-class premier made it clear to those African leaders who had long gone cap in hand to Paris in the knowledge that they could expect to be bailed out of financial crises with the help of the treasury, that France would assess assistance with their financial affairs only on the recommendation of the International Monetary Fund and the World Bank. "Under Balladur, the IMF and World Bank roles were allowed to replace the special relationship with the CFA zone."[19]

Even prior to the call for political change made at La Baule, and the demand for economic reform and probity implied by the devaluation of the CFA franc, the character of the French role in its former colonies had not meant that Paris could fully determine the direction of the regimes with which it had forged ties. The relationship was indeed Franco-Franco-African, and at the heart of it lay links between metropolitan governments, with their state-to-state interests derived from their respective needs for credibility on the world stage. The assertion that the motivation for these ties lay in common history, from which was derived the absurd idea that African school children should refer to the French as "nos ancêtres gaullois" (our ancestors, the Gauls), amounted to nothing more than confusing and potentially damaging propaganda.

Meanwhile, the legacy of Foccart's strategy, which depended upon the close personal ties between heads of state, was in fact a major hindrance when the major contradiction in the relationship—that of a democratic European republic having military defense pacts and aid programs with a gang of corrupt dictators—emerged out of the obscurity and mystification of the Cold War years. In the same breath as Mitterrand declared at La Baule that France would tie aid to democratization, he also told the gathering: "La France continuera d'être votre amie, et si vous le souhaitez, votre soutien,

sur le plan internationale, comme sur le plan intérieur." (France will continue to be your friend, and if you wish it, your supporter, on the international level as much as on the internal level.) His confidence was in itself a
mark of how he still regarded the French need for Africa, as a *pré carré*, the
preserve of French interests. Mitterrand had also made it clear at La Baule
that "chaque fois qu'une menace extérieure poindra, qui pourrait attenter a
votre indépendance, la France sera présente a vos côtés. . . . [Mais] notre role
à nous . . . n'est pas d'intervenir dans des conflits intérieurs. . . . [La France]
n'entend pas arbitrer les conflits."[20] (Each time an external threat appears,
which could threaten your independence, France will be at your sides. . . .
[But] our own role . . . is not one of interfering in internal conflicts. . . .
[France] will not be the arbitrator in conflicts.) By making this distinction,
Mitterrand had handed the gathering of despots the opportunity to make a
decision for themselves as to how they wanted to see the Franco-African relationship evolving, and also left them to decide on the pace of "development" as the precursor to "democratization."

By giving such leeway to leaders who later proved themselves determined
to cling to power for as long as they could and at more or less any cost,
France became trapped—between a wish to see greater democracy, and the
realization that such moves were not in the interests of its closest friends
among the leaders of Africa. Moreover, what Mitterrand does not appear to
have assessed accurately was the extent to which determination of the continent's political direction had already begun to slip out of the hands of those
gathered at La Baule. He also had yet to reveal the extent to which the
French humiliation at British hands at Fashoda in September 1898 still
played a part in his thinking and underpinned France's suspicion of the
Anglo-Saxon threat to its interests. His 1957 accusation against "British
agents" suggested that the spirit was still strong sixty years after Fashoda. By
1990 he felt confident that the pré carré was just that, even after La Baule
had rocked the political boat and the devaluation had started the process of
preparing francophone Africa for economic detachment. Then a rocket fired
at a presidential plane over Kigali on 6 April 1994, shook the very foundation on which all these best-laid plans had been resting.

GUNSHIP DIPLOMACY

The trap into which Mitterrand had thrown French policy had steadily begun to close after the RPF invaded northern Rwanda from Uganda on 1 October 1990. The existence of military assistance pacts, which bound France
to aid its friends if they came under external attack, had only been made public in 1990, though several had been signed in the 1970s. At La Baule, Mitterrand had reaffirmed the French willingness to assist. The RPF invasion—
led by English-speakers ostensibly backed by the "model" anglophone

leader, Uganda's president Yoweri Museveni—raised a question that came to haunt French policy: Was it a *foreign* invasion, or the launch of a *civil* war? Was the determination of the Rwandan refugees in Uganda to return home, a domestic issue? If Mitterrand, fresh from declaring that "our own role . . . is not one of interfering in internal conflicts," had decided that the invasion was a matter for Rwandans alone, the entire history of Central Africa in the 1990s would have been different.

Uganda vehemently denied assisting the RPF, and most analysts of the link between the rebel force and the government in Kampala lean toward doubting that Uganda masterminded the invasion. It was an internal Rwandan affair, and the RPF merely took with it the weapons to which it had access in Uganda as a result of its leaders' deep involvement in the armed force that had brought Museveni himself to power. Initially, France sent troops to protect foreigners.[21] But the decision to assist Habyarimana with weapons, supplies, and troops then led to the dispatching of a 30-member *détachement d'assistance militaire et d'instruction* (DAMI), designed to provide military training to the Rwandan army. By 1993, the DAMI had been expanded to 69 men,[22] while weapons supplies and the provision of military helicopters piloted by French personnel[23] marked an escalation of the French military role. By the time a ceasefire had been agreed upon by the warring parties on 9 March 1993, France had 291 military personnel in Rwanda and had provided military assistance valued at FF137 million.

Just as it was necessary for France to define the character of the threat posed by the RPF—external threat or internal conflict?—so it was necessary to define the character of the RPF itself. Was it simply an attempt by the Tutsi exiles to force their return to Rwanda and their reestablishment in the political life of the country after thirty-one years of Hutu rule? Accusations from many quarters, both within France and among its many critics abroad, stung the French government in the wake of the 1994 genocide. As the horrifying reality of the genocide found its way into the media, the close ties between France and Habyarimana's regime became more widely known. The provision of arms to the regime cemented the idea in the minds of many that France had behaved foolishly in supporting a regime within whose ranks were extremists who had long been planning the mass slaughter of the Tutsi. The major challenge to France, however, came from within, in the form of the National Assembly *Mission d'information sur le Rwanda* (Information Mission on Rwanda), the only official published French study into France's role in the region in 1990–1994.

At the heart of the French analysis of the genocide was the view that ethnicity was the key issue. "[Le] mouvement de démocratisation avait fait apparaître des tensions régionalistes ou ethnique extrêmement dangereuses."[24] (The democratic movement has led to the appearance of extremely dangerous ethnic and regionalist tensions.) Thus Bruno Delaye, an adviser to Mitterrand, spoke of the broader shift toward democracy on the continent in the early 1990s. The identification of the emergence of democracy as a cause of ethnic tensions across the continent was a key pillar of French official thinking. It was also what set France on a collision course with the RPF and left France on the sidelines as the political-military roller coaster launched by the genocide led to the subsequent collapse of the entire Great Lakes region and the eventual toppling of Mobutu Sese Seko in Zaire in 1997.

As discussed in Parts 1 and 2 of this book, ethnicity in much of Africa is much more significant as a tool in the armory of politicians than as the foundation of a deep-rooted culturally-based conflict. Of course there are examples of genuine cultural difference. But it is rare that ethnic tensions are stirred up from the bottom. More common is that they are the result of deliberate provocation by those at the top of the social, political, or military hierarchies. The RPF, while drawing its major support from the minority Tutsi, long argued that the ethnic argument was disingenuous. The ethnic exclusivism of Habyarimana was not derived from pure tribalism, but from a tendency toward dictatorship, which had split the Hutu community itself between northerners and southerners and between democrats and authoritarians, almost as violently as it had damaged the Hutu-Tutsi relationship. From the RPF's point of view, France appeared to have swallowed the disingenuous tribalist arguments of ethnic elites, as Paul Kagame, the RPF military leader and now Rwanda's president, told me three months before the genocide erupted:

> For the French I think there's a kind of sickness in the way they handle problems on the African continent. For them Habyarimana was a friend, whatever he was doing to the population. In this meddling in African politics there are lot of things to look at. They support dictatorship. What was left behind by colonialism is maybe being redressed by the removal of dictatorship. But the former colonial powers want to keep their man in power. . . . [In] the rush for power people are ready to play on any divisions, on ethnicity, on religion. If you rush into elections the winner takes everything and you get back to the same questions. First you have to politicize the population. They have to understand what the process means to them. The whole thing is a disaster if it's not mainly generated from within the countries.[25]

The process of democratization in Rwanda, which followed the signing of the Arusha accord, had in fact diluted many of the ethnic differences that had previously been highlighted, because democratization made obvious that the more important division was between those with a real dedication to democracy and the others. Although the main victims of the genocide were clearly Tutsi, their mass slaughter obscured another aspect of the reality—that the challenge to the northern Hutu elite presented by the RPF was a challenge to the system of government, not only because that system was tribally biased but because it was a politically bankrupt dictatorship. Overthrowing that dictatorial power was necessary if the Tutsi refugees were ever to return to Rwanda. But this challenge was political, not ethnic. The Tutsi leaders of the RPF have never suggested that they intend to reinstall the monarchy and instigate the suppression of Hutu rights in the manner that the Belgian colonialists had essentially depended upon them to do throughout the colonial period. The ability and readiness of the extremists within the Rwandan government to make the Hutu population believe that this was indeed what the RPF intended was the fuel for the explosion of genocide.

By tending toward the ethnic explanation for the conflict that erupted following the RPF invasion in 1990, France was failing to see that the challenge to Habyarimana represented a demand for a much more profound change in the practice of government in the stagnant political environment of Rwanda. French officials, long after the genocide, sought to portray France as having spoken bluntly with Habyarimana about the choices facing him, and thus to deflect criticism of its policies in Africa: "La diplomatie française a consisté a se mettre 'les mains dans le cambouis.'. . . Cette politique se traduisait a l'époque, non par un soutien au régime en place, mais au contraire par une précision continue et opiniâtre de la France sur le Président Juvenal Habyarimana pour que celui-ci partage son pouvoir et que les autres partis y accèdent."[26] (French diplomacy meant getting your hands dirty. . . . This policy, at that point in time, meant, not support for the incumbent regime, but on the contrary a continued and stubborn insistence by France to President Juvenal Habyarimana that he should share power and that the other parties should accede to it.) That was how Hubert Vedrine, France's foreign minister, later defined the French approach. Bruno Delaye said that "une véritable course contre la montre s'est engagé entre la logique de paix et celle des armes, entre la survie du dialogue et le basculement dans le chaos."[27] (There was a real race against time between the choice of peace and that of violence, between the continuation of dialogue and the collapse into chaos.) France, the National Assembly in Paris was told by many of the key policymakers within the French political establishment who gave evidence to the mission d'information hearings, had only been trying to help.

Such presentations of the French role barely stand up to scrutiny.

The military assistance France provided to the Rwandan government in 1990–1994 must be seen less as an honorable fulfillment of a promise of assistance, and more as the bolstering of an ally whom Paris regarded as worthy of support because of the anglophone character of its enemy and whose needs would allow senior officers in the French military to assert their worthiness as soldiers and flex their muscles on African soil. This view is most clearly asserted in the report of the French National Assembly. While emphasizing the ethnic element as lying at the heart of the unfolding crisis in Rwanda, the report sets great store by the theory that the missile that brought down Juvenal Habyarimana's aircraft—the event which led to the unleashing of the genocide—was fired by the RPF. It thereby casts doubt on the view that the crash that killed both Habyarimana and Cyprien Ntaryamira, the Burundian president, was the work of Hutu extremists who believed that Habyarimana had conceded too much to the RPF at the talks from which he was returning when he was killed.

Although the report comes to no definitive conclusion as to who was responsible, the assertion that the RPF infiltrated the Rwandan army barracks at Kanombe, or an area near it, then fired a missile, scored a perfect hit, and then escaped undetected is beyond belief. For an official government report to make its bias so stark is revealing of the sentiment that lay at the heart of French official thinking. "La zone de Kanombe était essentiellement tenue par l'armée hutue. . . . [Il] est peu probable qu'un tel missile ait été tiré en dehors de la zone controlée par les FAR."[28] (Kanombe zone was essentially in the hands of the Hutu army. . . . [It] is hardly likely that one of these missiles was fired from outside the zone controlled by the FAR.) To anybody present in Kigali at that time, as I was a few days after the aircraft had been shot down, it was clear that the Kanombe zone was the site of the largest government barracks in Kigali, and was *entirely* and not *essentially* under the control of the Forces Armée Rwandaise (FAR). The grudging tone of the inquiry report seems loaded with vagueness and uncertainties where they do not exist.

Although it is obvious that the RPF had once sought a military victory, it had subsequently engaged in peace talks that had brought it major negotiating success, in part as a result of the weak negotiating skills and questionable credibility of its main interlocutor—Habyarimana. The RPF had most to gain by keeping Habyarimana in place. The extremists within the army, meanwhile, had most to lose by negotiations. Militarily, the RPF was entirely unprepared for the violence that erupted after the 6 April attack. Aware that the small garrison it had been permitted to maintain in Kigali as part of the Arusha peace process would be of limited effectiveness, the RPF would logically have prepared its troops encamped in the north of the country for an advance south prior to the attack, if it had been planning to assassinate the president. But it had not done so, and its advance south to Kigali revealed the cost of its inability to protect the people it would naturally have sought to protect—the Tutsi victims of the genocide.

By raising the possibility of RPF culpability in the 6 April attack in such a tone, the French report reveals the defensiveness of the French political establishment and betrays the superficial signs of the much deeper mix of humiliation and guilt with which France emerged from the horrific months of the genocide. It sought to deflect blame for what followed the assassination at the hands of the architects of the genocide—with whom Paris had been on such intimate terms—and to somehow spread the blame by a mix of equivocation and finger pointing at the group that it nevertheless admits would have found the attack most difficult to carry out.

THE *PRÉ CARRÉ* BECOMES A *ZONE HUMANITAIRE*

After the ceasefire of 9 March 1993, there was never really a war between the RPF and the Rwandan army. The million dead in Rwanda were not the victims of a war. The RPF marched through the country in April–June 1994, while the government army retreated. Before the RPF achieved its goal of occupying the entire territory, the Hutu extremist civilian militias had done their work, backed up by the army when the civilians refused to be killed easily. On 8 April 1994, Jacques-Roger Booh-Booh, the former Cameroonian foreign minister appointed by Boutros Boutros-Ghali as UN special representative in Rwanda, wrote in a cable to Kofi Annan and Marrack Goulding, respectively heads of peacekeeping and political affairs at UN headquarters, that the situation in the country was "calm, although tense." He then stated that the Rwandan Presidential Guard had seized members of the opposition, including the prime minister. He then noted that ten Belgian UN peacekeepers had been murdered.

The naiveté of his conclusion was thus astounding. Moreover, Booh-Booh cannot claim to have had no idea what was taking place, as the rest of the same cable, written by General Romeo Dallaire, the Canadian head of the peacekeeping force, read—in capital letters—thus:

THE APPEARANCE OF A VERY WELL PLANNED, ORGANIZED, DELIBERATE AND CONDUCTED CAMPAIGN OF TERROR INITIATED PRINCIPALLY BY THE PRESIDENTIAL GUARD SINCE THE MORNING AFTER THE DEATH OF THE HEAD OF STATE HAS COMPLETELY REORIENTED THE SITUATION IN KIGALI. AGGRESSIVE ACTIONS HAVE BEEN TAKEN NOT ONLY AGAINST THE OPPOSITION LEADERSHIP BUT AGAINST THE RPF (BY FIRING AT THE CND), AGAINST PARTICULAR ETHNIC GROUPS (MASSACRE OF TUTSI AT REMERA), AGAINST THE GENERAL CIVILIAN POPULATION (BANDITRY) AND AGAINST UNAMIR (DIRECT AND INDIRECT FIRE ON U.N. INSTALLATIONS, VEHICLES, PERSONNEL AND AFFILIATED AGENCIES (I.E., UNDP)) WHICH HAS RESULTED IN FATAL AND NON-FATAL CASUALTIES. THE PARTICULARLY BARBAROUS MURDER OF THE 10 CAPTURED BELGIAN SOLDIERS EMPHASIZES THIS SITUATION.[29]

There is no doubt that the United Nations headquarters was being told of what was really taking place in Rwanda, despite what amounts to the mixture of ignorance, incompetence, and bias in favor of the Rwandan government that Booh-Booh—a member of the Cameroonian political elite, which enjoys close ties to France—had become known for by the time the violence erupted. Why did it take Boutros-Ghali until 4 May to admit that "here you have a real genocide, in Kigali"? By waiting he freed the signatories to the 1948 Convention on Genocide from their responsibility to intervene during April. "The U.S. effort to prevent the effective deployment of a UN force for Rwanda succeeded, with the strong support of Britain," Boutros-Ghali writes in his memoir, *Unvanquished: A U.S.-UN Saga*.[30] His account, written after U.S. objections to his standing for a second term as UN secretary-general, is highly revealing. Madeleine Albright, then U.S. ambassador at the UN, is cited as telling the U.S. House of Representatives Foreign Affairs Committee: "Sending a UN force into the maelstrom of Rwanda without a sound plan of operations would be folly."[31]

The debacle in Somalia, from which the incoming Clinton administration was still at that time trying to extricate itself, was a nightmare that the United States did not want to repeat. The "Mogadishu Line" should not be crossed, and the Somalia scenario was an excuse that freed the United States from the responsibility to intervene. To free it of its international obligation to intervene to stop genocide, the U.S. State Department instructed U.S. officials to avoid describing the killings as "genocide" and to acknowledge only that "acts of genocide may have occurred." Only when this directive was exposed and ridiculed in the *New York Times* was it reversed.[32] No U.S. effort was meanwhile made to develop a "sound plan of operations," and Albright in particular, during the UN Security Council debates on Rwanda, gave the impression of being completely unmoved by what was being reported of the genocide. President Clinton seemed even worse, joking with Boutros-Ghali about totally unrelated subjects when the secretary-general raised the issue of Rwanda at the White House.[33]

Boutros-Ghali's condemnation of U.S. failures should also be regarded as a preparation for his unequivocally positive account of the French decision to launch *Opération Turquoise*. "In the absence of a ceasefire, France's only options were either to withdraw its troops from Rwanda or to establish a safe humanitarian zone where the population would be protected from the fighting," he wrote in the introduction to the official UN account of UN involvement in Rwanda.[34] Such a representation of the French determination to extend its involvement is a horrifying sign of the extent to which the bilateral relations between foreign powers had sealed Rwanda's fate. The slaughter was always secondary to the rival concerns of the UN Security Council's leading members. This was obvious in the comments of Jean-Bernard Mérimée, the French ambassador to the UN, during the French inquiry into France's involvement in Rwanda. Asked to explain the UN Security Council's 21 April 1994 decision to reduce the size of its peacekeeping force in Rwanda despite the escalation of violence, Mérimée said it was a result of cowardice and cynicism: "lâcheté, parce que les gens avaient peur d'y aller, des soldats belges avaient été massacrés et les Américains étaient sous le syndrome somalien; cynisme, parce que toute présence internationale était considérée par la plupart des membres du Conseil de securité comme un obstacle au progrès du Front patriotique"[35] (cowardice, because people are afraid to go there, with the Belgian soldiers having been killed and the Americans under the influence of the 'Somalia syndrome'; cynicism, because any international presence was regarded by most of the Security Council members as an obstacle to the progress of the [Rwandan] Patriotic Front).

To suggest that the other Security Council members were prepared to deny the Rwandan population UN military protection in the interests of encouraging an RPF victory exposes the state of mind of those engaged in deciding Rwanda's fate from abroad. The determination of the French—on both the diplomatic and military levels—to thwart the RPF is made clear by Gérard Prunier in his account of the genocide, which also details his personal involvement in the planning team of soldiers and diplomats which prepared the launch of *Opération Turquoise*. "There seemed to be a mental stumbling block in French official thinking where the RPF was concerned, caused by the dreaded Anglo-Saxon enemy's proximity,"[36] Prunier wrote, in reference to the initial failure of French officials to meet with the RPF when it became clear that the mission to establish a safe zone in Rwanda, to which civilians could run, would require the acquiescence of the RPF. Even after the launch of *Turquoise*, Prunier said, "there were still extremist officers in the French force who itched for a chance to get at the RPF and help their old friends,"[37] the most prominent of whom was Colonel Thibaut, a pseudonym for a former French secret service officer named Thauzin who had been a military adviser to Habyarimana; he was initially sent as part of the French force but later recalled after making openly aggressive statements about the RPF.[38]

Only by the time the two-month *Turquoise* operation was launched, on 22 June 1994, had France started to become skeptical about the wisdom of supporting the interim Rwandan government led by Theodore Sindikubwabo. "Leur résponsibilité collective dans les appels au meutre . . . me parait bien établie. Les membres de ce Gouvernement ne peuvent, en aucun cas, être interlocuteurs valables d'un règlement politique,"[39] (The responsibility it has for calling upon people to commit murder . . . seems well established. There are no cases in which members of this government could be credible players in a political solution) so a senior French official based in Goma, Zaire, wrote on 6 July 1994. Despite this recognition, the safe zone created by *Opération Turquoise* was essential in allowing the leaders of Rwanda's genocide to escape the RPF advance and reach Zaire.

During early to mid-July, Sindikubwabo wrote to Mitterrand to demand that the French extend their military presence beyond the southwest of the country, because, Sindikubwabo said, "la France aura ainsi sauvé près de quatre millions d'habitants aujourd'hui menacés de massacre par le front patriotique rwandaise."[40] (France would in doing so have saved four million people threatened with being massacred by the Rwandan Patriotic Front.) French officials rebuffed this and other attempts by the ministers of the interim government to make contact, according to testimony presented to the French National Assembly hearings. Even so, the interim government sought refuge within the zone occupied by the French troops as the RPF advanced. A telegram sent to Sindikubwabo's officials stated that they could pass through the zone on condition that they act so as to "éviter toute activité politique ou militaire qui changerait la nature de la zone où notre présence n'a qu'une vocation humanitaire"[41] (avoid all political or military activity that would change the nature of the zone where our presence has a solely humanitarian role). Both Sindikubwabo and Jean Kambanda, the prime minister, moved into the zone. Just as French troops had cited the absence of a mandate when they refused to intervene to stop the killings in Kigali in April during the evacuation of foreigners, so the troops in the *Opération Turquoise* zone cited the absence of a mandate to arrest members of the interim government when they came within their jurisdiction. Thus, the architects of the genocide were, directly or indirectly thanks to France, able to flee Rwanda to a plush hotel in Goma, and remain at large across the African continent and beyond, until they were slowly rounded up, arrested, and brought to trial at the UN International War Crimes tribunal, which started in 1997, in Arusha, Tanzania.

THE END OF THE AFFAIR?

The general condemnation, within France as well as among Rwandans, of the links between French officialdom and the Habyarimana government in Rwanda forced a review of how and—more importantly—why France should retain a policy of engagement in African affairs. One key event in this period of reflection was the National Assembly mission to establish—at least from the French perspective—what Paris should be held accountable for. The conclusion was that its policy in Rwanda had been one of excessive military involvement.[42]

The politics of personality, the intimate ties, the long secret flights by luxury jet or on chartered Concorde from Paris to the *domaines présidentielles* of Omar Bongo's Gabon, Mobutu's Zaire, or Yamoussoukro to discuss common interests way out of the public eye, are perhaps now a thing of the past. Nevertheless, the horrors of the genocide focused attention on the relationship between France and the perpetrators, in a manner that was bound to lead to relationships with other regimes—just as bad in their own way as Habyarimana's regime—being overlooked. Who knows how many lives would have been saved from death through illness if the Mobutu regime had invested money in health care, rather than stealing the national finances and spending it on luxuries?

More people die every year in Africa from malaria than died during the Rwandan genocide—with the full knowledge of the numerous corrupt governments, who should be seen as largely responsible for the absence of development and the inadequacies of health care systems. Neither France nor any other country is condemned for dealing with these "peaceful" crooks, despite their contribution to the ravaging of the continent and its people, in ways less dramatic than the genocide but ultimately just as destructive.

"There were very strong personalities at the heart of it: Foccart, who died in 1997, was at the heart of the personalization of politics," said the same former French ambassador I quoted earlier.[43]

> [Now] France is losing a clientele at the United Nations, among the African countries that supported us. We are losing that. We are losing markets which were previously exclusively French. That's disappeared. For the language, the *francophonie*, people in Africa are saying that they shouldn't remain solely with French. We have certainly lost. The *pré carré* is not possible, because we don't have the means to preserve it.[44]

For France, the experience of the genocide in Rwanda has been particularly influential in forcing it to examine its own motives for action. Above all, it has exposed the absence of sound policy. The perceived threat to *French* interests by the onward march of the RPF in Rwanda was derived from the notion that the Fashoda complex, which France held onto as a reminder of the need to defend its interests as a cultural force, was still relevant a century after its birth. "For Mitterrand the Fashoda complex was important. It is incontestable that it played a major role [in his thinking]."[45] According to one senior French official, whose views I have already quoted, all the diplomatic traffic passed between embassies in the Great Lakes region and Paris in 1990–1994 "cited the Fashoda issue." The great error of judgment lay in the assessment of the nature of the supposed threat to French interests: "It's not the English themselves, or the Americans. But we sense that the language is an issue. It's seen as a loss. But the genocide really ended the idea of French engagement. It was an era that won't ever be repeated."[46]

The *franco-franco african* foundation of the policy was in fact the cause of the political failure. Ultimately, bad leadership is bad because it fails to act in the interests of the people. The Habyarimana regime, along with the perpetrators of the genocide within its ranks, was ultimately concerned more with its own survival than the development of Rwanda. As French policy was deliberately built on ties with the elites of the African political scene, it would inevitably suffer as those elites crumbled in the face of their own detachment from the needs of ordinary people. All it needed was somebody strong enough to push them out. The absence on the part of those elites of any reason to believe it was in *their* interest to regard the defense of *la francophonie* against an "Anglo-Saxon" onslaught as essential to their own survival seems obvious. If the RPF had been French-speaking Tutsis, backed perhaps by the French-speaking Tutsi-dominated army in Burundi, would the Fashoda complex have been evoked? For Habyarimana, it did not really matter where the threat came from. Any reason was a good one to call for French assistance. Trapped by its own myopia and vanity, France obliged. On the African side—in this case, the Habyarimana side—the relationship was exposed as purely opportunistic.

However, it is only since the genocide that France itself has been able to come to terms with the fact that there has to be more real substance to its relations with African countries. The changing nature of the African political elite—for better or for worse—has been the key element in forcing a change in the way in which African countries are perceived. The need for a new kind of relationship has not been lost on French policymakers; as one key French player said, "Countries have become more independent. In the 1960s they became *officially* independent. But since 1997 and beyond they have become *really* independent."[47] By implication that "independence" means independence from France, leaving them thus exposed to greater influence from France's supposed rivals for influence. Since the genocide in Rwanda, much analysis has centered on the nature of that rivalry. Although the National Assembly study of the Rwanda crisis does not really answer the fundamental question as to why France was in Rwanda in the first place, it does not shy away from the conclusion that there was really no threat whatsoever from the Anglo-Saxons, and that "il apparait que la France a mené au Rwanda une politique classique lui permettant d'étendre son influence dans le champ élargi de la francophonie sans que cette présence lui ait jamais été véritablement contestée par les puissances anglo-saxonnes"[48] (it seems that France launched a policy in Rwanda allowing it to exercise its influence in the larger francophone area without it ever really being the case that it was being opposed by the Anglo-Saxon powers.)

French readiness to accept that the threat to its influence was not what it claimed, and that France had taken the alarm simply because the RPF happened to launch its attack from an English-speaking country, is perhaps the first step toward establishing the new parameters within which French action in Africa is likely to be exercised. Meanwhile, 6,000 French troops remain based on the continent at barracks in Côte d'Ivoire, Senegal, Chad, Gabon, and Djibouti as a "security" for the 114,800 French nationals living across Africa. France had misunderstood the nature of the threat represented by the RPF, which was political rather than cultural or linguistic. This realization has subsequently forced a major shift away from the Foccart view that the links with Africa should essentially be used to bolster French standing on the world stage—the *franco-franco african* logic—to the view that those links should be reciprocal. The most recent policy statement issued by the French government, in its efforts to define its position, stresses noninterference in internal affairs and a focus on development.[49] The same document highlights the joint visit to Ghana and Côte d'Ivoire in March 1999 by Hubert Vedrine and Robin Cook, respectively the French and UK foreign ministers. The visit was perhaps a sign—if one were necessary—that the Fashoda complex and the rivalry that lay behind it is truly over, and that France is now resigned to the fact that a new policy must have African interests at its heart.

EPILOGUE

The Center Cannot Hold

Turning and turning in the widening gyre
The falcon cannot hear the falconer;
Things fall apart; the centre cannot hold;
Mere anarchy is loosed upon the world.

W. B. Yeats

CHINUA ACHEBE'S CHOICE of title for his 1958 novel, *Things Fall Apart*, seen in context, suggests some period of stability preceding the collapse; before, things were together, then they fell apart. Structures collapsed, people turned on each other, what had been built was destroyed, the center could not hold. The enduring sense is that something has been lost on the way. The process of destruction and decline has plagued much of the African continent, plunged into chaos as it was by colonialism, then promised a kind of freedom after independence, only to find that freedom was in fact a new form of bondage, albeit with African heads of state to lead it.

Understanding the impact of foreign involvement in Africa is important for several reasons, if the turmoil current in much of the continent is to be assessed as a phase that will pass. Colonialism created a kind of schizophrenia: The European model was ordained as superior, despite precolonial traditions having retained a vital importance in the areas of normal life that succeeded in remaining untouched by the colonial infection. Meanwhile, the European model was taught as something to be envied and admired, while by design remaining an elusive goal, beyond the reach of the mass of the colonized. The postcolonial period, dominated by the Cold War, thrust the

continent into a global political conflict in which it played no profound role
and was merely the abused stage upon which other peoples' wars were
fought, using African bodies as cannon fodder. Africa became engaged due
largely to the overpowering capacity of the superpowers to enforce that engagement, as well as to the opportunism of the array of outrageously bad
leaders that too many African countries have had the misfortune to throw up
in the past four decades.

Since 1990 and the end of the superpower conflict, the catastrophic
legacy of this poor leadership has truly been seen in its failure to build enduring institutional foundations. But the 1990s has also been the decade in
which the backlash against that legacy and its causes has started to be felt.

The reassessment of postcolonial relationships, the resurgence of a real
nationalism derived from a readiness to embark on strategies that are likely
to cement a break with the past and leave little prospect of later returning to
past practices of government, as well as a strong and growing sense that political risks are essential if the spiral of decline is to be halted, these are the
foundations of Africa's political future. As the World Bank asserted in a relatively hard-hitting report in 2000:

> [The] new century offers a window of opportunity to reverse the marginaliza-
> tion of Africa's people—and of Africa's governments, relative to donors, in the
> development agenda. Political participation has increased sharply in the past
> decade, paving the way for more accountable government, and there is greater
> consensus on the need to move away from the failed models of the past. With
> the end of the Cold War, Africa is no longer an ideological and strategic battle-
> ground where "trusted allies" receive foreign assistance regardless of their
> record on governance and development.[1]

Vital to exploiting the "window of opportunity," if indeed it exists, is a re-
alignment of relations with donors such as the World Bank and, in particular, the IMF. As the experience of Zaire shows, the IMF knowingly contributed to the corruption of the Mobutu regime. Such a scandalous use of
resources, purely to prop-up a U.S. ally, is an aspect of the dire and destructive legacy of foreign involvement in Africa. The "failed models of the past"
are as much a result of foreign involvement as they are a result of the ineptitude or corruption of numerous African governments. If these failures of institution building, economic reform, infrastructure development, and political leadership are to be fully recognized, the failure on all sides must be
admitted.

Now, however, there are clear signs that the wider political participation of
the past ten years has brought with it intense pressure within most African
countries for improvements in governance. This pressure has not emerged

primarily from the foreign donors who have watched their money siphoned off to numbered bank accounts in that sleazy haven for kleptocrats—Switzerland—but from the African populations who are the victims of bad government. Karl Maier quotes a Nigerian anticorruption campaigner, Bilikisu Yusuf, as saying, "It's not enough for us to say, 'Ah, the leadership is corrupt, government is corrupt.' We have not internalized the message of probity, accountability and transparency. If we are going to hold people to account and really make meaningful change . . . we must first begin with ourselves."[2]

But in this emerging atmosphere of heightened nationalism, internal criticism, and political participation, are there the makings of bonds that will renew the power of the center to hold?

Change in the institutions of the nation state is unlikely to bring profound improvement to the lives of the peoples of Africa unless it is carried out in a manner that responds to reality as the participants themselves discern it. When the West decided the time was right for Africa to democratize, African countries were expected to follow the decision promptly. However, the modalities of nation statehood, the language of democracy, systems of economic management, and the tenor of foreign relations, all require models. The extent of state collapse in parts of Africa in the 1990s, as a result of political crises, personal rivalry, economic devastation, or a combination of all these elements, must in part be seen as aspects of the wider world's legacy in Africa. But in drawing up responses to these problems, the advocacy of the democratic solution has drawn upon less rather than more knowledge of African society, and revealed a failure to understand the genesis of the problems. By pressuring for the overthrow of single-party rule, were Western countries seeking to overthrow aspects of the traditional exercise of power, upon which that rule had drawn? Or were they appealing to the long-buried "democratic virtues inherent in the traditional African political systems,"[3] which had perhaps existed in the precolonial era? It is hard to believe that Europe and the United States were genuinely discerning and responding to a sudden upsurge in the desire of Africans to improve their lot by democratic means. A minority had long voiced that desire when Europeans and Americans armed and equipped the dictators. The fact that the West had ignored indigenous calls for democracy when it suited it during the Cold War was rarely if ever dwelt upon after the Cold War was over.

For many African states, the question remains as to whether or not single-party rule on the continent was really the product of the Cold War, and thus ripe for dissolution once the Cold War was over, or whether in fact it was a form of rule that derived its justification from an African tradition of the warrior-chief. If the former, then clearly an alternative had to be found. If the latter, than why should it be dissolved, just because the Berlin Wall had fallen down?

The weakness of many African states at the beginning of the twenty-first century owes much to their inability to evolve naturally through assimilation and evaluation during *long* periods of stability. The deliberate abuse of ethnicity has meanwhile prolonged the experience of nation building—in Mobutu's former Zaire, in Kenya, in Rwanda and Burundi. The slow process of marrying apparently contradictory cultural traditions is prolonged by the lack of long-term stability and the absence of uninterrupted experience.

Even against a background of instability, despair, and dashed hopes, it is still essential to regard the turmoil of the past decade as part of a transition. The great risks people across the continent have taken in an effort to bring better government, and with it a better life, are proof enough of how strongly they want these things. For the outsider, the outward signs of that transition—street battles, the signs of intolerance, the horrors of war, genocide, and conflict—often obscure the substance of what is being sought. For the non-African observer, shocked by appearances and ill-informed about the substance behind them, impressions of the continent have continued to be superficial. It is a key purpose of this book to show that the enormous problems much of Africa faces are far from being entirely of its own making, but that with determination and courage it is the population of the continent that is now seeking to take those problems in hand.

"We are taking from a story that we heard when we were young, and we're trying to transform that story. When I was young the story was being told. It wasn't being painted then. It was being written down."[4] The interior of the long wooden hut glimmered with a red-gold light from a bright autumn sun, which was sinking over the lush hills even though it was only mid-afternoon. There was a bed covered by a brightly covered patchwork bedspread, and shelves cluttered with tubes of oil paint, pots of emulsion, rolled canvases, hundreds of brushes crammed into jars giving off the faint odor of turpentine, and on a paint-splashed easel the first brush strokes of a new work.

Meek Gichugu pulled canvasses from beneath his bed, one by one, unrolling them and laying them on the bedspread, where shards of sunlight shone upon the eyes and teeth, the frightened faces, the strange landscapes, the tortured expressions of his subjects. He was dressed in bright green trousers and a pink T-shirt, and it was hard to make the connection between the overpowering imagery and violence of the paintings and the young Kenyan painter who had conceived and created them. In a calm tone, he carefully, quietly explained the immense complexity of the emotional turmoil, religious crises, tribal conflicts, despair, anger, and obsessions that lay in the colors, the figures, the tales behind each canvas as he pulled them out from beneath his bed, while outside the hut, cattle hooves scraped the soft mud of the track, sheep bleated, and the twitter of a bird occasionally threw music into the solitude of Ngecha.

"There was a Prophet, I can't remember his name. It was said he would come with moving objects, spitting fire. So, there are cars and guns in the painting. The Prophet would come with a thing that could kill. So, there's a car, a Bible, a clock. This is something that will come. It's in the Kikuyu tradition." He stroked a small hand across the vast landscape of the canvas. Where was the landscape from which this was drawn, I wondered? The overpowering beauty of Kenya, of Kikuyuland where we were talking, among the hills and valleys of central Kenya thirty miles or so northwest of Nairobi, was nowhere to be seen. All was stark, harsh, with bright, violent colors, a world dominated by torment and disconnected symbols woven into a single, haunted landscape. "The Prophets say that there are people who will come who will not have ears to hear. They are here. The figures have already come. The war has come."

Meek was only in his early twenties, though he spoke with the thoughtfulness and wisdom of a sage. The dynamism of his paintings, the drama, the extraordinary and fantastical imagination at work in devising the vast and terrifying landscapes he had created, all seemed the work of a long-tortured craftsman. His intensity, hidden behind a tranquil, grinning veil of modesty, exploded in the paintings, hidden there under the bed of the long wooden hut, on the other side of the *shamba*, the small plot of land, where his mother lived.

"The war has come," he repeated. "The clashes have been prophesied. They have said that there will come a war, and that there will be smoke. Then the prophecy said that there will come a very small tribe which will rule by force, and that to remove that small tribe from power will not be easy. And then it will be very hot." The anger was there—his anger, the anger all around him, the anger that had brought chaos, the anger that nobody seemed able to voice in a manner which could prevent it from intensifying.

The clashes, the violence engineered by the government against the Kikuyu, Luhya, and Luo to force them out of the Rift Valley, had left the country scarred. His was the quietest voice, with perhaps the loudest message. The government's war on its own people, the betrayal—these were what lay behind the anger and violence of his paintings. Before his own eyes he could see the unfolding of a story he had heard when he was young, which had only been written down but which now he was capturing for the eye. The stories of slavery, power abused, people afraid and lost, it was all there to be seen. Meek drew upon the history he had inherited for a sense of purpose that gave a meaning to the drama of his paintings, which migh 331t otherwise have seemed excessive and irrational. Now there was a war in the next valley, his own people being killed by the government, by the nation whose laws he was bound to obey. In such a situation, what was there left to believe in, but the lasting symbols of his own ethnic patrimony?

He laid a mounted canvas out flat in the light of the remaining sun. It depicted some men in a boat rowing between two islands. "The men are the small tribe, rowing to push everything else aside." A man with wings was offering a gift, "in the hope that it will appease the men in the boat," he explained. Others had tried to offer gifts to the big man, but their boats had sunk. "Until God accepts for the men in the boat to fall down, nothing can stop them." He pointed to a bird. "The bird has been bought, to sing the praises of the big man: to sing the *gicukia*, the Kikuyu praise song. In Kikuyu tradition, the bird is symbolic. In the painting the bird is the Kikuyu. When the bird sings for you, all you need to do is give it a good cage and food and water. So, part of the Kikuyus have been bought. That is what has happened to my people." The bird is round, because he has a full belly, and his claws have been replaced by two double-barreled shotguns. "But the man in the boat isn't taking care where he is heading to. He is just rowing the boat. He is trying to cross from one island to another island. The islands symbolize the passing of time. The former president tried to bring up the Kikuyus. The current president is trying to turn them back. I don't see any future for his people. I doubt that they are as hungry as I am. Only a few have benefited from his rule. Flying fruits: there are always fruits to be had, which everybody is trying to take for themselves."

The man in the boat, the helmsmen, the *father-chief*, the ruler, is depicted as a pathetic, lost, aimless figure, unable to make sense of the world, unable to relate to the people around him. Lost among the islands of his rule, the leader is isolated, leading a dwindling crowd of sycophants who have no more hope from following than that some of the fruits might one day fall into their hands. Stark in Meek's paintings was the sense that even if one leader were overthrown, any replacement would be just as bad. None was represented as capable of disentangling the knots of history and reordering the mass of tensions, resentments, and anxieties that surged from the canvases. Rolled up, bound with a ragged ribbon and standing on end in a tall cupboard, was a figurative montage that trumpeted this message of disillusionment. He had called it "Royalty."

> My topic then was slavery. Slavery [in Africa] didn't start with the outside world. But if you look at slavery from the outside, it was much worse [than enslavement by other Africans]. But I was looking at the ministers, the leaders, and democracy, and I was wondering whether the leaders would be merciful. But they won't be merciful. If Moi goes, the person who will come after him will be much more harsh than him. The king can bring good things or bad things.

His powerful disillusionment was barely diminished by the unique chance he had to express it in his paintings. The urgency of his need to draw upon the richness of traditional, established culture, to throw past and present into relief against each other, had evolved as the immediate reality—the politics, the abuse of power, the bitter rivalry—had come to be dominated by the aimlessness of leadership, the power without purpose, which had lost any clear direction. He showed me a painting he had entitled "The Spider," *Komite Ta Kabubui.*

There's a traditional saying:

> . . . to be as satisfied as a spider. When I want to talk about the white man, he is always satisfied. He brings. He doesn't take. He brought the gun and sword, so the spear couldn't be used for war. So, he is satisfied. And he brought the Bible. In the painting, I had two hands. He had many hands and feet. They can kick you. They can cut you to pieces. They can do anything. [But] he brought us assimilation. Both the figures are living: One is strong, one is weak. But they are both living in the same world. This is a painting about before and after independence, and the time to come. The black man is trying to kill the white man. But he can't. The tactics of the black man mean that he can't. The high heels on the white man—they are Western civilization. The Bible—it talks about mountains. I think we all have to be Christian. We have been assimilated through Christianity. Religion is a significant thing. In churches we can find all sorts of people. The clock/Bible—as time goes on, people are growing up to have many churches. People are saying: Jesus is coming. But he has never come. Do you think he is going to come? I never saw him. But The Spider is a religious painting.

Across the field a thread of smoke twisted into the early evening sky. Meek locked the hut, and one step outside seemed as if into a wholly different world lying beyond the hearth. The cattle and sheep were silent. Only the birds twittered in the stark sky. The cold, drifting across the high hillside, swept away the raw pain of the paintings; the beauty of the land neutralized the harsh colors, the violence, the nightmarish anxiety. We walked across the *shamba* and into his mother's home, which was warm and dim and smelled of wood smoke. His mother, Lois Wangui, sat in a room where the walls were hung with family photographs. The contrast with her son's studio was startling, and her manner of expressing her appreciation of his work humanized its drama and overpowering impact. "I feel it's nice. I like to look at the paintings. He is my child, and whenever a parent sees what their child is doing, it makes them happy," she said. "We learn from the paintings. We can use the paintings to show our children and the white people what Africa was like. It's a happiness to me. I feel happy to see my son doing things which are fine."[5]

NOTES

PROLOGUE

1. At the polls, on 1 June 1993, Melchior Ndadaye won 64.8 percent of votes as leader of the Front pour la démocratie au Burundi (Frodebu: Front for Democracy in Burundi), compared with the 32.4 percent won by Pierre Buyoya, leader of the Union pour le progrès national (Uprona: Union for National Progress), and the 1.4 percent by Pierre-Claver Sendegeya of the Parti de réconciliation du peuple (PRP: Party of Reconciliation of the People).

2. Frodebu won 65 of the 81 seats, or 71 percent of the votes, compared with Uprona's 16 seats, or 21 percent of the votes, while four other parties failed to gain the minimum 5 percent of the votes necessary to secure a single seat.

3. In September 1991, Maj. Pierre Buyoya, Burundi's military ruler, who had seized power in 1987, presented a report on "national democratization," which was to lay the basis for Burundi's shift to democratic rule after twenty-six years of single-party rule. On 16 April 1992, a law was passed lifting a ban on political parties.

4. A. O. Ikelegbe, "Checks On the Abuse of Political Power," in *African Traditional Political Thought and Institutions*, edited by Zaccheus Sunday Ali, John A.A. Ayoade, and Adigun A.B. Agbaje (Lagos: Centre for Black and African Arts and Civilization, 1989), p. 151.

5. Ali A. Mazrui and Michael Tidy, *Nationalism and New States in Africa* (Nairobi: Heinemann Kenya, 1984), p. 187.

6. Ibid.

7. Ibid., p. 190.

8. See Ibid.

9. Eghosa E. Osaghae, "The Passage from the Past to the Present in African Political Thought: The Question of Relevance," in *African Traditional Political Thought and Institutions*, edited by Zaccheus Sunday Ali, John A.A. Ayoade, and Adigun A.B. Agbaje (Lagos: Centre for Black and African Arts and Civilization, 1989), p. 68.

10. A. O. Ikelegbe, op. cit., pp. 148–151.

11. Olufemi A. Akinola, "The Colonial Heritage and Modern Constitutionalism in Africa," in *African Traditional Political Thought and Institutions*, edited by Zaccheus Sunday Ali, John A.A. Ayoade, and Adigun A.B. Agbaje (Lagos: Centre for Black and African Arts and Civilization, 1989), p. 270.

12. Amadu Sesay and Abiodun Alao, "Democracy and Security in Africa: The Changing Nature of a Linkage," in Adebayo Oyebade and Abiodun Alao, *Africa After the Cold War: The Changing Perspectives on Security* (Trenton, N.J., and Asmara, Eritrea: Africa World Press, 1998), p. 51.

13. U.S. Government policy statement: "Africa: Guidelines for United States Policy and Operation," 1963, quoted in Edgar Lockwood, "Carter's Sometime Southern Africa Policy," in *American Policy in Southern Africa*, second edition, edited by René Lemarchand (Lanham, Md.: University Press of America, 1981), p. 470.

14. For a lucid study of this phenomenon see Liisa H. Malkki, *Purity and Exile: Violence, Memory, and National Cosmology Among Hutu refugees in Tanzania* (Chicago: University of Chicago Press, 1995), chapter 2.

15. Basil Davidson, *The Black Man's Burden* (New York: Times Books, 1992), p. 101.

16. Abiodun Alao and Funmi Olonisakin, "Post Cold War Africa: Ethnicity, Ethnic Conflict and Security," in Adebayo Oyebade and Abiodun Alao, *Africa After the Cold War: The Changing Perspectives on Security* (Trenton, N.J., and Asmara, Eritrea: Africa World Press, 1998), p. 125.

Chapter One

1. Parts of this chapter appeared in Mark Huband, Michael Holman, and Jimmy Burns, "How Mobutu Built Up His $4bn Fortune," *Financial Times*, 12 May 1997, p. 2.

2. Erwin Blumenthal, "Zaire: Report on her International Financial Credibility," unpublished (Washington, D.C.: International Monetary Fund, 1982).

3. John Stockwell, former CIA chief of base, Lubumbashi, Zaire, and chief, CIA Angola Task Force, interview by author, 4 May 1997.

4. Madeleine G. Kalb, *The Congo Cables: The Cold War in Africa from Eisenhower to Kennedy* (New York: Macmillan, 1982).

5. Ibid., p. 7.

6. Ibid., p. 25.

7. William Burden, U.S. ambassador in Brussels, in a cable to the U.S. State Department, 19 July 1960, cited in Kalb, op. cit., p. 27.

8. Crawford Young and Thomas Turner, *The Rise and Decline of the Zairean State* (Madison: University of Wisconsin Press, 1985), p. 364.

9. William Colby, former CIA director, quoted in Michael G. Schatzberg, *Mobutu or Chaos: The United States and Zaire, 1960–1990* (Lanham, Md.: University Press of America, 1991), p. 3.

10. Ibid., pp. 16–17.

11. This isolation was particularly marked when the Soviet Union sought to counter a U.S.-sponsored resolution put before the UN Security Council banning foreign military assistance to all sides in the Congo. African states sided with the United States, undermining Soviet claims to be speaking on behalf of the newly liberated states of Africa.

12. Lawrence Devlin, CIA station chief, Leopoldville, U.S. Congress, Senate, Select Committee to Study Governmental Operations with Respect to Intelligence Activities, *Interim Report: Alleged Assassination Plots Involving Foreign Leaders*, 94th Congress, 1st Session, 20 November 1975, quoted in Stephen Weissman, "The CIA and U.S. Policy in Zaire and Angola," in *American Policy in Southern Africa*, edited by René Lemarchand (Lanham, Md.: University Press of America, 1981), p. 412.

13. Stephen Weissman, "The CIA and U.S. policy in Zaire and Angola," in *American Policy in Southern Africa*, second edition, edited by René Lemarchand (Lanham, Md.: University Press of America, 1981), pp. 444–445.

14. Kalb, op. cit., p. 101.

15. Ibid.

16. Weissman, op. cit., p. 421.

17. René Lemarchand, "The CIA in Africa: How Central? How Intelligent?" in *American Policy in Southern Africa*, op. cit., pp. 401–402.

18. Kalb, op. cit., p. 96.

19. Ibid.

20. Weissman, op. cit., p. 160.

21. Stockwell, op. cit.

22. Kalb, op. cit., p. 141.

23. Ibid., p. 163.

24. Patrice Lumumba, to his friend Anicet Kashamura, 25 November 1960. The entire quotation in translation reads, "If I die, no matter. Congo needs martyrs." Quoted in ibid., p. 157.

25. Ibid., pp. 195–196.

26. Michael G. Schatzberg, *Mobutu or Chaos: The United States and Zaire, 1960–1990* (Lanham, Md.: University Press of America, 1991), p. 26.

27. Kalb, op. cit., p. 205.

28. Quoted in ibid., p. 371.

29. Steve Askin and Carole Collins, "External Collusion with Kleptocracy: Can Zaire recapture its stolen wealth?" *Review of African Political Economy*, no. 57, 1993, pp. 72–85, quoting a variety of sources.

30. Lemarchand, op. cit., p. 404.

31. Young and Turner, op. cit., p. 378.

32. Ibid., n. 31, p. 379.

33. Winsome J. Leslie, *The World Bank and Structural Transformation in Developing Countries: The Case of Zaire* (Boulder: Lynne Rienner Publishers, 1987), p. 72.

34. See Huband, Holman, and Burns, op. cit.

35. Stockwell, op. cit.

36. Roger Morris, "Our Man in Kinshasa," *New Republic*, 7 May 1977.

37. Stockwell, op. cit.

38. Blumenthal, op. cit.

39. Jean-Louis Remilleux, *Mobutu: Dignity for Africa, Interviews with Jean-Louis Remilleux* (Paris: Albin Michel, 1989), p. 182.

40. Blumenthal, op. cit., p. 9.

41. Nguza Karl-i-Bond, *Mobutu ou l'incarnation du Mal Zairois* (London: Rex Collings, 1982), p. 134, my translation.

42. Ibid., p. 136.

43. The Special Drawing Rights (SDR) are the currency equivalent used by the IMF, which at the time of the report converted at a rate of SDR 1: $1.15.

44. Blumenthal, op. cit., p. 10.

45. Askin and Collins, op. cit.

46. Ibid.

47. John Stockwell, letter to Admiral Stansfield Turner, director, CIA, *Washington Post*, 31 March 1977.

48. Ibid.

49. Young and Turner, op. cit., p. 382.

50. Stockwell, op. cit..

51. S. N. Sang-Mpam, "Understanding the Crisis in Peripheral Countries: The Case of Zaire," in *The Crisis in Zaire: Myths and Realities*, edited by Nzongola-Ntalaja (Trenton, N.J., and Asmara, Eritrea: Africa World Press, 1986), p. 47.

52. René Lemarchand, "Zaire: The Unamanageable Client State," in *American Policy In Southern Africa*, op. cit., p. 159.

53. Young and Turner, op. cit., p. 389.

54. *Washington Post*, 21 June 1978.

55. *Washington Post*, 25 June 1978.

56. Young and Turner, op. cit., p. 383.

57. Quoted in Remilleux, op. cit., p. 33.

58. Young and Turner, op. cit., p. 392.

59. Mabele Musamba, MIBA deputy managing director, interview by author, Mbuji-Mayi, 23 October 1994.

60. M. Amuri, Central Bank of Zaire official in charge of diamonds provided this figure, interview by author, Kinshasa, 20 October 1994.

61. Janet McGaffey, *The Real Economy of Zaire: The Contrbution of Smuggling and Other Unofficial Activities to National Wealth* (Philadelphia: University of Pennsylvania Press, 1991), p. 18.

62. Jonas Kadiata Mukamba, president of MIBA, interview by author, Kinshasa, 21 October 1994.

63. Kalb, op. cit., p. 185.

64. Kassembe Etete, vice-governor of East Kasai, interview by author, Mbuji-Mayi, 22 October 1994.

65. Tchbobo Mfuamba, MIBA technical director, interview by author, Mbuji-Mayi, 22 October 1994.

66. Kalonji Mbwebwe, interview by author, Mbuji-Mayi, 23 October 1994.

67. François Kabilenge Mukendi, interview by author, Mbuji-Mayi, 23 October 1994.

68. Louis Kabungo Mukendi, UDPS official, interview by author, Mbuji-Mayi, 23 October 1994.

69. Kengo wa Dondo, prime minister of Zaire, interview by author, Kinshasa, 25 October 1994.

70. Blumenthal, op. cit., p. 13.

71. Gen. Singa, interview by author, Kinshasa, 20 October 1994.

72. Etienne Tshisekedi, interview by author, Kinshasa, 18 October 1994.

Chapter Two

1. Katia Airola, interview by author, Luanda, 26 August 1993.
2. Joe Schriver, U.S. embassy spokesman, interview by author, Luanda, 27 August 1993.
3. The phrase is that of John Stockwell, former chief, CIA Angola Task Force. See John Stockwell, *In Search of Enemies: A CIA Story* (New York: W. W. Norton, 1978; Bridgewater, New Jersey: Replica Books, 1997), chapter 3.
4. Stockwell, op. cit., p. 67.
5. Gerald Bender, "American Policy toward Angola: A History of Linkage," in *African Crisis Areas and U.S. Foreign Policy*, edited by Gerald J. Bender, James S. Coleman, and Richard L. Sklar (Berkeley: University of California Press, 1985), p. 111.
6. Ibid., p. 113.
7. Stockwell, op. cit., pp. 67–68.
8. George Wright, *The Destruction of a Nation: United States' Policy Towards Angola since 1945* (London: Pluto Press, 1997), p. 36.
9. Fernando Andresen Guimaraes, *The Origins of the Angolan Civil War: Foreign Intervention and Domestic Political Conflict* (New York: St. Martin's Press, 1998), p. 183
10. Ibid., p. 63.
11. Fred Bridgeland, *Jonas Savimbi: A Key to Africa* (London: Coronet Books, 1988), p. 143
12. Ibid., pp. 143–144.
13. Stockwell, op. cit., p. 113.
14. Bridgeland, op. cit., p. 149.
15. William Minter, *Apartheid's Contras: An Inquiry into the Roots of War in Angola and Mozambique* (Atlantic Highlands, New Jersey, and Johannesburg: Zed Books and Witwatersrand University Press, 1994), p. 145.
16. Guimaraes, op. cit., p. 163.
17. Ibid.
18. Stockwell, op. cit., pp. 180–181.
19. Chester Crocker, interview by author, Georgetown, 4 February 1993.
20. Stockwell, op. cit., chapter 10.
21. Mario Pinto de Andrade, speaking at the 32nd meeting of the UN Special Commission on Territories under Portuguese Administration, Leopoldville, 24 May 1962. Quoted in Guimaraes, op. cit., p. 169.
22. Quoted in Bridgeland, op. cit., p. 19.
23. Guimaraes, op. cit., p. 176.
24. Ibid., p. 169.
25. Ibid., p. 162.
26. Ibid., p. 172.
27. Ibid., p. 189.
28. Stockwell, op. cit., chapter 8.
29. Ibid., p. 85.
30. Guimaraes, op. cit., p. 185.
31. Leonid Brezhnev, the Soviet leader, and U.S. president Gerald Ford, did at points consider this possibility. Brezhnev appears to have been the most hawkish, portraying the foreign role not as engagement in a civil war but a direct U.S.-USSR confrontation. See Guimaraes, op. cit., p. 175.
32. Ibid.
33. Ibid.
34. Minter, op. cit., p. 103.
35. Ibid., p. 104.
36. Wright, op. cit., p. 58.
37. Ibid.
38. Guimaraes, op. cit., p. 63.
39. Ibid.
40. Bridgeland, op. cit., p. 137.
41. Minter, op. cit., p. 90.
42. Ibid., p. 93.
43. Stockwell, op. cit., p. 90.
44. Wright, op. cit., p. 59, and Guimaraes, op. cit., p. 191.

45. *Africa Report*, no. 19, May–June 1976.

46. Bender, op. cit., p. 114.

47. Republican senator Bill Symms to Congress, 11 June 1985.

48. Wright, op. cit., pp. 128–129.

49. George P. Schultz, Preface, in Chester A. Crocker, *High Noon in Southern Africa: Making Peace in a Rough Neighbourhood* (New York: W. W. Norton, 1993), p. 10.

50. David E. Kyvig, *Reagan and the World* (New York: Praeger, 1990), p. 129.

51. Minter, op. cit., p. 161.

52. Chester Crocker, interview by author, Georgetown, 4 February 1993.

53. The results were issued on 17 October 1992. The United Nations special representative to Angola, Margaret Anstee, concluded that, although there were some irregularities caused by error and inexperience, the result was the conclusion of a free and fair process.

54. Jonas Savimbi, interview by author, Abidjan, 15 December 1990.

55. Ibid.

56. Guimaraes, op. cit., pp. 197–199.

57. Karl Maier, *Angola: Promises and Lies* (London: Serif, 1996), p. 157.

58. Xavier Da Sirva, interview by author, Beira des Salinas, 27 August 1993.

59. To use Karl Maier's devastatingly poignant phrase.

60. Honorio van Dunem, Unita parliamentarian, interview by author, Luanda, 24 August 1993.

61. Maria N'guare, interview by author, Vindongo, southern Angola, 29 August 1993.

62. Domingues Kalende, interview by author, Vindongo, southern Angola, 29 August 1993.

63. Warren Clark, Current Policy no. 1217, October 1989, quoted in Wright, op. cit., p. 149.

64. Crocker, op. cit., p. 61.

65. Ibid.

66. Ibid., p. 64.

67. Minter, op. cit., p. 161.

68. This figure was from a Belgian geologist, Luc Rombouts, who visited Unita areas. The figure is cited in *Africa Confidential*, vol. 40, no. 20.

69. "A Warlord's Best Friend," *Financial Times*, 20/21 May 2000, p. 7.

70. See, for example, Paul Hare, *Angola's Last Best Chance for Peace: An Insider's Account of the Peace Process* (Washington, D.C.: United States Institute for Peace, 1998), pp. 108–109. Hare, a former senior U.S. diplomat, is clear that Savimbi's ambitions were not satisfied by the promise of the second vice-presidential position in the power-sharing government and that consequently the agreement faltered.

71. *Africa Confidential*, vol. 40, no. 21, p. 6.

Chapter Three

1. Chester Crocker, U.S. Assistant Secretary of State for African Affairs (1981–1988), interview by author, Georgetown, 4 February 1993.

2. Parts of this chapter are based on Mark Huband, *The Liberian Civil War* (London: Frank Cass, 1997), chapter 3.

3. Crocker, op. cit.

4. Ibid.

5. Ibid.

6. Senior U.S. State Department official, interview by author, Washington, D.C., 3 February 1993.

7. A. Doris Banks Henries, *The Liberian Nation: A Short History* (Macmillan: New York, 1966), p. 19.

8. Crocker, op. cit.

9. Ibid.

10. Ibid.

11. Herman Cohen, U.S. Assistant Secretary of State for African Affairs (1988–1993), interview by author, Washington, D.C., 9 February 1993.

12. Herman Cohen arranged for Doe to go into exile in Togo.

13. Confirmed by Cohen, op. cit.

14. U.S. State Department official, interview by author, Washington, D.C., 3 February 1993.

15. Crocker, op. cit.

16. James Bishop, former U.S. ambassador to Liberia, interview by author, Washington, D.C., 4 February 1993.

17. U.S. State Department official, interview by author, Washington, D.C., 3 February 1993.

18. Bishop, op. cit.

19. Former senior Liberian minister, interview by author, Freetown, Sierra Leone, 3 November 1990.

20. Crocker, op. cit.

21. Former senior Liberian minister, op. cit.

22. Crocker, op. cit.

23. Senior U.S. State Department official, interview by author, Washington, D.C., 3 February 1993.

24. Memorandum from Maj. John G. Rancey, minister of state, to President Doe, 22 March 1983, copy in author's collection.

25. Senior U.S. State Department official, op. cit.

26. Harry Moniba, interview by author, Freetown, 13 November 1990.

27. Crocker, testimony to U.S. Senate, Foreign Relations Committee Subcommittee on African Affairs, Washington, D.C., 10 December 1985.

28. James Bishop, op. cit.

29. Senior U.S. State Department official, op. cit.

30. Senior U.S. State Department official, op. cit.

31. Former senior Liberian government official, interview by author, Freetown, 14 November 1990.

32. At that time, the Liberian dollar was pegged at a rate of one to one with the U.S. dollar.

33. The project was officially known as the Liberia Economic Stabilization Support Project.

34. Final Report on the Liberia Economic Stabilization Support Project (AFR-0213-C-00-8001-00), (Washington, D.C.: Louis Berger International, 19 May 1989).

35. Ibid., p. 3.

36. Ibid., p. 16.

37. Ibid., p. 21.

38. Crocker, op. cit.

39. Charles Taylor, letter to President Doe, 10 January 1984. Copy in author's collection.

40. Ibid.

41. Tonia King, interview by author, Abidjan, 12 November 1991.

42. Former Liberian NPFL trainee, interviews by author, Abidjan, October–November 1991.

43. Ibid.

44. Herman Cohen, U.S. Assistant Secretary of State for African Affairs (1988–1993), interview by author, Washington, D.C., 9 February 1993.

45. Confirmed by Cohen, ibid.

46. Chester Crocker, op. cit.

Chapter Four

1. Gali Gata N'gothe, interview by author, N'djamena, 16 May 1992.

2. The transition in Nigeria under General Ibrahim Babangida stands out as the most substantial example of this. For an account of this transition see Larry Diamond, Anthony Kirk-Greene, and Oyeleye Oyediran, eds., *Transition Without End: Nigerian Politics and Civil Society Under Babangida* (Boulder: Lynne Rienner Publishers, 1997).

3. This figure is inexact, and is based on estimates by foreign observers and is that used by Catherine Watson, in *Transition in Burundi: The Context for a Homecoming* (Washington, D.C.: U.S. Committee for Refugees, 1993), p. 11. The Burundi government said the number of dead was 80,000.

4. The figure is that of the U.S. State Department, though other estimates put the number of dead at 20,000. See: Catherine Watson, *Transition in Burundi: The Context for a Homecoming*, (Washington D.C., U.S. Committee for Refugees, 1993), p. 15.

5. Sylvie Kinigi was a Tutsi member of the largely Hutu government and also a member of the Parti de l'Union et du Progrès Nationale (Uprona: Party of Union and National Progress). She had been appointed prime minister by Ndadaye as a mark of his determination to create national reconciliation.

6. Martin Sindaru, interview by author, Karengura, Burundi, 27 October 1993.

7. The Twa or BaTwa are the third tribe of Burundi and Rwanda, representing less than 1 percent of the population in both countries.

8. Interview by author, Ngozi, Burundi, 27 October 1993.

9. Burundi was at that time home to 50,000 Rwandan refugees, the vast majority of them Tutsi who had fled Rwanda, either in 1959 when the Hutu majority seized power in Rwanda, or subsequently in 1990 following the invasion of Rwanda by the mainly Tutsi Rwandan Patriotic Front (RPF).

10. Jean-Marie Ngendahayo, information minister in the Ndadaye government, interview by author, Bujumbura, 28 October 1993.

11. The army numbered 15,000 troops.

12. René Lemarchand, *Burundi: Ethnic Conflict and Genocide* (New York: Woodrow Wilson Center Press, 1994), p. 10.

13. Ibid., chapter 1. See also Watson, op. cit., p. 5.

14. Figure provided by Médecins Sans Frontières-Belgium. The United Nations High Commissioner for Refugees put the figure at 324,000 in Rwanda, 214,000 in Tanzania, 21,000 in Zaire, and 100,000 displaced within Burundi's borders.

15. The issue of intervention will be examined closely in Part 4.

16. In November 1871, Stanley, a journalist working for the *New York Herald*, reported that he had "found" Dr. Livingstone at Ujiji on the eastern shore of Lake Tanganyika, while the latter was attempting to find the "fountains of Herodotus," which were the southernmost sources of the River Nile. By the time Stanley discovered Livingstone, the latter had long been presumed to have died of fever.

17. His last words, inscribed on his tomb at Westminster Abbey, London, were: "All I can add in my solitude, is, may heaven's rich blessing come down on everyone, American, English or Turk, who will help to heal this open sore of the world."

18. Thomas Pakenham, *The Scramble for Africa* (London: Abacus Books, 1991), p. 2.

19. Interview by author, Bononi, Burundi, 29 October 1993.

20. Bututsi is the traditional name given to a swathe of the southern part of the country, of which Bururi town is the center. In fact the official name for the province is Bururi, not Bututsi.

21. Father Balthazar Bacinoni, interview by author, Butwe, 29 October 1993.

22. Frederick Nimbesha, interview by author, Murama, Burundi, 30 October 1993.

23. Interview by author, Yanza, Burundi, 30 October 1993.

24. *Africa Confidential*, vol. 34, no. 25, p. 7.

25. Ibid.

26. Burundi's army is essentially designed for domestic security purposes rather than national security. As with most security services in military dictatorships, the primary role of the army is to crush domestic opposition to the incumbent regime.

27. The figure was provided by church officials in Gitega, who were also providing food for those living in the camps.

28. Interview by author, Gitega, Burundi, 30 October 1993.

29. These officers were Lt. Col. Charles Ntakije, the defense minister, Lt. Col. Gakoryo, defense adviser to the presidency, Lt. Didace Nzikoruriho, and Lt. Col. Jean Bikomagu, the army chief of staff. See *Africa Confidential*, vol. 34, no. 25, p. 175.

30. Ibid.

31. Capt. Augustin Nkunda, interview by author, Gitega, Burundi, 30 October 1993.

32. The defense minister was at that time in hiding, having opposed the coup but not feeling confident about reasserting his authority over the military.

33. Cyprien Ntaryamira was killed on 6 April 1994, along with the Rwandan president Juvenal Habyarimana, when the latter's aircraft was shot down over the Rwandan capital, Kigali, the event that led to the beginning of the Rwandan genocide.

34. Ahmedou Ould Abdallah, *La Diplomatie Pyromane: Burundi, Rwanda, Somalie, Bosnie: Entretiens avec Stephen Smith* (Paris: Calmann-Levy, 1996), pp. 35–36. My translation.

Chapter Five

1. Ahmedou Ould Abdallah, *La Diplomatie Pyromane: Burundi, Rwanda, Somalie, Bosnie: Entretiens avec Stephen Smith* (Paris: Calmann-Levy, 1996), pp. 26–27. My translation.

2. René Lemarchand, *Burundi: Ethnic Conflict and Genocide* (New York: Woodrow Wilson Center Press, 1994), p. 16.

3. Ibid., pp. 10–12.
4. Ibid., p. xii.
5. Ibid., pp. 38–39.
6. Ibid., p. 40.
7. Ibid., p. 57.
8. Ibid., p. 62.
9. Samuel Decalo, *Coups and Military Rule in Africa: Motivations and Constraints*, second edition (New Haven: Yale University Press, 1990), p. 4.
10. Lemarchand, op. cit., p. 5.
11. Decalo, op. cit., p. 6.
12. Eghosa E. Osaghae, "The Passage from the Past to the Present in African Political Thought: The Question of Relevance," in *African Traditional Political Thought and Institutions*, edited by Zaccheus Sunday Ali, John A.A. Ayoade, and Adigun A.B. Agbaje (Lagos: Centre for Black African Arts and Civilization, 1989), p. 72.
13. Annual gross domestic product per head in Burundi in 1993 was $259, while in neighboring Rwanda it was $290. Cited in: Glynne Evans, *Responding to Crises in the African Great Lakes*, Adelphi Paper 311 (London: International Institute for Strategic Studies, 1997), p. 20.
14. Pierre Buyoya, interview by author, Bujumbura, 14 January 1994.
15. Sylvie Kinigi, prime minister of Burundi, interview by author, Bujumbura, 31 October 1993.
16. Olufemi A. Akinola, "The Colonial Heritage and Modern Constitutionalism in Africa," in *African Traditional Political Thought and Institutions*, edited by Zaccheus Sunday Ali, John A.A. Ayoade, and Adigun A.B. Agbaje (Lagos: Centre for Black African Arts and Civilization, 1989), pp. 271–273.
17. Pierre Buyoya, interview by author, Bujumbura, 29 March 1995.
18. Pierre Buyoya, interview by author, Bujumbura, 14 January 1994.
19. Lemarchand, op. cit., p. 18.
20. Buyoya, op. cit. (1994).
21. Therese Minani, interview by author, Kigani Camp, Rwanda, 14 January 1994.
22. David Nkurikiye, interview by author, Kigani Camp, Rwanda, 11 January 1994.
23. Manda Tukahataza, interview by author, Burenge Camp, Rwanda, 11 January 1994.
24. Buyoya, op. cit. (1994).
25. Lemarchand, op. cit., pp. 31–32.
26. Lemarchand, op. cit., p. xii.
27. John Hanning Speke, *Journal of the Discovery of the Source of the Nile* (1863; reprint, Mineola, N.Y.: Dover, 1996), p. 241.
28. Ibid., pp. 241–242.
29. Ibid.
30. Ibid.
31. Ibid., p. 244.
32. The phrase is Lemarchand's, from René Lemarchand and David Martin, *Selective Genocide in Burundi* (London: Minority Rights Group, 1974).
33. Liisa H. Malkki, *Purity and Exile: Violence, Memory and National Cosmology among Hutu Refugees in Tanzania* (Chicago: Chicago University Press, 1995), p. 31.
34. Ibid., pp. 59–70.
35. Ibid., p. 68.
36. Ibid., p. 242.
37. Pierre Buyoya, interview by author, Bujumbura, 29 March 1995.
38. Buyoya, op. cit. (1994).
39. Lemarchand, op. cit., p. xxiii.

CHAPTER SIX

1. For the purpose of this analysis I shall use the name Zaire until events reach the point in 1998 when the name was changed to the Democratic Republic of Congo, which I shall refer to as Congo.
2. Etienne Tshisekedi, leader of Union démocratique pour le progrès sociale (UDPS), interview by author, Kinshasa, 29 July 1991.

3. *Dignity for Africa* is part of the title of a flattering series of interviews with Mobutu: Jean-Louis Remilleux, *Mobutu: Dignity for Africa, Interviews with Jean-Louis Remilleux* (Paris: Albin Michel, 1989).

4. Thomas Turner, "Zaire: Flying High Above the Toads: Mobutu and Stalemated Democracy," in *Political Reform in Francophone Africa*, edited by John F. Clark and David E. Gardinier (Boulder: Westview Press, 1997), p. 248.

5. Crawford Young and Thomas Turner, *The Rise and Decline of the Zairian State* (Madison: University of Wisconsin Press, 1985), p. 189.

6. Ibid., p. 208.

7. Ibid.

8. Mobutu Sese Seko, *Mobutu: Discours, allocutions, messages, 1965–1975, Part 2* (Paris: Editions J.A., 1975), pp. 100–101, quoted in Young and Turner, op. cit., p. 211.

9. Ibid., p. 215.

10. See Ibid.

11. Nguza Karl-i-Bond, leader of the UFERI, interview by author, Kinshasa, 30 July 1991.

12. Tshisekedi was appointed on 21 July 1991.

13. Etienne Tshisekedi, interview by author, Kinshasa, 29 July 1991.

14. Senior foreign military officer, interview by author, Kinshasa, 29 October 1991.

15. Ibid.

16. Michael G. Schatzberg, *The Dialectics of Oppression in Zaire* (Bloomington: Indiana University Press, 1991), p. 58.

17. Ibid., pp. 55–56.

18. Ibid., p. 67.

19. Ibid., p. 68.

20. Ibid., pp. 69–70.

21. A presidential ordinance initiating the restructuring was issued on 17 October 1991.

22. Mulumba Lukodji, prime minister of Zaire, interview by author, Kinshasa, 27 September 1991.

23. Ibid.

24. Kabuya Lumuna, professor of sociology, Kinshasa University, and later an adviser to President Mobutu, interview by author, Kinshasa, 3 October 1991.

25. President Mobutu, radio address, Kinshasa, 25 September 1991.

26. General Singa Boyenge, interview by author, Kinshasa, 20 October 1994.

27. Ibid.

28. Ibid.

29. Etienne Tshisekedi, interview by author, Kinshasa, 5 October 1991.

30. *Libération* 7 October 1991.

31. Tshisekedi, op. cit. (October, 1991).

32. President Mobutu, interview by author, N'Sele, Zaire, 27 October 1991.

33. C. Odumegwu Ojukwu, *Biafra, Random Thoughts of C. Odumegwu Ojukwu, General of the People's Army* (New York: Harper and Row, 1969), pp. 140–142.

34. Samuel Decalo, *Coups and Military Rule in Africa: Motivations and Constraints*, second edition (New Haven: Yale University Press, 1990), p. 2.

35. Larry Diamond, Anthony Kirk-Greene, and Oyeleye Oyediran, *Transition Without End: Nigerian Politics and Civil Society Under Babangida* (Boulder: Lynne Rienner Publishers, 1997), p. 3.

36. Jimi Peters, *The Nigerian Military and the State* (London: International Library of African Studies, Tauris Academic Studies, I. B. Tauris, 1997), p. 167.

37. Ibid., p. 169.

38. Paul A. Beckett, "Elections and Democracy in Nigeria," in *Elections in Independent Africa*, edited by Fred M. Hayward (Boulder: Westview Press, 1978), p. 104, quoted in Peters, ibid., p. 172.

39. Peters, op. cit., p. 167.

40. Gen. Buhari explained this motivation at a press conference on 1 January 1984. Ibid., p. 187.

41. Ibid., p. 189.

42. Ibid., pp. 188–190.

43. Ibid., p. 217.

44. Adigun Agbaje, "Mobilizing for a New Political Culture," in Diamond et al., op. cit., p. 143.

45. J. Bayo Adekanye, "The Military," in Diamond et al., op. cit., p. 59.

46. Ibid., p. 64.

47. Ibid., p. 65.

48. Ibid., p. 66.

49. Ibid., p. 72.

50. Ibid., p. 66, quoting an address by Gen. Babangida given at the chief of army staff annual conference, 25 January 1988.

51. Structural Adjustment Program, which was introduced in June 1986 and was widely denounced as an overly harsh method of trying to reverse Nigeria's economic decline.

52. Adekanye, op. cit., p. 75.

53. Chief Moshood Abiola, the presumed winner of the 1993 election.

54. Abiodun Alao and Funmi Olonisakin, "Post Cold War Africa: Ethnicity, Ethnic Conflict and Security," in *Africa After the Cold War: Changing Perspectives on Security*, edited by Adebayo Oyebade and Abiodun Alao (Trenton, N.J. and Asmara, Eritrea: Africa World Press, 1998), p. 137.

55. Toyin Falola, A. Ajayi, A. Alao, and B. Babawale, *The Military Factor in Nigeria, 1966–1985*, African Studies, vol. 35 (Lewiston, N.Y.: Edwin Mellen Press, 1994), p. 72.

56. Ibid., p. 74.

57. *Africa Confidential*, vol. 33, no. 4, p. 3.

58. Bola A. Akinterinwa, "The 1993 Presidential Election Imbroglio," in Diamond et al., op. cit., p. 260.

59. *Africa Confidential*, vol. 34, no. 14, p. 1.

60. Gen. Ibrahim Babangida, address to the nation, 26 June 1993.

61. *Africa Confidential*, op. cit. (34).

62. Ken Saro-Wiwa, a writer, was the leader of the Movement for the Survival of the Ogoni People (Mosop), whose lives and livelihoods were and remain severely threatened by the environmental degradation of the Niger delta caused by the activities of national and international oil companies in the area. Mosop demanded $10 billion in compensation from the Nigerian federal government. To silence the organization, Saro-Wiwa and eight other Ogoni activists were hanged in November 1995, after being found guilty of what was widely believed to have been a trumped-up murder charge.

63. Amadu Sesay and Abiodun Alao, "Democracy and Security in Africa: The Changing Nature of Linkage," in Oyebade and Alao, op. cit., p. 47.

CHAPTER SEVEN

1. Parts of this chapter are adapted from Mark Huband, *The Liberian Civil War* (London: Frank Cass, 1997), chapters 14 and 15.

2. Basil Davidson, *The Black Man's Burden* (New York: Times Books, 1992), pp. 245–247.

3. A. O. Ikelegbe, "Checks on the Abuse of Political Power," in *African Traditional Political Thought and Institutions*, edited by Zaccheus Sunday Ali, John A.A. Ayoade, and Adigun A.B. Agbaje (Lagos: Centre for Black and African Arts and Civilization, 1989), p. 142.

4. Ibid., p. 141.

5. Davidson, op. cit., p. 245.

6. Charles Taylor, press conference, Bamako, 29 November 1990.

7. Bamako, 27 November 1990.

8. For a full account, see Huband, op. cit.

9. President Samuel Doe was killed after being captured in Monrovia by the Independent National Patriotic Front of Liberia led by Prince Johnson, on 9 September 1990. The INPFL had split from Taylor's NPFL a few days after the December 1989 incursion.

10. The name given to troops sent to Liberia in late August 1990 by countries of the Economic Community of West African States (Ecowas), the main West African regional grouping.

11. Stephen Ellis, "Liberia's Warlord Insurgency," in *African Guerillas*, edited by Christopher Clapham (Oxford and Kampala: James Currey and Fountain Publishers, 1998), p. 163.

12. Huband, op. cit., pp. 52–59.

13. Ibid., pp. 48, 51–62.

14. Secret Ecomog report on Doe's visit to the Ecomog headquarters in Monrovia, 9 September 1990 (author's collection). Doe was captured by Prince Johnson's INPFL during this visit and later tortured. He died from his wounds.

15. Amos Sawyer, president of the IGNU, interview by author, Freetown, 6 November 1990.

16. Dogolea died in suspicious circumstances in 2000, amid accusations that he had been poisoned. Taylor vigorously denied any responsibility.

17. Inaugural sermon for the installation of Charles Taylor as the self-styled president of Liberia, Gbarnga, 23 October 1990.

18. See Huband, op. cit., chapter 3, as well as discussion in Chap. 3, above.

19. Ibid., chapter 4.

20. Most significant among them was Samuel Dokie, a former minister under Samuel Doe, who had fallen out with Doe and gone into exile. Dokie was a Mano from Nimba county, and was instrumental in organizing support for the NPFL among the Mano. See Huband, op. cit., pp. 32–33 and chapter 6.

21. See Huband, op. cit., chapters 9–14.

22. Two tribes from northern Liberia, whose members were generally sympathetic to the NPFL.

23. Gen. Henry Dubar, AFL chief of staff before Bowen.

24. The southern Liberian tribe, of which President Samuel Doe and many senior military officers were members.

25. Charles Taylor, interview by author, Gbarnga, 23 October 1990.

26. See Huband, op. cit., p. 212.

27. Isaac Roberts, AFL officer, interview by author, Monrovia, 7 April 1992.

28. Among the tribes who were victimized by the Krahn were the Gio, Mano, and Loma.

29. See Huband, op. cit., pp. 137–138, 175, 204.

30. J. Barcee Cooper, AFL officer, interview by author, Monrovia, 8 April 1992.

31. Stephen Ellis, *The Mask of Anarchy: The Destruction of Liberia and the Religious Dimension of an African Civil War* (London: Hurst, 1999), p. 214.

32. A zoe is a traditional elder of the Poro society, a secret brotherhood through which individuals can evoke ancestral power. Women have an equivalent in the Sande society.

33. Ellis, op. cit., (1999) p. 261.

34. Ibid., pp. 263–264.

35. Bowen, General Hezekiah, interview by author, 2 April 1991.

36. Elijah McCarthy, NPFL fighter, interview by author, Monrovia, 6 April 1992.

37. John Nimley, National Readjustment Commission, interview by author, Monrovia, 6 April 1992.

38. Boima Brown, AFL fighter, interview by author, Monrovia, 7 April 1992.

39. For discussion of the significance of dreams in Liberian culture, see Ellis, op. cit., (1999) p. 267.

40. Isaac Roberts, INPFL fighter, interview by author, Monrovia, 8 April 1992.

41. An example of the diminution of this traditional authority came in early 1990, when a traditional country devil, also called a Bush Devil (a figure who traditionally plays the role of arbiter, as well as being a link with the power of the ancestors) was invited to try and heal the rift which led to the Liberian rebel movement, the NPFL, splitting. The attempt failed, and the country devil was shot at by one of the sides.

42. Ibid.

CHAPTER EIGHT

1. Monsignor Classe, an adviser to the Belgian colonial administration, writing in 1927. Quoted in Gérard Prunier, *The Rwanda Crisis: History of a Genocide* (London: Hurst, 1995), p. 26.

2. For more discussion of this issue see Chapter 5, above.

3. Alain Destexhe, *Rwanda and Genocide in the Twentieth Century* (New York: New York University Press, 1995), p. 40.

4. Ibid., p. 41.

5. Liisa H. Malkki, *Purity and Exile: Violence, Memory, and National Cosmology Among Hutu Refugees in Tanzania* (Chicago: University of Chicago Press, 1995), p. 28.

6. See Prunier, op. cit., pp. 14–15.

7. Rwanda gained independence on 1 July 1962.

8. Malkki, op. cit., p. 31.

9. Newbury's spelling. See note 10 following.

10. Catharine Newbury, *The Cohesion of Oppression: Clientship and Ethnicity in Rwanda, 1860–1960* (New York: Columbia University Press, 1988), p. 51.

11. Ibid., p. 52.

12. Ibid., p. 212.

13. My italics.

14. Prunier, op. cit., p. 21.

15. Ibid., p. 31.

16. Ibid., p. 34.

17. Ibid., p. 42.

18. Michel Elias and Danielle Helbig, "Deux milles collines pour les petits et les grands," *Politique Africaine*, vol. 17, no. 42, June 1991, quoted in Destexhe, op. cit., p. 43.

19. See Prunier, op. cit., pp. 61–63, for discussion of these figures.

20. The Belgian colonialists had worked on the basis of a population which was 84 percent Hutu, 15 percent Tutsi, and 1 percent Twa.

21. Ibid., p. 82.

22. Literally "cockroaches" in Kinyarwanda.

23. For full accounts of the Rwandan role in the NRA, see Ogenga Otunnu, "An Historical Analysis of the Invasion by the Rwandan Patriotic Army (RPA)," in *The Path of a Genocide: The Rwanda Crisis from Uganda to Zaire*, edited by Howard Adelman and Astri Suhrke (New Brunswick, Can.: Transaction Publishers, 1999), pp. 31–49, and Prunier, op. cit., pp. 67–74.

24. Prunier, op. cit., pp. 71–72.

25. See Prunier, op. cit., chapter three; Dixon Kamukama, *Rwanda Conflict: Its Roots and Regional Implications*, second edition (Kampala: Fountain Publishers, 1997); Colette Braeckman, *Rwanda: Histoire d'un genocide* (Paris: Fayard, 1994); Ogenga Otunnu, op. cit.

26. Bruce D. Jones, "The Arusha Peace Process," in *The Path of a Genocide: The Rwanda Crisis from Uganda to Zaire*, edited by Howard Adelman and Astri Suhrke (New Brunswick, Can.: Transaction Publishers, 1999), p. 136.

27. The five main opposition parties, with dates of foundation and founding leaders: Union du Peuple Rwandais (UPR: Union of the Rwandan People), 1990, Silas Mayjambere; Mouvement Démocratique Républicaine (MDR: Democratic Republican Movement), 1991, Faustin Rucogoza; *Parti Social Démocratique* (PSD: Social Democratic Party), 1991, Frederick Nsamwambaho; Parti Libéral (PL: Liberal Party), 1991, Justin Mugenzi; *Parti Démocrate Chrétien* (PDC: Democratic Christian Party), 1991, Nayinzira Nepomuscen.

28. The Rwandan Patriotic Army was officially the armed force of the RPF political movement.

29. Joan Kakwenzire and Dixon Kamukama, "The Development and Consolidation of Extremist Forces in Rwanda 1990–1994," in Adelman and Suhrke, op. cit., p. 71.

30. Ibid., p. 73.

31. That is, the Hutu.

32. Nkiko Nsengimana, interview by author, Kigali, 10 January 1994.

33. Maj. Gen. Paul Kagame, vice chairman of the RPF and chairman of the RPA military high command, later minister of defense of Rwanda, then president, interview by author, Mulindi, Rwanda, 8 January 1994.

34. Justin Mugenzi, leader of the Parti Libérale and minister of commerce, interview by author, Kigali, 10 January 1994.

35. Ibid.

36. Prunier, op. cit., p. 152.

37. Kagame, op. cit.

38. Ibid.

39. Prunier, op. cit., pp. 194–195.

40. The Clan de Madame was composed essentially of Agathe Kanzinga's three brothers, Col. Pierre-Celestin Rwagafilita, Protais Zigiranyirazo, and Seraphin Rwabukumba, as well as her cousin Elie Sagatwa, and three other close confidantes: Col. Laurent Serubuga, Noel Mbonabaryi, and Col. Theoneste Bagasora.

41. Prunier, op. cit., p. 167.

42. Janvier Afrika, interview by author, Nairobi, 7 June 1994.

43. Afrika, op. cit.

44. Ibid.

45. Kajuga was given a Toyota dealership and a Mercedes by Habyarimana, and he led the militia despite the fact that his uncle was a leading member of the RPF.

46. Afrika, op. cit.

47. Ibid.

48. The United Nations Assistance Mission to Rwanda (UNAMIR) was created by UN vote on 25 September 1993, and the first troops arrived in November 1993.

49. Charles Ntampaka, secretary-general, Rwandan Association of Jurists, interview by author, Kigali, 10 January 1994.

50. Literally, a "state of rights," meaning a state with constitutional rule.

51. Kagame, op. cit.

52. Patrick Mazimpaka, RPF first vice president, interview by author, Mulindi, Rwanda, 9 April 1994.

CHAPTER NINE

1. With the outbreak of violence on the night 6 April 1994, few Rwandan journalists remained in contact with the agencies, newspapers, and broadcast media to which they had supplied news. The sole foreign journalist in Kigali at that time was Lindsay Hilsum of the BBC.

2. Theogene Rudasingwa, secretary-general of the RPF, interview by author, Mulindi, Rwanda, 8 April 1994.

3. Ibid.

4. Reference to the 600-strong RPF battalion stationed at the CND building as part of the Arusha accord. When the genocide erupted and the government forces launched an attack on the CND, the RPF troops stationed there became the front line forces of the RPF until reinforcement troops reached the city, as the RPF occupied territory in April and May 1994.

5. Patrick Mazimpaka, RPF first vice president, interview by author, Rwamagana, 3 May 1994.

6. Ibid.

7. For an assessment of the different theories regarding the shooting down of Habyarimana's aircraft, see Prunier Gérard, *The Rwanda Crisis: History of a Genocide* (London: Hurst, 1995), pp. 213–229.

8. Captain Bruno Vandriessche, interview by author, Kigali, 11 April 1994.

9. Ibid., p. 229.

10. Prunier says, though without giving details, that some elements of the Rwandan army actively attempted to stop the slaughter on 7–8 April and fought with the Presidential Guard to this end. It is not clear whether these elements within the army were Tutsi.

11. The term used by Hutu extremists for the Hutu majority, to justify Hutu domination of the kind that motivated the 1959 revolution.

12. MRND(D) was the party led by President Habyarimana, also abbreviated to MRNDD.

13. Prunier, op. cit., p. 231.

14. Col. Theoneste Bagasora, *Chef de Cabinet*, Ministry of Defense, interview by author, Kigali, 13 April 1994.

15. Maj. Gen. Romeo Dallaire, commander of the UNAMIR military observer force, interview by author, Kigali, 14 April 1994.

16. *Observer*, 1 May 1994, p. 12.

17. Therese Uwiligyamana, interview by author, Rukara, 30 April 1994.

18. Agathe Nsengimira, interview by author, Gahini, 30 April 1994.

19. Perhaps leaving aside the slaughter of Japanese when the United States dropped atomic bombs on Hiroshima and Nagasaki in 1945.

20. Capt. Diogene Mudenge, RPF, interview by author, 30 April 1994.

21. Marcel Gerin, interview by author, Gahini, 30 April 1994.

22. During early May 1994, Benaco became home to 250,000 mainly Hutu refugees, fleeing the advance of the RPF.

23. Interview by author, Rusumo, 1 May 1994.

24. Maj. Philbert Rwigamba, RPF, interview by author, Gasogi Hill, 2 May 1994.

25. Faustin Nsengimana, interview by author, Kabuga, 2 May 1994.

26. Maj. Gen. Romeo Dallaire, interview by author, Kibungo, 2 May 1994.

27. Mazimpaka, op. cit.

28. Theogene Rudasingwa, RPF, press conference, Nairobi, 26 May 1994.

29. Maj. Gen. Paul Kagame, interview by author, Rusumo, 4 May 1994.

30. Agnes Nyamahore, interview by author, Rwamagana, 7 May 1994.

31. Frederick Rubwejanga, bishop of Rwamagana, interview by author, Rwamagana, 7 May 1994.

32. Lt. Wenceslas, Gendarmerie Nationale, Kigali, interview by author, 13 May 1994.

33. Robert Kajuka, interview by author, Kigali, 13 May 1994.

34. Ibid.

35. Abdul Kabia, executive director, Unamir, interview by author, Kigali, 13 May 1994.

36. George Ruggiu, official at Radio Libre des Milles Collines, interview by author, Kigali, 14 May 1994.

37. Bernard Kouchner, interview on Radio Rwanda, Kigali, 14 May 1994.

38. Festus Byaruhango, interview by author, Kamonyi, Rwanda, 14 May 1994.

39. Jean Kambanda, prime minister of the Rwandan interim government, interview by author, Muvambi, 15 May 1994.

40. Ibid.

41. Col. Theoneste Bagasora, interview by author, Muvambi, 15 May 1994.

42. Theodore Sindikabwabo, Rwandan interim president, interview by author, Muvambi, 15 May 1994.

43. Severin Mugenzi, interview by author, Kirundo, Burundi, 25 May 1994.

44. Interview by author, Ngenda, 26 May 1994.

45. Annonciata Umupfasoni, interview by author, Nyamata, 26 May 1994.

46. Col. Alexis Kanyarangwe, RPF chairman, interview by author, 27 May 1994.

47. Cecile Uwamwezi, interview by author, Kicikiru, 28 May 1994.

48. Maj. Gen. Paul Kagame, interview by author, Kabuga, 28 May 1994.

49. Joseph Bukwavu, interview by author, Kabuga, 28 May 1994.

50. *Africa Confidential*, vol.35, no.9, p. 5.

51. Felicien Turatsinze, interview by author, Kabuga, 28 May 1994.

52. Justin Mugenzi, interview by author, 10 January 1994.

53. Julienne Mukanyarwaya, interview by author, Kabuga, 28 May 1994.

54. Justin Mbongata, interview by author, Kabuga, 28 May 1994.

CHAPTER TEN

1. Henri Konan Bedie, president of Cote d'Ivoire, 1993–1999, in a speech, Abidjan, Cote d'Ivoire, date unknown.

2. For a lucid study of this phenomenon, see Liisa H. Malkki, *Purity and Exile: Violence, Memory, and National Cosmology Among Hutu Refugees in Tanzania* (Chicago: University of Chicago Press, 1995).

3. Basil Davidson, *The Black Man's Burden* (New York: Times Books, 1992), p. 101.

4. Ibid., pp. 182–183.

5. Abiodun Alao and Funmi Olonisakin, "Post Cold War Africa: Ethnicity, Ethnic Conflict and Security," in *Africa After the Cold War: The Changing Perspectives on Security*, edited by Adebayo Oyebade and Abiodun Alao (Trenton, N.J., and Asmara, Eritrea: Africa World Press, 1998), p. 125.

6. René Lemarchand and David Martin, *Selective Genocide in Burundi* (London: Minority Rights Group, 1994), p. 183.

7. Ibid., p. 187.

8. "Between a brother and a friend, the choice is clear," President Mobutu said in an address to the United Nations on 4 October 1973, when he announced that Zaire was cutting off diplomatic relations with Israel, on the implied grounds that his basic loyalty was to his Arab "brothers" rather than to his Israeli friends. The phrase was subsequently applied to many other aspects of Mobutism, in particular with regard to the tribal inner circle he retained as his closest advisers and confidantes.

9. Crawford Young and Thomas Turner, *The Rise and Decline of the Zairian State* (Madison: University of Wisconsin Press, 1985), pp. 142–143.

10. Ibid., p. 147.

11. For the most detailed and fascinating account of this period see Madeleine G. Kalb, *The Congo Cables: The Cold War in Africa from Eisenhower to Kennedy* (New York: Macmillan, 1962).

12. Mwabila Malela, "Pour une relecture de la sociologie à la lumière de la théorie de la dépendance," in *La dépendance de l'Afrique et les moyens d'y remédier*, edited by V. Y. Mudimbe (Paris: Berger-Levrault, 1980), pp. 266–267, quoted in Young and Turner, op. cit., pp. 161–162. Translation mine.

13. Kabuya Lumuna, interview by author, Kinshasa, 3 October 1991.

14. Johannes Fabian, *Language and Colonial Power: The Appropriation of Swahili in the Former Belgian Congo, 1880–1938* (Berkeley: University of California Press, 1986), p. 137.

15. 30 July 1991.

16. Young and Turner, op. cit., p. 157.

17. Ibid.

18. Nguza Karl-i-Bond, interview by author, Kinshasa, 30 July 1991.

19. See Chapter 6.

20. Gen. Singa Boyenge, interview by author, Kinshasa, 20 October 1994.

21. Ibid.

22. The term is Michael G. Schatzberg's. See Michael G. Schatzberg, *The Dialectics of Oppression in Zaire* (Bloomington: Indiana University Press, 1991), chapter 5.

23. Nguza Karl-i-Bond, interview by author, Kinshasa, 26 September 1991.

24. Nguza Karl-i-Bond, *Mobutu, Ou l'Incarnation du Mal Zairois* (London: Rex Collings, 1982), p. iii, my translation.

25. Ibid., p. 39, my translation.

26. Mobutu's declaration of himself as Maréchal of Zaire was the closest he came to adopting the role of a sovereign.

27. Kengo wa Dondo, interview by author, Kinshasa, 2 October 1992.

28. Ibid.

29. Ibid.

30. The abacost was a form of formal dress introduced following the inauguration of authenticité in 1973. It was intended to mark a departure from European forms of dress, the name literally derived from the phrase *à bas le costume*, "down with the suit." The abacost consisted of a jacket that buttoned to the neck and had a wide collar, made either from plain material or in brightly colored fabric.

31. Albert-Henri Buisine, interview by author, N'sele, Zaire, 2 November 1991.

32. Mobutu Sese Seko, president of Zaire, interview by author, Kamanyola, N'sele, Zaire, 2 November 1991.

33. Nguza Karl-i-Bond, interview by author, Kinshasa, 30 July 1991.

34. Father Jose Mpundu, interview by author, Kinshasa, 4 August 1991.

35. Ibid.

36. Lumuna, op. cit.

37. Kengo wa Dondo, op. cit.

38. Ibid.

39. Mashala Kabumba, interview by author, Likasi, Shaba, 5 October 1992

40. Choni Claude Mwana, president of the refugee commission in Likasi, interview by author, Likasi, 5 October 1992.

41. Ibid.

42. Two inquiries were launched into the violence, one sent by the national conference and the other by the security forces.

43. Jacques Kote Tshilembe, provincial director of the UDPS party in Shaba, interview by author, Lubumbashi, 4 October 1992.

44. Gabriel Kyungu wa Kumwanza, governor of Shaba, interview by author, Lubumbashi, 4 October 1992

45. Tshilembe, op. cit..

46. David Throup and Charles Hornsby, *Multi-Party Politics in Kenya* (Oxford and Nairobi: James Currey and East African Educational Publishers, 1998), p. 80.

47. George Kamwesa, deputy secretary-general of the National Council of Churches of Kenya, interview by author, Eldoret, 21 April 1993.

48. Ibid.

49. Of these, 188 were elected and 12 nominated by the president.

50. Throup and Hornsby, op. cit., p. 175.

51. Kenya had been a multiparty state on independence in 1960. A multiparty state existed until 1964. Multipartyism was then revived between 1966 and 1969, when the Kenya Peoples' Union was banned and the single-party state under Jomo Kenyatta reimposed.

52. When FORD's creation was officially announced on 4 July 1991, its executive revealed the extent to which a balanced tribal-regional character lay at the heart of the party planners' strategy. Thus,

all but two of Kenya's eight provinces were represented, in the form of Jaramogi Oginga Odinga (Nyanza), Martin Shikuku (Western Province), Masinde Muliro (Rift Valley), Philip Gachoka (Central Province), George Nthenge (Eastern Province), Ahmed Salim Bamhariz (Coast Province).

53. Throup and Hornsby, op. cit., p. 163.

54. Paul Muite, first vice chairman of FORD, interview by author, Nairobi, 31 July 1992.

55. Ibid.

56. Raila Odinga, FORD executive committee member, interview by author, Nairobi, 23 August 1992.

57. This phrase was coined by William ole Ntimana, the minister for local government, as reported in *Weekly Review*, Nairobi, 13 September 1991, pp. 5–15.

58. Kitale, interview by author, 23 April 1993.

59. National Council of Churches of Kenya, *The Cursed Arrow: Organised Violence Against Democracy in Kenya* (Nairobi: National Council of Churches of Kenya, April 1992).

60. So called owing to the committee chairman being J. Kennedy Kiliku, M.P.

61. Republic of Kenya, *Report of the Parliamentary Select Committee to investigate Ethnic Clashes in Western and other parts of Kenya* (Nairobi: Republic of Kenya, September 1992), p. 75.

62. Mark Mereng, Pokot herdsman, interview by author, Kolongolo, Trans-Nzoia, Kenya, 24 April 1993.

63. Isaac Baraza, interview by author, Trans-Nzoia, 24 April 1993.

64. Paul Kibate, interview by author, Endebess Camp, Trans-Nzoia, Kenya, 25 April 1993.

65. Kamwesa, op. cit.

66. Father Peter Elun'gata, interview by author, Burnt Forest Catholic Church, Uasin Gishu, Kenya, 23 April 1993.

67. The other areas were Molo and Londiani.

68. The GSU is a paramilitary unit of the Kenyan security forces. It is renowned for its brutality and is regularly used by the government to attack and intimidate political opposition.

69. Tribal oathing is widespread in Kenya. By taking an oath, an individual promises to defend the tribe against all external threats.

70. Elun'gata, op. cit.

71. Olushola Isinkaiye, "African Presidential Systems," in *African Traditional Political Thought and Institutions*, edited by Zaccheus Sunday Ali, John A.A. Ayoade, and Adigun A.B. Agbaje (Lagos: Centre for Black African Arts and Civilization, 1989), p. 309–311.

72. Throup and Hornsby explain KANU's victory in 1992 as the result of the divisions in the opposition, of KANU's more widespread presence having been established, and of electoral fraud on a sufficient scale to ensure that genuine contests went KANU's way. See Throup and Hornsby, op. cit., p. 453.

73. Chinua Achebe, *Anthills of the Savannah* (London: William Heinemann, 1987), p. 141.

Chapter Eleven

1. Garry Wills, "Bully of the Free World," *Foreign Policy*, vol. 78, no. 2, March/April 1999, p. 59.

2. Samuel P. Huntington, "The Lonely Superpower," *Foreign Policy*, vol. 78, no. 2, March/April 1999.

3. Parts of this chapter have been adapted from Mark Huband, *Warriors of the Prophet: The Struggle for Islam* (Boulder: Westview Press, 1999).

4. Huntington, op. cit.

5. Koran, surat 43, verse 61.

6. J. Spencer Trimingham, *Islam in the Sudan* (London: Frank Cass, 1949), p. 151.

7. P. M. Holt and M. W. Daly, *The History of The Sudan, From the Coming of Islam to the Present Day* (London: Weidenfeld and Nicholson, 1979), p. 148.

8. Omar Hassan el-Bashir, president of Sudan, interview by author, Khartoum, 15 December 1993.

9. Hassan el-Tourabi, interview by author, Khartoum, 15 December 1993.

10. Ghazi Salah Eddin Atabani, minister of state for foreign affairs, Sudan, interview by author, Khartoum, 29 April 1995.

11. Interview by author, Nairobi, 19 April 1995.

12. The Oslo agreement, brokered by the Norwegian government and signed by the Palestinian Liberation Authority and Israel, established the principle that Israel would withdraw from areas of Palestine it had occupied during the 1967 Arab-Israeli war and would recognize the establishment of an independent Palestinian state in the West Bank and Gaza Strip. In return, Arab states would move toward the normalization of their relations with Israel, including measures to allow Israel to be assured of its external security.

13. Mounir Said, Khartoum representative of the Palestinian Hamas Islamic Resistance, interview by author, Khartoum, 30 April 1995.

14. Baha Al-Din Hanafi, interview by author, Khartoum, 13 December 1993.

15. Yossef Bodansky, *Bin Laden: The Man Who Declared War on America* (Rocklin, Calif.: Forum, 1999), p. 67.

16. Ibid., p. 69.

17. Ibid., p. 68.

18. Ibid., p. 72.

19. Mohamed Farah Aideed, interview by author, Bardera, Somalia, 20 September 1992.

20. Bodansky, op. cit., p. 55.

21. Ibid., p. 83.

22. Ibid., pp. 85–86.

23. Osama Bin Laden, "Declaration of Jihad On the Americans Occupying the Country of the Two Sacred Places," Khurasan, Afghanistan, 23 August 1996. Unpublished. In the author's collection.

24. Hassan el-Tourabi, interview by author, Khartoum, 3 June 1997.

25. Mohamed Ahamed Abdelgadir al-Arabab, a former provincial state minister who fled the country in March 1995, interview by author, Asmara, Eritrea, 5 May 1995.

26. Idriss Mohamed Idriss, activist in the Eritrean *al-jihad al-islamiyya* movement, interview by author, Kashm el-Girba, Sudan, 3 May 1995.

27. Ibid.

28. Even Bodansky admits this, in part blaming the failure of the ill-fated U.S. attempt to capture Mohamed Farah Aideed, on 3 October 1993, on an intelligence tip which "was only a trap set for the Americans." Bodansky, op. cit., p. 85.

29. Abel Aleir, *Southern Sudan: Too Many Agreements Dishonoured* (Exeter, UK: Ithaca Press, 1990), p. 267.

30. Ibid., p. 268.

31. Ibid., p. 284.

32. Donald Petterson, *Inside Sudan: Political Islam, Conflict and Catastrophe* (Boulder: Westview Press, 1999), p. 139.

33. Ibid., p. 177.

34. Osman Khalid Mudawi, interview by author, Khartoum, 26 August 1998.

35. Hassan Maki Muhammed, dean of the Centre for Research and African Studies, The International University of Africa, interview by author, Khartoum, 26 August 1998.

36. Ibid.

37. This was confirmed to me by a British diplomat in Khartoum.

38. This was confirmed to me by a senior Sudanese minister in Khartoum.

39. European diplomat, interview by author, Khartoum, 25 August 1998.

40. Ghazi Salah Eddin Atabani, interview by author, Khartoum, 25 August 1998.

41. Amr Moussa, Cairo, 21 August 1998.

42. Hassan el-Tourabi, interview by author, Khartoum, 26 August 1998.

43. Susan Rice and David Scheffer, "Why Sudan's Charm Offensive Puts U.S. Off," *The East African*, 28 September 1999.

44. See, for example Human Rights Watch/Africa, *Civilian Devastation: Abuses by All Parties in the War in Southern Sudan* (New York: Human Rights Watch, 1994).

45. Rice and Scheffer, op. cit.

46. Statement by Peter Bell, president of Care USA, *Atlanta Journal-Constitution*, 7 October 1999.

47. Jimmy Carter, ibid.

48. Former CIA officer, telephone interview by author, 8 October 1999.

49. Ali Osman Taha, minister for external relations, letter to Madeleine Albright, 15 February 1997. Copy in author's collection.

50. Madeleine Albright, secretary of state, letter to Ali Osman Taha, 15 May 1997. Copy in author's collection.

51. Lt. Gen. Gutbi el-Mahdi, director general, External Security Bureau, letter to David Williams, Middle East and North Africa Dept., FBI, 2 May 1998. Copy in author's collection.

52. David Williams, letter to Lt. Gen. Gutbi el-Mahdi, 24 June 1998. Copy in author's collection.

53. Yahia Babiker, deputy secretary-general, Sudan Intelligence Service, interview by author, Khartoum, 17 October 1999.

54. Senior U.S. official, telephone interview by author, 8 October 1999.

55. Babiker, op. cit.

CHAPTER TWELVE

1. Chris Giannou, interview by author, Baidoa, Somalia, 9 August 1992.

2. Jeffrey A. Lefebvre, *Arms for the Horn: U.S. Security Policy in Ethiopia and Somalia, 1953–1991* (Pittsburgh: University of Pittsburgh Press, 1991), p. 199.

3. Ibid.

4. Ibid., pp. 228–231.

5. Ibid., p. 211.

6. Ibid., p. 226.

7. Ibid., p. 241.

8. Donald K. Petterson, "Somalia and the United States, 1977–1983: The New Relationship," in *African Crisis Areas and U.S. Foreign Policy*, edited by Gerald J. Bender, James S. Coleman, and Richard L. Sklar (Berkeley: University of California Press, 1985), p. 203

9. *Africa Confidential*, July 1987, cited in Anna Simons, *Networks of Dissolution: Somalia Undone* (Boulder: Westview Press, 1995), p. 68.

10. Mohamed Sahnoun, *Somalia: The Missed Opportunities* (Washington, D.C.: United States Institute of Peace Press, 1994), pp. 54–55.

11. John Drysdale, *Whatever Happened to Somalia? A Tale of Tragic Blunders* (London: Haan Associates, 1994), p. 3.

12. Boutros Boutros-Ghali, *An Agenda for Peace*, second edition (New York: United Nations, 1995), p. 39.

13. Ibid., p. 44.

14. Steven Hurst, *The Foreign Policy of the Bush Administration: In Search of a New World Order* (London: Cassell, 1999), p. 221.

15. David Bassiouni, representative of UN Department of Humanitarian Affairs, interview by author, Mogadishu, 4 August 1992.

16. Boutros Boutros-Ghali, *Unvanquished: A U.S.-UN Saga* (New York: Random House, 1999), p. 96.

17. Ibid., p. 53.

18. Said S. Samatar, *Somalia: A Nation in Turmoil* (London: Minority Rights Group, 1991), p. 6.

19. Boutros-Ghali, op. cit., p. 58.

20. Ibid., p. 97.

21. United Nations, *The United Nations and Somalia 1992–1996*, United Nations Blue Book Series, vol. 8 (New York: Department of Public Information, United Nations, 1996), p. 41.

22. Ibid., p. 41.

23. Boutros-Ghali, op. cit., p. 59.

24. "Report of the Commission of Inquiry established pursuant to resolution 885 (1993) to investigate armed attacks on UNOSOM II personnel," S/1994/653, 1 June 1994, in United Nations, op. cit., p. 382.

25. Cited in Stanley Meisler, *United Nations: The First Fifty Years* (New York: Atlantic Monthly Press, 1995), p. 300.

26. Ibid.

27. Boutros-Ghali, op. cit., p. 60.

28. Hassan Mahmud Mohammed, interview by author, Bardera, 28 November 1992.

29. Abdukader Yassin, interview by author, Bardera, 28 November 1992.

30. Brig. Gen. Imtiaz Shaheen, interview by author, Mogadishu, 9 December 1992.

31. Ibid.

32. First Lt. Robert Van Hoesen, interview by author, Baledoglay, 11 December 1992.

33. Boutros-Ghali, op. cit., p. 95.

34. Ibid., p. 95, and United Nations, op. cit., p. 272.

35. "Report of the Commission of Inquiry," op. cit., p. 383.

36. General Mohamed Farah Aideed, press conference, Mogadishu, 11 June 1993.

37. Brig. Ikram-ul-Hasan, interview by author, Mogadishu, 14 June 1993.

38. General Mohamed Farah Aideed, interview by author, Mogadishu, 13 June 1993.

39. Admiral Jonathon Howe, UN special representative to Somalia, press briefing, Mogadishu, 16 June 1993.

40. Abdirazak Hassan Ali, interview by author, Mogadishu, 3 October 1993.

41. Hassan Issa Ahmed, interview by author, Wardhiigley, Mogadishu, 4 October 1993.

42. Mike Durant, interview by author, Mogadishu, 8 October 1993.

Chapter Thirteen

1. François Mitterrand, French minister of justice and later president, 1957, cited in *Mission d'information sur le Rwanda*, no. 1271 (Paris: Assemblée Nationale, 15 December 1998), p. 21. Web site version: http://www.assemblee-nationale.fr/s/dossiers/rwanda/ r1271.htm

2. François Mitterrand, *Présence française et abandon* (Paris: Plon, 1957), cited in: Jean de la Guérivière, *Les Fous d'Afrique: Histoire d'une passion française* (Paris: Seuil, 2001), p. 187. All translations in this chapter mine.

3. Ibid.

4. Jacques Chirac, interview by Jean Lacouture, in ibid., p. 231.

5. French foreign ministry figures, cited in Ministère des Affaires Etrangères, "La politique africaine de la France," 11 January 2001, at http://www/diplomatie.fr/actuel/dossiers/polafricaine/index.html

6. Hubert Vedrine, French foreign minister, cited in ibid., p. 23.

7. Former French ambassador, who served in several African countries, interview by author, Paris, 21 February 2001.

8. Philippe Gaillard, *Foccart parle: Entretiens avec Philippe Gaillard* (Paris: Fayard/Jeune Afrique, 1997), vol. 2, p. 506

9. For the most detailed description of this network see Stephen Smith and Antoine Glaser: *Ces Messieurs Afrique 2: Des reseaux aux lobbies* (Paris: Calmann-Levy, 1997), pp. 33–63.

10. Ibid., p. 36.

11. Gaillard, op. cit., p. 506.

12. Antoine Glaser, editor of *Lettre du Continent*, interview by author, Paris, 23 February 2001.

13. Ibid.

14. Gaillard, op. cit., p. 496.

15. Antoine Glaser and Stephen Smith, *L'Afrique sans Africains: Le rêve blanc du continent noir* (Africa without Africans: The white dream of the black continent) (Paris: Stock, 1994), p. 154. My translation.

16. Ibid., p. 188.

17. François Mitterrand, 16th Franco-African summit, La Baule, France, 20 June 1990.

18. Glaser and Smith, op. cit., p. 198.

19. Glaser, interview, op. cit.

20. Mitterrand, op. cit.

21. *Mission d'information sur le Rwanda*, op. cit., p. 72.

22. Ibid., p. 101.

23. Human Rights Watch, "Arming Rwanda" (New York: Human Rights Watch, 1995), pp. 23–24.

24. Bruno Delaye, councillor at the French presidency, 1992–1995, cited in *Mission d'information sur le Rwanda*, op. cit., p. 33.

25. Maj. Gen. Paul Kagame, then vice chairman of the RPF and chairman of the RPA military high command, later president of Rwanda, interview by author, Mulindi, Rwanda, 8 January 1994.

26. Hubert Vedrine, French foreign minister, cited in *Mission d'information sur le Rwanda*, op. cit., p. 107.

27. Delaye, cited in ibid.

28. Ibid., p. 141.

29. Cable from Booh-Booh/Dallaire to Annan/Goulding, cited in Human Rights Watch, op. cit., p. 626.

30. Boutros Boutros-Ghali, *Unvanquished: A U.S.-UN Saga* (New York: Random House, 1999), p. 138.

31. Ibid., p. 136.

32. Douglas Jehl, "Officials Told to Avoid Calling Rwanda killings 'Genocide,'" *New York Times*, 10 June 1994.

33. Boutros-Ghali, op. cit., p. 137.

34. Boutros Boutros-Ghali, *The United Nations and Rwanda, 1993–1996* (New York: United Nations Department of Public Information, 1996), p. 55.

35. Jean-Bernard Mérimée, French ambassador to the UN, March 1991–August 1995, cited in *Mission d'information sur le Rwanda*, op. cit., p. 166.

36. Gérard Prunier, *The Rwanda Crisis: History of a Genocide* (London: Hurst, 1995), p. 288.

37. Ibid., p. 293.

38. Ibid., p. 294.

39. Unnamed French representative in Goma, writing on 6 July 1994, cited in *Mission d'information sur le Rwanda*, op. cit., p. 186.

40. Theodore Sindikubwabo, letter to François Mitterrand, cited in ibid., p. 187.

41. French telegram to Sindikubwabo government, ibid.

42. Ibid., p. 193.

43. Former French ambassador, interview by author, Paris, 22 February 2001.

44. Ibid.

45. Ibid.

46. Ibid.

47. Senior French official, interview by author, Paris, 22 February 2001.

48. Ibid.

49. Ministère des Affaires Etrangères, op. cit.

Epilogue

1. World Bank, *Can Africa Claim the 21st Century?* (Washington, D.C.: World Bank 2000), p. 2.

2. Karl Maier, *This House Has Fallen: Nigeria in Crisis* (London: Allen Lane, 2000), p. 303.

3. Olushola Isinkaiye, "African Presidential Systems," in *African Traditional Political Thought and Institutions*, edited by Zaccheus Sunday Ali, John A.A. Ayoade, and Adigun A.B. Agbaje (Lagos: Centre for Black African Arts and Civilization, 1989), p. 309.

4. Meek Gichugu, interview by author, Ngecha, Kenya, 22 September 1994.

5. Lois Wangui, interview by author, Ngecha, Kenya, 22 September 1994.

BIBLIOGRAPHY

BOOKS

Abdallah, Ahmedou Ould, *La Diplomatie Pyromane: Burundi, Rwanda, Somalie, Bosnie: Entretiens avec Stephen Smith* (Paris: Calmann-Levy, 1996).

Achebe, Chinua, *Anthills of the Savannah* (London: William Heinemann, 1987).

Alao, Abiodun, *The Burden of Collective Goodwill: The International Involvement in the Liberian Civil War* (Aldershot, UK: Ashgate, 1998).

Aleir, Abel, *Southern Sudan: Too Many Agreements Dishonoured* (Exeter, UK: Ithaca Press, 1990).

Berkeley, Bill, *Liberia: A Promise Betrayed* (New York: Lawyers Committee for Human Rights, 1986).

Bodansky, Yossef, *Bin Laden: The Man Who Declared War on America* (Rocklin, Calif.: Forum, 1999).

Boutros-Ghali, Boutros, *An Agenda for Peace*, second edition (New York: United Nations, 1995).

———, *The United Nations and Rwanda, 1993–1996* (New York: United Nations Department of Public Information, 1996).

———, *Unvanquished: A U.S.-UN Saga* (New York: Random House, 1999).

Braeckman, Colette, *Rwanda: Histoire d'un genocide* (Paris: Fayard, 1994).

Bridgeland, Fred, *Jonas Savimbi: A Key to Africa* (London: Coronet Books, 1988).

Crocker, Chester A., *High Noon in Southern Africa: Making Peace in a Rough Neighborhood* (New York: W. W. Norton, 1993).

Davidson, Basil, *The Black Man's Burden* (New York: Times Books, 1992).

Decalo, Samuel, *Coups and Military Rule in Africa: Motivations and Constraints*, second edition (New Haven: Yale University Press, 1990).

Destexhe, Alain, *Rwanda and Genocide in the Twentieth Century* (New York: New York University Press, 1995).

Diamond, Larry, Anthony Kirk-Greene, and Oyeleye Oyediran, eds., *Transition Without End: Nigerian Politics and Civil Society Under Babangida* (Boulder: Lynne Rienner Publishers, 1997).

Drysdale, John, *Whatever Happened to Somalia? A Tale of Tragic Blunders* (London: Haan Associates, 1994).

Ellis, Stephen, *The Mask of Anarchy: The Destruction of Liberia and the Religious Dimension of an African Civil War* (London: Hurst, 1999).

Evans, Glynne, *Responding to Crises in the African Great Lakes*, Adelphi Paper 311 (London: International Institute for Strategic Studies, 1997).

Fabian, Johannes, *Language and Colonial Power: The Appropriation of Swahili in the Former Belgian Congo, 1880–1938* (Berkeley: University of California Press, 1986).

Falola, Toyin, A. Ajayi, A. Alao, and B. Babawale, *The Military Factor in Nigeria, 1966–1985*, African Studies, vol. 35 (Lewiston, N.Y.: Edwin Mellen Press, 1994).

Gaillard, Philippe, *Foccart parle: Entretiens avec Philippe Gaillard*, vol. 2 (Paris: Fayard/Jeune Afrique, 1997).

355

Glaser, Antoine, and Stephen Smith, *L'Afrique sans Africains: Le rêve blanc du continent noir* (Paris: Stock, 1994).

Guérivière, Jean de la, *Les Fous d'Afrique: Histoire d'une passion française* (Paris: Seuil, 2001).

Guimaraes, Fernando Andresen, *The Origins of the Angolan Civil War: Foreign Intervention and Domestic Political Conflict* (New York: St. Martin's Press, 1998).

Hare, Paul, *Angola's Last Best Chance for Peace: An Insider's Account of the Peace Process* (Washington, D.C.: United States Institute for Peace, 1998).

Henries, A. Doris Banks, *The Liberian Nation: A Short History* (Macmillan: New York, 1966).

Holt, P. M., and M. W. Daly, *The History of The Sudan, from the Coming of Islam to the Present Day* (London: Weidenfeld and Nicholson, 1979).

Huband, Mark, *The Liberian Civil War* (London: Frank Cass, 1997).

_____, *Warriors of the Prophet: The Struggle for Islam* (Boulder: Westview Press, 1999).

Human Rights Watch, *Leave None to Tell the Story* (New York: Human Rights Watch, 1999).

Human Rights Watch/Africa, *Civilian Devastation: Abuses by All Parties in the War in Southern Sudan* (New York: Human Rights Watch, 1994).

Hurst, Steven, *The Foreign Policy of the Bush Administration: In Search of a New World Order* (London: Cassell, 1999).

Kalb, Madeleine G., *The Congo Cables: The Cold War in Africa from Eisenhower to Kennedy* (New York: Macmillan, 1982).

Kamukama, Dixon, *Rwanda Conflict: Its Roots and Regional Implications*, second edition (Kampala: Fountain Publishers, 1997).

Kaplan, Robert, *The Ends of the Earth: From Togo to Turkmenistan, from Iran to Cambodia, a Journey to the Frontiers of Anarchy* (New York: Vintage Books, 1997).

Karl-i-Bond, Nguza, *Mobutu ou l'incarnation du Mal Zairois* (London: Rex Collings, 1982).

Kyvig, David E., *Reagan and the World* (New York: Praeger, 1990).

Lefebvre, Jeffrey A., *Arms for the Horn: U.S. Security Policy in Ethiopia and Somalia, 1953–1991* (Pittsburgh: University of Pittsburgh Press, 1991).

Lemarchand, René, *Burundi: Ethnic Conflict and Genocide* (New York: Woodrow Wilson Center Press, 1994).

Lemarchand, René, and David Martin, *Selective Genocide in Burundi* (London: Minority Rights Group, 1994).

Leslie, Winsome J., *The World Bank and Structural Transformation in Developing Countries: The Case of Zaire* (Boulder: Lynne Rienner Publishers, 1987).

Maier, Karl, *Angola: Promises and Lies* (London: Serif, 1996).

_____, *This House Has Fallen: Nigeria in Crisis* (London: Allen Lane, 2000).

Malkki, Liisa H., *Purity and Exile: Violence, Memory, and National Cosmology Among Hutu Refugees in Tanzania* (Chicago: University of Chicago Press, 1995).

Mazrui, Ali A., and Michael Tidy, *Nationalism and New States in Africa* (Nairobi: Heinemann Kenya, 1984).

McGaffey, Janet, *The Real Economy of Zaire: The Contribution of Smuggling and Other Unofficial Activities to National Wealth* (Philadelphia: University of Pennsylvania Press, 1991).

Meisler, Stanley, *United Nations: The First Fifty Years* (New York: Atlantic Monthly Press, 1995).

Minter, William, *Apartheid's Contras: An Inquiry into the Roots of War in Angola and Mozambique* (Atlantic Highlands, New Jersey, and Johannesburg: Zed Books and Witwatersrand University Press, 1994).

Mission d'information sur le Rwanda, no. 1271 (Paris: Assemblée Nationale, 15 December 1998). Web site version: http://www.assemblee-nationale.fr/s/dossiers/rwanda/r1271.htm

Mobutu Sese Seko, *Mobutu: Discours, allocutions, messages, 1965–1975, Part 2* (Paris: Editions J.A., 1975)

National Council of Churches of Kenya, *The Cursed Arrow: Organised Violence Against Democracy in Kenya* (Nairobi: National Council of Churches of Kenya, April 1992).

Newbury, Catharine, *The Cohesion of Oppression: Clientship and Ethnicity in Rwanda, 1860–1960* (New York: Columbia University Press, 1988).

Ojukwu, C. Odumegwu, *Biafra: Random Thoughts of C. Odumegwu Ojukwu, General of the People's Army* (New York: Harper and Row, 1969).

Pakenham, Thomas, *The Scramble for Africa* (London: Abacus Books, 1991).

Peters, Jimi, *The Nigerian Military and the State* (London: International Library of African Studies, Tauris Academic Studies, I. B. Tauris, 1997).

Petterson, Donald, *Inside Sudan: Political Islam, Conflict and Catastrophe* (Boulder: Westview Press, 1999).

Prunier, Gérard, *The Rwanda Crisis: History of a Genocide* (London: Hurst, 1995).

Remilleux, Jean-Louis, *Mobutu: Dignity for Africa, Interviews with Jean-Louis Remilleux* (Paris: Albin Michel, 1989).

Republic of Kenya, *Report of the Parliamentary Select Committee to Investigate Ethnic Clashes in Western and Other Parts of Kenya* (Nairobi: Republic of Kenya, September 1992).

Richards, Paul, *Fighting for the Rain Forest: War, Youth and Resources in Sierra Leone* (London: International African Institute), 1996.

Sahnoun, Mohamed, *Somalia: The Missed Opportunities* (Washington D.C.: United States Institute of Peace Press, 1994).

Samatar, Said S., *Somalia: A Nation in Turmoil* (London: Minority Rights Group, 1991).

Schatzberg, Michael G., *The Dialectics of Oppression in Zaire* (Bloomington: Indiana University Press, 1991).

_____, *Mobutu or Chaos: The United States and Zaire, 1960–1990* (Lanham, Md.: University Press of America, 1991).

Simons, Anna, *Networks of Dissolution: Somalia Undone* (Boulder: Westview Press, 1995).

Smith, Stephen, and Antoine Glaser: *Ces Messieurs Afrique 2: Des reseaux aux lobbies* (Paris: Calmann-Levy, 1997).

Speke, John Hanning, *Journal of the Discovery of the Source of the Nile* (1863; reprint, Mineola, N.Y.: Dover, 1996).

Stockwell, John, *In Search of Enemies: A CIA Story* (New York: W. W. Norton, 1978; Bridgewater, New Jersey: Replica Books, 1997).

Throup, David, and Charles Hornsby, *Multi-Party Politics in Kenya* (Oxford and Nairobi: James Currey and East African Educational Publishers, 1998).

Trimingham, J. Spencer, *Islam in the Sudan* (London: Frank Cass, 1949).

United Nations, *The United Nations and Rwanda, 1993–1996* (New York: United Nations Department of Public Information, 1996).

_____, *The United Nations and Somalia, 1992–1996*, United Nations Blue Book Series, vol. 8 (New York: Department of Public Information, United Nations, 1996).

United Nations Development Programme, *UNDP Human Development Report 1995* (New York: Oxford University Press, 1995).

Watson, Catherine, *Transition in Burundi: The Context for a Homecoming* (Washington, D.C.: U.S. Committee for Refugees, 1993).

World Bank, *Can Africa Claim the 21st Century?* (Washington, D.C.: World Bank, 2000).

Wright, George, *The Destruction of a Nation: United States' Policy Towards Angola Since 1945* (London: Pluto Press, 1997).

Young, Crawford, and Thomas Turner, *The Rise and Decline of the Zairean State* (Madison: University of Wisconsin Press, 1985).

ARTICLES

Abdullah, Ibrahim, and Patrick Muana, "The Revolutionary United Front of Sierra Leone: A Revolt of the Lumpenproletariat," in *African Guerrillas*, edited by Christopher Clapham (Oxford and Kampala: James Currey and Fountain Publishers, 1998).

Adekanye, J. Bayo, "The Military," in Larry Diamond, Anthony Kirk-Greene, and Oyeleye Oyediran, *Transition Without End: Nigerian Politics and Civil Society Under Babangida* (Boulder: Lynne Rienner Publishers, 1997).

Agbaje, Adigun, "Mobilizing for a New Political Culture," in Larry Diamond, Anthony Kirk-Greene, and Oyeleye Oyediran, *Transition Without End: Nigerian Politics and Civil Society Under Babangida* (Boulder: Lynne Rienner Publishers, 1997).

Akinola, Olufemi A., "The Colonial Heritage and Modern Constitutionalism in Africa," in *African Traditional Political Thought and Institutions*, edited by Zaccheus Sunday Ali, John A.A. Ayoade, and Adigun A.B. Agbaje (Lagos: Centre for Black African Arts and Civilization, 1989).

Akinterinwa, Bola A., "The 1993 Presidential Election Imbroglio," in Larry Diamond, Anthony Kirk-Greene, and Oyeleye Oyediran, *Transition Without End: Nigerian Politics and Civil Society Under Babangida* (Boulder: Lynne Rienner Publishers, 1997).

Alao, Abiodun, and Funmi Olonisakin, "Post Cold War Africa: Ethnicity, Ethnic Conflict and Security," in *Africa After the Cold War: The Changing Perspectives on Security*, edited by Adebayo Oyebade and Abiodun Alao (Trenton, N.J., and Asmara, Eritrea: Africa World Press, 1998).

Askin, Steve, and Carole Collins, "External Collusion with Kleptocracy: Can Zaire Recapture Its Stolen Wealth?" *Review of African Political Economy*, no. 57, 1993, pp. 72–85.

Bender, Gerald, "American Policy toward Angola: A History of Linkage," in *African Crisis Areas and U.S. Foreign Policy*, edited by Gerald J. Bender, James S. Coleman, and Richard L. Sklar (Berkeley: University of California Press, 1985).

Bin Laden, Osama, "Declaration of Jihad On the Americans Occupying the Country of the Two Sacred Places," Khurasan, Afghanistan, 23 August 1996. Unpublished.

Blumenthal, Erwin, "Zaire: Report on her International Financial Credibility," unpublished (Washington, D.C.: International Monetary Fund, 1982).

Devlin, Lawrence, CIA station chief, Leopoldville, U.S. Congress, Senate, Select Committee to Study Governmental Operations with Respect to Intelligence Activities, *Interim Report: Alleged Assassination Plots Involving Foreign Leaders*, 94th Congress, 1st Session, 20 November 1975, cited in Stephen Weissman, "The CIA and U.S. Policy in Zaire and Angola," in *Dirty Work: The CIA in Africa* (London: Zed Press, 1980).

Elias, Michel, and Danielle Helbig, "Deux milles collines pour les petits et les grands," *Politique Africaine*, vol. 17, no. 42, June 1991, pp. 39–44.

Ellis, Stephen, "Liberia's Warlord Insurgency," in *African Guerrillas*, edited by Christopher Clapham (Oxford and Kampala: James Currey and Fountain Publishers, 1998).

Huband, Mark, Michael Holman, and Jimmy Burns, "How Mobutu Built Up His $4bn Fortune," *Financial Times*, 12 May 1997, p. 2.

Human Rights Watch, "Arming Rwanda" (New York: Human Rights Watch, 1995).

Huntington, Samuel P. , "The Lonely Superpower," *Foreign Policy*, vol. 78, no. 2, March/April 1999, pp. 35–50.

Ikelegbe, A. O., "Checks on the Abuse of Political Power," in *African Traditional Political Thought and Institutions*, edited by Zaccheus Sunday Ali, John A.A. Ayoade, and Adigun A.B. Agbaje (Lagos: Centre for Black and African Arts and Civilization, 1989).

Isinkaiye, Olushola, "African Presidential Systems," in *African Traditional Political Thought and Institutions*, edited by Zaccheus Sunday Ali, John A.A. Ayoade, and Adigun A.B. Agbaje (Lagos: Centre for Black African Arts and Civilization, 1989).

Jehl, Douglas, "Officials Told to Avoid Calling Rwanda killings 'Genocide,'" *New York Times*, 10 June 1994.

Jones, Bruce D., "The Arusha Peace Process," in *The Path of a Genocide: The Rwanda Crisis from Uganda to Zaire*, edited by Howard Adelman and Astri Suhrke (New Brunswick, Can.: Transaction Publishers, 1999).

Kakwenzire, Joan, and Dixon Kamukama, "The Development and Consolidation of Extremist Forces in Rwanda 1990–1994," in *The Path of a Genocide: The Rwanda Crisis from Uganda to Zaire*, edited by Howard Adelman and Astri Suhrke (New Brunswick, Can.: Transaction Publishers, 1999).

Kaplan, Robert, "The Coming Anarchy," *Atlantic Monthly*, February 1994.

Lemarchand, René, "The CIA in Africa: How Central? How Intelligent?" in *American Policy in Southern Africa*, second edition, edited by René Lemarchand (Lanham, Md.: University Press of America, 1981).

———, "Zaire: The Unamanageable Client State," in *American Policy In Southern Africa*, second edition, edited by René Lemarchand (Lanham, Md.: University Press of America, 1981).

Lockwood, Edgar, "Carter's Sometime Southern Africa Policy," in *American Policy in Southern Africa*, second edition, edited by René Lemarchand (Lanham, Md.: University Press of America, 1981).

Ministère des Affaires Etrangères, "La politique africaine de la France," 11 January, 2001, official publication of the foreign ministry: http://www.diplomatie.fr/actuel/dossiers/ polafricaine/index.html

Morris, Roger, "Our Man in Kinshasa," *New Republic*, 7 May 1977.

Osaghae, Eghosa E. , "The Passage from the Past to the Present in African Political Thought: The Question of Relevance," in *African Traditional Political Thought and Institutions*, edited by Zaccheus Sunday Ali, John A.A. Ayoade, and Adigun A.B. Agbaje (Lagos: Centre for Black African Arts and Civilization, 1989).

Otunnu, Ogenga, "An Historical Analysis of the Invasion by the Rwandan Patriotic Army (RPA)," in *The Path of a Genocide: The Rwanda Crisis from Uganda to Zaire*, edited by Howard Adelman and Astri Suhrke (New Brunswick, Can.: Transaction Publishers, 1999).

Petterson, Donald K., "Somalia and the United States, 1977–1983: The New Relationship," in *African Crisis Areas and U.S. Foreign Policy*, edited by Gerald J. Bender, James S. Coleman, and Richard L. Sklar (Berkeley: University of California Press, 1985).

"Report of the Commission of Inquiry established pursuant to resolution 885 (1993) to investigate armed attacks on UNOSOM II personnel," S/1994/653, 1 June 1994, in United Nations, *The United Nations and Somalia, 1992–1996*, United Nations Blue Book Series, vol. 8 (New York: Department of Public Information, United Nations, 1996).

Rice, Susan, and David Scheffer, "Why Sudan's Charm Offensive Puts U.S. Off," *The East African*, 28 September 1999.

Sang-Mpam, S. N., "Understanding the Crisis in Peripheral Countries: The Case of Zaire," in *The Crisis in Zaire: Myths and Realities*, edited by Nzongola-Ntalaja (Trenton, N.J., and Asmara, Eritrea: Africa World Press, 1986).

Sesay, Amadu, and Abiodun Alao, "Democracy and Security in Africa: The Changing Nature of a Linkage," in *Africa After the Cold War: The Changing Perspectives on Security*, edited by Adebayo Oyebade and Abiodun Alao (Trenton, N.J., and Asmara, Eritrea: Africa World Press, 1998).

Shearer, David, "Private Armies and Military Intervention," Adelphi Paper 316 (London: International Institute for Strategic Studies, 1998).

Turner, Thomas, "Zaire: Flying High Above the Toads: Mobutu and Stalemated Democracy," in *Political Reform in Francophone Africa*, edited by John F. Clark and David E. Gardinier (Boulder: Westview Press, 1997).

Lockwood, Edgar, "Carter's Sometime Southern Africa Policy," in *American Policy in Southern Africa*, second edition, edited by René Lemarchand (Lanham, Md.: University Press of America, 1981).

Weissman, Stephen, "The CIA and U.S. policy in Zaire and Angola," in *American Policy in Southern Africa*, edited by René Lemarchand (Lanham, Md.: University Press of America, 1981).

Wills, Garry, "Bully of the Free World," *Foreign Policy*, vol. 78, no. 2, March/April 1999, pp. 50–60.

INDEX